S0-BBM-609

CONFLICT AND CONSENSUS IN LABOUR'S
FOREIGN POLICY, 1914–1965

# CONFLICT AND CONSENSUS IN LABOUR'S FOREIGN POLICY 1914–1965

MICHAEL R. GORDON

*Stanford University Press, Stanford, California* *1969*

*Stanford University Press*
*Stanford, California*
© *1969 by the Board of Trustees of the*
*Leland Stanford Junior University*
*Printed in the United States of America*
*L.C. 69-18494*

*To My Parents*

# Preface

Why has the Labour Party suffered recurringly and for prolonged periods from angry conflict over foreign policy?

The question draws attention to an important though little understood area of Labour's behavior. In whatever period of the party's history one turns to, be it during World War I or in the 1930's or the aftermath of World War II—for that matter the situation is not much different today—foreign policy has persistently generated controversy and discord. Not that it has been unique in this respect. In varying degree, nearly every sphere of policy making has been infected with strife, Labour partisans succumbing again and again to an apparently irresistible impulse to overlay even minor disputes with the vehement rancor of ideological argument. With few exceptions, however, scholars have focused on the struggles raging in matters of domestic socialism; as a result we know less than we should about the noisy clashes that have repeatedly erupted over foreign policy. The point of the present inquiry is to make good this deficiency. It attempts to account for the nature of the conflict and to identify the conditions responsible for its stubborn recurrence.

The inquiry pursues its objective in two overlapping analytical steps. First, it describes a distinctive outlook in foreign policy that has been peculiar to the Labour Party and that, following normal party usage, I have termed socialist foreign policy. In Chapter 1 this policy is clarified by being broken down into its constituent principles; I have isolated four of them, and tried to show how they embody basic beliefs about international politics and the forces at work within it, moral values affording a powerful vision of a new and better international system, and appropriate symbols calculated to arouse desired emotional responses. Historically, these principles were assumed by Labour to be identical with the principles comprising its domestic socialism; they were simply projected onto the international scene and rephrased accordingly. Just as the commitment to socialism at home carried definite programmatic implications, so too did the commitment to a socialist policy abroad. The importance of that commitment can scarcely be exaggerated. It meant that Labour's hostility to the kind of foreign policy traditionally conducted by the capitalist parties in Britain was no less uncompromising than its opposition to their domestic policies. As Clement Attlee, leader of the party, asserted in 1937: "There is no agreement on foreign policy between a Labour Opposition and a Capitalist Government."[1] The point could hardly be put more bluntly, and the mass of the party plainly concurred. Until 1945, scarcely anyone could be found who questioned outright the soundness of the socialist commitment, much less the likelihood of its being fully honored once Labour achieved full power. What happened after 1945 is another matter, and a subject of major concern in these pages.

Two further points relating to the descriptive task ought to be made. First, in identifying what I regard as distinctive about socialist foreign policy, I have found it profitable to analyze Labour's utterances and behavior in terms of three fairly distinct periods. In the first three chapters I have concentrated on the party's development up to the end of World War II, during which time socialist foreign policy matured into a body of coherent doctrine. The next five chapters probe the crucial years between 1945 and 1951, the period encompassing the two Attlee governments, when the socialist commitment was at long last put to a test. Finally, I have examined the fierce controversy that flared up after 1951. Historical comparison of this sort is of inestimable value. It permits us to generalize about the conflict over foreign policy against the background of widely varied historical circumstances and in the presence of different party spokesmen, and thereby to decide whether a recurrent pattern can be isolated and explained. Clearly, as my previous remarks suggest, I believe that such a pattern can be discerned.

The second point is that the inquiry emphasizes political culture as a determinant of political behavior. It assumes that a fruitful way to study Labour's foreign policy troubles is to examine the values, beliefs, and symbols that party members share: hence the emphasis on socialist principles. But the reader must not be misled by this. Nowhere is it claimed that there has been a one-to-one correspondence between the principles and Labour's actual behavior —between theory and practice. After all, political culture is only one determinant of behavior; also important is the objective environment, what Karl Popper has called the "logic of the situation," which can constrain the range of choice and even lead intended actions astray by producing unforeseen consequences. An inescapable problem of all sound policy making is to recognize the environmental constraints and to make the necessary adjustments to them. Obviously, were the inquiry to stress the cultural variables of Labour's behavior to the point of neglecting the environmental determinants, it would be lacking in realism, and so I have been at pains to take the latter into account.* Indeed I have done more than that. For precisely one of our more substantial findings is that whenever Labour has been in office, its foreign policy has invariably been controlled not by socialist ideology but rather by continuous adjustment to environmental determinants—in other words, by the logic of externally imposed demands and pressures. And this finding, far from calling into question our predominant emphasis on political culture, actually vindicates it by baring a major clue to the party's recurrent conflict.

Thus the first step of the inquiry. The second step involves an effort at classification. Nearly always in political analysis, to describe something is to attempt to classify it in some manner or another. For instance, the assertion that socialist foreign policy needs to be broken down into underlying principles is in effect an assertion that it becomes clarified through classification. But this is a simple, perhaps self-evident point, and there is no reason to belabor the obvious. What I principally wish to make clear is that this inquiry aims at developing a typology of foreign policy in British politics. In doing so it distinguishes two contrasting

---

* As perceptive students of international relations theory will have already recognized, the inquiry is in no small part an exercise in grappling with the level-of-analysis problem.

types—socialist foreign policy and what, for want of a better term, is called "traditional foreign policy."* Together, these two types seem to exhaust the alternatives that recent British political actors have been able to define as meaningful orientations in the conduct of foreign affairs. And drastically different alternatives they are. Indeed, it will be seen that socialist foreign policy originated as a self-conscious reaction to the principles constituting traditional policy (principles that, like their socialist counterparts, embody beliefs, values, and symbols).

Are these two types of foreign policy really distinctive, coherent doctrines as I have implied? Mirrored in each, to be sure, one can find varied interpretations of this or that principle in response to changing historical circumstances, as well as changing policy emphasis according to the policy makers and the objective international situation in any one period. This is particularly true of traditional foreign policy, something hardly surprising, of course, in view of its longevity. In recent times some of its practitioners have preferred to cultivate a "free hand" (Salisbury, the Foreign Office and Admiralty until the 1920's, probably the Lloyd George Coalition), others to create an imperial superstate (Cromner, Milner, Amery, perhaps the Suez Group), yet others to cultivate a special relationship with America (Balfour, Churchill, almost any Conservative minister since 1940). Yet these have been differences over tactics, not underlying principles; their doctrinal unity is attested

* The term "traditional," it needs to be said, is ambiguous and may lead to some confusion unless clarified. A full definition is attempted in Chapter 1, but the following should perhaps be said at this point. What makes the term ambiguous is the Weberian overtones it has acquired in the social sciences. Because of such association, it may seem that when I speak of traditional foreign policy I mean to imply that the policy is generically different from its socialist counterpart: that it is free of ideological taint, something transcending history and partaking of eternal wisdom. I want emphatically to state that this is not my belief. Traditional foreign policy is no less historically and socially conditioned than socialist foreign policy. If I employ the term despite the ambiguity, it is because from one important perspective "traditional" is more than appropriate: it expressly captures what the partisans of the policy themselves ardently believed. To their way of thinking, traditional foreign policy was indeed nonideological, the embodiment of permanent wisdom and immemorial truth, repudiation of which would be tantamount to infinite folly. As Sir Harold Nicolson told the Commons in October 1938: "For 250 years at least the great foundation of our foreign policy, what Sir Eyre Crowe called a 'law of Nature,' has been to prevent by every means in our power the domination of Europe by any single Power or group of Powers."

by the heavy overlap of membership in all three of these factions. In short, whatever the variations in emphasis and interpretation according to the situation at hand, traditional and socialist foreign policies can each be shown to form a unified and coherent pattern, a recognizable and distinguishable body of interconnected beliefs and values that persisted without fundamental change down to 1945. Whether the same can be said of each type since then is a matter to be probed in these pages.

Constructing the typology has at least two virtues. For one thing, it has implications that are probably far-reaching enough to be of value in other, more general studies of British foreign policy. In terms of the present inquiry, its usefulness is that it helps to illuminate a perennial dilemma dogging Labour that we have already touched on: the dilemma that, in office, the party has invariably resorted to traditional means of constant adjustment and compromise in policy making, allowing adaptation to environmental constraints to override socialist principles. Yet to say this is only another way of saying that Labour governments have ended up pursuing a traditional rather than a socialist foreign policy. The typology, by elaborating the distinctions between the two types, suggests why; it shows that where the two policies contrast most strikingly is precisely on the issue of cultural versus environmental determinants of behavior. As Arnold Wolfers has observed, theories of international politics have exhibited a persistent dualism as between a "philosophy of choice" and a "philosophy of necessity."[2] Socialist foreign policy exemplifies an extreme philosophy of choice. Postulating that statesmen enjoy almost unlimited freedom to follow the right path in foreign affairs (at any rate, as much as they do in domestic affairs), it draws the conclusion that the essential problem of foreign policy is almost wholly a matter of intention—of applying morally correct principles with sufficient motivation to make them effective in action. Traditional foreign policy, by way of contrast, occupies a position somewhere between a philosophy of choice and a philosophy of necessity. Unlike (say) *Realpolitik*, it does not insist that wise statesmanship consists solely of recognizing and then acting according to necessities of state, but assumes that there is always some room for free choice and the play of moral convictions; yet unlike socialist foreign policy, it is sensitive to the unique complexities of international politics and to the fact that these make the international environment appreciably different from the political setting within the British nation. For this reason, the principles underlying traditional policy reflect an awareness of the inescapable constraints limiting the range of action in foreign affairs. Socialist policy, on the other hand, is oblivious of—or at any rate indifferent to—environmental constraints. To the extent that it considers the international system as a distinct political environment at all, it does so mainly in terms derived from Labour's experience with the British political system. Hence the familiar criticism, not made by Tories alone, of parochialism on Labour's part.[3]

One final observation. The systematic nature of the socialist challenge separates it from all previous controversy over foreign policy. Disagreement in this area, even angry and far-reaching disagreement, is nothing new; it has been as persistent a feature of British policy as the famed continuity of that policy from one government to the next.[4] Not only have radical dissenters been attacking traditional policy since the seventeenth century, rejecting its aims, its methods, its principles, and excoriating its practitioners as ignorant and class-selfish scoundrels; what is more, they have castigated it in the name of superior moral and intellectual insight. To this extent, the Labour Party's challenge has drawn on an ancient and venerable legacy in British politics. But socialist foreign policy differs from previous dissent in one crucial sense: it offers a comprehensive, coherent, well-defined alternative to existing practice. Previous dissenters, by way of contrast, "were more concerned to attack an existing policy than to state their alternative." Their outlook was essentially nonsystematic, "little more than an automatic reaction to events."[5]

The only exception was the Manchester School as exemplified by Bright and Cobden. Yet their ideas never became official Liberal doctrine; instead of capturing the party, they remained, at most, a powerful tendency within it. Gladstone himself specialized in *ad hoc* contriving, and could never make up his mind between extreme nonintervention and an equally extreme crusading interference nearly everywhere. But this is only to say that the clash between socialist and traditional foreign policies is not to be confused with the arguments between Liberals and Conservatives during the nineteenth century and down to 1914. These arguments were genuine enough and often engaged basic national interests. But, to quote Taylor again, "they were differences, not Dissent— differences of tactics, not of fundamental strategy."[6] Nothing could be further from the nature and spirit of the systematic socialist challenge; its rejection of traditional policy is total, without quali- fication. Its quarrel with traditional practitioners cannot even be said to turn on conflicting interpretations of the national interest, because it rejects that concept as a serviceable guide to good pol- icy. Socialist foreign policy differs from Liberalism as much as La- bour's collectivist orientation at home represents an abrupt break with nineteenth-century individualism and piecemeal meliorism.[7] In both areas, domestic and foreign, Labour owes heavy debts to its predecessors on the left. But in both areas it has also inter- jected a completely new dimension of "system-thinking" into Brit- ish political culture, with all its attendant consequences.

### ACKNOWLEDGMENTS

I owe a heavy debt to Professor Samuel H. Beer of Harvard for his penetrating comments on earlier drafts of the manuscript. Profes- sor Norman Gibbs, All Souls, Oxford, made helpful suggestions in connection with the first five chapters. To the Warden and Fellows of St. Antony's College, Oxford, I want to reiterate my apprecia- tion for a pleasant year's stay that enabled me to use British librar- ies and to interview academics, politicians, and journalists.

M.R.G.

# Contents

CONFLICT AND CONSENSUS IN LABOUR'S
FOREIGN POLICY, 1914–1965

*Chapter one*

# The Nature of Socialist Foreign Policy

### TRADITIONAL FOREIGN POLICY

Socialist foreign policy originated in the Labour Party's repudiation of traditional British foreign policy. Logically, therefore, our first task would seem to be to describe traditional policy and then to discover what Labour found objectionable about it.

The policy was traditional in the sense that by the time of Labour's origin, it had been guiding the conduct of British foreign affairs for well over a century. In the process it had come to be considered almost part of the nature of things, a near-inviolable law embodying timeless wisdom. "Continuity of British foreign policy," "policy transcending party preferences," or more simply "*the* British tradition"—call it what you like; what is important is not so much the slogans as the idea they all convey of permanent factors and permanent objectives, with its subtle overtones of inevitability. Briefly, the policy reduced to self-regarding promotion of national interests, defense of a far-flung imperial and commercial network, and management of a European balance as a condition of British security—all backed, whenever necessary, by the application of force.[1] Thus traditional policy was rooted in considerations of British geography, national independence, and economic and strategic needs; and British statesmanship had acquired, in the course of its application, a formidable reputation for realism and success—so formidable, indeed, that an unassailable consensus appeared to characterize all elite opinion on the subject. Always there were dissenters, and always therefore debates among the larger public concerning this or that feature of British

policy in any one situation. But the consensus remained firm, unshaken; the crosscurrents of public discussion washed against a
granite wall. Even most Liberal politicians subscribed to the policy, with at most, perhaps, altered emphasis. Gladstone, greatest
Liberal of all, was no exception. Though his Midlothian stump
pronouncements are sometimes taken to be a rejection of Disraeli's
traditionalism, they are nothing of the sort. His quarrel was not
with traditional tenets but with Disraeli's application of them,
which he regarded as a misapplication. Indeed, his speech at West
Calder in 1879 reaffirming Liberal beliefs could read like a crib for
Foreign Office applicants at the time of Eyre Crowe.[2]

As with socialist foreign policy, we can conveniently regard traditional policy as weaving together fundamental principles that
serve to fix priorities and to provide standards for making appropriate choices among perceived alternatives. Maintenance of the
European balance was the most crucial: not only did British security rest directly on its successful operation, but equally important,
it was the indispensable precondition for a vigorous imperial policy. As long as possible enemies remained balanced against one
another, no one power could dominate Europe, and Britain was
free to turn toward the sea and its Empire beyond. But control of
the Empire itself posed additional problems, whose solution became incorporated into further traditional principles. One was in-
direct rule: in much the same way that British policy makers
played off one European state against another, they divided native groups, won some to Britain's side, and transformed them into
instruments of British will. Governing client states and colonies in
this manner conferred innumerable advantages; chief among them,
it facilitated the husbanding of precious British capabilities. At
the same time, these capabilities had to be kept in ready condition,
available for immediate and effective use against either foreign
threats or internal imperial disturbances. Hence the third principle dominating traditional policy: British supremacy of the sea,
together with a string of bases and garrisons at strategic points
around the globe. In this way Britain, like Rome before, could
meet its responsibilities and defend its interests by superior mo-
bility—the capacity to direct military power rapidly, efficiently, to
widely scattered areas.

A fourth principle, evolved through the application of the first three, was flexibility and self-restraint. Fluidity of commitment, resiliency in identifying possible enemies, avoidance of advance alliances, willingness to compromise rather than fight, preference for a peripheral rather than frontal military strategy should a fight materialize: such was the style behind British behavior on the world scene, a style assiduously cultivated not only for reasons of foreign policy but also because it suited nicely the pragmatism of domestic politics. It was this flexibility, practiced moderation, and undogmatic attitude that accounted for much of the nation's success as balancer among the European nations: in effect, by eschewing territorial demands on the Continent and remaining aloof from conflicts there until the alignment of others crystallized fully, British statesmen could pick the moment, at their choosing, when and on which side to intervene as the decisive factor. As the Continentals saw it, this behavior smacked of perfidy; to the British traditionalists, it was the source of Britain's success. Certainly the traditionalists were not bothered by reproaches directed at the self-regarding nature of their policy. As Palmerston observed in a phrase aptly capturing the spirit of the enterprise, Britain had neither eternal allies to help nor perennial enemies to fight but rather only permanent interests to promote. The overall upshot of this flexibility is a well-known story: British power succeeded in underpinning a stable international system in which Europe enjoyed a century of general peace after Waterloo and the Empire grew and flourished. Traditional policy was successful power politics.

I hasten to add that the above account is a simplification. For our purposes it has to be, because, in order to facilitate comparisons with socialist foreign policy, we need to reduce traditional practices to a manipulable model and all models must necessarily simplify. By a model I do not mean, of course, a highly formalized analogy such as used in the natural sciences, still less a mathematical-logical theory. I mean the term only in the sense of an ideal-type, which emphasizes certain features of a complex reality and deemphasizes others, all in an effort to distill its "inner logic" and thereby to educate our judgment and understanding of it.* Thus

---

* As Weber observed, an ideal-type "is not a description of reality, but wants to provide unequivocal means for expressing such description" (pp. 190–91).

the question is not whether my depiction of traditional foreign policy is a simplification, an abstraction that reduces the blurred grays of British diplomacy to a picture in sharp blacks and whites. This it obviously is, just as any model is bound to be. Accordingly, one would not have a difficult time in casting about for exceptions to the above ideal-typical abstractions: Palmerston's swagger and fanfaronade during the shoddy Don Pacifico affair, to cite one such instance, comes immediately to mind. The pertinent question is rather this: by appropriate use of the model, are we helped to penetrate to the underlying rationality behind most British foreign policy during, say, the nineteenth century? I suggest one further, and to my way of thinking, clinching piece of evidence in reply. This is that an episode like the Don Pacifico affair stands out so glaringly precisely because it is exceptional. On balance, indeed, Palmerston's career can be pretty accurately assessed in the light of traditional principles as depicted here.[3]

As previously noted, traditional foreign policy was a successful policy of power politics. But it does not follow that traditional policy was mere successful *Realpolitik*. *Realpolitik* is, in effect, power politics for the sake of power; grounded in the assumption of implacable enmity among nations, it denies the relevance of any moral considerations to foreign policy because statesmen are regarded as having no choice other than to act out of necessity, according to the laws of *Staatsräson* or even a *höhere Sittlichkeit*. British statesmen did not normally act as though they thought in terms of irreconcilable enmity. In their realism, it is true, they recognized that the competitiveness of the existing system prevented policy from being judged mainly according to ethical criteria. Conflict was an ever present danger, and British interests had to be backed, where necessary, with force or at least its threatened application. As a specific example, willingness to use force was an indispensable ingredient in managing a balance of power in Europe. At the same time, traditional practitioners were flexible enough to recognize that it was only *prudent* to make the most moral choice that circumstances seemed to warrant—in other words, to temper self-regard with regard for the interests of others. A more aggressive policy, as Eyre Crowe warned, would invariably be to Britain's disadvantage: it would arouse the fear and the jealousy of others and probably drive them into anti-British coalitions. Prudence dictated, therefore, that protecting British commerce mean freedom of the seas for all; that operating a European balance entail respect for the rights of other nations, especially the independence of small powers; and that defending the status quo involve a willingness to let it change peacefully, in response to new circumstances.

Traditional foreign policy was thus successful power politics tempered by vigilant prudence.

### LABOUR'S REPUDIATION

There are two basic notions which, if we understand them properly, express Labour's attitude toward traditional policy. The first is the notion of selfish class politics. The Labour Party was no sooner founded, at the turn of this century, than its spokesmen began assaulting the whole edifice of traditional practices on this ground. Not that they were blind to certain of the policy's merits. On the contrary, they willingly granted that Britain had often championed the cause of liberal nationalism in Europe and defended the rights of small powers against the encroachments of great powers. They even, understandably enough, took pride as Englishmen in this record. All the same, despite this and other acknowledged virtues, Labour partisans denounced traditional policy as something shot through with immoral power politics and arrogant imperialism, which was calculated to further, not the well-being of the entire British people—still less peace and cooperation among the nations of the world—but rather the selfish interests and privileges of the capitalist ruling classes. The most penetrating analysis of these matters was worked out by J. A. Hobson, more than a decade before his conversion to the Labour Party, in his monumental study of imperialism. But it was among Labour's ranks that his ideas found their most enthusiastic reception and elaboration. "The whole corrupting system should be swept away," Ramsay MacDonald noted at one point about traditional diplomacy. "It stands like a dirty old slum area, full of vermin and disease, in the midst of a district cleared and improved."[4] In the name of superior morality and intellectual understanding, the Labour Party thus rejected traditional policy's acknowledged merits as little more than accidental by-products of an otherwise evil state of affairs. It proclaimed that it wanted nothing to do with traditional principles; it would repudiate foreign policy as soon as the power to do so was available. In 1937 Clement Attlee articulated the party's profound feelings when he insisted: "There is a deep difference of opinion between the Labour Party and the capitalist parties on foreign as well as on home policy, because the two cannot be separated. The foreign policy of a Government is the reflection of its internal policy. . . . Particular instances of action which can be approved by Socialists do not affect the proposition that there is no agreement on foreign policy between a Labour Opposition and a capitalist government."[5]

The second notion followed automatically from the first: an emphasis upon reform. In place of traditional policy, Labour proposed to conduct the nation's affairs according to socialist principles which would aim at nothing less than a thorough transformation of international relations. The champions of traditional principles prided themselves on their sense of realism, but socialists were not interested in coming to grips with the so-called realities of the existing international system. What they desired was to change the realities, to uproot the system, and to put the relations among nations on an entirely new and better footing. Reform of what kind, however? As Attlee's statement discloses, Labour believed that foreign and domestic policy should (and do) mirror one another. It followed that socialist foreign policy was conceived of as the international equivalent of the party's commitment to socialism at home. In the words of Arthur Henderson, Foreign Secretary in the 1929 Labour government: "Labour's policy at home and abroad forms one organic whole, because our foreign policy is a function of our domestic policy and both spring from our faith that the future belongs to Socialism."[6] Thus, in line with this reasoning, socialist foreign policy aimed at reforming the international system in such a way that it would come to embody those socialist objectives—economic organization, social justice, fraternity, and cooperation—that Labour stood for in Britain itself. Socialist foreign policy rested, in the last resort, on a powerful and inspiring vision of how relations among nations *ought* to be conducted.

Labour took its commitment to transform the international system no less seriously than its commitment to transform British society. The two were seen as a unit, it being generally assumed in party circles that the full triumph of socialism at home was in part conditional upon its victory abroad. To quote Henderson again: "We know that Socialism in any one country will live poorly and dangerously so long as the rest of the world is prey to capitalist anarchy."[7] More eloquent was Hugh Dalton, junior minister at the Foreign Office under Henderson, when he asked: "What use to create an Earthly Paradise that enemy aircraft will bomb to smoking ruins, or to begin the building of a Socialist Commonwealth on a foundation of planks stretched across a precipice?"[8] Socialist foreign policy was the opposite, in theory at least, of the belief in socialism in one country.

The overriding stress on reform meant that Labour accorded scant respect to those considerations taken to be the very hallmark of wisdom in traditional policy making. The traditionalists insisted that foreign policy had to rest on careful power considerations if it were to be realistic. "It is in our willingness to face realities which we cannot change, and to make the best of them," Neville Chamberlain taunted the Opposition in 1938, "that the difference lies between this side and the other side of the House."[9] The taunt did not sting much. Labour could not have cared less about being thought realistic in this sense: such realism struck it as decidedly of the crackpot variety. The party was certain that in playing power politics, no matter with what skill, traditional policy makers exhibited a complacent obtuseness of political judgment: sooner or later they were bound to miscalculate and to overshoot their mark, and the result would be general war. What else, after all, could one expect from a system of anarchy? The party was not in the least reassured by the success enjoyed by traditional policy during the nineteenth century. Success, it felt, was a wasting asset, and indeed the outbreak of war in 1914 seemed striking proof of this. Henceforth Labour was more than ever convinced that the only wise foreign policy was one that aimed at overcoming the sordid game of power politics and infusing the relations among nations with the spirit of socialist ideals.

Again and again Labour assailed the traditionalists for being wrongheaded and shortsighted in straining to adapt to the impossible conditions of anarchy. And never were the attacks more vocal than after 1918, when the traditionalists, far from turning out to have recanted, gave every sign of intending to remain lodged in their familiar mental habitat. In Labour eyes, nothing could compare in absurdity with Tory efforts to conduct foreign policy during the interwar period as though the old system had been or even could be restored. Restoration was impossible: the old system had broken down in bankruptcy and a new one required nothing short of a revolution in imagination. Yet this was exactly what the Conservatives could not bring themselves to understand. As Attlee told the Commons in 1937, the perennial trouble with British policy in the interwar period had been the fact that "the Government have always tended to give too narrow a view to what are really British interests. The true British interests are the preservation of peace, the support of international law and democracy. The British Empire can survive in the world only insofar as it serves greater interests than our own."[10]

### THE FOUR SOCIALIST PRINCIPLES

The foregoing comments all assume that there has been a distinctive Labour doctrine in foreign policy. This assumption runs counter to many recent studies of the Labour Party. It became fashionable, during the 1950's and early 1960's, to insist that Labour has been merely a broad coalition of interest groups, with the socialists only one among many, and that accordingly the beliefs and values shared by these groups have of necessity been vague, amorphous, without design or pattern. This familiar view, however, has been persuasively challenged by the publication of Samuel Beer's work. He argues that Labour claimed historically to be more than just a broad coalition, and indeed it was. It was a party cemented together by a commitment to a particular orthodoxy, a comprehensive socialist philosophy, which had, moreover, strong programmatic implications.[11] And what was true of socialist orthodoxy at home was equally true of socialist orthodoxy in matters of foreign policy, the latter being regarded—as we have just seen—as merely the application of the former to the international scene.

So far, the character of this foreign policy has only been hinted at. It will be necessary, if the concept is to have much analytical value, to be more rigorous. As in the case of traditional policy, this requires reference to its underlying principles.[12]

It will be helpful, as a start, to clarify the theoretical status of these socialist principles. Labour's socialism has never reduced to a sharply defined, authoritative, totalistic doctrine—explicitly inculcated, like Marxism-Leninism, through repeated indoctrination.

The variegated emphases of the party's creed are easy to demonstrate, even during what Beer calls "the socialist generation."* All the same, the beliefs and values held by Labour members were not randomly distributed; if they did not form an inflexible dogma, they were sufficiently bound together by some form of psychological constraint or functional interdependence to fall into a definite pattern, a distinctive attitudinal syndrome. As a result, knowing that Labour members were favorably disposed toward (say) extensive public ownership, an observer would be able to make reasonably valid predictions about their attitudes toward high income taxes, generous social welfare, educational opportunity, distribution of wealth, and so forth. The most reliable way to isolate the elements of this syndrome would be, of course, through the use of survey techniques. But for our purposes, a survey study is ruled out by virtue of the historical slant of this book; one cannot ask dead men to make themselves available for detailed interviews. Nor, unfortunately, are there available past surveys—at any rate, prior to 1945—for filling the gap. This leaves only one other recourse: generalizations about Labour's cultural patterns, inferred from observations of party members' behavior in its historical setting.

The validity attaching to such generalizations increases if two conditions are met. First, *identifiable* behavioral patterns on the part of Labour members (including, of course, their verbal and written utterances) need to be isolated *over a long period of time.* If they are, we have good reason to believe that the members' behavior reflects underlying attitudes, one of the key characteristics of an attitude (behavioral predispositions toward political objects) being persistence over time. Second, as a further check on the reliability of these observations, the behavioral patterns in question must also be found to reappear *under widely differing* conditions. Such repetition suggests that Labour behavior as a group is not being conditioned by particular environmental forces or institutional arrangements only. In fact, the more divergent the conditions, the more we are entitled to assume that party behavior is also being shaped by a stable and powerful set of consistent, underlying attitudes, which are deeply embedded in members' minds.

* Writing in 1925, Tawney observed: "To the British Socialist the realization of this Socialism presents itself not as the application of a clearly conceived and sharply defined theory, but as a tendency . . ." *The British Labour Movement*, p. 162.

At this point a third operation is advisable. Since the attitudes isolated in the above manner are likely to be numerous, some more central than others, there is a need to pick out the more significant and lump them together under the heading of principles. This step involves selection, simplification, abstraction; its aim is to generate a manageable analytical framework for use as an explanatory device. In taking this step, we are in effect treating the socialist principles used here as ideal-typical abstractions. Like traditional principles, then, socialist principles are to be understood as constructs with empirical referents, checked by satisfying the above two conditions; but their formulation is such that they purposely emphasize, even exaggerate, in an effort to distill the inner logic—the underlying rationality—of a complex reality. Only when the apparently disparate facts and events of Labour's history are fitted against a framework of this sort can they be seen as essentially manifestations of general and recurring processes. The framework simplifies, to be sure. But there is a simple test of its analytical usefulness—how well does it account for the most important facts of Labour's history, and how adequately does it lead to generalizations of reasonable validity about them?

As in all discussions of the political culture approach, moreover, the isolated cultural patterns can also be viewed in functional terms. From this standpoint, socialist principles will be assumed to have served two indispensable psychological needs—the cognitive and the evaluative.* On the one hand, the principles formed a cognitive map of international relations; they wove together a theoretical pattern of beliefs and ideas guiding Labour partisans to an understanding of the political forces at work in the existing international system, and suggesting at the same time how these forces might be manipulated to operate differently and so produce a new system. These ideas and beliefs may be only partly true (as confirmed by logical and empirical methods), but that is beside the point; all that matters is that they have appeared true to Labour partisans themselves. On the other hand, the principles incorporated a consensus of moral feelings and socialist aspirations affording a compelling vision of what this new international sys-

---

* Some political scientists distinguish a third dimension as well: the affective, which refers to the emotional feelings of political actors toward political objects. Here, however, it is more simple and convenient to lump together the affective and the evaluative dimensions.

tem ought to look like. In this sense, the principles performed a vital normative function: they provided the party with standards for evaluating international events in terms of good and bad, right and wrong. Presumably, then, an observer who grasps these standards would be well situated to predict the consequent emotional response of a cross section of Labour members—or he would, at any rate, until 1945, after which the socialist consensus broke down.

There is a one-sided tendency, in approaching belief systems or ideologies in functional terms, that we would do well to avoid here. The tendency is to concentrate exclusively on the furtive sociopsychic functions that ideologies serve (maintain group solidarity, integrate the personality, ease inner doubt, etc.), as though they are nothing but systems of "deformed"—"distorted," "warped," "contaminated," "pathological"—thought that require merciless exposure. But to adopt this one-sided tendency is to rob the whole concept of ideology of analytical value; it becomes thoroughly evaluative (that is, pejorative), as Mannheim discovered to his dismay. No doubt, Labour's socialist principles may have performed other, less consciously acknowledged functions than the two I have singled out. They may well have mirrored such things as projections of repressed anxieties, disguises for ulterior motives, and communal expressions of group solidarity. But the essential point is that whatever else the socialist principles may have done, most distinctively they have functioned historically to form a configurative map of problematic reality and a persuasive chart to collective action.[18] In the minds of Labour partisans, they rendered meaningful the uncertain flux of international events and made possible purposeful collective action in relation to them.

This conclusion can be brought into sharper focus by an additional consideration: the role that the principles seem to have played in the policy-making processes of the party (again before 1945). Ernest May, in a recent study of American foreign policy, has contrasted means-ends calculations with what he calls "historical axioms" in fixing priorities and providing broad standards of choice among perceived policy alternatives. By historical axioms he means basic tenets that have evolved out of the national experience in international relations, and that have come, as a result, to condition powerfully the outlook of Washington policy makers. May concludes, on the basis of certain important decisions, that these axioms exercise the determining influence in national behavior; they have controlled major policy outcomes even to the point of swamping initial inclinations to act differently, in terms of more technical means-ends calculations: "Calculated policies are much more volatile, altering with a shift in weight in any integer, while axiomatic policies vary only as history grows and takes new shape, as the makers of policy, including private citizens who mold public opinion, see the past in different light or with different eyes, or as the American conscience or character changes."[14] Labour's socialist principles can be viewed in a similar light. Like May's historical axioms, they are bound up with the party's whole historical experience as a collectivity pursuing distinct ends, and like them, they have been the controlling factor in determining the broad objectives of Labour's pivotal policy decisions as well as the means it used in implementing these decisions. To put the point more specifically: the particular objectives that Labour pursued at any one moment (prior to 1945) can be understood as having flowed from the application of the principles to the generalized situation confronting the party. In any such situation, the principles conditioned the partisans' perception of the alternatives available; at the same time they provided the partisans with broad standards by which to choose one alternative as the desired objective. Similarly, the selection of means (policy instruments) can be understood as governed by the fact that the principles led the party to prefer some means over others as intrinsically better and more effective (e.g., moral suasion as against military force).

There is one final observation, a point about chronology, worth making. Beer emphasizes that a socialist orthodoxy in domestic affairs did not originate until 1918, but the origin of socialist foreign policy needs to be dated earlier, placed at least sometime before World War I. The reason is that foreign affairs required a more distinctive Labour orientation than party leaders found necessary within the domestic sphere. At the very time when the Parliamentary Labour Party (PLP) was content to pursue MacDonald's strategy of limited objectives and tactical advances at home, the party joined the Second International, pledged itself to direct action as a means of stopping war, denounced the Liberal government's foreign and defense policies as contributing to the existing international anarchy. As MacDonald observed as early as

1907, "socialism has a great part to play immediately in international politics: it alone can banish national jealousies from the Foreign Offices; it alone offers the guarantees of peace which are a necessary preliminary to disarmament."[15] In like manner, the party leadership worked out a theoretical case against the bipartisan notion of continuity in foreign policy.[16] Hence it was no accident, when war finally erupted in 1914, that MacDonald and other prominent Labour spokesmen displayed a militant socialist bias against British involvement. None of this is to deny that the war itself had a tremendous impact on Labour thought in foreign policy, still less to deny that the influx of ex-Liberal intellectuals led to a more explicit formulation of socialist principles after 1918. But it is to say that one can legitimately refer to a socialist foreign policy in the pre-war period. A pertinent observation by Henderson's biographer adds to our perspective here: provincial as Henderson was, in the days before the war, "he yet had the *feel* of internationalism in his bones."[17] The difference by 1918 was that Henderson's feeling—and the feeling of untold others—became more systematically articulated.

## THE FOUR PRINCIPLES DEFINED

### Internationalism

Among other things, traditional foreign policy stood condemned in Labour eyes for being nationalistic. That it was nationalistic was indeed something beyond dispute, for the policy was singularly concerned with promoting national interests, however flexibly or reasonably these might be defined. To Labour's way of thinking, nationalistic egoism of this sort was an unmitigated disaster. The whole notion of vital national interests struck it as a monstrous ruse, "a cynical saving phrase, dear to the practitioners of the old diplomacy [which could be] stretched to cover almost any dispute at the discretion of the disputant."[18] Nationalistic egoism meant that British policy, by failing to transcend parochial self-interest, only intensified the competitiveness of the existing nation-state system and heightened the degree of power politics bound up with it. This nation-state system was held to be no less perilous than that state of nature envisaged by Thomas Hobbes, where life was "solitary, poor, nasty, brutish and short." As party propaganda vividly put it, the system was riddled with capitalist anarchy. And, of course, in anarchy war would inevitably occur because there was nothing to prevent it. Therefore, just as socialism at home would aim in the first instance at smashing the hold of capitalism on the economy, so in foreign policy the first step would have to be directed at destroying the grip of nationalism on policy making.

The party assumed that the root of the trouble was the entrenched value laid on national sovereignty. So long as the nation-state refused to acknowledge a higher moral authority than its own arbitrary will, the international system would remain fragmented into multiple autonomous units and so be conducive to endemic conflict, turmoil, and war. It was thus necessary to go beyond the nation-state, to aim at a more encompassing community. "The mere existence of a State is not an end in itself," MacDonald told the House in 1923; separate national identity is justified only so far as it "means a great moral lead to the other nations of the world."[19] Others in the party, especially the more theoretical-minded, balked at the notion of even morally rehabilitated nations. Nothing justified the existence of separate nation-states; to believe otherwise was to fall prey to the Liberal "inspiration of anarchy and individualism." For H. N. Brailsford, who raised this objection in a work of wide-ranging influence, nationalism and proletarian internationalism were irreconcilably at odds; even the principle of self-determination, as enshrined in the League of Nations, was suspect as a "politics of the Tower of Babel . . . a weakening of constructive and creative power, a decline in civilization."[20] On the whole, however, predominant Labour thinking stopped short of this extreme position. Most party propaganda did not attack the idea of separate national development, let alone the right of any people to a distinct national identity. What grated was the excessive fusion of nation with state power, which resulted in assertive nationalism and consequent anarchy in the international system. If, on this view, the various nations advanced to a higher moral level, becoming increasingly democratic, socialist, and peaceful, they would simultaneously advance toward ever more intimate cooperation; at some point the whole process would culminate in a "socialist world community," organized along confederal lines, each nation retaining its own identity, but all recognizing their interlocking destinies. Henderson concisely formulated Labour's convictions when he wrote: "The inevitable corollary to a national policy which aims at the creation of a Socialist community [at home] is an international policy which is directed towards the establishment of a Cooperative World Commonwealth. . . . British Labour would put this country's influence, in its dealings with all other countries, behind a truly international policy, which will develop the League of Nations in the direction of world government."[21]

The experience of World War I cemented the party's conviction that the existing nation-state system was a disaster. For the first three years, the Independent Labour Party (ILP) alone championed a vigorous internationalism. But the prewar majority had not repudiated the party's prewar attitude; as Winkler aptly observes, an ideological internationalism "was still taken for granted by most of its leaders."[22] As a result, when war weariness reached its numbing peak, in late 1917, the rest of the party did not have much difficulty in catching up with the ILP vanguard. December marked the crucial turning point: a specially convened Labour conference gave near-unanimous approval to the "Memorandum on War Aims," an official policy statement in which ringing demands for a "supra-national authority," "a society of nations," bulked large.* The impact of promotional groups like the League of Nations Society and the Union of Democratic Control can also be discerned here, and these were not exclusively—or even predominantly—Labour in composition. But Labour spokesmen had been active in them from the beginning; what was more, the dissentient Liberals who had been equally prominent in their operations began crowding into Labour's ranks, toward the end of the war. By 1918, therefore, the Labour Party was the most powerful political force in Britain behind the drive for a League of Nations. And as we would expect, its concrete plans for a very comprehensive League "stemmed from a vision of the future."[23]

The League that materialized fell short of the party's high expectations and stirred widespread disillusion. As Labour partisans saw it, the existing organization was too identified with the puni-

---

* The Labour statement was adopted, with certain refinements, by the Allied Socialist Conference which met two months later in London. Among the refinements was even greater emphasis on creation of a League of Nations, but this was entirely to the liking of the Labour delegates, and the party subsequently regarded the inter-Allied memorandum as the most complete statement of Labour ideas on the question of future international organization.

tive peace settlement and the consequent French endeavor to underpin an unjust status quo. But the spurt of Labour misgiving was short-lived, and by 1922 a more favorable evaluation was setting in. The annual conference hailed the League as a commendable first step toward a better world; in a "strengthened and democratised" League of Nations would be found "the most hopeful official machinery for the preservation of international and social peace."[24] Thereafter the Labour leadership concentrated on schemes for improving the organization, the work of Arthur Henderson, who was emerging as one of the party's most influential commentators on foreign affairs, figuring prominently in this campaign.[25] By the late 1920's the party percolated with enthusiasm for the League cause. The notion of national interests, suspect to begin with, now became all the more myopic and wicked. "You have to put loyalty to the League of Nations above loyalty to your country," Attlee informed the Commons in 1933.[26]

The party fully realized that the League itself was not a comprehensive supranational institution, let alone a world government. But it was optimistic, especially in the early interwar period, that a breakthrough in this direction was imminent—perhaps too optimistic. At any rate, Labour spokesmen continually referred to the League as the focus of an already existing "community of nations." Peace was indivisible, international cooperation was inevitable, world opinion was real and could be counted on; such slogans appeared and reappeared in Labour propaganda throughout the whole of the interwar period. It was as though the party, despite its keen alertness to the excesses of nationalism, did not fully appreciate how overwhelmingly powerful a force it still was. Instead, the assumption was apparently made that the loyalty and allegiance that the League required to operate effectively were already in existence and could be relied on—or if not already in existence, just beneath the surface, straining to break through. All that was needed to complete the growth was a firm moral lead from a great power; give that lead and the other nations would automatically follow. Naturally, in Labour's view, that power had to be Great Britain. The party demanded that the League become the heart and center of all British foreign policy; no major objectives should be envisaged outside its context. As Attlee put it in 1938, the traditional-minded had to be made to appreciate "the immense feeling there is behind the principles of the League and the immense differences it makes to people whether they are to be called upon to make sacrifices for an ideal or for a little bit of British property."[27]

Attlee's utterance is more than suggestive. It helps explain why Labour anticipated, during the 1930's, an automatic response by others to a British call for collective action; why it put only the most favorable construction on the status of contemporary nationalism and underplayed the adverse but nonetheless real aspects of national egoism; why, in short, it expected statesmen to violate so easily and willingly their deepest instincts for freedom of maneuver, for tailoring their nation's foreign policy to the exigencies of the moment, merely because a system of collective security was nominally established. For if, as Attlee assumes, people's loyalties are internationalist to begin with, then the whole problem of instituting an *effective* collective security system fades. The subjective patterns in men's orientations do not have first to be radically altered; it is not necessary, as a precondition, to remold their minds by replacing national symbols and values with international equivalents. Instead, taking an internationalist consciousness for granted, the Labour Party also took it for granted that national interests and international obligations coincided. But then what about the actual behavior of nations: why the huge discrepancy between what they really did and what Labour expected of them? This question, which Labour's opponents posed over and over again, did not vex party members very much. If national behavior was still governed by self-regarding considerations, it was only because existing statesmen had such little faith and limited vision— they could not appreciate the extent and magnitude of the inescapable challenge confronting them. But Labour could, and as soon as control of a great power like Britain fell into its grip, the consequent British lead would bring practice into line with the common people's present aspirations. Men would be brought to see, conclusively and strikingly, that peace was indeed indivisible, that what was good for the world was automatically good for the individual nation.

Airy fancies? Utopian longings that the party recognized had at best a chance to materialize in some vague and distant future? Anyone with this view of the matter has a shallow understanding of Labour thought during the interwar period. Far from considering these ideas feckless speculation, party members were unassailably convinced of their underlying realism. It was the traditionalists, with their threadbare cynicism, who spluttered nonsense, not Labour, which penetrated beneath the surface of things to capture the drift of history. The old system was bankrupt; its atavistic remnants were being daily discredited. Only a new system organized on lines of international cooperation, economic sharing, and social justice was tailored to meet the overarching needs of the moment. "We Socialists do not believe in keeping ideals and facts in watertight compartments," Henderson observed in a stern rebuke of traditionalist shortsightedness. "We derive our ideal [the establishment of a cooperative World Commonwealth] from a realistic analysis of the facts, and the existence of our ideal is itself a tremendous fact which will shape the course of world events."[28]

There is one additional facet of Labour's internationalism worth comment: anti-imperialism. The party objected to imperialism both because it denied the equality of peoples and nations and because it was supposed to be the form that capitalism invariably took in its international aspect. To fight against capitalism at home was thus willy-nilly to be committed to struggle against imperialism abroad. Right down to 1945 and beyond, the writings of not only J. A. Hobson (one of the prominent Liberal converts to Labour after World War I) but Karl Kautsky and Lenin continued to exercise considerable influence in Labour circles. Colonial native populations were regarded as fellow sufferers from the evils of predatory capitalism. As late as 1952, Denis Healey was moved to comment that "though war is at least 3,000 years older than capitalism, many socialists believe that capitalism is the only cause of war."[29]

From the very outset, most of Labour's more prominent leaders translated their anti-imperialist sentiment into concrete policy pronouncements, denouncing the Boer War as a shoddy imperialist adventure. It was, said Keir Hardie, a sordid affair aiming at the "enslavement of Black Labour and the pauperization of white Labour."[30] A few party spokesmen had a different opinion. These were chiefly Fabians, whose Society, with the publication of *Fabianism and the Empire*, expressed somewhat guarded but nonetheless explicit statements in approval of European (especially British) imperialisms. In Fabian eyes, the rest of Labour as well as Liberal anti-imperialists like Hobson had confounded imperialism and jingoism, and attributed the evils of the latter to the former.[31] "The majority of the Socialist leaders," according to Sidney Webb, who had in mind the Independent Labour Party, were hopeless Little Englanders, high-minded men of inaction who "proved to be, with regard to the British Empire, mere administrative Nihilists."[32] The first Labour conference passed a scorching anti-imperialist resolution all the same. Imperialism was termed bluntly a "reversion to barbarism." Though none of the resolutions approved by subsequent conferences before World War I were quite so categorical, there could be no mistaking the thrust of most Labour sentiment. The major impetus behind the campaign for colonial trusteeships under League auspices, for instance, was furnished by the Labour Party during the war. And like the rest of socialist policy, the anti-imperialist strain intensified in the interwar period. It spread even to the point of accounting, in Labour minds, for the deteriorating international scene in Europe itself. Behind fascist expansion were economic causes; fascism *was* capitalism in acute, unadorned form, capitalism grown desperate. Views such as these cut across the lines between the radical Left and the majority in the Labour Party in the mid-1930's. Attlee, in a Geneva speech, expounded a doctrine that no Leninist could object to.*

## International Working-Class Solidarity

The second socialist principle manifested itself in broadly two ways over Labour's history prior to World War II. On one level, it took the form of class-consciousness by which capitalist policy

* "Briefly our analysis is that production for profit invariably leads to a struggle for markets. It is of the essence of capitalism as we know it that it fails to distribute purchasing power among the masses of the workers in the country where it operates. The capitalist has to find a market for his production outside his own country. He exports goods as loans for the development of countries less industrially advanced than his own. The continuance of his system of production depends on finding ever fresh markets as the old ones become saturated, and sooner or later this brings him into rivalry with the capitalists of other nations. In the struggle for markets and concessions the rival groups of interests enlist the support of their respective Governments, which is exerted by diplomacy and threats of war. Ultimately war breaks out." "The Socialist View of Peace," pp. 98–99.

makers at home came under severe suspicion and, at the same time, international socialist organizations were participated in. On another level, following the Russian Revolution, it crystallized as ardent pro-Soviet sentiment. Each deserves to be examined in detail.

Labour, in harmony with its firm belief that socialism at home could not be safe in the presence of international anarchy, was convinced from its outset of the need for working-class cooperation across national borders to prevent war. It was only natural then for the party to seek membership in the Second International, just as it was natural for the party to endeavor to resurrect the International in 1919—though the creation of the Third International and the Vienna Union, the Two-and-a-Half International to which the ILP affiliated itself until 1923, sorely complicated matters by that date. In reality, these same complications existed in 1907 when Labour first applied to the Second International, though in less acute form than at the end of World War I. Labour's application was blocked for a year, and the reason had to do with the doubts of many Continental socialists about the party's credentials. What most puzzled them was Labour's aloofness from Marxism, particularly from its insistence on class warfare. Hyndman's Social Democratic Party, affiliated since 1904 (like the ILP), added to the resistance. The following year, however, Kautsky devised an ingenious formula that overcame the doubts of his colleagues. "The English Labour Party," it read, "is to be admitted to the International Socialist Congress because, although it does not avowedly recognize the class struggle, it actually carries it on; and because the organization of the Labour Party being independent of the bourgeois parties is based upon the class struggle." The formula was perhaps a bit too resourceful. It rested on an academic hairsplitting between class war (*Klassenkrieg*) and class struggle (*Klassenkampf*).[33] The distinction was meaningless because Labour, while committed to furthering working-class interests, adhered to the Fabian notion of class solidarity, not class struggle. Capitalism, Hardie wrote in exasperation after attendance at the 1904 congress of the International, was the "product of selfishness," and socialism would make "war upon a system, not upon a class."[34] What united Labour to the rest of the International was thus not class struggle but rather a shared sense of working-class solidarity and a shared conviction that capitalist anarchy had to be combatted on an international basis.

As a member of the International, Labour was pledged to support the 1907 Stuttgart Resolution on direct action as a means of war prevention. The 1912 annual conference reaffirmed the party's commitment, and the 1913 conference did so in even stronger language.[35] Needless to say, these were all exercises in futility. A general strike proved chimerical, a will-o-the-wisp to the last; the Second International came down in a crash during the August 1914 crisis. The resulting surge in nationalist feeling among the pro-war Labour members threatened to compromise the party's socialist principles, but the spirit of working-class solidarity never entirely died out, and weariness with the carnage of war began rekindling it in 1917. It was by no means mere coincidence that the episode which caused Henderson's resignation from the Cabinet, freeing him to become the vital link in the reunification of the pro- and anti-war factions, involved the Stockholm Peace Conference —attempted revival, however feeble, of prewar solidarity. Henderson's "international outlook, before dim and rather conventional, now gradually became vivid and personal."[36] He told the Trades Union Congress, in September, that though Stockholm might be dead, the idea of "an International Conference of workers" was not: "We belong to the class which has given most and suffered most, and we shall not allow this matter to rest in the hands of diplomatists, secret plenipotentiaries, or politicians of the official stamp."

Labour was rapidly radicalized in the course of the next few months. The ILP view of the war diffused rapidly among the party's ranks. Snowden observed in January 1918: "The turn around to the position of the ILP on the war has been so extraordinary within the last few months that we can confidently await the influences which have wrought this conversion to complete their work."[37] On one issue the ILP and the Labour Party continued, for five years, to differ somewhat. Though both were convinced at the war's end of the need to resurrect the International, the Russian Revolution made its revival a tricky matter. Labour, rejecting all overtures of the Third International, was instrumental in reviving the old Second, or at any rate what remained of it. The ILP, less willing to acknowledge an irreparable fissure in working-class solidarity, affiliated to the Vienna Union as a hopeful means of reforging unity. But by 1923 the effort was abandoned as hopeless, the Union collapsed, and the ILP and the Labour Party were joined together, however briefly, as common members in the new Labour and Socialist International.

After this brief burst of activity, the International receded into the background as a subject of interest. Only in the 1930's did Labour's attention perk up: this involved the Popular Front campaign, though even then the role of the two Internationals was still severely circumscribed. Otherwise nothing of consequence ensued. The Labour and Socialist International held meetings, published memoranda, sent fraternal greetings to Labour's annual conferences. But its Secretariat, though seated in London, dared make not even the slightest effort to interfere in intra-party disputes.[38] There is an unequivocal measure of Labour's lack of concern here. G. D. H. Cole, diligent historian of the Second International, makes no reference to it past 1923 in his comprehensive—and partly firsthand—account of the party's development.[39]

None of this should be taken to mean, however, that class consciousness waned as a factor in Labour foreign policy. On the contrary, a sense of class grievance and solidarity climbed considerably (although somewhat discontinuously) after 1918—only its focus shifted to the British scene and remained there. This was something new. In the pre-1914 period, Labour had always been a laggard as compared with Continental socialist parties in pursuing a distinctly class-biased line. The meetings of the International resounded with envenomed denunciations of capitalists; Labour delegates returned more convinced than ever of the ethical bonds uniting men across class boundaries. The International adopted blistering war resistance resolutions; Labour added its signature without ever working up much enthusiasm. But the upsurge in class feeling following the war brought a change; the party could no longer be accused of insufficient zeal, at any rate so far as its utterances went. Militancy, an acrid class animus, was very much in evidence when matters of foreign policy arose. In sharp revulsion to Versailles and Allied intervention in Russia, Labour began veering leftward. What, it was angrily asked, had been the point of the war if these were the sordid results? The 1922 conference gave one emphatic answer: Labour would henceforth oppose "any war entered into by any government, whatever the ostensible object of the war."[40] The 1926 conference went further still; it resolved that "the workers will meet any threat of war, so-called defensive or offensive, by organizing general resistance, including the refusal to bear arms."[41] Labour's commitment to direct action was reaffirmed at the 1933 Hastings Conference. The National Executive Committee (NEC) accepted, without a vote, a resolution instructing it to conduct anti-war propaganda, to map specific plans for a general strike, and to "work within the Labour and Socialist International for an uncompromising attitude against war preparations."* The last instruction illustrates our chief point more than adequately. Once again it was Labour that was in the lead and the International that was behindhand, in need of prodding.

But what about the 1924 government: are its actions not evidence to the contrary? It is true that the parliamentary leadership decided against "bold socialist measures"; as a minority government, the Cabinet was more concerned to demonstrate its responsibility, its "fitness to govern."[42] But its major initiatives in foreign policy, modest though they seemed, were fully in accord with Labour's received doctrine and program: diplomatic recognition of Russia, mediation of the Ruhr dispute, and conciliation of other Franco-German differences, not least support for the "Geneva Protocol" with firm deemphasis on its coercive elements and even firmer emphasis on its internationalist features. Moreover, to the extent that the government appeared to waver in its socialist zeal, it came under a drumfire of criticism from the rank and file. What Beer has argued about the running MacDonald-ILP quarrel in domestic policy at the time applies with even greater force to the area of foreign policy: the controversy was thrashed out within limits set by the party's consensus.[43]

The argument concerning Labour's radicalization finds additional support in a breakdown of attitudes according to important

---

* *LPCR*, 1933, pp. 185–92. Dalton, *Memoirs, 1931–1945*, argues that the resolution was passed with a possible Anglo-Russian war, not fascist aggression, in mind. Dalton should know; he accepted the resolution on behalf of the Executive, though even so his interpretation is not entirely supported by a reading of the conference report. In any case, the point to grasp is that the party showed an obsessive concern with British Tories, not German Nazis.

sections of the party. The ILP of course was consistently militant, its members bitter-enders, and not much needs to be said by way of amplification. What is worth reemphasizing, however, is its decisive impact on Labour after 1918; its systematic anti-capitalism —especially in connection with the origins of the war and the precariousness of the peace—was incorporated wholesale into Labour's foreign policy pronouncements.[44] The new Liberal recruits were almost equally militant, in spite of—or perhaps because of— their middle-class backgrounds; their influence in Labour circles, for almost a decade, was generally radical.[45] E. D. Morel, an uncompromising firebrand who expected to become Foreign Secretary in 1924, sought to organize a rank-and-file revolt against MacDonald's diplomacy.[46] It is a measure of his hold on Labour minds that, had he not died in the autumn, he might have gone on to pose a serious challenge to MacDonald's leadership.[47] By the late 1920's one could no longer so easily identify a distinct ex-Liberal viewpoint. Some of the converts were pursuing a more moderate tack; together with Henderson, they tried to make the League and piecemeal improvement function as the dominant dynamic in Labour's policy. But one must not be misled here; between the moderates and their more doctrinaire colleagues there was no fundamental principle at issue—only a matter of emphasis. All of the recruits, as Angell once observed, regarded "some form of Socialism as the best hope of saving the world from that madness which threatens to send whole nations down the steep places to destruction."[48] As for a third major section, the trade unions were in a combative frame of mind for the first decade and were closely attuned to the ILP view in foreign policy. In 1924, for instance, they tended to line up behind Morel, not MacDonald. Given their aggressive industrial activity at the time, their posture in foreign policy was only natural; all-out emphasis on class struggle became the rule, culminating in the 1926 general strike. Thereafter the unions' reconsideration regarding industrial matters left them with neither time nor energy to engage in disputes over foreign policy. The muddle and indecision prevailing in the party during the mid-1930's forced certain union leaders to intervene, and their intervention was of a moderating sort. But the early militancy of the unions had left its mark all the same, if only in the sense of reinforcing the radical upsurge that was touched off after 1918. Taking the Labour Party as a whole, then, it must be said that Kautsky's distinction no longer seemed so fanciful.

The party's leftward drift picked up momentum under the combined impulse of the Depression and the alleged MacDonald betrayal. For the first time in Labour's history, its intellectual spokesmen began questioning the strategy of gradualism. The fear haunted them that parliamentary democracy was a sham, an ideological smoke screen for the preservation of an increasingly obnoxious capitalist order. Twice Labour had come to power by parliamentary means; twice it had not edged one inch closer to the socialist utopia. Would the future, bleak as the present was, prove any better? The response of the more moderate pessimists was to try binding the leadership in advance: either a new Labour government would proceed directly to comprehensive socialist legislation or it would resign and refuse to come to terms with the existing order.* The more glum-ridden—Laski, Cripps, Strachey, Bevan, to name just a few—were filled with ominous premonitions; they asked themselves whether socialism could ever be implemented by constitutional means. Even Tawney insisted, at one point, that socialist measures would involve "a pretty desperate business."[49] In 1932 these fears and obsessions found expression in the Socialist League, created in the void left by the disaffiliation of the ILP. Under the guidance of left-wing stalwarts, the Socialist League evolved into a vehicle of unqualified class warfare in Labour's midst. It mounted savage attacks on *For Socialism and Peace*, the most comprehensive and radical programmatic statement adopted in Labour's history, as being insufficiently bold;[50] championed direct action by the workers "to prepare resistance to War declared by their own Governments";[51] blasted the League of Nations—a "tool of satiated imperialist powers";[52] and advocated a united front with the Communists as a means of staving off fascism abroad and capitalism at home, which were one and the same enemy.

So far as foreign policy was concerned, the strained mood of class antagonism noticeably complicated the Labour Party's effort to develop a practical policy in response to the fascist threat. Most

---

* This was the gist of Sir Charles Trevelyan's resolution, *LPCR*, 1932, pp. 204–5, which was carried without a vote.

of all the National government came under biting class-biased suspicion, until it seemed scarcely less wicked than fascism itself. Could such a government dare be trusted with arms? To the members of the Socialist League and their sympathizers, the question had only to be posed in order to be dismissed as absurd. In approving British rearmament, the Labour Party would merely be encouraging right-wing reaction to make use of its added strength for the purpose of crushing the organized working-class movement. As Cripps proclaimed in 1935: "I am not opposed to working class rearmament if it is necessary to provide protection for the workers against their class enemies in this or any other country, but I certainly am opposed most bitterly to rearming the British National Government for the purpose of increasing their power, so that they may do more evil in the future than they have done in the past."[53] The nature of this extremist opposition to rearmament might be best dubbed "class pacifism," in order to distinguish it from the ethical pacifism of figures like George Lansbury, the leader of the PLP from 1931 to 1935.

The Socialist League's irreconcilable die-hardism, it should be emphasized, never became the official Labour line. Even in its moments of bitterest despair, the official leadership never equated Toryism with fascism. Thus the 1933 annual conference approved a trade union–sponsored resolution which, while fiercely critical of British capitalism, hastened to emphasize that Britain was one of the few countries left in Europe still enjoying political liberty.[54] When the Socialist League continued to press energetically for a united front, launching a massive unity campaign in 1937, the Labour NEC moved to disaffiliate it and to denounce the whole idea of cooperation with the Communists.[55] All the same, if the Socialist League's class animosity never became the officially sanctioned party attitude in the 1930's, its harsh cynicism concerning the National government spilled lavishly over onto other party circles. Until late in the decade, the bulk of Labour members acted as though the government could not be trusted in matters of rearmament. "The Party won't face up to realities," Dalton complained in 1936. "There's much more anti-armament sentiment and many are more agin' our own Government than agin' Hitler."[56]

As previously noted, the focus of Labour's class consciousness shifted to Britain itself in the interwar period. This observation is only generally, not strictly, correct, for there was one exception. The principle of working-class solidarity also found expression in pro-Soviet sentiment and influenced Labour's behavior accordingly.

The term "sentiment" is important. Essentially the tie joining Labour's sympathy to the Soviet cause was emotional, an assumed identity of common status as underdogs. The identity grew out of certain harsh experiences that both seemed to share in the war's aftermath—or so, at any rate, Labour partisans came to believe, which in the end amounted to the same thing. The impression seized hold of the party that the new Soviet state and itself suffered the implacable enmity of a common foe: international capitalism, especially in its virulent British form at the time.[57] "Russia, prime object of Capitalist fear and attack, became, inevitably, the rallying centre of Labour sentiment."[58]

For all its one-sided subjectivity, Labour's impression was partially rooted in reality. Two related chains of events between 1918 and 1920 reinforced the party's instinctive sympathy with a workers' government. First, the Lloyd George government appeared to be masterminding the Allied intervention campaign against the Bolsheviks. Labour firmly opposed intervention; however great the gulf dividing the Soviet Bolshevik and the British socialist parliamentarian, the party had jubilantly welcomed the collapse of czardom and insisted that the new Soviet regime be given opportunity to make real its socialist aspirations. When, therefore, three major unions (the Triple Alliance) demanded in April 1919 a British withdrawal on pain of a general strike, the effect on the party was electric and the annual conference emphatically endorsed the ultimatum. Thus, owing to events within the Soviet Union and to British foreign policy, a showdown between Labour and the established order loomed clearly and menacingly ahead. Second, a clash was made all the more likely because the Lloyd George government had become repellent to Labour for other, though related, reasons. Lloyd George, master intriguer and incomparable political maneuverer, fought the 1918 election on a shrill patriotic note, arousing nationalist passion and then exploiting it to the disadvantage of his foes, among whom Labour of course figured prominently. He had endeavored, among other things, to frighten the electorate with innuendos and barely veiled allusions that Labour and Bolshevism were stealthy bedfellows. The Labour Party was "run by the extreme pacifist, Bolshevist group," he harangued at one point on the hustings. "Look at what has happened in Russia."[59] Amidst this highly charged demagogic atmosphere, the election resulted in a sharp blow to Labour fortunes. Of 361 candidates that the party ran, only 57 managed to edge into Parliament; among the defeated were all of its preeminent leaders save for J. R. Clynes.

It was thus not surprising, given these two chains of events, that the Labour Party reacted as it did. Labour's detested political enemies at home were trying to engineer the destruction of the new Soviet regime and for what appeared to be the same motive animating their unscrupulous assaults on socialism in Britain itself— their half-hysterical zeal to preserve the status quo, the class-ridden and decadent capitalist order, no matter what the cost. Under such circumstances the party felt that if its own cause at home was henceforth to be salvaged, it had to champion the Soviet cause as well.

Nor was this all. The emotional tie was strengthened, in 1920, when Labour intensified its campaign against intervention and moved more dramatically to the verge of direct action. By then the British government had itself pulled out of Russia, but Labour suspected (rightly) that the government was continuing its anti-Bolshevik vendetta by way of covert financial support to the Poles, then at war with the Soviets. In mid-summer the war abruptly changed course and the collapse of the Polish armies seemed imminent; rumors flew in Britain that the Government, rather than suffer a Red victory, was prepared to dispatch a large British force. Faced by the threat of general war, Labour was galvanized into a fury of activity. It established an ominous-sounding "Council of Action," with responsibility to map final plans for the long-expected general strike. As things turned out, no strike crystallized. It was not necessary. A collision with the established forces was averted when Lloyd George backed off and offered assurance of his restraint. Labour was exhilarated. The old order had surrendered; its foreign foe, weak and isolated, had been saved. Seen in retrospect, the Government's decision to retire was probably prompted more by a sudden upturn in Polish military fortunes than by any fear of a showdown with Labour, but the party itself did not see matters in that light. It was decidedly convinced that its boldness at home had been the decisive factor in rescuing the Russian Revolution from destruction.[60]

Henceforth Labour enthusiasts displayed the same benevolent, paternalistic attitude toward the Soviet Union that a protector adopts toward an underdog whom he has saved from the clutches of an overbearing bully. This emotionally charged state of mind made it impossible for the majority of Labour partisans to view subsequent Soviet development in perspective. Roy Jenkins has referred to the party's historical "wallowing in vague, emotional feelings of solidarity with the Soviet Union."[61] Less harshly, R. H. S. Crossman has employed the term "Russian Complex" to describe the prevailing mood.[62] Not all Labour spokesmen were beguiled, of course. Bertrand Russell became an early antagonist of the Soviet dictatorship. Arthur Henderson retained a skeptical outlook dating from his 1917 Moscow mission. MacDonald was characteristically ambivalent (or confused). In *Foreign Policy for the Labour Party*, which he wrote in 1923, he denounced Soviet Communism's "queer non-moral mentality," only in the next breath to denounce "nine-tenths of anti-Communist propaganda" as a "wild whirl of forgery, of ignorance, of fake." But there was no confusion or ambivalence among the mass of the party. Any wavering by the leadership in support of the Soviet cause was sure to provoke outbursts of protest. As Dalton observed, "Russia is still, in the whole field of foreign affairs, the subject on which we are under most pressure from our own Party for quick action."[63] The 1930's brought little change. The Comintern, forced collectivization, labor camps, dictatorship, purges—these might not have existed for all many Labour partisans cared. Indeed, some grew more enthusiastic as time went on—the Webbs, for instance, whose *Soviet Communism: A New Civilisation?* uncovered a kind of promised land, a socialist future in operation, with dedicated puritan administrators toiling busily on behalf of the common weal.

Labour's benevolence toward the Soviet Union did not extend to the British Communist Party, even though its creation was, of course, a direct consequence of the Russian Revolution. In 1921, the Comintern ordered the British Communists to seek affiliation with the Labour Party; but Labour, whatever its sympathy for Communism in Russia, wanted nothing to do with the homegrown equivalent, and by 1925 the annual conference adopted a constitutional resolution proscribing all Communist links.[64]

Of the multitude of reasons that would account for Labour's unmitigated antagonism to British Communism, two bulk largest. In the first place, the party prided itself on its democratic character, and this meant that the leadership did not take kindly to Communist officials who dutifully switched their line according to the whims of a foreign agency, even one located in Moscow. At the same time, the leadership realized that Labour's only hope of ever winning power in Britain was through convincing the electorate of its fitness to govern; quite obviously, even remotely appearing to consort with the Communist Party would be calculated to produce the exact opposite effect. In the second place, the British trade union movement soon developed staunch anti-Communist views in face of repeated Communist attempts to infiltrate it—again, a strategy for which the Comintern was plainly responsible.[65] Tough-minded, hardened union leaders like Ernest Bevin, Walter Citrine, and Charles Dukes were not prepared to stand idly by while Communist agitators diligently proceeded to wrest control of their unions; and there ensued a running battle between the two sides that raged throughout the whole of the interwar period.[66]

Most Labour partisans apparently saw no contradiction in sympathizing with Communism in Russia and yet resolutely opposing it in Britain. The connection between the two might as well have been fortuitous, a coincidence of no great import. There was one standout exception. A number of trade union leaders, including the ones just mentioned, gradually swung round to the realization that their movement would remain vulnerable to Communist penetration so long as enthusiasm for the Soviet Union remained itself at high pitch in the minds of average trade unionists.

By the early 1930's, as a result, the Trades Union Congress (TUC) General Council was pressing the Labour leadership for a firmer stand on the Soviet regime. A notable instance occurred in 1933 when the annual party conference endorsed Citrine's report condemning all totalitarianism, whether of the Left or of the Right.[67] The hardening of will in leadership circles was also evinced in the Executive's steadfast hostility to the united front campaign. When approached by the ILP and the Communist Party in this connection in February 1934, for instance, the Executive observed that the Communists' real aim was "to destroy the Labour Party's influence and to disrupt its membership."[68]

On balance, however, the emotional link connecting Labour to the Soviet Union did not snap. Party members still continued to distinguish between Communist antics at home and Soviet Communism; still continued—in Dalton's phrase—to make the Soviet Union the subject on which the leadership came under the most pressure for quick action.* Indeed, Soviet prestige climbed rapidly in proportion to the growth in the fascist menace; this was especially the case once the Soviets adopted the rhetoric of collective security and won admission to the League of Nations. Hitherto, in Soviet utterances, the League had loomed as a capitalist sham; overnight it became the focus of all freedom-loving, progressive-minded men. Most Labour partisans were not bothered by this inconsistency. What they saw was a welcome addition to the anti-fascist camp, and not even the outbreak of purges in 1935 notably altered their view. Soviet support for the Spanish Republicans—or, rather, what was widely believed about this support, despite the disturbing reports sent home from Spain by Orwell and other socialists—seemed far more important and in character. Who could doubt that the Soviet Union was a major progressive force in the world? Only two months before the Nazi-Soviet Nonaggression Pact, the Chairman of the party assured the Labour Conference that "Moscow is the custodian of peace."[69]

*Anti-Capitalism*

Until 1918, Labour's commitment to a new political and social order at home was never spelled out and remained obscure. Time and again socialist intellectuals pressed the party to adopt a detailed declaration of ultimate socialist objectives, and time and again the bulk of the party resisted. But in 1918 the situation was fully transformed. In adopting the present party constitution, Labour specifically stated that its ultimate aim was to establish a socialist society based "on the common ownership of the means of

---

* Even Bevin, blistering anti-Communist though he was, apparently adhered to this distinction. See his observation quoted in Bullock, I, 559.

production, distribution, and exchange." And directly central to
this distinct commitment was a thoroughgoing hostility to capitalism. This hostility did not, in the manner of traditional reformist agitation, merely fasten on a few features of contemporary
capitalism; it did not single out only this or that aspect as obnoxious and in need of reform. Labour's antagonism was without
qualification. It repudiated capitalism as a system, condemning it
as the source of all social wrongs and evils.[70]

So far as socialist foreign policy was concerned, this anti-capitalism made itself felt in at least three ways. Two have already
been touched on and can be quickly disposed of.

The first was conviction that traditional foreign policy amounted primarily to a vehicle to serve the interests of the capitalist ruling classes. "The modern foreign policy of Great Britain," J. A.
Hobson observed in 1902, "is primarily a struggle for profitable
markets of investment." Financial capitalism did not, by itself,
constitute "the motor-power of Imperialism" on the Hobson view;
in addition, capitalism was partly allied with "patriotism, adventure, military enterprise, political ambition, and philanthropy,"
and partly their manipulator for its own interests. But whatever
the causal link here, maldistribution of wealth, over-saving, and
repeated outward economic thrusts were the odious consequence
of any capitalist order.[71] Attlee put the matter more simply when
he asserted, in *The Labour Party in Perspective*, that "the foreign
policy of a Government is the reflection of its internal policy."
Just as at home the established order was engaged in all sorts of
devious practices to keep itself in power, so secret diplomacy and
the like were manifestations of capitalist intrigue on an international level. Even reform-minded Liberals came under suspicion:
had not the Asquith governments manufactured secret treaties,
and had not their machinations driven the nation into war in
1914? In Labour's view, the only way to hold in check the ruling
classes was to tie their hands, to "democratize" foreign policy;
secret diplomacy had to be abolished, all treaties should receive
the prior approval of Parliament. The Union of Democratic Control (UDC), E. D. Morel its driving force, was a powerful vehicle
in campaigning for change. More and more the old tried system
of diplomacy fell into disrepute; even Lloyd George showed only
contempt for the professionals at the Foreign Office. With the ad-

vent of the 1924 Labour government, the right of prior Parliamentary review was formalized in the Ponsonby rule—named after Arthur Ponsonby, ex-Liberal recruit, UDC luminary, and current Under-Secretary at the Foreign Office.

But democratization of foreign policy, however welcome in itself, was not construed by Labour to spell the end of capitalist influence. The root problem was social and economic, not just political; so long as there were capitalist nations, there would *most likely be* imperialist expansion, imperialist competition, and consequent war. Here, then, was the second manifestation of Labour's anti-capitalism: a profound conviction that peace could be made fully secure until capitalist anarchy in the whole international system was overcome. Tampering with the Foreign Office, limiting the latitude of permanent officials, increasing the role of Parliament in policy making—these were all desirable steps, but they were also only initial steps, steps that had to be supplemented by more systematic socialist measures. As the International Advisory Committee observed in 1920: "Capitalism, given over to its extreme phase of Imperialism and militarism, is shattering the material basis of civilisation. Our task is not to deflect the Foreign Office a little from its crazy path. Our task is to make the masses understand the ruin wrought in the world by Imperial capitalism."[72] Even if by chance a situation of peace existed, war could erupt at any moment because suspicion, cynicism, scheming, and intrigue were built into the very core of capitalist nations. So entrenched was this feeling that Harold Laski tried tapping it as late as 1946; as he told the annual conference in his capacity as chairman of the Executive, "let capitalist nations mistrust one another: that mistrust is inherent in capitalist society."[73] By the converse of such reasoning, socialist regimes would be instinctively peaceloving. Judicious collective reorganization of the domestic economy would remove any economic reason for aggressive international behavior. Instead of trying to escape from economic crisis and class struggle at home, socialist regimes would end that struggle, would employ the nation's resources for the general welfare, would, in short, prepare the groundwork for that ultimate transformation of the international system that socialist foreign policy had as its goal.

Logically, Labour's suspicion of capitalist regimes should probably have entailed an unqualified refusal to cooperate with any capitalist government or coalition of such governments, even for the purpose of preventing a particular war. In fact, however, the party evinced some ambivalence on this score. The more radical groups, increasingly numerous after 1931, regarded imperialism as an *inevitable* consequence of capitalism and therefore, by extension, wars among imperialist nations as no less inevitable. As a Socialist League manifesto said flatly, "war is inherent in the economic structure of Capitalist Society."[74] It followed, on this view, that efforts to prevent war in a capitalist world were foredoomed, little more than pious hangovers from nineteenth-century liberalism. Cooperation with even the League of Nations was ruled out; to the radical-minded, that body also "inevitably reflected the economic conflicts of the capitalist system and of the governments which compose the League."[75] On the other hand, many party theorists rejected what Leonard Woolf called the "fatalistic view of history."[76] Capitalism was bad; capitalism produced imperialism; capitalism led to war. But it did not do so "inevitably." As Hobson had stressed in his original study, imperialism was a *likely* policy of any capitalist order, not an inescapable consequence. The difference in the degree of probability was not an academic matter. Depending on which view he took, a Labour member might, however great his suspicion of capitalist governments, still decide that some were less warlike than others and that, accordingly, socialists might have to join cause with them under certain regrettable circumstances. Attlee spoke for this viewpoint when he said in 1934: "Ultimately we shall not get peace until we have world socialism, but we have to deal with things as they are today."[77]

The third way, finally, in which anti-capitalism entered into socialist foreign policy did not matter a great deal before 1945. This was a general uneasiness about the United States, a stronghold—if not the citadel—of world capitalism. On the left wing of the party, this nervous feeling approached outright apprehension, especially during the 1930's. Whether it could be described as "anti-Americanism," though, is another question; for the fact is that before World War II the United States figured as a topic of only minor interest in most Labour circles. So long as the United States remained on the periphery of international life, in semi-isolation, Labour was far more concerned with, say, capitalist France; and during the 1920's the "wild anti-German chauvinism of French capitalist-militarists" became an obsessive concern to the party. Only after 1945, when the United States functioned as one of the two poles of international activity, did Labour interest in it shoot upward. Then party opinion became sharply agitated. Then, indeed, it was correct to talk about a significant anti-American current. And since the degree to which the party became agitated had roots in the interwar period, Labour's traditional attitude toward the United States deserves diagnosis no matter how vague and ill-defined it remained.

Among British liberals and radicals in the nineteenth century, the United States had enjoyed a favorable image. They saw it as a benign force in history, a happy augury of Britain's own future; they lavished praise on American egalitarianism, marveled at its democratic openness, and extolled its universal educational system.[78] By the time of Labour's founding, however, the American image had already begun to sour; party partisans now seized on the newly discovered sordid features and added their own twists. Now it was the conservatism of American life that was underscored, mercilessly exposed, and placed in socialist perspective. Two features were regarded as particularly disturbing. The first involved the apparent singleminded concern of most Americans with economic development—a concern that loomed as doubly repulsive to Labour's early spokesmen, themselves unwavering critics of a narrow-minded economic perspective that created Britain's own social evils. The United States, as increasingly reconstructed in the writings of socialist intellectuals, appeared crass, materialistic, a capitalist's paradise. Nor was this picture composed of only ILP efforts, though ILP members were at the forefront. The Fabians also had a strong negative view. To their administrative and orderly minds, the United States was bureaucratically outlandish, and its people "infantile" in all that concerned the machinery of government.[79]

The second feature of American life that rubbed wrong was the failure of an American version of the Labour Party to take root. The failure puzzled Labour observers all the more in that numerous socialist groups flowered over the American countryside prior to 1914. The party did not, for the most part, attempt to appreciate the reasons for this peculiar political development, nor could most Labour partisans have cared less about them; what mattered was the failure of socialism and that alone, and hence the United States had to be hopelessly and irretrievably anti-progressive, political democracy notwithstanding. By the interwar period the United States occupied a sinister place in left-wing demonology. It towered in the eyes of the party's numerous radicals as a bulwark of capitalist reaction, a haven for the ruthless exploiters of workers. As a measure of Labour opinion, it is worth noting that radical American writers like Jack London, Frank Norris, and Upton Sinclair had become *de rigueur* for aspiring British socialists.

By the early 1930's the more militant in Labour's ranks were writing off the American ability to remain outside the fascist fold. Several, singly or in groups, risked journeys to the United States in order to observe at first hand the effects of the Depression there. Would Americans seek salvation from the devastating economic crisis by swerving at long last to the socialist left or—more likely—by plunging headlong into extreme right-wing reaction? A third alternative was simply unimaginable. "From all signs visible," wrote Jennie Lee (Aneurin Bevan's wife), "it is Fascism, not Socialism, which is most likely to overtake the American masses."[80]

Not even the vigor of the New Deal improved the Left's opinion very much. Capitalism was capitalism, whether tempered by a New Deal or not, whether stabilized by Keynesian economics or not, whether found in America, Britain, Spain, Italy, or anywhere. Aneurin Bevan was an instructive case. As a backbench member of the PLP, Bevan had an impeccable militant reputation: stalwart of the Socialist League and even disaffiliated in 1939 by the Labour Executive. To Bevan, capitalism was nothing less than a huge monolithic structure of international character which could tolerate political democracy for only so long. In a capitalist society, "either poverty will use democracy to win the struggle against property, or property, in fear of poverty, will destroy democracy."[81] To the extent that Bevan granted that American capitalism differed somewhat from the pre-1945 European kind, he found it all the more evil and obnoxious, for it was bigger and stronger, and so more viable. No less illustrative of an uncompromising anti-capitalist mentality was Harold Laski, a long-standing member of the National Executive before becoming its chairman in 1945. Laski's voluminous writings did much to spread and diffuse an unfavorable American reputation in party circles. Like Bevan, he did not see the New Deal as much of a redeeming feature. According to one widely read work of his, the New Deal eventually lost its momentum, and lapsed into dependence on the whims of city political bosses who "are, for all practical purposes, simply the affiliates of Big Business, acting as their agents in municipal affairs."[82]

It needs to be emphasized, however, that the Left's apprehension never received official sanction. The more moderate elements in the Labour Party, so far as they gave America consideration at all, managed to preserve a more balanced outlook. This was especially true of many trade unionists, owing in no small part to the lesser hold of socialist ideology in their ranks. Several union leaders maintained harmonious relations with their American counterparts, and the belief was widespread that American workers were like the hard-working, democratic-minded workers in Coventry or Glasgow. Hence, as long as there was a strong and independent trade union movement in the United States, the average British trade unionist was satisfied that things could not be too bad there.[83] The cautious phrasing of the last five words is purposeful. It is one thing to argue that British trade unionists had a more open-minded attitude than their socialist colleagues, quite another thing to argue that they were pro-American. The latter argument would be inaccurate. With but few exceptions, even moderate trade unionists were not left untouched by the misgivings of Labour intellectuals. Bevin, who can be considered representative of their type, was a case in point. For all his contacts with American unionists, his trips there, his respect for American organizational methods, he still thought "American civilisation crude, noisy, boastful and materialistic."[84]

All in all, the further left on the political spectrum a Labour partisan was located, the more likely he was to display nervous mistrust of the United States. This was true even before 1945. Indeed the conviction seeped into the minds of many, left-wing or otherwise, that Wall Street had been involved in toppling the Labour government from power during the August 1931 crisis. Henceforth it was easy to hold American capitalism nearly as guilty as British capitalism for Britain's domestic plight.

*Anti-Militarism: Antipathy to Power Politics*

Of all the aspects of traditional foreign policy that Labour objected to, none aroused its rancor more than reliance on force as a major policy instrument. That British statesmen had generally employed force with restraint, and more often than not for defensive purposes, did not alter Labour's powerful feeling one bit. The party was certain that a foreign policy backed by force was not only immoral but inexpedient, that it would sooner or later provoke general war. The only genuine security lay in trust of others and in devotion to the ideals of international cooperation and justice. "Moral means," "the proper position," "rightness of position," "conciliation," "scientific political and economic policy," "disarmament," "ruling justice"—these are all terms taken from the utterances of J. R. MacDonald during the 1920's, but they were in intense circulation throughout the whole of the party and formed part of the accepted mode of discourse for Labour partisans. Add to them the terms "direct action" and "war resistance," which were the specialty of the more militant-minded, and you have an ample vocabulary for describing the alternatives with which Labour proposed to replace force as an instrument.

Well before World War I, Labour had directed a broad attack against traditional policy on these grounds. To the traditionalist way of thinking, skillful balancing of power could and would maintain general stability and peace; and it was precisely owing to this belief that British governments after 1900, sensing the mammoth upswing in German power and ambitions, had edged round to entangling relationships with France and Russia. With dismay and apprehension Labour watched the Anglo-German naval race, the two Moroccan crises, the rise in European tension unfold. As party spokesmen saw it, British attempts to keep the scales of the balance adjusted would invariably fail, indeed produce the opposite of the desired effect. Again and again they pointed to the increase, not decrease, in the likelihood of war that was resulting. To avert war, Labour contemplated direct action by the organized working classes. The workers, as MacDonald put it in 1911, were not going to stand passively by while disaster overtook them. They were no longer "content to be pawns in the game of diplomats and financiers"; they—or, rather, Labour as their spokesman—

demanded slashes in military expenditure, open diplomacy, and a new moral sense in high places.[85]

The 1912 and 1913 conference resolutions pledging direct action remained, of course, in the realm of fantasy when war erupted. The majority of Labour partisans proved to be patriotic; they supported British intervention and trooped off to the trenches. To the anti-war minority, this was a betrayal of socialist principles; the ILP alone had "withstood the onrush of war passion" and "refused to identify itself and Socialist and Labour principles with the foreign policy that led the country into war."[86] Yet, in defense of the Labour majority, it should be said that they did not regard their actions as betraying the party's principles. Once the initial passions subsided, the majority took a more sober view of the war; in January 1916, the first regular annual conference reaffirmed Labour's hostility to secret diplomacy, balance-of-power politics, and militarism.[87] The pro-war majority supported the British effort chiefly for one reason: like their German counterparts, they saw themselves as fighting a defensive war on whose outcome the future of civilization hinged. Their belief might have been mistaken—indeed, many Labour partisans by 1918 were more than willing to concede this; but the point is that, except for the British Workers' National League, a right-wing splinter group, Labour opinion remained international-minded—opposed to a war of imperialism, expansion, or revenge.

In 1918, under pressure of revulsion to the war, the party regained its unity. More than by anything else, it was now tied together by a common anti-militarist outlook and a conviction that socialists must never again support a policy of force. The prestige of the anti-war group shot up rapidly; its most prominent member, Ramsay MacDonald, was elected leader in 1922 in no small measure owing to his pacifist reputation.[88] By the early 1920's, moreover, the international situation seemed a source of decided hope for breakthroughs in pacification and disarmament. Power politics appeared to be well along the way to becoming an anachronism, a museum relic; the League system was heartening evidence that force was being eliminated from international relations, yielding gradually but assuredly to reasoned discussion and the rule of law. Party spokesmen, if queried why it was that they were so optimistic on this score, invariably pointed to the ghastly suffering of 1914–18 as proof of a fundamental change in men's minds. The terrible experience of those four years had demonstrated, beyond any doubt, the total unprofitability of war; an intellectual grasp of this fact was alone sufficient to set the nations in irreversible motion toward a new and better era.

There were, it is true, some Labour spokesmen with a more sober-minded view of things; they understood that the League system could not rely just on men's goodwill, that its success required a firm undergirding of meaningful collective security. Angell, for instance, began campaigning in 1924 for recognition of force as a permanent factor in international relations; the issue was not force versus no force, but the purposes for which it would be used.[89] And Angell was joined by several ex-Liberals, by Henderson, even—it seemed—by MacDonald in pressing the Geneva Protocol. But how much did their view count? Did they themselves take seriously the prospect that force, even force under collective auspices, was an indispensable ingredient in the massive effort to overhaul the international system? The answers are hardly in doubt; Labour remained as hostile as ever to hardheaded power calculations. The party was convinced that force was losing its rationale—losing it no matter what individual men or regimes themselves did, including either acceptance or rejection of the Geneva Protocol. Conciliation, pacification, disarmament: the world was marching steadily in that order toward a system of lasting peace and justice.

What reasons underlay the party's unshakable faith on this matter? In posing this question, I mean those reasons quite apart from the international situation itself—in other words, intellectual and emotional reasons. Here it is necessary to try to get at Labour's understanding of discord and conflict in political life. The party's ideas on the subject were of pivotal importance not only in relation to the anti-militarist principle but concerning the whole of socialist foreign policy.

To put it simply, the party regarded conflict as unreal, illusory, mistaken. The term itself is not particularly important; in point of fact, Labour partisans used all three interchangeably, even though they are not, of course, equivalent. But to the partisans all three expressed a profound truth about life: namely, when two or more individuals (or nations for that matter) fell out with one another, the resulting discord was unnecessary. It was a mistake—the disputants didn't really understand or appreciate each other's objectives. Or it was due to shortsightedness—they were only taking the short-run view of their interests. Or it was a result of insufficient knowledge—they lacked adequate information to predict the outcomes of their initial actions. The list is endless: misperception, easily removed prejudices, faulty images, etc. The point underlying all these variations—the point that was at the heart of Labour's understanding—is that harmony (cooperation, accord) was alone natural. Any other sort of relationship was unnatural: the disputants had only to discover the common good which was at the same time their own highest good, and they would immediately see that they had every reason to modify their position and to overcome their discord.

There was nothing new about this notion. Far from Labour inventing it, a doctrine postulating an ultimate harmony of interests was part and parcel of the whole Liberal metaphysic that sprang out of the eighteenth-century enlightenment.[90] In laissez-faire economics, for instance, the doctrine maintained that there was an inevitable harmony between an individual entrepreneur's self-interest and the nation's overall interest in maximizing economic wealth. By the middle of the nineteenth century, Bright, Cobden, and other Liberal speculators had elaborated a comprehensive theory of international relations along this very line. As they saw it, the ultimate harmony pertained no less to the international community (the whole) and to individual nations (its component parts); each in pursuing its own interest would maximize the common good of all, on the crucial assumption that *peace* was equally in the *long-run interest* of everyone. No matter how much one nation's circumstances differed from another's, no matter if one were rich and the other poor, if one were territorially satisfied and the other not, they all had a "true," a "real," a "transcendent," an "ultimate" interest in avoiding war and reaching peaceful conciliation in any dispute. The problem (which was considered tractable) was simply to get statesmen to understand this vivid truth.

It is hardly surprising that Labour absorbed this doctrine, given its intellectual indebtedness to classical liberalism in so many areas of its thought. The doctrine, for instance, plainly colored the party's stand on class relations: the "natural" relation between capitalists and workers was one of cooperation, not (as Marxists insisted) conflict. For that matter, the whole rationale of a strategy of gradualism and Parliamentary advance was founded on the doctrine: you didn't have to seize power, knock heads, destroy wicked capitalists; you could win support by persuasion, appealing to people's natural sense of justice. Labour, to be sure, did not imbibe the Liberal metaphysic indiscriminately. We have already noted how the party broke sharply with Liberalism in one crucial sense: it rejected piecemeal reform in favor of systemic reform which aimed at a thoroughgoing regeneration of society. But the doctrine about natural harmony it absorbed, fully, without qualification. So manifestly self-evident did the Liberal assumption about peace seem to Labour that in 1944, as bombs were still falling on London, the annual conference approved a resolution that stated: "We are confident that the vital interests of all nations are the same. They all need peace."[91]

But why, then, were there wars? Liberalism was not blind to international conflict; it only held that such conflict was unnecessary, unreal, always avoidable. If it therefore happened that two or more disputants were unable to perceive the transcendent common good in any situation and so stumbled into war, this had to be due to the folly of statesmen who blocked the path to harmony: they were too shortsighted, narrow-minded, indeed class-biased, to grasp the basic truth of life. To overcome these intellectual and moral defects, certain reforms had to be implemented within the nations. These comprised, of course, the standard Anglo-American liberal program: democratization of foreign policy, the end of secret diplomacy, settlement of the nationality problem, and reduction of military establishments.

They also comprised the Labour Party's program. But—and this is the significant point—only part of that program: for to this list of reforms was added one powerful and distinct socialist component. If Liberalism argued that, to end anarchy and secure harmony, it was necessary to institutionalize the four measures just mentioned, Labour argued that a fifth was no less important: socialization of the economy. Only then would anarchy—that is, discord, conflict, strife, alienation—be truly overcome, for anarchy and capitalism were all of a piece. There are countless examples of Labour's reasoning in this regard. As MacDonald observed after identifying the sources of international difficulties: "the need, therefore, was for disarmament, the end of the prevailing political system of Europe, open diplomacy, and the genuine international-ism of socialism."[92] Once the nations were democratically social-ized, force as a factor in their relations would automatically dis-appear. Indeed, the desire for its use would have faded.

By and large, Labour's behavior during the interwar period ex-emplified these convictions. Not only did the party pass three doc-trinaire anti-war resolutions (in 1923, 1926, 1933); it also unwaver-ingly pressed for disarmament through the League of Nations and sent Arthur Henderson to head the Disarmament Conference in 1932. "The prime purpose of the League of Nations," Arthur Greenwood wrote in 1929, is "to organize the world for peace, to find a method of settling international differences without recourse to war, and to lift from the nations the oppressive burden of com-petitive expenditures on armaments."[93] Despite the changes in the international situation, despite the fierce tussles over rearmament in the late 1930's, the party clung to its belief that force was always suspect no matter what the purpose behind its use. This belief backed the party, as we shall see, into a dilemma of mammoth proportions; and it found that the only way to retain even a tenu-ous grip on reality was by way of compromise. Yet right down to the spring of 1939, it refused to countenance conscription as a means of meeting the advance of war. What MacDonald had writ-ten in 1923, "We have to abandon absolutely every vestige of trust in military equipment"; what Attlee had echoed in 1935, "It is impossible for us to get any kind of security through rearmament"; what, indeed, almost all Labour spokesmen had said again and again, even when grudgingly approving British rearmament, still provided a powerful impulse in party thought on international relations.[94]

#### SOCIALIST FOREIGN POLICY AS PARTY ORTHODOXY

Together, the four principles dissected here added up to a distinct socialist commitment in foreign policy, a party orthodoxy. This orthodoxy was maintained in its essentials right down to World War II and even after that. Different sections, different spokesmen and leaders, might emphasize this facet or that facet, depending on the temperament of the persons in question and the circumstances involved. It is even proper, probably, to distinguish between a militant and a moderate variation—between whole-hoggers and go-slowers. Hence the eruption of conflict in 1924 and in the 1930's. But always the differences between the two sides turned on tactical matters, not fundamentals. How could the principles be applied to the problems at hand? And if no immediate application seemed feasible, how far could a good socialist go in tempering his commitment out of consideration for the realities of the moment? These—and not fundamentals of the orthodoxy—were the questions that Labour partisans posed to themselves again and again between 1900 and 1939. They were the questions that separated the anti-war and pro-war factions in 1914, Morel and MacDonald in 1924, the Socialist League and the League of Nations proponents in the mid-1930's. To the one side, compromise with a capitalist international system was unthinkable or at any rate dangerous; the attempt would invariably make things worse and divide the socialist camp in the process. To the other side, it might be true (as Attlee said in 1934) that "ultimately we shall not get peace until we have world Socialism"; all the same, "we have to deal with things as they are today."

Note Attlee's choice of words. The fundamentals of the socialist orthodoxy are taken for granted; peace and capitalism are ultimately irreconcilable. It was the problem of "things as they are today" that divided the two sides, and this—to employ an apt military metaphor—was a matter of tactics, not strategy. Or as A. J. P. Taylor has put it, in his inimitable way: "Until 22 August 1939 the Labour movement from Right to Left retained its old principles or, if you prefer, its old illusions. It still held that outlook of Keir Hardie, and E. D. Morel, of Brailsford and J. A. Hobson. No issue of principle divided Attlee from Cripps so far as foreign policy was concerned. Two simple sentences expressed it all. Imperialist capitalism was the cause of war. Socialists should oppose both war and capitalism."[95]

*Chapter two*

# The Crisis of Socialist Foreign Policy in the Interwar Period

For all the conflict that tore through Labour's ranks during World War I, the status of socialist foreign policy as party doctrine was itself never seriously at stake. Neither faction at the time, the pro-war majority any more than the anti-war minority, ever called the four socialist principles into question, and the unity that was re-found in 1918 rested in large part on their emphatic reaffirmation. For several years a near unassailable consensus prevailed and with it party unity. Occasional rumblings of discord were audible, especially in 1924. But consensus, even firm consensus, does not necessarily imply full harmony; in any large party some disagreement is inevitable, if only over the tactics and the speed with which to move toward commonly accepted objectives. So it was for the most part with the 1924 controversy: a dispute over means and timing, not over fundamentals of the orthodoxy. The controversy soon petered out, and by 1929 the second Labour government seemed to be moving from one socialist success to another, though by that time party attention was riveted on domestic problems in any case. But harmony did not last. A fresh conflict, protracted and intense, slashing directly to fundamentals for the first time, was touched off when the turmoil of the 1930's struck. Labour's unity was shaken as it had not been since 1914. One year after another, party partisans veered and backed in uncertain response; the quicker the international situation deteriorated, the deeper the party sank in internal strife. It is no exaggeration to speak of a crisis during this period—a crisis with wide-reaching consequences for Labour's future.

The crisis as it developed turned essentially on the question of socialist foreign policy's realism. This was something new. Though the question had always been bandied about in one form or another, it had been largely academic before 1918 and remained in the background. Until then Labour spokesmen had been free, by and large, to ignore the practicability of their proposals; as spokesmen for a party nowise close to power, they had not often found themselves challenged to demonstrate that what they preached could be readily put into practice. Following World War I, this convenient state of affairs was irreversibly transformed. Labour became first His Majesty's official Opposition and then His Majesty's actual Government, and the issue of socialist policy's realism moved accordingly to the fore. Willy-nilly the leadership now had to show that socialist principles were not only theoretically superior to traditional principles, but also a reliable guide for hard-pressed statesmen wrestling with intractable problems. This change in the party's situation cannot be overstressed. In the past Labour had enjoyed the luxury of saying, in effect, that its policy recommendations would effectively surmount the existing difficulties of international relations *if* only they were implemented, the practical question posed by the *if* being treated as largely irrelevant—a matter not directly bearing on the theoretical evaluation of the recommendations. Henceforth the two issues could no longer be treated separately; Labour had to grapple, whatever the consequences for party harmony, with the problem of transforming theory into practice. Or—to pose this problem in terms employed by party propaganda at the time—could socialist policy really accomplish what Labour claimed it could accomplish: open diplomacy, an ever stronger League of Nations, international arbitration and cooperation, universal disarmament, and the elimination of war?*

The contrasting answers at which Labour partisans themselves arrived was what largely triggered the conflict in 1924 and even more so in the 1930's. The question of socialist foreign policy's realism proved inescapable—and agonizing.

An additional observation that will underline much of the anal-

* These were the party's "Six Pillars of Peace" as presented in the 1929 election manifesto, "Labour and the Nation."

ysis needs to be made explicit here. Speaking generally, the interwar years can and should be divided for analytical purposes into
two distinct periods, the 1920's and the 1930's, each decade characterized by contrasting environments; and it is only against the
background of this distinction that the issue of socialist policy's
realism, and hence Labour's internal unity, can be fully appreciated. The distinction helps to explain, for instance, why socialist
policy fared well enough in the earlier but not in the later decade,
and why party accord was affected in consequence. The 1920's were
a period during which prospects for realizing objectives similar to
the "Six Pillars of Peace" seemed reasonably optimistic. Not only
did there set in a far-ranging revulsion against power politics,
against almost every aspect of traditional international relations;
but what is more, millions of people, socialist or not, expressed
faith in the compelling force of world opinion and in that opinion's essential decency, in an international community centered at
Geneva, and in the near-realization of the ultimate harmony of
interests among nations. If the British people were ever ripe for a
policy of conciliation, pacification, and disarmament, it was then.
By way of contrast, the 1930's were a decade of dismal prospects,
with strife and hate more and more the dominant international
mood. This, at any rate, is clear enough in retrospect. It is also
clear that others at the time recognized the enormous shift in the
environmental situation and adjusted their policy positions accordingly. Whether Labour itself recognized it, however, is something else again.

#### THE PROBLEM OF COLLECTIVE SECURITY

The most urgent international problem of the interwar period was
raised by the soaring menace of fascist aggression. To repulse aggression of any kind, the Labour Party was categorically pledged
by the late 1920's to uphold a system of collective security. This
being so, the question of socialist policy's realism may be conveniently rephrased to read: how did Labour interpret its pledge and
so act in relation to it? The question as stated encompasses the
two crucial variables of the argument: Labour partisans' attitudes
on the one hand and their consequent behavior on the other.

Labour's commitment to collective security followed from its
zeal for the League of Nations. By 1922 the party began shedding

its initial misgivings about the organization. In 1924 the MacDonald government unpacked a League-centered foreign policy and edged toward firm endorsement of a collective security notion by further unpacking proposals later incorporated in the Geneva Protocol. The last inhibitions on the subject were shattered by 1929; "Labour and the Nation," the election manifesto for that year, spoke eloquently about "pooled security" to halt aggression. At the same time party spokesmen were denouncing the efforts of those nations seeking security through balance-of-power maneuverings. Labour demanded an end to this practice. Statesmen had to realize that security as well as general peace was indivisible, dependent on the collective workings of an authoritative League. "To my mind," Attlee said in 1935, "the essential thing about the League is that any one member of the League should feel that the other States have an obligation towards it whether it is a near neighbor or not, or whether this or that State has any particular interest of its own."[1]

### Labour's Policy of Pacification

The party fully realized by the mid-1920's that for the League to function effectively as a war-preventive system, certain defects in the Covenant as it was initially organized had to be remedied. What particularly worried many Labour spokesmen were the famous gaps in Articles 10 and 16. Together, these were the parts of the Covenant committing member nations to collective responsibility for each other's integrity; but the guarantees they provided in this regard were so vague and ambiguous as to make it possible for the members not only to sidestep the obligation to apply military sanctions in the event of aggression, but even to go to war with one another should their disputes prove unamenable to peaceful solution.[2] The need to fill these gaps appeared all the more urgent because of the insatiable French quest for security, which was driving that nation to create a sprawling alliance system outside the League's jurisdiction. Was not the danger growing daily that European affairs might inexorably slide back into the horrible morass of competitive alignments, mutual suspicions, and futile power balancing? The question had only to be asked in order to send shivers down Labour backs. Military alliances were a "grain of mustard seed," which grows "until at last the tree pro-

duced from it overshadows the whole of the heavens and we shall
be back in exactly the military position in which we found our-
selves in 1914."[3] The French occupation of the Ruhr and the unremitting disruption of the German economy in 1923 made it all
the more imperative in Labour eyes that something decisive be
done on behalf of pacification and conciliation.

When the MacDonald government took office in 1924, it was
pledged to arrest the dangerous regression to the anarchy of the
old international system. A two-bite strategy evolved from its de-
liberations. For a start, there was an overriding need to end the
French occupation and to clear the menacing atmosphere prevailing between France and Germany. The MacDonald solution,
pressed at the London Conference in July, did both: the Dawes
Plan was accepted, the reparations problem eased, the French
troops withdrawn. On a more general level, the government appreciated that Franco-German differences could not be seen apart and
in isolation from the whole issue of collective security. At a stroke
it hoped, in accord with socialist prescriptions, to satisfy the French
yearning for security, to pacify the Germans, and to boost internationalism by amending the Covenant and enhancing the League's
authority.

These were ambitious goals. As it turned out, Labour pondered
two alternative schemes for revamping the League's machinery before choosing the one that most accorded with socialist attitudes.

The first scheme was to concentrate on improving the League's
ability to punish aggression to the certain point where no nation,
however powerful in its own right, would dare defy it. This course
would involve action to supplement the Covenant so that, first,
the Council came to enjoy broad powers of inquiry to designate
the aggressor promptly in cases of hostilities and, second, the application of economic and military sanctions came to be automatic
and solemnly binding. In this way—so the argument went—the
international community centered at Geneva would invariably
enjoy preponderant power whenever disputes arose; such collective preponderance in turn would tend to discourage potential
aggressors; and so the vicious circle would be finally broken in
which, under a balance-of-power system, one state's security meant
another state's insecurity. Action along these lines was essentially
what the Draft Treaty of Mutual Assistance proposed. Drawn up

in the League's Temporary Mixed Commission and submitted to
the Assembly in September 1923, the Draft Treaty was the product
of individual delegates rather than official governmental delega-
tions. Indeed, the initial exploratory ideas had been broached by
Lord Robert Cecil, a very untypical member of the Conservative
Party who eventually became adviser to the League delegation
sent by Labour in 1929; but Cecil's ideas had been considerably
modified under pressure from French delegates, and it was France
which became the Draft Treaty's staunchest champion.[4] In addition to provision for increased Council authority, regional security
pacts, and automatic sanctions, the Draft Treaty included a plan
for future disarmament, but it occupied a decidedly secondary role
and created doubts regarding the seriousness of its intent. What
the French and others liked was the stress on effective and superior
power available for collective defense of the status quo.[5]

Labour, however, with its instinctive suspicion of power, shrank
from going along with the Draft Treaty. The MacDonald government uncovered what it regarded as serious shortcomings in the
scheme, many—though not all—of them in conflict with socialist
principles. Henderson derided the emphasis on military assistance
as contrary to the ideals and spirit of the League.[6] MacDonald was
more categorical; he branded the Draft Treaty as "essentially a
war preparation document," a shored-up holdover from the old
system.[7] The worst defects were generally held to be a failure to
provide for peaceful settlement of disputes, and a confusion of
priorities which mistakenly put security before disarmament.* If,
according to party spokesmen, genuine security on a collective
footing were to be attained, these defects had to be eliminated
and their remedies incorporated in a new and more imaginative
scheme. At a minimum, it would be necessary to draw up a comprehensive program for universal disarmament, complemented by
plans for effective League conciliation and arbitration of all disputes. Once the first measure was implemented, then presumably

---

* "Worst," that is, from the perspective of socialist principles. This qualification is worth adding since MacDonald, his own Foreign Secretary, mingled
practical as well as theoretical objections in his letter to the League Secretary-
General announcing the government's rejection of the Draft Treaty. Foreign
Office, *Correspondence between H.M.G. and the League of Nations respecting
the proposed Treaty of Mutual Assistance,* 1924, pp. 10–14.

no nation would have the capacity to impose its will on another, whereas once the second was implemented, none would have either need or desire to do so. The era of universal peace, of cooperation and communal harmony, would then ensue—and all on the basis of socialist prescriptions.

It was roughly with this interpretation in mind that MacDonald himself appeared in September at the Fifth Assembly of the League to plead for an alternative to the abortive Draft Treaty. The League responded; after a month of verbal infighting between French and British delegates, the Geneva Protocol on the Pacific Settlement of International Disputes was hammered out. Stripped to its essence, the Protocol incorporated MacDonald's ideas by envisaging an elaborate system of arbitration as the vital link in the equation of disarmament and collective security. Arbitration, to be sure, could work only to the extent that conflicting parties were willing both to submit their disputes to an arbiter and then to abide by his decision. This consideration was taken fully into account by the Geneva Protocol: following MacDonald's reasoning, it provided that any nation that proved recalcitrant on either point be branded an aggressor and so become subject to the automatic imposition of sanctions by League members. Thus the complicated arbitration scheme not only provided a precise definition of aggression, but specified binding collective coercive measures for dealing with it.

In theory Labour fully endorsed the principles of the Protocol, including its provision for collective force as the *ultima ratio*.* But the point is—only in theory. In actual fact there was scarcely a prominent Labour spokesman who seemed to take seriously the commitment to use force against aggressors. The defenders of the Protocol ignored the coercive element when they could, or severely downplayed it when they could not, or at any rate rationalized it out of existence. MacDonald dismissed the possibility of military sanctions as a sop to French fears, "a harmless drug to soothe nerves."[8] Henderson too was seized by doubt.[9] And what Labour spokesmen argued in Britain only duplicated their reservations

---

* *LPCR*, 1925, p. 252. Twelve years later Attlee wrote in *The Labour Party in Perspective* (p. 150): "The Labour Government fell, and the Conservatives refused to ratify the Protocol. Subsequent events have shown that Labour's policy was right."

and misgivings at Geneva when working out the Protocol's details. Thus Lord Parmoor, the most important member in the delegation aside from Henderson, proved elusive in face of worried French queries concerning British willingness to commit armed forces for League use.[10] When Henderson proved no more forthcoming, the French had to settle for the vague assurance of "loyal and effective cooperation."[11] In short, the Labour Party still shied away from the prospect of using force even for collective reasons. Its members were as convinced as ever that revulsion against war would simply make aggressive behavior improbable and impossible—once, that is to say, this revulsion could be translated into concrete disarmament measures, underpinned by a system of conciliation and sanctified in the eyes of public opinion. As MacDonald observed in *Protocol or Pact*, the Protocol would eventually obviate the entire need for national armed forces. It would not even require collective force, for it would become self-enforcing, its own sanction: "So soon as it has been worked once or twice it will be impossible for a nation to defy it—impossible not owing to the menace of force but to habit and other psychological and moral reasons. The nations will simply accept it. The era of peace will have come at last."

The difference between French and Labour interpretations of collective security was fundamental, a matter of basic outlook. The French view was essentially a modified version (French vintage) of traditional foreign policy, except that the French recognized the gain to be had from identifying their own interests in stabilizing the Versailles status quo with the supposedly like-minded interests of the League of Nations. At the bottom of their view was a root assumption on international relations. They did not see harmony and cooperation as the natural condition; far from it, they regarded tension, discord, and conflict as inevitable so long as the international system was comprised of sovereign nations which valued their independence above all other considerations. Hence the only way to preserve some minimal order was through being realistic about these matters: through accepting the status quo, backing it with preponderant power, and relying on the consequent deterrent effects to contain the ambitions of others. Labour's view, on the other hand, was fully in keeping with socialist foreign policy. Fear and distrust were not inevitable in relations among nations; they arose out of misunderstandings and removable injustices, and the only realistic approach to order and peace was through tackling conflict there, at its very source. To lay stress on military preparations rather than on the underlying causes was irredeemably short-sighted, a typical defect of traditional habits; and to dress up these preparations in collective garb did not much improve matters—militarism was militarism, international or otherwise.

It is important to appreciate Labour's reasoning here because it profoundly colored the party's outlook on the international situation in the early 1930's. The party, as its spokesmen claimed, did indeed become committed to collective security. But the hearts of Labour partisans were not in it; their commitment remained formalistic. This was the reason why the 1926 annual conference could, only one year after the previous conference endorsed the Protocol, pass a resolution of a doctrinaire war-resistant sort. To the overwhelming majority of Labour partisans, there was no contradiction involved, since conciliation, pacification, arbitration, and disarmament—not collective security—constituted the core of the Protocol's provisions. More than ever, the party continued to read the international system in light of the British political system. More than ever, it assumed that a genuine international *community* existed, centered at Geneva, and more than ever it looked forward to the not very distant day when this international community would function exactly like an integrated national community—that is, according to effective law, with peace and order maintained as a matter of course. Again and again this analogy between a national community and the international community was drawn in such a way as to obscure the striking differences in the two environments. Was there really a need for international police forces, ready and alert to stifle aggression as the French wanted? But "my protection really is, not that there is organized force around me, but that there are involuntary social habits around me. . . . It is not so much the policeman that one depends on as public opinion."[12] MacDonald expressed this sentiment during the war as a lonely rebel against his party's line. But in 1925 he spoke for the party as leader and former Prime Minister when he returned to the same theme. "Give us ten years of the working of the Protocol," he confidently told Parliament, "and we will have Europe with a new habit of mind."[13]

*A Flurry of Rank-and-File Unrest*

Labour's prevailing frame of mind on these questions is so
charged with significance for the party's subsequent behavior that
it is worth exploring from a different angle. I am thinking here
particularly of the stormy reactions provoked among the ranks by
the government's diplomacy.

At first blush the commotion seems strange. After all, we have
just observed how diligently the PLP leadership endeavored to
underplay the coercive features of the Protocol and to present it
as a socialist victory. But the point is that the leadership could not
underplay those features enough to prevent acute misgivings from
arising all the same. To many influential backbenchers and extra-
Parliamentary spokesmen, the government had inexcusably strayed
too far from socialist principles. Indeed, seen against the background of its other actions—its sluggishness in accommodating
Soviet trade demands, its sell-out to French revanchists at the London Conference, its suspicious dependence on the permanent officials at the Foreign Office—did not its effort to sneak militarism
into Labour's policy betoken something much more devious? Betrayal perhaps?

Such was the embittered charge raised repeatedly by E. D. Morel
during the summer of 1924. Writing in the *New Leader* on 25
July, he insisted that the government's shocking behavior forced
him to but one conclusion: it was overturning the "convictions
and pledges which have been the inspiration of the party for the
last five years." Morel, who could rely on considerable support
from ILP, UDC, and trade union circles in directing an incessant
drumfire at the MacDonald leadership, had been keyed up to expect the worst ever since he had been passed over for the post of
Foreign Secretary, which he had come to expect as his right.[14] Yet
no more than with Bevan, when he was passed over for the same
post in 1951, can Morel's protests be reduced to personal frustration. As Morel saw the situation, a matter of principle was involved. Had not MacDonald revealed his true hand when, right
at the outset, he openly repudiated Henderson's electoral pledge
to revise the Versailles Treaty?[15] And then look at what happened.
First the dreary and protracted haggling with the Soviet Union,
a trade agreement being finally reached—so Morel proclaimed—

only when he and six other backbenchers had the courage to intervene as a salvaging force in the negotiations.[16] Then endorsement
of the Dawes Plan, which legitimized greedy French claims to unlimited German reparations. Then the Geneva Protocol, which,
disguise the fact as the leadership might, was a nasty bit of militarism. And on top of it all the "Red Letter" episode, which Morel
saw as clinching evidence of a Foreign Office conspiracy. He wrote
with characteristic verve: "The 'Foreign Office' as the nation is
content to tolerate it with the occultism and secrecy which sur-
round it, its mysterious links with the Secret Service, the newspapers and 'society,' and its uncontrolled disposal of Secret Service
funds, is an increasing menace to Democratic Government, a permanent obstacle to the effective control of foreign policy."[17] We
have already had occasion in the previous chapter to note that
Morel was by no means voicing eccentric unease in these matters.
The air was thick at the time with speculation that, had he lived,
he would have posed a serious challenge to MacDonald's leadership.

This rank-and-file edginess corresponds closely to the whole pattern of recurring conflict under examination here. On the one side
was a pressing international environment, with all its constraints
restricting the freedom of maneuver, the latitude of choice, open
to Britain. On the other side were Labour Party members striving
to make sense of the environment, striving to find *realistic means*
of relating socialist principles to inescapable situational demands.
As in 1914 and during the 1930's, opinion in the party divided
sharply in face of that pivotal question concerning realistic means.
As in the other cases, eventually one group decided that such
means were simply not at hand. The situation was too demanding;
the party could not afford the luxury of further search; action was
necessary now, at that very moment, even if this meant compromise
with the party's principles. As in these other cases, however, another group of party members, instinctively mistrustful of appeals
to realism or necessity, chafed at the reasoning of the first group.
It found the latter's action deplorable, close to betrayal—a hasty
and needless sellout.* The leadership in the MacDonald govern-

---

* The harshest judgment was meted out by the pseudonymous author
"U.D.C.," in a piece entitled *The Diplomacy of Mr. Ramsay MacDonald*. Indicating that MacDonald's assumption of office had presaged "a revolutionary

ment was, needless to say, the first group, and the Morel-inspired critics the second group. As far as these critics were concerned, the various arguments brandished by the government were all pieces of manufacture calculated to rationalize its devious behavior. Like the rank-and-file critics of Bevin after 1945 and the Bevanites in the 1950's, they had nothing but contempt for so-called socialists who succumbed, immediately upon taking power, to the utterly muddled notion that there were "responsibilities of office" requiring compromise.*

All the same, we would do well not to overestimate the extent and magnitude of the 1924 conflict. For a number of reasons it was more easily contained than had been the case in 1914 or would be the case in the 1930's. To begin with, the government's record in foreign policy was by no means barren of measures that its defenders could represent as socialist in inspiration. Settlement of the Ruhr crisis, improvement in the atmosphere surrounding German-French relations, enthusiastic support for the League of Nations, diplomatic recognition of Russia and an Anglo-Soviet trade agreement—these measures, if not necessarily socialist, were in any case in harmony with socialist principles, and to that extent the leadership could mobilize considerable rank-and-file sentiment in meeting its critics head-on. In the second place, the government had a convenient excuse when the controversy shifted to the charge

---

change in our foreign policy, a break with the follies of the past," "U.D.C." went on to observe that the Prime Minister–Foreign Secretary actually turned out to be "a man with no grasp of principles, no equipment of knowledge . . . an actor who was his own perpetual and admiring audience."

* Quite apart from MacDonald's initial speech repudiating Henderson's electoral hints at treaty revision, there were several other instances of government spokesmen invoking the theme of responsibilities as an argument against undue innovation. It is not hard to imagine, to cite just one example, the derision that J. H. Thomas, the Colonial Secretary, incited among the critics' ranks when he told the Newport Chamber of Commerce: "You have for the first time a Government composed in the main of humble working men, men who hitherto have played the role of propagandists and who are now face to face not only with the responsibilities of office, but with the responsibilities of the knowledge of what this great Empire means. Men faced with these responsibilities can never again be the indifferent propagandists that they were in the past. They must remain for all time responsible politicians keeping only in mind the great interest of the country." Quoted in Miliband, p. 112. Though Miliband dubs this speech "crude . . . imperial rhetoric," the fact is that Thomas was only drawing attention to a factor that he and his colleagues found impossible to ignore in their policy calculations.

of its being insufficiently bold in going beyond these steps: as a minority government, just how bold could it possibly be and still retain crucial Liberal support in Parliament? Here was a formidable point in the leadership's favor, not only in 1924 but between 1929 and 1931 as well.

In the third place, the government never *formally* adopted the Geneva Protocol for the simple reason that it fell from office before the need arose. This meant that the Cabinet leadership, known to have been somewhat divided itself on the question, did not have to debate its critics with its own disunity bared to view. Instead the debate over the Protocol was thrashed out on entirely different grounds when the Baldwin government, recoiling from a League-fixed course, scuttled the Protocol in preference for the more traditional-inspired Locarno Pact.* The upshot was predictable: the Labour leadership could point to a common threat, and in face of this new danger, the rest of the party had a decided incentive to close ranks. Fourth and finally, the character of the international situation at the time had a settling effect. For however ominous certain of its features loomed in Labour eyes, the general situation was in fact more encouraging than had been the case for a generation of European affairs. There was no prospect of military aggression in sight, no towering menace of a sudden and fitful crisis on the order of July 1914; and not even the most convinced Francophobe expected Paris to be mad enough to unleash preventive war against a Germany currently unarmed and down and out. By 1925, indeed, Labour's ranks were thick with high hopes of irreversible progress. The Dawes Plan, for all its drawbacks to the left wing, reversed Germany's sagging economic fortunes and gave a lift to prosperity elsewhere. The Locarno Pact, for all its traditionalism, had noticeably calmed French fears and

---

* Actually the Locarno Pact represented a new departure in traditional British policy, since it had been a cardinal tenet of the balance-of-power policy to avoid advance commitments on the European continent which limited British freedom. The Pact was a sign that the Baldwin government appreciated the wisdom of reappraising this traditional tenet in light of the recent war's lessons. But if Britain could no longer afford to remain indifferent to the day-to-day flow of European diplomacy, the Pact and not the Protocol represented the least alteration of traditional policy. Thus F. S. Northedge is right to refer to the Baldwin government's "traditionalist mental background" in his recent comprehensive account of interwar British diplomacy, *The Troubled Giant*, p. 245.

removed the last obstacles to German entrance into the League.
Never were statesmen more eager to profess their devotion to the
League Charter. Never did they speak more earnestly of conciliation, pacification, arbitration, cooperation. With some justification
Labour partisans could look forward to the next round when it
would be in office, ready once more to hasten the universal movement toward lasting peace.

### The Realism or Unrealism of Labour's
### Policy of Pacification

The problem round which Labour's conflicts of the interwar
period all whirled was how to find realistic ways to relate socialist
principles to the continuous and uncertain succession of baffling
international events. Except for inveterate traditionalists, the
problem of realism is never easy to handle, and Labour's difficulties at the time were by no means unique. To the hardheaded traditionalist, realism and power—especially military power—are all
of a piece; the realistic course is always the one that promises to
maximize one's power position vis-à-vis the positions of others. But
are such ruthless, coldhearted calculations really any more profound than Labour's diametrical conviction that power could be
slighted as a factor in foreign policy? The fact is that what is realistic or unrealistic cannot be answered in the abstract. Realism is
always a matter of circumstances—of the prevailing international
climate. If the situation facing the nation seems threatening, then
vigilance and military preparations may be in order. If, on the
other hand, the situation seems more promising, then a policy of
pacification and appeasement may be exactly what is warranted.

Seen in this light, there was nothing necessarily fanciful about
Labour's interpretation of collective security, nor was it necessarily
less realistic than the French interpretation. If realism is a question
of circumstances, then the key circumstance, at least during the
1920's, reduced to their divergent attitudes toward the existing
status quo. The French saw the Versailles status quo as sacred,
something that had to be preserved at all costs, if only for the reason that it was organized to the decided French advantage and the
German disadvantage. The whole thrust of French policy was directed at underpinning the existing power distribution; and given
that aim, the French view of collective security needs to be judged
as well-tailored to French needs at the time. But to Labour the pre-

vailing status quo was anything other than sacred. From the outset the party had denounced the Versailles Treaty for imposing a draconian peace, and it continued to demand revision well into the 1930's, though after 1925 with, perhaps, somewhat less fervor than before.[18] There was thus nothing unrealistic in Labour's refusal to espouse an interpretation of collective security that it felt to be in the interest of the status quo powers only. Given the party's overall aim of reforming the international system and its rooted conviction that agreement and cooperation were always possible, its aversion to military sanctions was no less suited to its aims than the contrasting French position was to French aims.

This point has been all too frequently overlooked in much of the commentary on Labour's policy during the 1920's. It became fashionable to dismiss the party's gropings toward pacification as airy-fairy utopian hankerings, and to chide not only Labour but all British opinion for not being more receptive to French ideas of security. Yet during the 1920's, a policy of conciliation and appeasement surely had at least as much chance to succeed in establishing a durable European settlement as a tougher-minded, security-conscious policy did. It may be true, as one observer has suggested, that Labour's belief in ultimate harmony led the party to evade the unpalatable fact "of a fundamental divergence of interest between nations desirous of maintaining the *status quo* and nations desirous of changing it."[19] It may even be true that maintenance of long-run peace is inseparable from defense of a general status quo.[20] Yet even if these two oversights in Labour's understanding of the European situation are granted, they do not loom as very serious drawbacks for the years between 1919 and 1929. Certainly they did not invalidate the rationale of a policy aimed at gradual revision, at meeting grievances and working for common points of agreement, and at establishing international machinery for the precise purpose of achieving objectives of this sort. During this period, after all, the revisionist power neither made outrageous demands nor as yet advanced them at gunpoint. A wise defense of the status quo that would have made ample allowance for its peaceful alteration—that would have accommodated others in a spirit of mutual give-and-take—might therefore have very well succeeded in forging a fairly stable settlement on the Continent. And it does not seem to be a compelling criticism to note that appeasement was in fact tried under British prodding, Conservative and Labour alike; to argue that the policy simply did not work because "German resentment was greater at the end than at the beginning"; and to claim that as long as France and Germany were vying for dominance in Europe, "it is futile to suppose that more concessions, or fewer, would have made much difference."[21] The false note in this criticism is its determinism. Was there really anything inevitable about Franco-German competition? Only an assumption that nations are invariably motivated by a drive toward hegemony would make an affirmative answer meaningful. Perhaps Imperial Germany evinced such motivation. Certainly National Socialist Germany did. But did Weimar Germany? Does present-day West Germany? At any rate, Robert Schuman and every French statesman since 1950 have calculated differently.

So, too, did Labour partisans in the 1920's. Far from sensing that "German resentment was greater at the end" of conciliation and pacification, they felt themselves entitled to draw vigorous satisfaction from the progress of the period. Evidence of a better atmosphere piled up impressively. Aside from such successes as the Locarno Pact, growing French moderation, and German membership in the League, even Russia, the one-time pariah, had partly rejoined the European fold by adding its signature to the Paris Pact and by participating in the League's preparations for disarmament. And as Labour partisans had expected, the MacDonald government that took office in 1929 devoted itself to intensifying the pace of agreement. Though Philip Snowden, Chancellor of the Exchequer, proved sticky at the Hague Conference on the matter of German reparations, no other incident of this sort marred the government's behavior. With Henderson at the Foreign Office, Britain reestablished diplomatic relations with Russia; it also exerted pressure on France to withdraw its occupational forces from the Rhineland, promised to work for further reductions in German reparations, and gave emphatic impetus to the cause of compulsory mediation and arbitration by signing a host of proposals like the Optional Clause of the Statute of the Permanent Court. Above all, the Labour government toiled indefatigably to achieve a breakthrough in disarmament. It was largely owing to Henderson's endeavors that the League's Preparatory Commission managed to set a specific date for a disarmament conference.[22]

A measure of the government's energy in striving after party-sanctioned objectives was the mildness of rank-and-file complaints. In part, no doubt, the greater accord in foreign policy as compared with the tussles of 1924 was a matter of accidental circumstances, chief among them preoccupation with domestic problems, especially soaring unemployment. But in large part it also attested to a widespread impression that this time the leadership took socialist principles seriously. Not that outbursts of ill will and accusation no longer occurred at all; they did, but in contrast with 1924, the point at issue was nearly always the *pace* of the government's acknowledged socialist advance. At the 1929 conference, for instance, a female delegate demanded "total disarmament" and the immediate abolition of British armed forces. Most delegates seemed satisfied with Arthur Henderson's skillful rejoinder that "we shall not attempt that which is practically impossible"—"I only wish that she, and other speakers, would tell the Conference what they mean by total or complete disarmament. If they will only think the problem out, they will see that they are asking for that which is impossible. What we must really try to get down to is a reasonable standard of policing forces. . . . I think that, in all the disarmament policies that have been gripping the public seriously, it is the policy that recognizes that you must have progressive disarmament down to a reasonable standard of policing forces that is most important."[23]

The absence of strident conflict at the time is suggestive. It indicates that just as most Labour partisans supported a domestic strategy of gradualism in moving toward the ultimate socialist utopia at home, so by the late 1920's they concurred on the wisdom of gradual (if continuous) socialist advance in foreign policy. The prospect of "continuous" advance was perhaps the snag. Only the quality of the future international situation would tell in this connection. But in 1929 the situation was no problem. It seemed to burst with opportunity; by early 1930 Europe appeared nearer to durable peace than at any moment since the end of World War I. There was thus ample reason for Labour members to expect the process of conciliation to continue unabated for years, until the ultimate transformation of the international system was at long last accomplished. In such circumstances it was only understandable that Hugh Dalton, Henderson's Under-Secretary, felt justified in confessing to the House of Commons: "I myself hope and believe that we are now entering upon a new and more hopeful phase of history. . . . I hope and believe that we shall be able, in the months and years that lie ahead, to make a forward movement in the direction of arbitration, disarmament, the better economic organization of the life of the world, and the general establishment of reconciliation between old enemies and firmer friendship between old friends."[24] Already Labour's "Six Pillars of Peace" appeared to be lodged firmly on their foundations.

### THE PERIOD OF CRISIS

And yet within only a matter of months Labour's optimism seemed like a giddy flight of fantasy. For in the interval, circumstances, the brute and inescapable facts of the international situation, had taken a fateful turn.

First the Great Depression struck, jeopardizing the whole foundation of the European economy. This, in turn, stirred economic nationalism, country after country resorting to ingenious beggar-my-neighbor policies in desperate efforts to save themselves at the expense of others. Eventually economic nationalism soured into nationalism pure and extreme, stimulating political reaction, swaggering militarism, and aggressive imperialism. Amidst the soaring tension, the policy of conciliating Germany began to backlash, each concession granted to it now indeed provoking only further demands, the one more blatant than the other. Moreover, in proportion as the German economy slumped, the political fortunes of the National Socialists rose. In August 1930, the Reichstag elections netted the hitherto insignificant party a gain of over one hundred seats; winner-take-all would be Hitler's prize a mere 30 months later. Nor was the effect of the Depression any less staggering on the other side of the world. In 1931 the Japanese strove to overcome internal unrest by invading Manchuria. When the League of Nations protested, the Japanese defied the world and staged a haughty withdrawal from that organization.

In the face of these momentous changes, what was Labour's reaction? Remarkably, if one searches through its major policy debates and pronouncements between late 1930 and 1933, the impression emerges that the party seemed hardly to take notice of them. "Remarkably" is perhaps inappropriate. To the student of socialist foreign policy, Labour's failure to adjust its stand to altered circumstances—even blatantly altered circumstances—seems in character: the decisive, fateful outcome of its preoccupation with reform to the neglect of the power realities of the moment. Insofar as the party did allow for the rapid deterioration in the international situation, it drew the apparent conclusion that there was now more urgent need than ever to press ahead with schemes that made sense only on the assumption of international goodwill. Disarmament—"immediate, universal, substantial, and controlled" —remained the party's preeminent objective.[25] To Philip Noel-Baker, Henderson's other Under-Secretary, military force was progressively becoming useless while moral force was on the upswing as the controlling factor in international relations.[26] Seizing on the London Naval Conference of April 1930 as a hopeful omen, the party did not appreciate that this modest measure of arms limitation was founded on quickly passing international conditions, and it hailed the announcement of the forthcoming World Disarmament Conference "as one of the most momentous events in the history of the world."[27] Optimism of this sort, however well-grounded as late as 1930, by 1932 risked making Labour members prey to all manner of illusions about themselves and the world around them. One might even detect withdrawal symptoms, but this is no doubt too glib. Labour's trouble was not psychological but intellectual. Socialist principles clouded the vision of party members on what was happening. Even Arthur Henderson, more hardheaded than most, more willing than others to appreciate the need for an organized system of League sanctions, "never really faced up to the problem of power relationships in Europe."[28] The Disarmament Conference had little promise, under existing circumstances, of achieving those noble aims the party hankered after. As things turned out, its major consequence was to worsen European relations, not to improve them, and it had the added drawback of intensifying mutual Anglo-French suspicion. In October 1933 Hitler finally showed what he thought of disarmament talk. Ordering a showy German walkout from the Conference, he waited a week and, when nothing happened, issued a second order to quit the League of Nations as well.

Here, it might have been supposed, was vivid, unambiguous warning of the dangers bound up with a policy of pacification in the present international situation. But the warning passed over the surface of party discussions without leaving much more than a ripple behind. In spite of all the menacing signs piling up, Labour

balked at any pressure to reconsider the realism of its existing
policies. Not only did it cling as resolutely as ever to an interpretation that equated collective security with arbitration and disarmament: it actually became more hostile to appeals for armed
security, more mistrustful of armaments, more keen to achieve a
spectacular breakthrough in pacification. To Hitler's defiance of
the Disarmament Conference, the party's International Advisory
Committee responded: "We must disarm down to the German
level."[29] The rest of the party shared this sentiment; at the October
meeting of the annual conference at Hastings, it reaffirmed the
1926 position on doctrinaire war resistance and urged preparations
for direct action.[30] For the majority of Labour partisans, the disaster that overcame Labour's general strike plans, pre-1914 vintage,
might as well have never taken place. There was nothing surprising about this behavior. As the Preface suggests, a vigorous "philosophy of choice" orientation in foreign policy envisages no in-
surmountable limits on the capabilities of human will to shape the
environment.

The foregoing argument has made no reference to Labour's attitude concerning the Manchurian Crisis: the temptation would be
to follow party propaganda too closely as a guide here, when in
fact much of what Labour spokesmen later claimed about the
party's position was exaggeration—an effort to score points off their
Tory opponents on the question of responsibility for the whole
decade of British appeasement. Our analysis of Labour's stubborn
adherence to its program of the 1920's helps to place things in perspective. It is true that the party condemned the Japanese invasion
and urged League reprisals; true, too, that its behavior was far
more vigorous in this regard than the National government's. But
then this was only to be expected. The Tories, who dominated the
government, had always been cynical regarding the possibilities of
collective League action, and they would remain cynical as the disastrous decade unfolded. Labour, in contrast, had been a staunch
supporter of a League-centered foreign policy since the early 1920's,
and its advocacy of League involvement agreed with this received
position. The relevant question is what sort of reprisals party members had in mind. In this connection the most comprehensive
statement was issued in February 1932 by the Joint Council of the
Labour Party and the Trades Union Congress. It urged (1) diplo-

matic rupture with Japan, (2) which would lead to "manifestations of world opinion" and (3) which, if need be, should be backed by "graduated measures of financial and economic constraint."[31] There the party halted. Time and again government spokesmen queried what would happen if diplomatic, moral, and economic pressures proved inadequate; and time and again Labour spokesmen shied away from answering. No one was willing to envisage military sanctions; military action was unnecessary or at any rate too provocative. George Lansbury, now head of the PLP and a firm advocate of economic and financial sanctions, insisted that Manchuria was "the acid test of the League of Nations as a guarantee against attack."[32] He also insisted that British ships and troops be completely removed from the Far East so as to preclude even accidental collision with Japanese forces.* In brief, world opinion, plus a short boycott, would do the trick.[33] Labour was still as opposed as ever to armed collective security.

The faster the international situation deteriorated, the more blatantly defective socialist policy seemed in relation to it. The international system was not supposed to work according to its own logic, with some fear and insecurity built into its structure; everything was rather a question of determination, of willpower and proper sentiments. Labour's increasingly ill-founded hopes for disarmament make sense only if viewed in this light. Examples abound, but one that is particularly striking can serve as illustration of the intellectual fog in which party members were stumbling at the time. Exasperated by the Disarmament Conference's growing deadlock, Henderson protested eloquently at one point: "The world wants disarmament. The world needs disarmament. We have it in our power to help fashion the pattern of future history. Behind all the technical complexities regarding manpower, gunpower, tonnage, categories and the like, is the well-being of mankind, the future of our developing civilisation." The emotion was genuine, the anguish justified. But, as Winkler observes, unhap-

---

* Cited in Tucker, p. 158. It does not seem that the Manchurian incident had much of a lasting effect on Lansbury. His biographer, at any rate, who was close to him at the time, has devoted only four or five sentences to the incident, concluding with the observation that "fortunately, the dilemma [should military sanctions be used if economic sanctions fail] was postponed." Postgate, pp. 286–87.

pily, behind these complexities that Henderson mentioned was also the growing reality of Franco-German antagonism—to which we can add fascist Italy's aspiration for an empire, Nazi contempt for civilized diplomacy, raucous Japanese militarism, and Soviet Russia's hostility to the bourgeois democracies like Britain itself.[34] In face of these smoldering animosities, faith in an ultimate harmony among nations was not enough.

### THE CONFLICT TO READJUST TO REALITY

Gradually Labour itself came round to this realization. But the party was not moved to greater realism overnight. The intellectual fog by the end of 1933 was thick, and it required a brutal struggle among different factions before the conversion, first to armed collective security, then to armed national security, was completed. As it happened, the conflict was waged for more than five years. And even then its final outcome remained obscure.

This last point is significant. A group can readapt its stand at any moment without at the same time repudiating the principles underlying it. From the viewpoint of ideological theory, there are all sorts of psychological mechanisms that serve to conceal from the believers the degree to which their beliefs may have been found inadequate in any particular situation, and to relieve the inner tension that the situation might have engendered. As we examine the course of conflict within the Labour Party, we therefore need constantly to ask what party members made of the series of policy readjustments. Did they see these readjustments as repudiating socialist principles? Do different sections of the party have to be distinguished in this connection? If so, what might be the long-run consequences of this divergence in outlook?

### The Left Wing

Three different factions caught up in the conflict can be discerned. One, not very large in number but whose influence cannot be reliably gauged on this basis alone, consisted of left-wing radicals who endeavored to win the party over to a program of class warfare. In terms of foreign policy, this program meant not only that the Soviet Union should be seen as the most reliable ally among the Great Powers, but that the struggle against fascism should be regarded as inseparable from the struggle against capitalism at home. "Our enemy is here," William Mellor said, and this was the sentiment governing the behavior of most other left-wing stalwarts.[35] By far the most prominent group embracing this viewpoint was the Socialist League.* It regarded a general strike as the workers' most effective weapon, agitated on behalf of unity with the Communists, dismissed the League of Nations as a "thieves' kitchen," and opposed British rearmament as calculated to harm the interests of the working class. Even though the Left's perverse equation of Toryism and fascism baffled most Labour partisans, its sense of outrage at the contemporary order did not. Quite the contrary, class-biased mistrust of the National government was widely diffused throughout the party and added measurably to its gropings and stumblings on the rearmament issue. The year 1937 recorded something of a turning point, however. By then the Socialist League was overreaching itself in energetically pressing for a united front with the ILP and the Communist Party. By then, too, more and more Labour partisans had edged grudgingly around to realize that cooperation with the National government—not class struggle against it—was imperative in at least some areas of defense. With this shift in attitude, the Left's fortunes plummeted. Cripps's biographer speaks of "the known hostility of the party in general."[36] The Labour Executive capitalized on this mood to proscribe the Socialist League and to warn its members against further united front agitation. That took most of the sting out of the Left's efforts. The League dissolved itself, and much of its membership abided dutifully by the party directive. For those who stubbornly did not, the punishment was severe: in 1939 Cripps, Bevan, Trevelyan, G. R. Strauss, and others were expelled, and several disloyal constituency parties disaffiliated.[37]

## The Majority Faction

A second faction, if it can be properly called that, comprised all those in the party who clung as long as they could to Labour's received policy of pacification. They were far and away a majority in Labour's ranks, and their continued espousal of disarmament coupled with arbitration after 1931 conformed perfectly to the anti-militarist principle. At the extreme this could lend itself to

* See above, pp. 25–26.

outright pacifism, such as the kind championed by George Lansbury, PLP head from 1931 to 1935, who refused on strict moral
grounds to countenance the use of force for any purpose whatever.[38] Lansbury attempted to convert the party to his uncompromising point of view, but in this he met with little success. Few
Labour partisans were themselves dyed-in-the-wool pacifists, opposed, without condition, to the use of force regardless of circumstances; and by the late 1930's, even Lansbury's friends watched
with dismay as his pacifism drove him to ever greater muddle and
confusion.[39] If, however, majority Labour sentiment was not pacifist, it showed an ingrained mistrust of force as an instrument of
foreign policy. It was this mistrust that underlay Labour's vacil-
lations all throughout the 1920's on the question of collective
security. It was the same mistrust that created the agonizing dilemma of the 1930's on the question of British rearmament. Henderson caught its spirit when he wrote in 1935: "The ultimate object
of Labour's disarmament *and security policy* is to abolish all national armed forces and to entrust the defence of world law and
order to an international police force, under the League of Nations."[40]

The words in italics draw attention to a major point of the argument: to most Labour partisans disarmament and collective security were at bottom one and the same thing. In their principled
view, either the League of Nations stood for conscience as opposed
to force, the rule of law as against power politics, and pacification
as contrasted with military establishments—or it stood for nothing
whatever. All the same, the members of the majority faction were
not irretrievably doctrinaire. Much as their initial reflex action
after 1931 was to retreat into ardent anti-militarism, they were not
so compulsively ideological as to be altogether immune to the re-
lentless pressure of new events; sooner or later their minds could
be penetrated by hard empirical evidence, however discordant
this evidence might be with prevailing socialist images. What was
needed to force a change in their outlook was a rupture in the
unanimity with which these images were held, so that at least a
few influential Labour spokesmen, themselves driven to an open-
eyed awareness of the crisis shaping up, would be able to agitate
from *within* the party for altered policies. Those Labour members
who fitted this category can be lumped together as comprising a

third distinct faction. It was this third faction, together with the
cumulative impact of successive international threats, that eventually succeeded in forcing the majority to back a harder-hitting
collective security.

An initial stir toward such a policy was discernible at the 1934
annual conference. Under prodding from the third faction, the
conference endorsed a NEC report, "War and Peace," which overturned the previous year's stand on war resistance. "War and
Peace" did not mark an unequivocal advance. Its language was
enshrouded in muzziness, though the fog was perhaps deliberate,
a smoke screen to conceal the extent of rupture with the past. Thus
on the one hand it renounced a general strike and proposed to
stiffen the League Covenant, only, on the other hand, to revert to
calls for full national disarmament—including all forces for self-
defense. Matters were not improved when Arthur Henderson, who
presented the report for the NEC, argued that it was "really a
restatement of Labour's old policy and attitude in international
relations." Even so, "War and Peace" was a significant document.
Despite strenuous objections raised by the Socialist League, it emphatically affirmed "the duty unflinchingly to support our Government in all the risks and consequences of fulfilling its duty to take
part in collective action against a peace-breaker."[41]

Labour's policy could be described, at this point, as full-fledged
support of the League of Nations as the mainstay of peace. But did
the policy as yet envisage the use of military sanctions? This is hard
to say. "War and Peace" left the matter in doubt; and judging from
a NEC manifesto issued shortly afterward in May 1935, the Executive itself remained uncertain. The manifesto talked boldly in one
part about "collective strength powerful enough to overcome" all
aggression, yet in another part dwelt on the disarmament theme
and railed at the National government for announcing increases
in British rearmament. No clear-cut answer was forthcoming, in
fact, for some months. Once again it took the combined impact of
worsening events and the efforts of the third faction before the
party was prepared to adjust.

The change was recorded at the October meeting of the annual
conference. With Italy on the verge of attacking Ethiopia, the delegates considered a new NEC statement demanding forceful British
support of strong League sanctions. The debate was long and

stormy, one of the most dramatic in Labour's history.[42] Cripps, representing the Socialist League, assailed the NEC position. So did Lansbury, still PLP leader, who warned that a League boycott could very well mean general war. Lansbury's stature, the genuineness of his fears, his skillful emotional appeal, all seemed at first to win the conference over. But he drew in rejoinder a vicious, slashing upbraiding from Ernest Bevin, the most outspoken member of the third faction, and despite its abuse, Bevin's speech rescued the NEC statement from defeat. Lansbury, a broken man, withdrew from the hall. He resigned the leadership within the week.[43]

Lansbury's resignation symbolized, in effect, Labour's repudiation of its pacification policy. The party had now come round to a position where it was unmistakably committed to collective security in terms of armed security. And plainly this new stance was more in touch with the harsh circumstances of the moment. Yet, however far Labour had moved beyond the lofty optimism of the previous decade, policy and reality still did not fully mesh. Events were not standing still, and as the whirligig of European relations turned faster and faster, the party was once again confronted with painful choices.

In particular, an anguishing dilemma was soon seen to inhere in the party's espousal of armed collective security. For though Labour members now acknowledged that support for the League might entail the use of force, most continued to distinguish sharply between force under collective auspices and force as a national instrument.[44] Yet sound as the distinction was in theory, it made no sense in practice. The League had no military establishment of its own; the only force it could draw on would have to be provided by its member nations. Did this not mean that so long as Britain and other members remained at a low level of armaments, a collective League stand against aggression was impossible? The answer seems clear in retrospect. It did not appear so to most Labour partisans at the time. To have replied affirmatively would have been unnerving; it would have signified the bankruptcy of the antimilitarist principle. So the party beat about, unwilling or unable to make an irrevocable choice. Faced with a soaring menace from abroad, party members at long last favored forceful collective action. Yet faced at home with a government whose motives seemed suspect, they flinched at the prospect of massive British rearmament—sole means of making collective action feasible.

Perhaps Labour's mistrust of the National government's motives was well founded.* Perhaps the government preferred to employ the arms for selfish national interests alone, in purely traditional fashion. All the same, in the absence of international armed forces, how was the League going to muster sufficient power to act unless Britain rearmed? Of course, Labour's dilemma would disappear in the event Labour itself took office; no Labour partisans need then worry whether British arms would be earmarked for solely League use. But the November 1935 general election returned the National government by a thumping margin, and the prospects for a Labour government within any reasonable span of time were dismal to say the least. The party's dilemma was inescapable.

The supporters of the National government were not laggard in exploiting the dilemma for their own purposes. It was impossible, they insisted, to do what Labour wanted to do: to distinguish between arms needed for Britain's own defense and arms needed to meet British obligations to the League. "You must," Austen Chamberlain said, "have your armaments and your defence, whether you are pursuing a policy of alliances, or a policy of isolation, or a League policy."[45] Labour, recalling the National government's past contempt for the League, remained dubious. Who could offer the necessary assurance that British rearmament programs would not in fact be used "along the old lines of balancing and comparison with other countries,"[46] thereby restoring "the old balance of power and the old armaments race?"[47] For that matter, who could guarantee that the National government, once armed, would not simply proceed from a position of strength to strike a bargain with the dictators?[48]

For more than two years, from 1935 to late 1937, the dilemma haunted the majority faction. And it became all the more agonizing once the League turned out by mid-1936 to be utterly incapable of stopping Italian aggression. Collective security, finally put to conclusive test, had failed. Plainly the British Government was in part responsible, betraying its electoral pledge regarding League

---

* Pertinently, no Labour leader was given access to confidential information about either foreign policy or the state of British rearmament until the spring of 1939.

sanctions. Yet the government had tried to end the Italian attack
on Ethiopia in the best way it knew how: according to traditional
principles of power-maneuvering and diplomatic negotiation, as
in the Hoare-Laval deal. This, naturally, was no consolation to the
Labour Party. The setback suffered by the League was a fateful
blow to its hopes for a collective stand against fascism. Only the
left wing remained undismayed. Maybe, it was asked, Cripps and
the others were right after all. Maybe the real enemy was to be
found here, in Britain, rather than abroad. . . . In the painful mood
of indecision and vacillation prevailing during the spring of 1936,
the PLP decided for the second consecutive year to oppose the government's rearmament program even while, at almost the same
moment, German troops were marching into the Rhineland.
Scarcely a Labour voice was raised in protest against the German
move. Even Hugh Dalton, who was blasting his colleagues for their
inability to "face up to realities," said: "The Labour Party would
not support the taking of military sanctions or even economic sanctions against Germany at this time, in order to put German troops
out of the German Rhineland."[49]

Hence, by the spring of 1936, Labour's struggle to adjust its
policy to the international situation had once more been outpaced
by the rapid passage of events. The party had moved considerable
distance since 1931 from pacification to support of armed collective security; yet the system of collective security was itself now in
shambles. Meanwhile the dictators were busy arming themselves
and capitalizing on the weakness of their adversaries. Amidst this
tense atmosphere Labour's dilemma had become more clear-cut,
but also more intolerable, than ever. Henceforth, if the party seriously desired to halt aggression, it would have to discard socialist
principles altogether* and sanction a vast rearmament program
not only devised but implemented by a capitalist government that
it despised.

### The Third Faction

That the Labour Party eventually supported British rearmament was due, in large measure, to the persistent agitation of the

---

* That is to say, this is how we as observers would define the situation. But
it is another matter whether Labour participants themselves interpreted the
situation and their subsequent behavior in similar terms.

third faction.* It consisted for the most part of certain powerful trade union leaders, together with a handful of PLP members, most notably Hugh Dalton. Ernest Bevin of the Transport Workers and Walter Citrine, TUC General Secretary, were the most influential of these trade unionists, but they could ordinarily rely on the support of colleagues like Charles Dukes of the Municipal Workers and John Marchbank of the Railwaymen. There is a suggestive barometer of the unions' powerful role in the struggle within the Labour Party at the time: the steady rise in left-wing alarm at trade union "bossism." To the left, each union's affiliation to the party as a national body was not only undemocratic but dangerous, and Bevan—the trade union leaders' most insistent critic in the postwar period—early arrived at the conviction that trade union affiliation should be exclusively through the local branches to the local divisional Labour Parties.[50]

What accounted for the prominence of trade union leaders in the third faction? The hatred that the organized working class had for fascism certainly bulked large as a reason. This, of course, was a feeling widespread in all Labour circles, but the trade union wing had added cause to detest fascist brutality and to clamor for strong action against it: since early 1933, its leaders had been forced to watch as one by one their counterparts in Central Europe were hounded, persecuted, and hauled off to concentration camps. The intense emotion aroused by this experience had an immediate, enormous impact on trade union circles, as the biographies and memoirs of trade union leaders readily attest, and it colored their outlook on the international situation for years to come. Many of them early concluded that war between fascism and anti-fascism was inevitable and that it was therefore senseless to waste time in preparing for it. Hence they had scant patience for those in the Labour Party who, whether out of pacifist convictions or concern with doctrinal subtleties, hindered its conversion to a resolute policy. If this meant support for British rearmament, then the price

---

* As was the case in discussing the majority faction, the use of the term "faction" is somewhat oversimplifying. Bullock is right when he says, for instance, that the agreement in viewpoint of Citrine and Bevin was less the result of prior and conscious deliberation than of coincidence (I, 590–91). Even so, it is the similarity of views that counted, something that Citrine himself still regards with some surprise (*Men and Work*, pp. 238–39).

simply had to be paid. "I say this to Sir Stafford Cripps," Bevin
shouted at one point during the 1936 Labour conference: "If I am
asked to face the question of arming this country, I am prepared
to face it. . . . Which is the first institution that victorious Fascism
wipes out? It is the trade union movement . . . we saw our Movement go down in Germany . . . our men shed their blood in Aus-
tria—and nearly every one of them was a trade unionist."[51]

To influence Labour policy making, the trade unions were well
situated by virtue of their strong position on the National Council
of Labour. Established in 1931 as the successor to the National
Joint Council, this was the body within the Labour movement that
had the task of coordinating Labour Party and TUC activity
wherever they overlapped; and of its thirteen members, seven
were from the TUC general council, including Bevin and Citrine.
Even apart from this institutional arrangement, determining influence in the party came increasingly to be exercised by the unions
owing to the enfeebled condition of the PLP during the lean years
following the 1931 debacle. But the National Council was a convenient and serviceable vehicle for making trade union views felt,
and Bevin and Citrine exploited it to good effect in their unrelenting effort to drive Labour round to an aggressive stand on
rearmament.[52] Its impact was particularly decisive in Labour's conversion to armed collective security between 1933 and 1935. Under
trade union pressure, for instance, the PLP and NEC representatives on the National Council were prevailed upon to acknowledge
that the 1933 Hastings general strike resolution was fanciful and
dangerous, and therefore should be repudiated. Again, a year later,
certain trade unionists spearheaded the campaign for an energetic
Labour stand in favor of League sanctions against Italy during the
Ethiopian crisis. Citrine, in arguing the case for sanctions at the
Trades Union Congress, expressed vividly and categorically the
sentiment mounting in trade union circles about the need to stand
up to the dictators: "There is only one way of dealing with a bully
and that is by the use of force. Moral resolutions are no good . . .
it may mean war, but that is the thing we have to face. There is no
real alternative now left to us but the applying of sanctions involving, in all possibility, war. But I say this. If we fail now, if we go
back now, war is absolutely certain. I ask you what will happen to
Germany, if Italy can treat with contempt the nations of the world

who have plighted their word to preserve peace?"[53] It was at the Labour conference in the following month that Dalton tore into Lansbury. Dalton wrote shortly afterward: "Everyone of the big guns of the General Council—Marchbank, Dukes and Bevin—thundered in our support" for a firm policy on collective security.[54]

By this time, the worried inability of the PLP to break the impasse over rearmament was proving wearying and exasperating to a number of trade unionists, and not least to Bevin himself. He was especially incensed when the next party conference, which met at Edinburgh in October 1936, once again proved unable to reach a clear-cut decision. The NEC presented a resolution on defense that still endeavored to distinguish between arms for collective security and arms as a national instrument: "The Labour Party," it read at one point, "declines to accept responsibility for a purely competitive armament policy."[55] Bevin had already demonstrated what he felt about such equivocation when he warned, at the TUC meeting of the previous month, that collective security was threatening to become "a shibboleth rather than a practical operative fact."[56] The party's wavering obviously was eating at his nerves. For a while he even regretted the ties binding the trade union movement to the Labour Party, fearing that the "intellectuals of the party" (his terms for the leaders of the political wing) completely lacked a sense of reality and would drive the British working class to disaster.[57]

Before the strains and tensions between the trade union and political wings developed to a breaking point, however, two events intervened to raise the rearmament problem to a more manageable level. The first was the Spanish Civil War, which erupted with shattering suddenness in mid-1936. The National Council of Labour, which initially followed the Blum government in France by backing nonintervention, did a turnabout when it realized how strikingly out of touch this policy was with party feeling, and in 1937 Labour began pressing the National government to lift the embargo on arms to Spain.* It was the Spanish Civil War that,

---

* Bullock, I, 586–88, 594–95; Citrine, pp. 357–59. It seems clear that the trade unionists were put off by the role of the Communists in the Spanish Republic; and though neither of the two works just cited admit this, Dalton, another member of the third faction, hints at it (*Memoirs, 1931–1945*, pp. 96–100). The subject is treated at length in Watkins, pp. 141–96.

more than anything else, wore down Labour's doctrinal scruples
concerning British rearmament, though even then it took the impact of the second event to prove decisive in this respect. The
event was a fortunate coincidence of personalities in Labour's
councils. In September 1936 Bevin was elected chairman of the
TUC general council, and a month later Dalton secured election
to the equivalent position on the NEC. Since Attlee, Lansbury's
successor as head of the PLP, enjoyed Bevin's confidence despite
his reputation as one of the intellectuals, it followed that two of
the three most powerful leaders in the Labour movement were
now outspokenly favorable to massive British rearmament, whereas the third at least proved amenable to their arguments. With
this change at the top, the party would have a harder time continuing to seek refuge in indecisiveness and muddle. The days of
extreme equivocation and soul-searching were numbered. In July
1937 the PLP finally ended its two and one-half years of opposition to rearmament, although even then it took the weight of
trade union MP's to overcome entrenched frontbench resistance.[58]
The left fumed, accusing Dalton, who engineered the change, of
"a piece of backstairs intrigue."[59] Harold Laski was no less severe
with Bevin and Citrine, whom he rightly regarded as sharing
preeminent responsibility for the change. As Laski saw it, Bevin's
power antics had an "undeniable fascist flavor" about them.[60] The
left's embittered resentment of Bevin would resurface, undimin-
ished, after 1945.

The PLP's decision reduced the party's dilemma to more manageable proportions. But there was no conclusive settlement, no
neat and clean solution; Labour's break with its past remained
halfhearted. For one thing, though the PLP ended its opposition
to the armament estimates, it did not thereby swing round in favor
of them; it simply decided to abstain. Even then, the majority was
tiny, the final vote a mere 45 to 39. Without the largely inarticu-
late trade union MP's, the opponents of rearmament would still
have prevailed; among the diehard, moreover, were to be counted
not just the members of the left, but most of the PLP leadership,
including Attlee and his two principal adjuvants, Morrison and
Greenwood. For another thing, the change in the party's tactics
was blurred in subsequent policy statements. Thus "International
Policy and Defence," a report that the National Council of Labour

prepared in July and submitted to the annual conference in October, treated the question of rearmament with the same familiar vagueness of previous reports. On some international issues it was frank and explicit: the League of Nations had been rendered ineffective "for the time being"; Britain needed new associates, like the United States; disarmament was still Labour's goal but had to await a better international climate. Yet on matters of national defense it proved, as Cole noted, a "most inadequate" guide.[61] Rather than confidently affirming the wisdom of British rearmament, it restricted itself to the inconclusive, almost grudging, observation that as long as the international situation remained menacing, a future Labour government "would be unable to reverse the present programme of rearmament."[62]

Plainly Labour remained torn between conflicting impulses. But if the party could still be rapped for preaching tough anti-fascism without fully practicing it, definite progress in bridging the gap had nonetheless been made. "Our best collective statement yet," as Dalton termed the new report, won both Trades Union Congress and Labour Conference support by thumping majorities.[63] For the first time the PLP had full authority to collaborate with the National government. How extensive that collaboration would actually be was another matter. Yet to the extent that any would be forthcoming at all, the third faction largely deserved the credit.

## THE TRADE UNIONS AND POWER

What explains the more developed sense of power shown by certain trade unionists during this period of fierce party conflict? Of the various reasons that might account for it, three stand out and deserve to be elaborated.

The first springs directly from the nature of a trade union leader's work. In collective bargaining with management, union negotiators are ordinarily alert to the need of operating from as strong a position as possible and of relating their demands to a skillful use of threats. Had the spokesmen for the trade union movement not appreciated the role of force and its threatened application in such bargaining, the movement would have been overwhelmed from the outset by the superior resources at the disposal of the owners of production. The conduct of a nation's foreign policy is somewhat similarly a matter of bargaining among self-interested parties, of pressing claims and relating them to threats (as well as to persuasion and promises); hence it was only natural for trade unionists to interpret international relations in terms of their experience with collective bargaining. How seriously they took the analogy between the two areas of activity can be illustrated by the statement made by the National Council of Labour in 1936: "Labour must be prepared to accept the consequences of its policy. A man who joins a trade union accepts the obligation of collective action in defence of its principles. A man who enjoys the collective security of a trade union must be prepared to take the risk of loyalty to his principles when a strike or lock out is threatened. Similarly, a Movement which supports the League system cannot desert it in a crisis."[64] No one was more profoundly influenced by his trade union background in his approach to foreign policy than Ernest Bevin. This was particularly evident in his keen appreciation of the power considerations in any situation. He found it hard to understand why others, with an entirely different background, had a different outlook on things: "From the day Hitler came to power, I have felt that the democratic countries would have to face war. I believe he was taken too cheap. We have been handicapped by the very sincere pacifists in our Party who believe that the danger can be met by resolutions and prayers and by turning the other cheek. While I appreciate their sincerity, I cannot understand anybody who refuses to face the facts in relation to the happenings in China, in Abyssinia, in Spain, all virtually disarmed countries. I cannot see any way of stopping Hitler and the other dictators except by force."[*]

The second reason is that the trade union wing was historically less carried away with enthusiasm for socialist foreign policy than the political wing was. This was in part because the occupational experience of the trade unionists conflicts somewhat with at least one socialist principle, but also because the British trade union

---

[*] Quoted in Bullock, I, 592. Bullock, in II, speaks on p. 104 of Bevin's "instinct for power" and contrasts it with the political wing's "distrust of power." Another experienced observer, W. N. Medlicott (p. 484), notes that Bevin "showed himself to be a power politician of some distinction when the need arose."

movement developed initially outside any socialist context. In contrast to the situation on the Continent, where trade unionism and socialism grew apace, British unions formed no close bonds with any one political party during their formative years. They were singularly interested in industrial matters, in improving their members' lot in whatever ways possible; if, politically, the Liberal Party seemed best suited to facilitate such gains, then they would support it—if not, then they showed themselves ready to turn to the Tories. The not surprising outcome was that the average British trade union leader was highly pragmatic and initially indifferent to the tug of ideology, and he carried this outlook into the Labour Party at the time of its founding.[65] Even when Labour became a programmatic socialist party, more than just a few traces of this state of mind lingered on in trade union circles and made for tension between them and left-wing enthusiasts.

The third and final reason is bound up with the situation of the British working class in the late nineteenth and early twentieth centuries. Of all the European proletariats, it was the least alienated from the mainsprings of national life—something, of course, that Marx himself appreciated.[66] Unlike working-class spokesmen on the Continent, therefore, British trade unionists never took very seriously such slogans as that the working class had no home. They were patriots, proud to be British; and though most trade union leaders came to speak Labour's internationalist rhetoric, they seemed less zealous in this regard than most Labour politicos and socialist intellectuals. It was thus no accident that those party leaders who were of working-class origin and retained a trade union style—J. R. Clynes, J. H. Thomas, and Bevin come readily to mind—not only were ever ready to profess patriotic sentiments but seemed, at times, to be decidedly assertive and boisterous in their Englishness. For all their internationalist talk, they could match any Tory major in expressing a pronounced dislike of foreigners, a stuffy insular indifference to foreign ways, and even a swaggering sort of nationalism.

### THE CRISIS OF SOCIALIST FOREIGN POLICY

With Labour's turnabout concerning rearmament in late 1937, the conflict within the party tended to peter out. The change in policy had not been easily accomplished; the tussling and wran-

gling were fierce, and at times the whole fabric of party organization seemed near to coming apart. At each step the majority faction endeavored to salvage what they could of socialist policy and
to convince themselves, and others, that events had not simply
rendered it ineffective. An enormous amount of self-induced
muddle was the consequence. More than once the party was so
bewildered that it was in effect pursuing contradictory objectives.
It stood for a strengthened League of Nations, collective security,
universal disarmament, opposition to fascism, appeasement, doctrinaire resistance to war, resistance to British rearmament, and both
nonintervention in Spain and victory for the Republican side.
What saved the party from total confusion, and hence ultimate
paralysis of will, were the unrelenting efforts of the third faction
to press it into abandoning preestablished positions once these
positions were overtaken by events. Under the constant stimulus
of this pressure, Labour renounced a familiar aspect of working-
class solidarity, the call for a general strike; qualified the principle of internationalism, conceding that the League was no
longer adequate to the tasks of the moment; overturned the principle of anti-militarism, endorsing a vast armaments program;
and compromised the anti-capitalist principle, supporting the National government as the trustee of British arms.

This poses a question of supreme importance. With the benefit
of hindsight, we would describe Labour's behavior in these terms.
But it is equally necessary to know how Labour partisans themselves construed their behavior at the time. Did they appreciate
how far they had actually gone in repudiating the four socialist
principles?

The answer spills over onto a complex epistemological problem, what some social psychologists call "reality-testing"—that is,
the ways in which men detect and eliminate errors in their images
of the world and so gradually revise them to approximate the
reality of a situation.* The problem arises every time an expectation (an image of the future) is disappointed by the actual course
of events. In such cases of noncorrespondence, the reasonable

---

* Hume, whose views on the interrelations of beliefs and action have colored
social science till recently, would no doubt have been surprised by this choice
of terms. As he saw it, we cannot approximate "reality," since there is no objective reality to know; all that we can do is compare one image with another.

thing would seem to consist of admitting the error in one's image and making efforts to adapt it. But except for scientific research, men's behavior is seldom so straightforward. The elimination of error is only one possible outcome. Instead, systems of beliefs and the images bound up with them may be more or less closed to new and unsettling evidence. The psychological and sociological mechanisms underlying a closed mind are complicated (see Chapter 6). The point to grasp here is that a gap between reality and image, or between behavior in regard to a situation and beliefs about it, not only is common but often goes undetected.

In Labour's case, it seems that a gap of just this sort arose in connection with the developments examined above. Instead of the fierce conflict over rearmament forcing changes in socialist images, with consequent reexamination of socialist principles, tenacious resistance to such changes appears to have resulted. True, "International Policy and Defence" was construed by the annual conference to mean endorsement of rearmament; true, too, the PLP behavior altered in accord with that interpretation. But the question is what these shifts in both policy and behavior signaled to Labour partisans. That they saw these shifts as signaling abandonment of socialist principles, however temporarily, and adoption of a traditional policy of force, however reluctantly, is doubtful. There were no doubt certain exceptions, especially those who belonged to the third faction. But as far as most Labour partisans were concerned, an easier and more psychologically comfortable course was to minimize the muddle, the drift, the angry squabbles of the period; eventually, perhaps, to stop thinking about them altogether; and to cling, instead, to the consoling belief that nothing fundamental had been at stake—only a slight adjustment, forced by unusual circumstances that proved nothing either way about the soundness of socialist principles.

There is an acid test of Labour's true state of mind in these matters: the government's limited conscription bill, introduced in the spring of 1939. The situation was deteriorating without respite. Few Labour partisans seemed to have any illusions that war was now unavoidable; even the appeasers in the government had been compelled to opt publicly for a firmer policy. Yet despite the approach of war and Labour's previous support for rearmament, the party balked. Conscription was too much to swallow. It became a kind of passion, the one subject on which left-wingers and right-wingers, Sir Stafford Cripps and Clement Attlee, Aneurin Bevan and Ernest Bevin, were able to agree. "It became clear last April," R. H. S. Crossman wrote a few months afterward, "that Labour's conversion to the use of armed force was only skin deep. Underneath all the trappings of collective security, a pacifist heart still beats."[67] The limtis of disagreement were thus reached. In Taylor's apt phrase, when war broke out "no principle divided Attlee from Cripps so far as foreign policy was concerned."

# Chapter three

# Socialist Foreign Policy and World War II

*During the Coalition the Labour members had learnt a great deal from the Conservatives in how to govern.*
—HERBERT MORRISON to King George VI, November 1945

If Labour entered World War II still enjoying a consensus in foreign policy, it confronted the subsequent peace in a far different mood. A cleavage in outlook developed during the war years, splitting the party into roughly two sections, each with distinct ideas about how to cope with the postwar situation. The result of this split was predictable; with consensus shattered, conflict swept through the party's ranks within a matter of months. Once more Labour's fate in foreign policy was tied to angry strife.

How did the line of cleavage slice through the party? One section, overwhelming in number because it included most of the rank and file, continued to peer at the world in mid-1945 through socialist eyes. Not only did few Labour partisans appreciate, when war erupted, the degree to which socialist principles had been responsible for the confused groping and stumbling of the late 1930's; in addition, there was scarcely anything said or done between 1939 and 1945 to encourage reconsideration of these principles in the light of recent experience. Right up to the end of hostilities, the thrust of party utterance fostered the widely diffused belief that socialist foreign policy was as intellectually sound and morally compelling as ever, and that, further, a future Labour government would no sooner take office than it would proceed to follow a bold socialist line. As Harold Laski, chairman of the party, insisted on the eve of the 1945 general election, "Labour has a foreign policy which in many respects will not be continuous with that of a Tory-dominated Coalition."[1] We shall see that most other Labour partisans believed no differently.

We shall also see that their belief was wrong. For by 1945 one small section of the party had other views on the subject; and though small, it was nonetheless the most influential of all—the Labour ministers in the Coalition government. For reasons to be unraveled, their long tenure in the Coalition transformed their outlook so that they came, by the time of the general election, to discard socialist principles as irrelevant to the towering international problems of the moment. It is not too much to say that their outlook was essentially traditionalist, barely distinguishable in most respects from Churchill's or Eden's. The gulf between the two sections was thus enormous. The rank and file fully expected a new departure in foreign policy, a break once and for all with the odious notion of continuity; yet, as it happened, Labour's accession to office made scarcely a difference. Against this background it was only a matter of time before anguished cries of betrayal, treachery, and sell-out were forthcoming.

### THE RANK-AND-FILE VIEW OF THINGS
*Labour's War Aims*

A recurring theme of the party's earliest pronouncements on the war was that Labour bore none of the responsibility for the blunders of British policy in the 1930's. The Tories had been in power throughout; therefore, they alone were guilty, they alone should be ashamed, they alone needed to reconsider the intellectual and moral premises of their actions. Labour, on the other hand, was innocent; and being innocent, it could continue to derive satisfaction from the knowledge that it had the right formula, the socialist formula, for remedying the world's problems. Such, in essence, was the message unpacked by a host of Labour utterances in 1939 and 1940, as for instance by Attlee on 8 November 1939. His speech, which stood as the official declaration of the party's war aims for several months, was largely "a justification of Labour's past policy."[2] All this was a diet, needless to say, on which socialist imagery eagerly fed. Nor were any of the other messages of the period better calculated to stimulate reconsideration of socialist foreign policy. Attlee in the speech just mentioned; the National Council of Labour with a publication entitled "Why Kill Each Other?"; Citrine speaking at the Trades Union Congress in September; the Party Executive with an official declaration of policy called "Labour, the War, and the Peace," issued in February 1940—all struck the theme of international working-class action, distinguishing sharply between the Nazi government and the German people and urging the latter to rise up and overthrow Hitler.[3] Not until 1944 did an official Labour statement admit the impracticality of drawing such a clear distinction.

Another topic of the time was the imperialist character of the war. For the most part discussion of it was confined to the extreme left wing of the Labour Party and to the Communist Party,* but it also seems to have influenced a wider audience, for the Labour leadership was sufficiently disturbed to urge Laski to produce a refutation. The choice was somewhat odd in that Laski himself seems to have shared this view. Still, he proceeded to write "Is This an Imperialist War?," which, while not denying the charge of imperialism, did exhort British socialists to support the war effort on the grounds that, since British imperialism was irreversibly in decline, whereas German imperialism was in its most aggressive stage of capitalist development, a British victory would be the lesser evil. Talk of an imperialist war, it goes without saying, became something of an anachronism following the German attack on the Soviet Union.

Such, in brief, was the way things more or less stood by the time Labour entered Churchill's Coalition government in the spring of 1940. On the whole, the rank and file approved the move, and it ordinarily supported the Coalition's foreign policies. There was one notable exception—a small, vigorous group of backbench MP's led by Aneurin Bevan, which began protesting, as early as 1942, against the alleged subservience of the Labour ministers to Tory views with respect to the postwar configuration in Europe. "It is not unity we have now," Bevan bitterly complained; "it is

---

* "Many intellectuals of the Left," Orwell observed in 1941, "were flabbily pacifist up to 1935, shrieked for war against Germany in the years 1935–1939, and then promptly cooled off when the war started." "England Your England," p. 279.

Was Orwell exaggerating? Another observer, John Maynard Keynes, wrote a letter to the *New Statesman* (14 October 1939) noting that "the intelligentsia of the Left were the loudest in demanding that the Nazi aggression should be resisted at all costs. When it comes to a show-down, scarce four weeks have passed before they remember they are pacifists and write defeatist letters to your columns."

a conspiracy against the future."* Except on isolated occasions near the end of the war such as during the intervention in Greece, the rest of the party did not agree. Even then they detected at most only misjudgment, not subservience, let alone conspiracy. They continued to believe in their leaders' fundamental devotion to socialist principles; and if it happened that the Coalition's policies lacked a socialist flavor, this—it was argued—could be easily explained by the fact of total war and the overriding necessity to cope with the bewildering problems at hand.† Besides, ample socialist reassurance could be found in official party propaganda statements. In marked contrast to what Labour leaders were saying as ministers, this propaganda continued right into 1945 to glow with socialist symbolism and imagery.

Nowhere was this more vividly evident than in Labour interpretations of the ideological issues at stake in the war. The peculiar twist, socialist style, that recurred in party statements was that the war, while on one level a struggle between democracy and fascism, was at a deeper level essentially the decisive and fateful clash between the forces of the old order and the international working class.[4] And by the old order was not meant just fascism but also capitalism in all its variations, the British included. The old decadent ruling classes were said to have not entered the war with enthusiasm, in any anti-fascist mood; they had been dragged in by heroic pressures of the common people, after having fallen over one another in a scramble to appease the dictators, and their preeminent concern was to survive intact, to squirm and edge their way back into power at the war's end. But in this their hopes would be rudely shattered. The old order was doomed. Whether fascist, monarchist, oligarchic, or Tory, it could not survive because the common people were determined for the first time in history to take control themselves. As "The Old World and the

---

* Quoted in Foot, *Aneurin Bevan*, pp. 434–35. In industrial and social matters, as distinct from foreign policy, the trade unions and many party members were less happy with Labour's role in the Coalition. Our concern, however, is strictly with foreign policy.

† "The war, whatever the ambitions of the Government or of its leader, had become so plainly a war for sheer survival of Great Britain as a self-governing country that this factor was all-important in most working people's minds and directed their sympathies and actions to the exclusion of everything else." G.D.H. Cole, *A History of the Labour Party from 1914*, p. 395.

New Society" put it, the defeat of the Axis powers would automatically entail "widespread revolution ... in countries which they now dominate." The instrument of the revolution would be the various resistance movements that had sprung up to fight fascism. Once the war ended, these movements would not meekly yield their arms and acquiesce in a return of the corrupt ruling classes; rather, they would seize power for themselves, sweep away the last decadent remains of the old order, and in its place establish a universal socialist commonwealth—"the new society." What, then, should be Labour's role in this epochal struggle? As the leading socialist party in the allied nations, it had a history-making obligation to aid the revolution wherever it needed moral encouragement or material assistance. In the words of "From a People's War to a People's Peace," "the new world must be built up through unremitting struggle and International Labour and Socialist Unity." All the same, despite such hellfire rhetoric, Labour did not envisage the need for violence everywhere. In nations with established parliamentary systems like Britain itself, socialism could prevail by gradualist means, since the electorates would be eager, at the war's end, to support left-wing parties promising them bold socialist programs. The overall result would still be the same: the commencement of the socialist commonwealth.

There is a special reason for dwelling on these propaganda themes, which is that they have usually received short shrift from other authors—as though Labour's difficulties over foreign policy after 1945 arose unexpectedly, overnight. Nowhere is this neglect more evidenced than in the memoirs or biographies of the Labour members of the Coalition. One searches in vain through Attlee's assorted reminiscences, Morrison's autobiography, and two biographies apiece of Cripps and Bevin for relevant commentary on the party's wartime propaganda. Even Dalton, who helped draft "The International Post-War Settlement," is of little aid, for though he devotes four pages to this topic in his memoirs, half of the commentary focuses on the Palestinian question and the other half recapitulates his views at the time on Germany.[5] In face of this neglect, one can only conclude that the Labour leadership never took the party's pronouncements very seriously or regarded them as harmless sop for the ranks. And yet this propaganda had its importance. Not only did it feed the rank-and-file impression that the Labour ministers retained a decidedly socialist outlook, despite Bevan's warnings that they did not; it also encouraged extravagant expectations about the postwar period that turned out to be based on little more than passing myths and airy fancies.

### *"Left Understands Left"*

In these exuberant hopes for the postwar world, the Soviet Union commanded a prominent role.

We have already seen how pro-Soviet sentiment remained ardent in party circles right down to June 1939. Over the next two years, however, owing to the Nazi-Soviet Nonaggression Pact and the subsequent Soviet attack on Finland, Labour's long established emotional links to the Soviet Union buckled for the first time and a new mood began to emerge. The Pact was denounced by the *Daily Herald* (24 August 1939) as amounting to "a bigger betrayal of peace and of European freedom even than Munich," and the condemnation was made formal by the next annual conference.[6] Yet the nature of that condemnation was instructive. Its hostile tone was restricted to the Pact itself, scarcely anything critical of the Soviet Union itself being mentioned, as though its recent exploit was accidental, an unfortunate but ephemeral aberration. The left-wing press, for its part, managed to uncover reasons for praising the Pact, as in the *Tribune*'s observation (25 August 1939) that it represented "a great reinforcement for peace in Eastern Europe." Only on the occasion of the Soviet-Finnish war did the emotional links come near to snapping outright. Censure was nearly universal, though it varied in degree of acridity; the National Council of Labour protested the most vehemently and helped set up a fund to aid the besieged Finns.[7] Yet the indignation, though genuine, soon faded in many circles. Shortly afterward party voices were again praising the Soviet Union,* demanding that the Coalition conclude an immediate alliance with

---

* Typical of the surging enthusiasm was a 1942 pamphlet of the Engineering and Allied Trades Shop-Stewards' National Council, which began with these ringing words: "For trade unionists, the Anglo-Soviet Treaty is a confirmation of the anti-fascist character of the war, emphasizing the indisputable fact that the destinies of the British workers are linked up with that of the Soviet peoples . . . our future social progress depends upon the complete smashing of Hitlerite Germany." The pamphlet, "How to Get the Best Results," is quoted at length in Coates and Topham, pp. 172–79.

the Kremlin—this at a time when the Kremlin showed no overwhelming desire to enter the war. In this context, it was hardly
surprising that the (still reluctant) Soviet entry in mid-1941 caused
tumultuous jubilation in the Labour Party. With the one socialist
nation now unequivocally on the anti-fascist side, Labour's interpretation of the ideological issues at stake seemed graphically vindicated.

Of course, for things to work out as predicted by party propaganda, the Soviet Union would have to share Labour's war aims.
Though few facts were available at the time concerning Soviet
intentions, they were enough to sour optimism if viewed dispas-
sionately. At any rate, there was no lack of British observers including, it would seem, the War Cabinet who realized what the
Soviets hankered after in Central and Eastern Europe. But Labour was hardly prepared to view the matter with detachment.
The Soviets had joined the anti-fascist struggle; were fighting
heroically, magnificently; spoke a progressive rhetoric. Who could
reasonably ask for more, given the uncertainties and imponder-
ables of the time? In approximately this way Soviet aims were
simply assumed to coincide, or at least converge, with Labour's.
Presumably, both aspired to the same sort of new order, wanted
the same sort of revolution, understood peace and cooperation in
the same sort of way. "Our chance of having Socialism in this country," the shop-stewards' conference proclaimed, "is bound up with
defence of the Soviet Union."[8] Roughly the same conclusion was
reached by a host of other Labour utterances after June 1941.
Wittingly or not, their effect was to foster a state of mind that
would welcome a Soviet-dominated Central and Eastern Europe
with equanimity.[9]

As the war neared its end, a final partisan touch was put on
this bright, reassuring picture. Party orators began insisting that
future Anglo-Soviet cooperation hung perilously on Labour's ability to win power immediately upon the war's cessation. Churchill
could not be permitted one moment longer in office, else, as the
old order started crumbling on the Continent, he and his Tory
cohorts might grow desperate, plunge into reckless adventures
aimed at arresting the inevitable revolutionary upswing, perhaps
even manuever to contain Soviet influence within a reconstructed
*cordon-sanitaire* propped up by British bayonets. It fell to Labour

to forestall this reactionary rearguard operation. Nerving itself for
the coming struggles, it had to make the British people realize that
only a Labour electoral victory could preserve Soviet friendship
and so preserve the peace. "Left understands left" was the way in
which a party slogan compactly expressed this widely diffused conviction.

### The Survival of Socialist Foreign Policy

If the various strands of the argument are now drawn together,
the following conclusion emerges: Labour's wartime propaganda,
official or otherwise, offered little or no incentive to reconsider the
soundness of socialist foreign policy. On the contrary, the average
party member had every reason to cling to socialist policy as accepted party doctrine and to expect that it would govern the behavior of future Labour governments. And by average member is
meant not just the proverbial wild-eyed zealots within the constituency party organizations, but almost everybody within the
party other than the Coalition ministers, most Labour MP's and
candidates decidedly included. As the 1945 general election study
noted, "much of the attention which they [Labour candidates]
gave to foreign policy in the nineteen thirties survives, and also
much of the spirit of that period."[10]

Just how much survived was made strikingly plain by the party's behavior as the election drew near. Very illuminating in this
connection was the annual conference, which assembled at Blackpool in May. The European war was already over, and events on
the Continent were unfolding in ways that seemed to vindicate
the party's predictions. Nearly everywhere radical resistance movements were emerging into prominence; the moment of the long
anticipated Revolution was at hand—or so it appeared to the ex-
cited throng of delegates. The conference hall resounded with the
uproar of exhilarated men. "Left understands left" sloganeering
filled the air: "Labour Election . . . Revolution . . . Big Three
Unity . . . Gallant Soviet Allies . . . Socialist Cooperation . . .
Movement of History . . . New Era. . . ." The heady mood and
spirit were well exemplified by a speech of Denis Healey, then a
major in the army, who demanded that "the crucial principle of
our foreign policy should be to protect, assist, encourage and aid
in every way the Local Revolution wherever it appears." Major

Healey granted that the Revolution might not be entirely to Labour's liking, that it might be nasty and violent, but the party
had to realize that there was often no other way for history to
progress. The penalty for hesitating, for entertaining reservations
about the overall desirability of the Revolution, he grimly warned,
would be that Labour would awake one day to find itself "running
with the red flag in front of the armoured car of Tory reaction."*

### THE LEADERSHIP'S VIEW OF THINGS

*Contrasted Mood*

Despite the mounting excitement over international prospects,
one section of the party preserved a more sober outlook: the
Labour ministers in the Coalition government. Attlee, head of
the party, was Churchill's Deputy Prime Minister and had pre-
sided, in his absence, for weeks on end over the War Cabinet. Of
the other important Labour leaders, Bevin was Minister of Labour and National Service, Morrison Home Secretary, Dalton
Minister of Economic Warfare and later President of the Board
of Trade, Cripps first Ambassador to Russia and then Minister
of Aircraft Production.

Before 1940, they had been luminaries in a party that had never
governed with an absolute Parliamentary majority and even then
for but two brief and somewhat unhappy spells. Thus they had
been comparatively unversed in the responsibilities of office, free
to formulate lofty policy declarations, free to moralize against the
stupidity of those in power. But joining the Coalition changed
all this. Where once they had been but leaders of a party almost
permanently in opposition, they now became the governors of the
whole nation, who were daily led deeper and deeper into the multitude of bewildering administrative tasks of total war, and who
were, moreover, privy to all the Coalition's major decisions.†
Hence, whatever their previous impulses in matters of foreign

---

* *LPCR*, 1945, p. 114. Metaphors of this sort, it should be observed, are
quite common in Labour oratory. At the 1921 conference (*LPCR*, 1921, p. 201),
for instance, a delegate insisted that the Lloyd George Coalition's foreign policy
was in effect "tying Britain to the chariot of French imperialism."

† This situation stands in sharp contrast to the party's experience during the
previous war, when a Labour leader (who was by no means the most prominent)
was brought into the War Cabinet only in December 1916, long after most key
decisions were made.

policy, they had no choice in their new roles but to keep ideas of British security, power, and national interests uppermost in their minds.

It is not hard to estimate the impact that this altogether new experience must have had on their appreciation of socialist foreign policy. Willy-nilly they had to do what the average Labour partisan himself was spared of doing: they were forced to rethink the premises of accepted socialist beliefs and values. Years later Morrison conveyed the psychological effect that the realities of governing can produce in these terms: "It is one of the first things that one learns when one becomes a Minister ... that you bump up against lots of facts which you wish you did not, but that is part of learning the facts of government."[11] Where foreign policy was concerned, this learning process evidently meant that the Labour Coalition ministers had to adjust their visions to the brute realities of the existing international system. No longer could the system interest them primarily as a matter for socialist reform; they had to learn to work with, not in indifference to, the facts of power. If, accordingly, the four socialist principles did not illuminate the vexing problems thrown up anew, day in, day out, by the vicissitudes of war; if they did not lead to penetrating diagnosis or suggest plausible solutions of an immediate sort, then the ministers apparently discarded them as irrelevant or useless. Of course, the principles had been equally discarded in the agonizing struggle to adapt Labour's policy in the late 1930's. The difference this time was that those directly involved as participants on the Cabinet level had no illusions about what they were doing. Bevin made this clear, for instance, when he pleaded in April 1945 "for foreign and defence policy to be put on a different footing outside the party conflict."[12]

What is the other evidence? Most striking of all, of course, is the foreign policy that the Labour government implemented *immediately* upon taking office in July 1945. Apart from it, we can single out the attitude of the leadership on the question of Labour's share of responsibility for the blunders of the 1930's. Unlike the rank and file, the ministers were willing to come to terms with this legacy, as in Bevin's avowal that Labour "refused absolutely to face the facts" of rearmament.[13] We can mention the intriguing case of Cripps, a zealot of socialist foreign policy dur-

ing the prewar period; his views were transformed by his experience in office no less than those of his colleagues—so much so, indeed, that his biographer assures us that by 1945 "his ideas on foreign policy matched with Bevin's."* For that matter they seemed
to have matched even before that, since he was one of the tiny
band of Labour MP's (23 in all) who voted with the Coalition in
support of its widely condemned Greek policy.[14] (The vote is also
valuable as further illuminating the gulf between the leadership
and the ranks, for 30 Labour MP's voted against the Coalition
while over 100 abstained.) We can, in the fourth place, mention
Bevin's point-blank admission when he became Foreign Secretary
that the Labour and Tory Coalition ministers had seen eye-to-eye
on *every* important decision in foreign policy made during the
war.[15] We can also mention a similar statement avowed by Attlee
months earlier.[16] And, finally, we can point to the concern that
Attlee shared with Churchill and Eden in the spring of 1945 concerning Soviet expansion into Central Europe.[17]

It has been said that one minister, Hugh Dalton, still retained
a socialist outlook in 1945.[18] Yet beyond an ambivalent speech
praising Labour as best situated to cooperate with Russia,[19] there
is little—or rather no—evidence to support such a contention; as
we shall see, even Bevin struck a "left understands left" note at
that same conference. Perhaps Fitzsimons has in mind Dalton's
large role in writing "The International Post-War Settlement."
If so, this proves nothing because Dalton did not in fact compose
it alone but had to compromise with many other views, including
Laski's. "But these I regarded as harmless additions," he later observed.[20] Though, regrettably, little else in his memoirs touches
on his attitudes in foreign policy, what he does say about Russia,[21]
together with his pro-rearmament stand during the 1930's, makes
the Fitzsimons-Watts assessment seem most doubtful.

### The Failure to Reeducate the Party

This leads to an obvious and intriguing question: Given the
profound change in outlook of the Labour ministers, why did

---

* Cooke, p. 358. See too p. 326 for an appraisal of Cripps's experience in the
Coalition, where Cooke observes that the ideas of Cripps's Tory friends concerning postwar government were "not enough" for him. This suggests considerable overlap.

they not strive to impart the lessons derived from their tenure
in office to the rest of the party?

With the benefit of hindsight, we know that the leadership
might have spared itself considerable pains in foreign policy after
1945 had it taken the task of reeducation more seriously. Precisely this conclusion was reached by at least one prominent Labour spokesman in the postwar period. Looking back on the deep
split in foreign policy that prevailed by the war's end, Roy Jenkins wrote in 1953 that "more attention should have been paid
to it by the party leaders—paid not by abandoning their own
realistic approach but by devoting a far greater part of their energies to seeing that the facts upon which they were basing their
policy were made equally real to their supporters." But the leadership did not take such pains, and "today," Jenkins ruefully
noted, "a heavy price is being paid for the failure to do this."[22]

If, however, the consequences of the leadership's neglect are
easy to document, the reasons for it are another matter. The subject is not even so much as alluded to by either memoirs or biographies, which in itself says something. Still, a plausible explanation
can be conjectured. Jenkins, for instance, singles out the leadership's "complacency"—its rooted conviction that party loyalty and
discipline could always be counted on to ensure that its views
would prevail. He grants that the conviction was not entirely ill-
founded; after all, whatever the controversy stirred up over foreign policy, the postwar Labour government was never in danger
of defeat at party conference. At a deeper level he is less satisfied,
for he notes that "support for the official policy was passive rather
than active," that, as a result of this complacency, "the foreign
policy of the Labour Government never bit deep into the consciousness of the party."[23] It seems doubtful, however, whether
Jenkins' explanation is entirely adequate. Complacency there no
doubt was, but at least two additional reasons need to be considered in order to round out the picture. First, the leaders of British
parties have nearly always preferred to avoid head-on confrontations with their followers, there being other, less risky and more
serviceable mechanisms by which they can try to keep order among
the ranks—not least a style of politics that plays down policy
disputes, cautiously shies away from dramatizing them, suggests
that it is better "to let situations develop until the near necessity

of decision blunts inclinations to quarrel about just what the decision should be."[24] Waltz aptly refers to this strategy as "the management of parties," something that we shall pick up again in Chapter 7. What this meant at the time seems fairly clear: the Labour ministers, sensing the gap between themselves and their followers, preferred to let the international situation develop rather than try to assault socialist convictions. Their hope, of course, was that events themselves would soon demonstrate the need for a more cautious, nonsocialist, postwar policy in Europe, especially where the Soviet Union was concerned. Second, in order to see the problem of education in its full setting, we must recall the exhausting duties that the leaders had as Coalition ministers. Since this role swamped all others, including partisan roles, the ministers were probably too absorbed in the tasks of governing, too caught up in the tangle of complex policy making and administration, to bother much with party concerns. Even when they found time to address party gatherings, their aim was nearly always to rally their followers' enthusiasm for the war effort. This meant not only that they tried to make unpopular Coalition policies appear palatable, but that they were reluctant to get tied down in discussions over fundamentals.*

Still, successful as these stratagems proved to be in keeping the ranks in line, they were not free of drawbacks. I have already mentioned the greatest drawback of all: the price paid in postwar disputes over foreign policy. Yet quite apart from it, there were certain shortcomings visible even before the war ended. For in trying to straddle the gap between Coalition measures for postwar Europe and socialist principles, the Labour ministers could find themselves subject to a strong two-way tug. This predicament was never very important so long as everyone's attention was preoccupied with the war itself. But as the outcome became evident and men began to speculate about the postwar situation, the predicament grew more acute and did not augur happily for the future of party harmony.

---

* "It is a cardinal point of policy for the government as a whole," Bevin weighed in with a retort to backbench Labour criticism during a Commons debate, "that neither interest, property, persons, nor prejudice will be allowed to stand in the way of our achieving that great objective [victory]." 376 *H.C.Deb.* 1342–43 (4 December 1941). For an example of another minister's view, see Dalton, *Memoirs, 1931–1945,* p. 334.

The most vivid example was the outrage that the British intervention in Greece generated among Labour's ranks, many of which
saw the move as nothing other than Churchill's initial attempt to
crush the European revolution in its formative stage. The sharp
division that immediately ensued within the PLP has already
been noted. At the annual conference which met shortly afterward, a strongly worded resolution in condemnation of the Coalition's policy was moved from the floor. Ernest Bevin, speaking
for his colleagues, tried to rebut the resolution, whereupon Aneurin Bevan jumped up to protest that only fascist Spain, fascist
Portugal, and the Tory Party were at all enthusiastic about British intervention.[25] The tone of Bevan's acrimonious attack seemed
attuned to the mood of the conference, and had the delegates felt
free to vote according to their dominant impulse, they would
probably have broken with their leaders. The fact was, however,
that they did not feel entirely free. Because the leadership had
publicly staked its prestige on the line, and because, too, "Bevin
had used his influence to secure the block vote of the major
unions," the conference voted "out of loyalty rather than conviction" in support of the Executive's position.* Even then, the
leadership's victory remained equivocal. Minutes later, the conference turned around and passed another resolution that approved the general European revolution in terms almost indistinguishable from those employed by the one dealing with Greece
alone.[26]

There occurred a second incident at the conference that illuminated the leadership's problems in a different way. Attlee, speaking for the Executive, praised a resolution that reaffirmed emphatically and without qualification all of the socialist principles.[27]
No doubt the rash of attacks on the Coalition's Greek policy gave
the leadership added incentive not to challenge a resolution of
this sort. All the same, such deft maneuvering, however aptly it
sidestepped the risks of the moment, was a false reassurance from
the rank-and-file viewpoint. It meant that any future showdown
might be only that much more explosive.

An ominous portent of just this sort of danger arose at the next
annual conference, held five months later at Blackpool. At long

---

* The quoted words are Alan Bullock's, II, 343.

last the Labour ministers seemed determined to set the postwar situation in proper perspective. What accounted for their new resolution? No doubt it was their knowledge that the Coalition had reached its breaking point. A general election would be imminent, and then, perhaps under Labour guidance, the nation would have to tackle the enormous problems of peacetime reconstruction and diplomacy.

Two speeches are of particular importance here, those given by Attlee and Bevin. The atmosphere at Blackpool was thick with heady optimism and intoxicating vistas of the coming era in Europe; "pro-Russian feeling," Jenkins notes, "was at its zenith," and there "already existed a sharp difference of outlook between the platform and the floor."[28] Attlee, who spoke first, tried to dampen the soaring enthusiasm by reminding the conference just how colossal the problems at hand were. He warned that the era of eternal peace had not arrived; "old suspicions die hard," and before socialist cooperation could materialize, it would first be necessary to reconcile different histories, different outlooks, different ideologies." Some day the world might perhaps be wise enough to permit Britain and the other peace-loving nations to dispense with armed forces—but that day was hardly upon them yet, and until then there would be need for caution, sober-mindedness, and vigilance.[29] Bevin was even blunter. He agreed that a wave of revolution was rushing across Europe. But revolutions, whatever else they might accomplish, would not change the hard facts of international politics; policy making would still have to consider geography, commercial needs, and national security and interests. It was, moreover, both dangerous and misleading to believe that doctrinaire economic theories could disclose which great power might be friendly to Britain and which might be hostile. Such theories degenerated into mere slogans—slogans that said that "all the people in one country are angels and in the other all devils." Britain genuinely desired to maintain good relations with the Soviet Union, but Britain alone could not determine the future of Anglo-Soviet relations; if the Soviets desired friendship, they should desist from the growing practice of presenting us with *faits accomplis* at the conference table. For that matter, Anglo-Soviet relations were not aided when Labour partisans regarded it as their supreme duty to apologize for Soviet brutalities in East-

ern and Central Europe. Finally, Bevin pleaded, Labour should
remember that it was committed to a policy of collective security.
"Collective security involves commitments and I do beg Labour
not to bury its head in the sand."[30]

These were hard-hitting words. But a mood built up, encouraged, and fed for five years was not easily punctured. Despite the
loud ovation that greeted Bevin's speech, Jenkins concludes that
"it is nevertheless doubtful to what extent the more sombre parts
of his message went home."[31] The speakers who followed Bevin
and Attlee either objected to their cautious assessments of the
world situation or simply ignored them. One irate delegate chas-
tised Attlee for failing to apply the proper socialist analysis to
things and instead talking in terms that "might have been applied by a very good Liberal statesman in those days of the League
of Nations when people sincerely believed that a League of capitalist governments would prevent war." It is true, of course, that
those who speak in conference debates are never entirely representative of those who do not speak. Jenkins, who admits this,
nonetheless insists that the split in outlook between platform and
floor was very real and that it remained as great at the end of the
conference as at the beginning.[32] How powerful a socialist steam
the delegates worked up was shown in other ways, too. Thus the
Executive, faced with evidence of the cleavage in opinion, found
it expedient "to take the greatest notice" of a resolution emphatically demanding a bold socialist approach to the postwar world,
indefatigable opposition to power politics, and unremitting support for the expected European revolution.[33] But the most graphic
illustration was the lingering impression taken away by most delegates that Bevin, for all his cautious utterance, had his heart in the
right, that is socialist, place, because at one point he supposedly
reaffirmed the voguish slogan, "Left understands Left, but the
Right does not." In fact, Bevin was referring to the leftward trend
in French politics at the time, though that was not how most delegates recalled the incident. They were convinced that he meant
the Soviet Union.[34]

### LABOUR ON THE EVE OF POWER

In view of Labour's bifurcated development over the previous five
years, there was nothing surprising about the gap between plat-

form and floor that existed at Blackpool. The surprise, indeed, would have been that the leadership could have succeeded in remedying its previous neglect of rank-and-file education within such a short span of time. But what does seem unexpected, at any rate in retrospect, was the extent to which the leadership encouraged rank-and-file illusions during the subsequent election campaign. Cripps, former Ambassador to the Soviet Union whose views now matched Bevin's, insisted at one point: "We must have a government that by sympathy and understanding believes in the objectives of the people of the Soviet Union."[35] A rhetorical flourish of this sort undoubtedly reinforced the mistaken impression of Bevin's "left understands left" reference at Blackpool. For that matter Bevin's election speeches were ambivalent enough to hearten the most militant rank-and-file enthusiast. If, at one point, he was quoted by *The Times* (23 June) as again avowing Labour's equal share of responsibility for the Coalition's foreign policy, he was quoted by the *Daily Worker* on 9 July as expressing the opinion that the Russians would unquestionably prefer a Labour government because "left can speak to left in comradeship and confidence."

No doubt it would be a mistake to make too much of these inconsistencies, the majority of which could be chalked up to campaign fever. But the trouble was that they only emboldened the ranks to boost their enthusiasm, their heady expectations, another notch or two. A fired-up activist in Glasgow or Manchester or Leeds might have been forgiven if he hung more eagerly on Bevin's "left understands left" notes than on his sober analyses of Britain's postwar problems. He might have been forgiven, too, for not appreciating the fine distinction between such slogans and the full-fledged radical logic behind the demands filling the pages, say, of the *New Statesman* at the time. After all, if the principal aim of Labour's foreign policy would be cooperation with socialist nations under any conditions, and if cooperation would be furthered to the degree left saw eye to eye with left, then did it not follow that a Labour government should spare no effort to make itself as radical as it could? Or as R. H. S. Crossman put it: "If we were ready to participate in the planned reconstruction of the European economy on a grand scale, we might find in the end that we had come to a real understanding with the Russians."[36]

From a charitable viewpoint, "Let Us Face the Future," the party's election manifesto, might be said not to have appreciably added to the growing store of confusion regarding Labour's intentions in foreign policy. This, however, was mainly because it said little about the subject and said it in harmless generalities. The section dealing with foreign policy was relegated to the very end, was sweepingly vague in terminology, and—while containing no easy promises—in effect reaffirmed the socialist principles. Thus at one point the manifesto related success in foreign policy to success at home in areas of full employment, housing, and welfare, while at another point it insisted that Labour's "one great asset" in dealing with other nations was its "common bond with the working peoples of all countries." In connection with Russia, it assailed the Tories' prewar fears of that nation and suggested that Labour would get along well with it. The studied vagueness, the rarefied generality, also set the tone of Labour's speeches on the stump. While 50 per cent of Conservative candidates linked foreign policy to matters of defense and the armed forces, the corresponding figure for Labour candidates was only 12 per cent.[37] At the same time Harold Laski, chairman of the party, was traveling about issuing declarations to the effect that Labour "does not propose to accept the Tory doctrine of the continuity of foreign policy because we have no interest in the continuity of Conservative policy."[38]

### The Result of the Election

The Labour Party emerged from the campaign with an imposing victory, its parliamentary strength swelled to 393—a majority of 146. From the standpoint of foreign policy, however, the victory was not an unmitigated blessing. Most of the Labour MP's were new, without previous experience in politics; they were young, enthusiastic, boundless in their expectations of what a Labour government could do, abroad no less than at home. Even to run a sufficient number of candidates, the National Executive had been compelled to approve scores of untested persons. Only 120 owed their seats to trade union sponsorship—that is, to the one section of the party that had shown itself in the late 1930's to be immune to some of the more utopian features of socialist foreign policy.

The scene was already set for trouble when the readers of the *New Statesman* learned in its columns that the very first socialist step taken by the new Labour government—Bevin's and Attlee's replacement of Eden and Churchill at Potsdam—had visibly improved the Anglo-Soviet atmosphere.[39] Thus socialist foreign policy was already reputed to be bringing in its promised dividends.

# Chapter four

## Conflict Again: The Initial Phase,
## August 1945–Spring 1946

> *Without the stopping power of the Americans the Russians might easily have tried sweeping right forward. I don't know whether they would, but it wasn't a possibility you could just ignore. It's no good thinking that moral sentiments have any sway with the Russians, there's a good deal of old-fashioned imperialism in their make-up you know....Some of our friends wouldn't see that.*
>
> —CLEMENT ATTLEE

Memoirs are, of course, a notoriously tricky source of information, but the only cause for complaint about Attlee's observation is his use of the term "some." Many, or perhaps most, would be more to the point, if what we have in mind is the party's stormy reaction to the Labour government's foreign policy during its first two to three years of development. Once again party harmony was shaken by angry controversy; once again party politics was a story of renewed confrontation, bitter strife, and temporary and inconclusive compromises in opinion and alignment. There is, however, nothing surprising about the renewal of turbulent conflict at the time, not at any rate in retrospect, given the two-sided history of socialist foreign policy during World War II—its tenacious survival among the party mass and its rejection by the leadership in the Coalition. Even by itself Attlee's observation more than just hints at the profound contrast in outlook prevailing at the war's end.* Less than 60 words in length, the excerpt quoted here is yet sufficient to overturn three of the four socialist principles. Pro-Soviet sentiment (working-class solidarity) is turned topsy-turvy, and the Soviets rather than the Americans (anti-capitalism) are accused of old-fashioned imperialism; the Americans are singled out by implication as the major bulwark against imperialism; and even more striking is the emphasis placed on the desirability of

---

* The observation was made in 1961, of course, but there is overwhelming reason to believe that Attlee felt no differently in 1945.

power balancing (a reversal of anti-militarism). We shall see that the fourth principle, internationalism, was treated no less brusquely by the new Labour government.

In direct opposition to this was the dominant outlook in the party itself. The rank and file, together with a large, probably overwhelming, majority of backbench MP's, approached the postwar era fully convinced that their leaders would proceed to implement a socialist foreign policy. The ambivalent behavior of the leadership during the election campaign only strengthened this conviction. Seen in this light, the dominant question was not whether there would be a collision between followers and leaders; it was rather when the collision would take place and how severe and far-reaching its consequences would be.

### FORETOKEN OF THE GOVERNMENT'S REVERSAL
### OF SOCIALIST FOREIGN POLICY

Had the readers of the *New Statesman*'s 11 August issue actually been present at the Potsdam Conference, they might not have so confidently assumed that the arrival of Labour ministers had "visibly" cleared the atmosphere. The assertive, almost aggressive front that Bevin presented to the conference set the tone, in many ways, of the government's foreign policy for the next few years. Bevin did not go out of his way to elicit the Soviets' cooperation, as "left understands left" sentiment would have dictated, any more than he invoked appeals to their "common" socialist background. On the contrary, he took so militant a view in defense of British interests that even the Americans wondered how it would be possible to get along with such an imperious Foreign Secretary.* The Soviets, for their part, scarcely concealed their disappointment that Labour instead of the Tories had won the General Election. "I knew from experience," Attlee later observed, "that the communists had always fought us more vigorously than the Tories because they thought we offered a viable alternative to Communism."[1]

---

* Byrnes, p. 79. On two of the most contentious issues at the conference, German reparations and the Polish western frontier, Soviet and British views clashed loudly; and far from the Labour ministers mediating as the party hopefuls back in Britain expected, it was an American initiative that broke the impasse and led to a compromise. See Woodward, pp. 560–67.

The immense differences between Soviet and Western attitudes surfaced with even greater dramatic force at the September meeting of the Council of Foreign Ministers. Soviet demands for enormous German reparations, Soviet behavior in Poland, the character of Soviet-imposed regimes in Bulgaria, Hungary, and Rumania, where, in Bevin's words, "one kind of totalitarianism is being replaced by another"[2]—all these disturbing indexes were transforming the spirit of the Grand Alliance, never very deep at any time, into an air of cumulative mistrust and suspicion. What particularly alarmed Bevin and the Cabinet was the disclosure of keen Soviet interest in Southern Europe and the Mediterranean, a prospect that had haunted the Coalition at least since 1943. This prospect loomed ominously at Potsdam when Stalin called, in effect, for British evacuation from much of the area, Soviet control of the Turkish Straits, and Soviet acquisition of ex-Italian colonies; and its shadow lengthened when Molotov returned to these demands with stubborn emphasis at the London meeting. Bevin became so enraged that at one point he likened the Soviet Foreign Minister to Hitler.[3] On other occasions he proclaimed, in the bluntest of terms, that the Labour government was absolutely opposed to any unilateral withdrawal from the Mediterranean. To the House of Commons he represented current Soviet policy as conspiring to slice "right across, shall I say, the throat of the British Commonwealth."[4]

Here again the Labour government manifested aloof indifference to socialist principles. With their denigration of national interests and their insistence that conflict between nations was the result of easily surmounted misunderstanding, the principles would presumably have dictated unilateral British concessions— to the point, indeed, where the Soviets would be convinced of British goodwill and begin to reciprocate. Even apart from the government's hostility to suggestions of this sort when they were advanced by party members, the character of its anti-Soviet policy can be brought out in another revealing way: to urge a more conciliatory attitude toward Soviet demands at the time, one did not have to be a socialist. This was for instance, essentially the attitude of the Americans, still under the influence of their wartime optimism that it was worth buying Soviet cooperation with professions of good faith and acts of kindness.

The deadlock at the London Conference made public, for the first time, the enormous differences separating East and West that had hitherto been papered over by the façade of Big Three unity. The revelation of discord had a lightning effect in Labour circles. Spokesmen for the party had argued, during the election campaign, that a Labour victory would ensure cooperation with the Soviet Union; Labour had won the election, yet the upshot was not increased harmony but rather a precipitate decline in Anglo-Soviet relations. Hugh Dalton, Chancellor of the Exchequer, observed in the early autumn that "already our relations with Russia, only a few months after the war, were not at all satisfactory."[5] Obviously something had gone amiss, and countless party members belonging to most circles in the party, but particularly on the left, did not dally in explaining what the trouble was.

These circles had been growing increasingly restless ever since Bevin's first speech as Foreign Secretary to the House of Commons in mid-August. For Bevin, far from repudiating continuity in foreign policy, had in effect repudiated a socialist policy as fantasy: he denied that ideology of any kind could serve as an adequate guide for the nation's affairs; refused categorically to alter the Coalition's policies either toward Spain or toward Greece; and added, for good measure, a forthright denunciation of the totalitarian regimes being set up in Eastern Europe under Soviet auspices.[6] (Significantly, even if by coincidence, on the same day Attlee demanded that Laski, the party chairman, refrain from issuing further pronouncements on what the government would or would not do in foreign policy.[7]) Bevin's address left much of the party dismayed, to gauge from the reaction it provoked. Only a few backbenchers dared to take issue with the Foreign Secretary on the floor of the Commons itself, but soon the "Letters to the Editor" columns of pro-Labour journals were inundated with messages from bothered Labour supporters protesting the government's alleged betrayal of socialist principles.[8] The protests, moreover, though strongest in the left-wing press (the *Tribune, New Statesman*, etc.), were by no means confined to that section of the party. When, a few weeks later at the London Conference, the Big Three failed even to keep their discord buried from public view, Bevin's unhappy critics knew what was wrong and who was to blame.*

The trouble was held to reside in the West's ingrained reluctance to meet legitimate Soviet demands, particularly the altogether unimpeachable Soviet desire for friendly nations on its borders. The Soviets—it was granted—might not be acting so unexceptionally in Eastern Europe as comfortable democrats in Britain would want, but then it was obviously wrong to suppose that the Soviets were therefore aggressive, imperialistic; this was impossible because the Soviet Union was a socialist state and so had no economic impulse toward expansion. Only a socialist critique could put this and everything else relating to East-West relations in proper perspective. Socialist diagnosis would disclose, for instance, that all current Soviet intransigence could be traced to Soviet fears of capitalist hostility—fears that were by no means groundless, given the sad history of East-West relations since 1918 and especially the recent brutal American refusal to share its nuclear secrets. If the two Western powers really desired peaceful cooperation, all that they had to do, therefore, was to cease acting in ways calculated only to confirm or heighten Soviet anxiety; at a minimum, they would have to come to terms with the irreversible Soviet presence in Eastern and Central Europe. The initiative in making a new departure fell by default, of course, to the Labour government, the United States, a bastion of capitalist reaction, being incapable on its own of appreciating the imperative of a more reasonable policy.

### THE GOVERNMENT'S SKEPTICISM

Bevin and apparently the rest of the Cabinet showed themselves to be of an entirely different mind.

It was the American government rather than the Labour government that decided to take the initiative in conciliating the Soviet Union. Largely because of American prodding, the Council of Foreign Ministers agreed to reassemble at Moscow in Decem-

---

* The left-wing press had no doubts whatever that Soviet demands raised at the conference must be legitimate. The argument unfolded in the next paragraph is a composite summary of the left's views as developed in the *New Statesman* and in the *Tribune* during late September and October, as well as in the statements of PLP backbenchers.

ber; largely owing to American concessions on peace treaty pro-cedures and on allied control in Japan, the Council when it did reconvene was able to break the existing deadlock and record some progress.[9] Ironically, the very government that the Labour left and its numerous supporters were denouncing as a capitalist-imperialist power, the ultimate source of East-West dissension, was outdoing the Labour government in searching for a basis on which to cooperate with the Soviet Union.[10]

But then the Labour government had good reason for not taking so detached a view as the Americans did: it believed the risk involved was too great. Britain, after all, was inextricably entangled in Continental affairs as a European power; not only did it have direct and immediate strategic interests in the area, but its security, its very fate as an independent nation, hinged in no small measure on how these interests would be defined and then defended. Hence the Labour government's intense reluctance to be optimistic, to make lighthearted concessions to Soviet de-mands. In its estimation, the cost might be prohibitive in terms of national security.

Did this mean that Bevin and his colleagues had abandoned hope of reaching a tolerable understanding with Moscow from the outset, scarcely before trying? This is hard to say with certainty, though the evidence cited above makes plausible an affirmative answer. And if we add mention of the Coalition's marked concern with Soviet expansion and the Labour ministers' avowed support for the Coalition's foreign policy, then our answer seems as clear-cut as it ever will be until the official documents become available. McNeill's assessment appears basically sound: "Whatever their differences over domestic matters, Bevin and Churchill saw nearly eye to eye with respect to British foreign policy."[11] McNeill, it should be added, arrives at this evaluation on the strength of Bevin's initial month in office. For these reasons, then, the argu-ment that Bevin did not decide that a break with the Soviets was irreparable until June 1947, the date of Marshall's offer of ex-tensive aid, is misleading unless the emphasis is on the term "irrep-arable," in which case it makes no difference for our purposes one way or another. For the issue is the Labour government's *initial* image of the terms that Moscow seemed to be demanding as the basis for any sort of understanding. Did it perceive the terms as acceptable or unacceptable? What price, in other words, did the Soviets seem bent on exacting, and was the price worth paying? To state the alternatives in such terms is to state them starkly, but doing so does not appear to misrepresent very seriously the way the Labour government itself probably defined them.* Nor does it seem a misrepresentation to say that the government *early* decided to reject the terms as intolerable.† In late November, for instance, Bevin told the Commons: "I cannot accept the view that all my policy and the policy of His Majesty's Government must be based entirely on the Big Three."[12] Since the Foreign Ministers' Council had not yet reconvened at Moscow to see whether the London deadlock could be broken, Bevin's statement of intent seemed to prejudge the outcome pretty sharply.

But then did the government believe that it had any other choice? Again, no matter what its predispositions toward the Soviets, the government probably did not and for a simple reason: Moscow, fully aware of American anxiousness to quit Europe, had made Britain the principal object of its belligerent diplomacy. All the initial East-West clashes were fought between Moscow and London, whether over Germany or about the Eastern Mediterranean, whether involving Iran or Indonesia, whether at the Foreign Ministers' conferences or at the first meetings of the United Nations. The first Western statesman publicly to indict the Soviets for their intransigence was Bevin, not Byrnes; the occasion was at the Security Council, where he exploded during an angry exchange with the Soviet representative: "The danger to the peace of the world has been the incessant propaganda from Moscow against the British Commonwealth and the incessant utilization of the Communist parties in every country of the world to attack the British people and the British Government, as if no friendship existed between us."[13]

No doubt there is a danger in reconstructing the Labour government's perceptions in such a categorical manner. No doubt the international situation presented itself with less clarity of outline, the initial development of the Cold War being not so much a tapestry as a hopelessly raveled and knotted mess of yarn. But if

---

* This point is elaborated in the following chapter.

† Which again contrasts with the American position, Roosevelt's or Truman's. See Feis, p. 599.

we have to pick out certain threads for the sake of exposition and follow them where they lead, the one that sticks out most clearly is that the Labour government, for all the uncertainties facing it, perceived a distinct Soviet threat from the very moment it took office. Moreover, it reacted instinctively to that perceived threat in the same way previous British governments under similar conditions had: it sought to prevent its adversary from attaining hegemony on the continent of Europe by means of a balance of power policy—that is, by constant adaptation and adjustment, based on power calculations and employing its own threats and counterthreats.* Thus, far from mediating between capitalist America and communist Russia, as Labour Party members had come to expect, the Labour government assumed the initial responsibility for checking the dynamic of Soviet expansion. It did so, moreover, almost entirely on its own. As Attlee later observed, "we were holding the line in far too many places and the Americans in far too few."[14]

## THE GOVERNMENT'S TWO-SIDED PREDICAMENT

### One Side of the Predicament

Thus the Labour government, fully sharing the Coalition's fears of Soviet hegemony, set out to correct the European power distribution prevailing at the end of the war. But it was obvious to Bevin and his colleagues that Britain alone could not successfully perform the task; the British economy was enfeebled, British power was badly overextended abroad, and the nation—as the 1947 *Economic Survey* commented gloomily—did not have "enough resources to do all that we want to do: We have barely enough resources to do all that we must do."[15] Only the United States possessed the necessary resources, the necessary power, to offset Soviet power and resources. An intimate Anglo-American alliance had evolved during the war, one so entangling as to be nearly indistinguishable from confederation in many respects, and the new Labour government had every reason to desire the continuation of such cooperation into peacetime: not least because, if it did, then American power could be harnessed for the creation

---

* Francis Williams, a close friend of Bevin at the time, interprets the motivation behind British policy along similar lines. *Ernest Bevin*, pp. 253–56.

of a new, less threatening power distribution in Europe. On all the evidence available, extensive Anglo-American collaboration was thus adopted as a policy objective of top priority by the Labour government from the very outset.*

And yet precisely herein lay one facet of its predicament. For the United States did not at all seem eager to play the international role in which the Labour government wanted to cast it.

American reluctance stretched back to the war years, when Washington had doggedly refused to couple American power to the Coalition government's various schemes for arresting the westward thrust of the Soviet Union. British soundings to this effect had first been made in early 1944, but they grew particularly insistent during the winter and spring of 1945 as Churchill, at wit's end, frantically implored the Americans to appreciate that "Soviet Russia had become a mortal danger to the free world."[16] The Americans proved unmovable. Roosevelt, in contrast to Churchill, remained "determinedly optimistic" that East-West harmony was not just possible but probable, provided that the two Western powers were willing to allay Soviet fears of their postwar intentions.[17] The divergence between these British and American viewpoints derived from conflicting orientations in foreign policy. Where Churchill thought in terms of spheres of influence, showing himself willing to strike a deal with the Russians but bent on shoving the line of demarcation as far east as possible, Roosevelt fixed his hope on winning Stalin over to universalist notions. As McNeill puts it: "Once he had proved to Stalin that the United States was really ready to be friendly and cooperative, he hoped (and he was willing to stake everything upon his hope) that the Russian leader would abandon the Communist world crusade and come to support of Roosevelt's plan for a liberal, democratic, and peaceful world order."[18] British observers have been severe in their judgments of this American policy, seeing it as irretrievably naïve and quixotic. Yet if the American approach was idealistic, it was so because of a conscious conviction that balance-of-power mechanisms were inherently defective, inherently incapable of produc-

---

* Francis Williams argues that "Bevin came fairly *soon after Potsdam* to the conclusion that in view of Russian policy the only hope for European security lay in American assistance." *Ernest Bevin,* p. 257 (italics added). See, too, p. 263; also Nicholas, pp. 33ff.

ing a stable, long-run equilibrium, inherently bound, in short, to disintegrate in another general war. Whether, in adhering to this conviction, the Americans were naïve is irrelevant for our purposes. But it is more than slightly ironic that Roosevelt, not the Labour ministers in the Coalition, thought of East-West cooperation in terms that could have been taken out of the pages of Labour's wartime propaganda.

In one regard British exasperation with the American position was well founded. This had to do with the anti-imperialist mentality prevailing in Washington during the war, a rooted state of mind that translated itself into lack of sympathy for Britain's likely postwar plight. Not only did Roosevelt and his staff regard the British and the Soviets as the major competitors in the postwar period and America as the arbiter, conciliator, and teacher who would lead the Europeans out of the wilderness of sordid power politics; in addition, they pressed the British to dismantle their Empire as a way of demonstrating to Stalin the West's faith in international organization and the new liberal order that would follow.[19] Thus the very last thing to which they were receptive were British complaints about Soviet intentions. Such complaints concealed sinister motives. They were designed to disorient American diplomacy; they aimed at transforming the United States into a reactionary mainstay of the decaying British Empire. Truman, who became President in April 1945, did not stray from the course plotted by his predecessor, either in his desire for Soviet cooperation or in his distrust of British imperialism.[20] As late as May 1945, his emissary, Joseph Davies, reported from London that the British were far more concerned with their power position in Europe than with preserving the peace.[21] Not even the fact that a Labour government took office shortly afterward, pledged to bestow freedom on the colonies, assuaged American suspicions much. On the contrary, growing Anglo-American discord over Palestine hardened the American impression that where British imperial policy was concerned, nothing fundamental had changed.

For all these reasons, then, Washington in mid-1945 was not just reluctant to help balance Soviet power; it was doubly reluctant to do so in conjunction with Britain. In fact, partly to convince the Soviets of its impartiality, the Truman administration proceeded to divest the closely knit Anglo-American wartime alliance

of its substance. In August Lend-Lease Aid was abruptly termin-
ated;[22] soon afterward Anglo-American economic pooling was
halted; and the Combined Chiefs of Staff, while never officially
dismantled, limped on as only a faint replica of its former self.
By the end of 1946, there still prevailed a spirit of amity between
the two nations, but the alliance itself existed in name only.[23]

The Labour government peered at these developments without
any illusions as to their meaning. Desperate as the government
was to secure American assistance, it understood that to prod
Washington too brusquely, to press its strategic aims too assertively, was to risk a fatal rebuff.[24] Several participants in American policy-making circles have themselves subsequently attested
to the period of uncertainty and mind-changing in Washington
at the time.[25] Thus, however painful the decision was, Bevin and
his colleagues concluded that they had no choice but to be patient
and bide their time, all the while staging a holding operation
against Soviet pressure until events themselves persuaded the
Americans of the wisdom of sharing the British burdens.*

### The Other Side of the Predicament

The Labour government, then, in striving to bring American
power back to Europe, had to contend with Washington's deep-
dyed inhibitions about "ganging up" against the Soviets. But
American inhibitions were only one obstacle to the successful execution of the government's policy. Another stumbling block was
created by the anxious objections to that policy being raised by
increasingly disgruntled Labour partisans.

The counterblasts directed at Bevin's policy by his nominal
supporters, both in and out of Parliament, completed the government's predicament. On the one hand, the government anxiously awaited the moment when the United States would decide
to align itself wholeheartedly with the British. For the Americans

* "It was to this purpose [bringing America back to Europe] that he [Bevin]
bent his major energies, knowing that time was short and his own resources
running out, but gambling, as he had often had to do in the past, on the other
side's making mistakes, banking on his conviction that Communist Russia,
contemptuous both of British weakness and of American quiescence, would
overplay her hand and disclose her purpose in time to bring American public
opinion to the point of action before too late. His job as he conceived it was to
hold on with grim patience for the right moment and the right issue." Williams, *Ernest Bevin*, p. 263.

to reach this critical decision, they would first have to grow weary of pursuing the will-o-the-wisp of Soviet cooperation, and this required precious time. Presumably, the Labour government had the power to hasten the arrival of the desired juncture; in a bold move, it might have sought to bring East-West tension to a head and force the Americans to act willy-nilly. On the other hand, a move of this sort was precisely what was ruled out by the government's pressing need to appease its Labour critics at home. The fierce attacks unleashed against it for refusing to repudiate Churchill's Fulton Address were sufficient warning, had it any lingering doubts on this score. In brief, the critics within the Labour Party represented a looming threat that could not be lightly ignored.

As already noted, the critics were made uneasy by East-West developments during the autumn of 1945. Their immediate reaction was to maintain a steady flow of barbed commentary about the government's alleged betrayal of socialist policy. At the same time certain socialist mainstays in the party appreciated the need for a positive approach as well. They recognized that it was not enough to continue hoping for socialist cooperation in present circumstances; a new, if temporary, strategy had to be found, one geared to the realities of the moment, even while socialist harmony between Russia and the West still remained the ultimate objective. As early as September, with the revelation of Big Three deadlock at the London Conference, certain left-wing journals and spokesmen in Parliament broached the theme of British neutrality as the lesser of evils now confronting the nation. When subsequently refined and elaborated, the theme matured into the policy of the third force, and we shall have occasion later to examine the policy in detail. What is worth stressing here are two of the principal assumptions behind its logic, on the reasonableness of which hinged the wisdom of neutrality itself: pro-Soviet sentiment and anti-American feeling. An examination of both assumptions will conveniently bring out the marked contrast in reasoning between the government and its critics regarding the international situation.

On the one hand, the critics had to show that a neutralist third force policy was a realistic policy by arguing that there was no need to balance Soviet power as the government obviously reasoned. This was because, in their view, there was no Soviet threat —a claim that required them to portray current Soviet policy in the most charitable light possible. We saw above (p. 106) one of the forms that such a portrayal could take, and there were several other variations, all of which added up to the picture of an essentially peaceful Soviet Union, whose surface belligerence did not lack good cause and was in any case transient and easily surmountable (surmounting it was, indeed, to be the principal task of the proposed third force). Arguing so and at the same time tapping all of Labour's traditional emotional attachment to Soviet symbols, the critics thus adopted a position with respect to Soviet intentions that conflicted sharply with the government's evaluation. On the other hand, the critics had equally to demonstrate the wisdom of neutrality with respect to the United States too. This necessitated that they depict American policy in the least charitable light possible so as to undercut any incentive for alliance. Bevin and the rest of the Cabinet had to be shown that the Americans were basically a provocative power, indeed the principal source of current East-West discord, and hence a dangerous nation to contemplate as an ally. Not only that; the government had additionally to be brought to realize that the United States, the remaining capitalist fortress, was by nature implacably hostile to British socialism and that for this reason an Anglo-American alliance would be not simply hazardous but possibly suicidal.

Armed with this interpretation of Soviet and American intentions, the Labour critics went on to expound how their distinctive frame of analysis could then put the whole of recent East-West relations in proper perspective. In a flash, the bewildering confusion and apparently haphazard progression of events was stripped away and shown to be following a definite pattern.

The critics began with American policy, relating the shreds of evidence pertaining to it so as to form a coherent theory of alleged American malevolence. The termination of Lend-Lease Aid, for instance, was widely depicted in Labour circles as a ruse by Washington designed to quash British socialism at the onset, in the same sort of way that Wall Street had engineered the financial crisis of August 1931. Long before the war's end, Aneurin Bevan had warned that "the United States will inherit Nazi Germany's position as bulwark and protector of world capitalism in the West";[26] after the war and as a result of the aid's termination, it became a standard left-wing belief that there was some sort of American plot against the government's socialist programs, di-

rected "by the most merciless champions of competitive capitalism left on the face of this planet."[27] The conditions stipulated by
the Anglo-American Loan Agreement of December also elicited
protests, such as Jennie Lee's objection that the sole beneficiary
would be "the hard-faced businessman's government" in Washington, now provided with a convenient channel for the outflow of
surplus capital.* If, therefore, the critics in the Labour Party were
able to detect American designs on British socialism, did it not
seem reasonable to suppose that the leaders of Soviet socialism were
doubly justified in fearing the United States? Who, after all, could
blame the Kremlin for acting rather uncooperatively, given the
"arrogant mood" of the "most merciless champions of competitive
capitalism" in control of a nation armed with nuclear weapons?
Posing rhetorical questions in terms of this sort overstates no doubt
the critics' own arguments, but the result is not a caricature; on
the contrary, the result conveys pretty faithfully the spirit of their
reasoning as unfolded in the pages of the *Tribune, New Statesman,* and even more moderate publications, and as expounded in
the statements of several backbenchers and party spokesmen outside of Parliament at the time. The government's critics were not
even shaken in their beliefs if someone pointed out that it was
Britain, not the United States, which was being repeatedly hammered at by Soviet policy. It was always open to them to assert
that the Soviets had simply not had enough time to appreciate the
fact that Britain had formally been a socialist nation since July
1945. As soon as this appreciation had worked its way into Soviet
consciousness, however, the Kremlin would learn to distinguish
between predatory American capitalism and a Britain full of
goodwill—always provided, of course, that by then Bevin had
realized the folly of his ways and publicly repudiated continuity
in foreign policy.†

Finally, in late autumn 1945, an event occurred that convinced

---

* 417 *H.C.Deb.* 670 (12 December 1945). The government itself was none
too happy with the terms of the agreement, but as Bevin observed, Britain
was "not in a position to dictate terms." 417 *H.C.Deb.* 728 (13 December 1945).
See too Dalton, *Memoirs, 1945–1960,* pp. 68ff.

† E.g., "We are convinced that Russia's chief fear is of American dollar imperialism. In attacking us diplomatically, she considers she is 'going for' the
weaker of the two Anglo-Saxon imperialisms. Unfortunately Bevin's words and
deeds give her some justification for the false assumptions that we are in the
American camp." Baird, *Left.*

the critics beyond a doubt of the complete soundness of their position: Washington's announcement that, pending agreement on an international atomic control system, the United States would retain exclusive monopoly of its nuclear secrets. Here, in a flash, was incontrovertible proof in the critics' estimation of East-West disharmony—the ultimate reason for the break-up of Big Three unity, the ultimate justification of Soviet fears, indeed the ultimate key to current Soviet behavior. To the socialist mainstays in the Labour Party, the American refusal to share its nuclear know-how was decidedly the preeminent cause of international tension. Certain left-wing journals even claimed to be able to trace the deadlock at the recent London Conference back to this single factor.[28] Anxiety over American intentions rose to such heights in Labour circles that by the time Attlee returned from Washington, in November, with an Anglo-American-Canadian declaration in his pocket advocating international control of atomic energy, he was hailed as the "savior of civilisation."[29]

### RENEWED CONFLICT

Thus the government's critics in the Labour Party, progressively disenchanted with its initial thrusts in foreign policy, had equipped themselves by the end of 1945 with an elaborate theory with which to criticize that policy and to analyze the current state of world politics. In all major respects, this theory accorded with the four fundamental principles of socialist foreign policy.

The theory held a particular social system, American capitalism, guilty for the international tension that prevailed—just as, conversely, it maintained that a socialist state, the Soviet Union, was inherently peaceful no matter what its actions appeared to be on the surface. The theory raised strenuous objections to the government's declared readiness to defend important British interests in the Mediterranean and on the Continent: thus *Forward*, a journal for which Harold Laski frequently wrote, advocated that Britain withdraw unilaterally from the whole eastern half of the Mediterranean as a symbolic gesture of its socialist goodwill.[30] The theory, in the form of third-force neutralism, reaffirmed the principle of working-class solidarity by urging the Labour government to create and to lead a European socialist bloc. Finally, the theory adhered faithfully to the principle of anti-militarism by denouncing the government's policy as naked power politics; according to a report in the *Manchester Guardian*, many Labour MP's thought that the policy was in fact indistinguishable from what Churchill advocated in his Fulton Address.[31]

Hence, setting one thing against another, the following conclusion emerges. Within a matter of months following the general election of 1945, there were actually two foreign policies vying with one another for the allegiance of the Labour Party. One was the policy being conducted by the Labour government; the other, a full-fledged version of socialist foreign policy, was championed by its critics in the mass party. These two policies were fundamentally opposed. They differed in their assessment of the international situation, conflicted in their objectives, and contrasted in the means they favored to realize these objectives. Those who espoused the cause of socialism saw the government's policy as nothing short of a betrayal of Labour's socialist principles, and by January 1946 the process of suspicion and distrust had acquired a cumulative momentum. A great deal of resentment was summed up in the exasperated complaint of one Labour MP who protested: "It is felt that when our policy meets with such hearty approval from the Opposition, there must be something wrong with it. It is felt that if the Tories applaud, it cannot be a Socialist Foreign Policy."[32]

# Chapter five

# The Reversal of Socialist Foreign Policy

*It is to the enduring credit of the Labour Government and of the Foreign Secretary, Ernest Bevin, in particular, that, by-passing party doctrines, they framed policies which were suited to strategic realities and to the national interest, as traditionally understood.*

—LORD WILLIAM STRANG

Repeatedly, from late 1945 on, the government's critics within the Labour Party denounced its foreign policy as a deliberate corruption of the party's socialist vision. Again and again Bevin and the Cabinet were charged with forsaking Labour's socialist principles, with pursuing an uncompromising traditional rather than a bold socialist course. In retrospect, this accusation—if pruned of its polemical bias—appears correct. The Labour government's conduct of British foreign affairs represented, as it turned out, an unsparing reversal of socialist policy—a reversal that, as Lord Strang notes, embodied traditional inspirations. As far as the critics were concerned, this reversal amounted to betrayal. As far as the government was concerned, it amounted to the realistic recognition that the party's socialist vision was utopian and therefore a poor and dangerous guide.

By use of a few simple concepts from decision-making theory, this reversal can be reconstructed in terms that accord with our general emphasis on political culture. We assume, accordingly, that to explain the government's foreign policy is to explain the way its principal policy makers approached and defined the international situation confronting Britain in 1945—in particular, how they *perceived* the situation, what *choices* of action they thought were available, and what they *expected* to gain for Britain by making the choices they did. Approaching the subject in this manner has several virtues. Most of all it enables us, by weaving a vast array of material into a new and revealing pattern, to underscore and elaborate the contrast between the two clashing ideologies competing for Labour's allegiances. It is only against some such background that the course of intra-party conflict during the postwar period—its eruption in 1945, decline between 1948 and 1950, eruption again in 1951, and stubborn if mercurial persistence into the 1960's—can be properly understood.

The analysis focuses mainly on the European context. As the major arena of conflict and the locus of the perceived Soviet threat, Europe was where the contrast between socialist and traditional principles was most sharply drawn and where, therefore, the government and its critics clashed the loudest. It is true that the Cabinet, fearing overcommitment, considered abandoning key positions on the Continent in the absence of American help;[1] true, too, that no definitive decision to fight on the Continent, in the event of war, was actually made until May 1948.[2] But the delay in arriving at the decision did not mean that the government slighted the European theater; it meant only that until May 1948 it was still wedded to an outmoded peripheral strategy that needed updating. As Attlee later observed, Europe always came first on the list of the government's strategic priorities.[3]

### PERCEPTION OF THE INTERNATIONAL SETTING

In terms of our proposed frame of analysis, the overriding fact concerning the international setting in 1945 was the shift of the European power distribution in favor of the Soviet Union. The new distribtuion was objectively signalized by the presence of millions of Soviet troops in Central and Eastern Europe, if by nothing else. The Russian Empire, which had been expanding for hundreds of years, was now four-fifths of the way from its prewar borders to the North Sea.

As far as national security mattered, policy makers in Britain could have perceived this setting in one of two ways.

On the one hand, they could have decided that the Soviet presence posed no danger to Britain because the Soviet Union had been a wartime ally and would likely remain so in peacetime. The majority of British people, accustomed as they were to the rhetoric of the Grand Alliance, had adopted roughly this view of things by mid-1945.[4] So, too, had the average Labour partisan, except that he went further and expected that Labour's electoral victory had enhanced the chances of future Anglo-Soviet cooperation to the point of near-certainty. From his standpoint, all that the Labour government had to do in order to guarantee the convergence of British and Soviet interests was to break totally with traditional foreign policy, redefine British security and interests in socialist terms, and then await generous professions of Soviet goodwill.

On the other hand, the policy makers could have decided that the existing power distribution in Europe did endanger British security—this for at least one of two reasons. In the first place, they might have regarded the Soviet Union as a basically aggressive and dangerous nation by nature, owing to its Communist political system. Or, second, they might have concluded that the real danger to British security was represented by the developing power balance itself, in which case it would not have greatly mattered what the political hue of the Soviet Union happened to be. What counted was that a power vacuum had emerged, with all the risks that had attended such situations in Britain's long diplomatic history. These two reasons were not exclusive, of course, and in fact they seemed to merge in Churchill's mind in accounting for the danger that he perceived on the Continent.

The same can be said of the Labour government, which continued the Coalition's policy without the slightest change. Bevin, for instance, sometimes located the major threat in the Communist leadership of the Soviet Union, considering it rigid and doctrinaire and limitlessly immoral. Thus Attlee has related that Bevin not only "hated" Molotov as the murderer of innocent peasants, but "could never get over this hatred."[5] The intensity of his emotion was no doubt very largely responsible for his angry outbursts—his repeated denunciation of Soviet totalitarianism, his comparison of Molotov with Hitler, his vehement exchanges with the Soviets at the first sessions of the Security Council. Firm anti-Communists like Senator Vandenberg, exasperated by Byrnes's high-minded efforts at mediation in the early meetings of the Council of Foreign Ministers, privately urged the American government to emulate Bevin's combative diplomacy.[6] Even Churchill had no complaints in this connection, confiding to James Forrestal, shortly after his Fulton Address, that Bevin as a Labour Foreign Secretary "was able to talk more firmly and clearly to Russia than he could have."[7] At other times, however, Bevin appears to have attached more significance to the power imbalance itself. As he told Smuts on one occasion, his fear was not that Stalin deliberately wanted war but that "the Soviet policy of expansion had engendered its own dynamic which may prove too strong for him [Stalin] in spite of all his shrewdness and power. I don't think he's planning for war, but he may be unable to control the forces he's started. We've always got to be prepared for that."[8] So stated, Bevin's analysis was identical to the standard rationale of a traditional balance-of-power policy: Nation X may not want war, but if its drive for greater power and influence goes unchecked, a cumulative process may result in which the security of Britain becomes jeopardized. That the Labour government's policy reflected both considerations, the anti-Communist thesis and the balance-of-power rationale, was graphically attested by its unremitting continuation of the Coalition's course in Greece. The imposition of a British client-government there averted a Communist take-over. At the same time it prevented the Soviet Union from absorbing all of the Balkans and obtaining access to the Mediterranean.

Bevin's statement to Smuts that he discounted a Soviet intent to war deserves brief elaboration, for some writers have drawn unwarranted inferences on this score and thereby misconstrued Labour's policy at the time. Citing, above all, certain observations of General Montgomery to the effect that Russia was too weak to want a deliberate war for at least a decade,[9] they have doubted that the Labour government saw a real Soviet threat at any moment before late 1947.[10] But to argue so is to miss what British policy makers, Montgomery decidedly included, actually perceived. The problem as they saw it was not so much imminent war as a cumulative Soviet diplomatic offensive aimed at wearing down Western resistance and eating away Western positions one at a time until Soviet hegemony resulted. As Montgomery himself noted at the time, "I reckoned that Russia was quite unfit to take part in a world war against a strong combination of allied nations." A strong combination of allied nations was the important proviso. It was precisely to create such a combination that the Labour government worked from the outset to keep American power available on the European continent as a counterpoise to Soviet power. There were no illusions whatever in Whitehall as to what would happen in the absence of an effective counterpoise. In Montgomery's words, Russia "would go as far as she could to get what she wanted, and if opposed only by weakness would be prepared to go a long way—short of actual war."[11]

### CHOICE OF POLICY WITH RESPECT TO SETTING

Even if the Soviet presence in Central Europe had been unanimously perceived as dangerous from the British perspective, agreement among Labour partisans on how that danger should be dealt with would not have automatically followed. Roughly two courses of action in response to the danger were conceivable: one that accorded with socialist foreign policy, the other with traditional foreign policy.

The socialist course of action was in fact proposed by many of the government's critics starting in mid-1946, after they (grudgingly) had recognized that Anglo-Soviet cooperation on the basis of "left understands left" was impossible for the time being. A fundamental tenet of socialist foreign policy is the belief that conflicts are essentially illusory, the outcome of miscalculation and shortsightedness: to resolve their dispute, the disputants have only to discover the common good, which is at the same time their highest good; consequently, it would presumably follow that if at least one of the disputants begins to manifest goodwill, if he starts to make *unilateral* concessions, the other is bound sooner or later to apprehend the common good and so commence to reciprocate. Beginning in mid-1946, left-wing critics of the government started to make policy recommendations along precisely this line, advocating unilateral Western concessions as the most effective means of arresting the unremitting deterioration in East-West relations. Thus "Keep Left" proposed in early 1947 a speedy British withdrawal from the whole disputed area of the eastern Mediterranean, including consent to the internationalization of the Dardanelles and the Suez Canal. With crisp socialist logic, "Keep Left" argued that such actions would have the merit of conclusively proving "the sincerity of our Socialist intentions" to the Soviet Union.[12]

The second course of action was to concentrate on correcting the European power imbalance. Labour's chief ministers, habituated by their Coalition experience to traditional modes of thought, appear to have opted for this course as though by reflex. The general direction of policy once affixed, specific objectives followed with bold, almost instinctive traditionalist logic:

*One was the decision to stage a holding operation against Soviet expansion at the periphery.* In addition to the initial jockeying and maneuvering discussed earlier, this objective came vividly to light during the Anglo-Soviet clash over Iran. Meeting with Soviet efforts to secure a foothold there, the Labour government did not hesitate to take up the historical British task of policing Russia's southern borders. At the 1945 London and Moscow Foreign Ministers' Conferences, at the United Nations Security Council in early 1946, and through official channels, Bevin and his colleagues applied steady, forceful diplomatic pressure to compel a Soviet withdrawal under terms of a 1942 treaty of joint occupation.[13] During one February Security Council debate, Bevin weighed in so vehemently against the Soviets that he was upbraided by the Secretary General for overboldness.[14] In the next month, the Labour government evidenced its determination in an equally revealing manner. More than 100 Labour backbenchers moved a strong motion of censure against Churchill's Fulton Address, the most detailed public exposition to date of the Russian threat. Despite the earsplitting outcry, the government refused to renounce the statement; the furthest it went toward allaying the critics' apprehensions was to have Bevin disclaim any "prior consultation"—and even then the disclaimer was tainted with equivocation.* East-West problems in Germany, particularly the Soviet demand for reparations on the order of 10 billion dollars, were approached no less resolutely. Government spokesmen argued that if this were to be the price of Soviet cooperation there, the cost was prohibitive, since payment of such an amount would be tantamount to having British taxpayers subsidize Soviet plunder. Concluding, ultimately, that reasonable agreement with the Kremlin

---

* Bevin's statement is quoted in *The Times*, 18 March 1946. Was there prior knowledge of Churchill's speech despite Bevin's disclaimer? This will not be known for certain until the official documents are available, but certain remarks in Williams, *A Prime Minister Remembers*, pp. 162–63, and by Churchill in Millis, *The Forrestal Diaries*, p. 144, suggest that there was not, at any rate, much of a gap between the government and the Leader of the Opposition.

was a will-o-the-wisp, the government preferred to risk a permanent East-West division of Germany by merging its zone of occupation with the American.[15]

During all of this, the government maintained the stubborn British holding operation against Communist-led insurgents in Greece. Neither the soaring unpopularity of its Greek policy in Labour circles nor Soviet propaganda onslaughts against it—indeed, initially not even the crushing economic burdens of the British commitment[16]—deterred Bevin and his colleagues from doggedly hanging on. Even when the staggering economic crisis of early 1947 necessitated withdrawal on pain of collapse at home, the government leaped at the subsequent American offer to assume British responsibilities in the area and agreed, despite the cost, to maintain British troops there until adequate American replacements could be scraped together.[17]

Labour's initial containment policy was capped in July 1947 by Bevin's decision to embrace Marshall Aid, irrespective of threatened Soviet reprisals. To an effort by Molotov to cow him into retreat with a verbal broadside, Bevin retorted: "My country has faced grave consequences and threats before, and it is not the sort of prospect which will deter us from doing what we consider to be our duty."[18] Enraged, the Soviets implemented their threatened retaliation; they formed the Cominform, tightened their grip on Eastern and Central Europe, and incited the West European Communist Parties to efforts at sabotaging the Marshall Aid program. Nevertheless the Labour government did not waver. Far from being intimidated, it proceeded on the one hand to spearhead the creation of the Organization for European Economic Cooperation, thus meeting the preconditions of American assistance, and on the other hand to counter the heightened Soviet challenge by organizing, a few months later, the regional defense of West Europe. At the height of tension in the cold war, namely the Soviet blockade of Berlin, the Labour government was found by Moscow to be as resolutely opposed as ever to unilateral concessions. To break the Soviet hold on the besieged city, Aneurin Bevan even proposed dispatching an armed land convoy.[19]

*A second objective was to organize an alliance system with Atlantic nations.* This goal followed automatically from the recognition that Britain could not by itself create a new European balance and that eventually American power had to be available for the task. The Labour government, aware of the initial American detachment from the European balance, concentrated on close Anglo-French ties as the first element in an encompassing alliance system.[20] But always it was the United States that remained the biggest prize.[21] Ambassador Harriman reported to Forrestal in July 1946 on the "passionate desire for military and diplomatic cooperation with the US."[22] A couple of months later, Montgomery, on a visit to Washington, pressed hard for extensive military collaboration.[23] Not until January 1948, however, did the Labour government feel bold enough to proclaim publicly that the "time is ripe for a consolidation of Western Europe."[24] The result was the Brussels Treaty, a defensive pact between Britain, France, and the Benelux countries, which—as Bevin's correspondence with Washington at the time indicates—was valued in London mainly as another device by which to lure American power back to Europe.* The treaty had scarcely been signed before the Labour government petitioned the Truman Administration for negotiation on an Atlantic-wide alliance.[25] As if to underscore the urgency of this objective, the government assented to certain far-reaching bilateral arrangements with the United States even while these negotiations were just getting under way. Most notable among them was an agreement relating to the stationing of American bombers on British soil, permission for which was given so promptly, and without any reservations, that American officials were set to wondering if London appreciated fully the radical implications of its decision.[26] Soon afterward Cripps and Attlee separately told Forrestal that, in the event of war, the United States should regard the British bases as the principal launching pad for a nuclear strike against the Soviet Union.[27]

The North Atlantic Pact was signed on 4 April 1949. In defending the treaty in the Commons, certain Labour spokesmen made

* Truman, *Memoirs*, II, p. 257. In his discourse, Bevin remarked at one point that the Labour government had abandoned the "traditional" British policy of maintaining a balance of power in Europe. Not only did the Brussels Treaty show that the remark was probably a sop for the left, but, according to Truman, Bevin was thinking in such traditional terms at the time that he even preferred to restrict Britain to bilateral rather than regional defensive agreements. Evidently it was Spaak of Belgium who first suggested a regional pact.

much of the claim that it aimed at establishing, not a traditional alliance, but rather a new, a bold, indeed almost a socialist-like coalition—in a word, a collective security arrangement which fully accorded with Article 51 of the UN Charter on regional pacts.[28] This claim, however sincerely made, was misleading. For although Article 51 provides for regional pacts, it refers explicitly, not to collective security, but instead to collective self-defense (in brief, collective defense), which it deems an inherent right of all nations. Collective defense is not the same as collective security, though confusion between them is common. Collective defense is an established part of traditional foreign policy, collective security a clean break with it; and those who identify the two often do so for reasons of propaganda, of making more palatable a jockeying maneuver in power politics.[29] In the case of those Labour spokesmen who confused the two policies, their presentation seemed intended, consciously or otherwise, to conceal the pronounced degree to which the North Atlantic Pact flew in the face of socialist principles. Yet the simple fact remains that the Atlantic Alliance represented a form of collective defense, a traditional alignment of nations which, fearing for their security, agreed to band together for mutual protection.

*A third objective was to back British diplomacy with as much military power as other pressing claims permitted.* A necessary feature of any balance-of-power policy is the practice of armed diplomacy, the intimate linking of military power to foreign policy, and in this sense the policy is what socialist critics contended it was: militaristic by nature. For Britain in 1945, the decision to offset Soviet power thus dictated the need to maintain large forces in being, and the need was made all the more urgent by the rapid American withdrawal. Left virtually alone, the Labour government had to draw on its own severely constricted resources for meeting the defense priorities that it drew up. It managed, despite the problems of economic reconstruction and vast welfare programs, to devote a greater proportion of GNP to defense than any other non-Communist nation in the pre-Korean period. In 1947 British defense expenditures amounted to 9.5 per cent of GNP, and American expenditures to 6.5 per cent; in 1950 they amounted to 7.7 per cent, American to 5.9 percent, and French to 5.0 per cent. Where defense manpower was concerned, it was the same story: in 1948 Britain had double the percentage of men under arms as the United States, and in 1950 still more than 50 per cent as much.[30] It is true that much of the British defense effort was directed at areas outside the European context. But equally true, as a recent study reaffirms, most of these British forces were used for "cold war conflicts."[31] Past all doubt, the Labour government —for all its concern with the economy and the welfare state— placed an extremely high value on military capabilities when ordering its budgetary priorities.

The government displayed no less vigor in tackling the shifting problems of defense organization and weapons production. Its record here was impressive, and by the time it left office in 1951, it had thoroughly reorganized the whole defense establishment, creating a new Ministry of Defence in 1946; had intensified research and development in weaponry of all sorts, most notably in connection with a large-scale nuclear program and a V-bomber force; had implemented the first peacetime conscription bill in British history; and had accepted the principle of West German rearmament.[32] In none of this was there the slightest trace, the minutest indication, of socialist hostility to militarism. On the contrary, if any one consideration served as a guide to the government's actions, it was proclaimed in a striking passage of "Cards on the Table," the party leadership's official rejoinder to "Keep Left": "A nation which puts domestic comfort before its own security and independence is condemned to a foreign policy of appeasement leading inevitably to capitulation or to war under unfavorable circumstances."[33]

### EXPECTATIONS IN TERMS OF SETTING

It remains for us to determine what the policy makers expected to gain for Britain by means of their policy choices. By the nature of things, their expectations have to be a matter of inference, though there is enough evidence at hand to be reasonably confident of what we are doing.

Was there a clear sense of purpose running through all of the Labour government's actions? The question may seem odd, particularly to those for whom international relations is mainly a matter of reflex, response, unintended consequence. "In my opinion, statesmen are too absorbed by events to follow a preconceived plan. They take one step, and the next follows from it."* In one sense, this is no doubt true—but in the sense of being platitudinous. Obviously, the effects of foreign policy are hard to predict or difficult to control, for the forces involved are subject to the manipulation of two or more nations. But suppose we alter Taylor's wording slightly; suppose, in place of "preconceived plan," we substitute the word "purpose"—that is, an image, however inchoate, in the minds of policy makers of a desired state of affairs that they would like to try to bring about by exercising influence in the international system. Does it still follow that foreign policy is only a question of instinctive reaction, with no inner sense of direction involved? Policy makers do not, after all, act at random. They normally have some goal in mind of how their behavior will help to preserve or modify a given situation. These goals need not be highly concrete, nor need they fit into an overall plan; they may be little more than tentative, ambiguous notions. But there is almost always an element of purposefulness that can be detected. Even "muddling through" involves a hope of getting through to some desired position.

In the case of the Labour government, the goals that its policy makers appear to have had in mind can best be portrayed as aiming at adjustment—continuous adaptation to the new circumstances of the postwar period. Now adjustment is an ambiguous term. In one sense it can come close to Taylor's view that all policy is responsive rather than goal-oriented, a question chiefly of passive, defensive reaction to outside pressures. At the extreme, a reactive policy of this sort deteriorates into strident defensiveness, a sullen and grudging submission to harsh facts of power that are perceived as brutal and inescapable constraints. But there is another kind of adjustment. The need to adapt to new circumstances can be tackled positively, dynamically, with resolute determination to extract the maximum advantage out of situations no matter how intolerable they may at first appear. As Stanley Hoffmann has observed, adjustment of this latter sort "implies far more than submission to irrefutable facts. The very task of statesmanship consists of selecting the most favorable interpretation of the facts, whenever the lessons they carry are ambiguous; of choosing the

---

* Taylor, *The Origins of the Second World War*, p. 69.

most subtle and dignified form of submission, when the lesson is beyond debate; and most importantly, of trying to change the facts whenever they are intolerable but it is in the nation's power to transform them."[34] Though Hoffmann has in mind French statesmanship, the substance of his remarks can be properly applied to the quality of the Labour government's foreign policy.

This policy, to be sure, was not free of shortcomings. Yet for all the wavering and miscalculation that one can find in the behavior of the Labour government, it did rethink Britain's international patterns, did draw several correct lessons from the power distribution prevailing after 1945, did seek to alter unpleasant facts whenever it could to the nation's advantage, all the while maintaining a large British influence on the world scene. Its active policy as a counterpoise to Soviet expansion was a notable case in point, as was its determination, despite criticism and economic pressure at home, to back that policy with the largest defense expenditures in the Western world. Looking beyond immediate problems, it endowed the nation with an atomic energy program and an advanced nuclear delivery system, the V-bomber force. Breaking with history, it introduced peacetime conscription, and its decision to commit the nation militarily in advance on the Continent was no less of a courageous break. Not least, it began the long process of colonial withdrawal and did it for the most part in an orderly way that left few residues of irreconcilable embitterment among the native elites. Taken together, these diverse actions enabled Great Britain to pass through an uncertain and threatening period with considerable diplomatic achievement to its credit. Muddle, indecision, mind-changing, perhaps even overreaching there no doubt were—but not timidity, still less sullen submission to a fate perceived to be harsh and implacable. Compared with the British record during the 1930's or after Suez, the nation's foreign policy between 1945 and 1951 radiated confidence and firmness of purpose.

Adjustment, it goes without saying, is a traditionalist strategy, socialist foreign policy scorning environmental constraints and the inescapable limits that they impose on a nation's margin of choice. For adjustment to work successfully, it was necessary:

1) *That the reality of Britain's position be faced up to.* The overarching reality in 1945 was Britain's greatly reduced status

on the scale of world power, a reduction that severely limited the opportunities open to the nation. That Bevin was keenly aware of the strict limits to initiative in policy, adapting his calculations accordingly, was reflected above all in his aversion to new and bold departures. Even before Labour took office, he had admonished the party not to let their enthusiasm blind them to certain hard facts. Labour would "have to form a government, which is at the centre of such a great Empire and Commonwealth of Nations, which touches all parts of the world, and which will have to deal, through the diplomatic, commercial and labour machinery, with every race and with every difficulty, and every one of them has a different outlook upon life."[35] Bevin ended this particular speech with an explicit plea that might be regarded as the leitmotiv of his subsequent policy declarations: "I do beg Labour not to bury its head in the sand." To mounting criticism in 1947 that Britain was sluggish in dealing with European economic recovery, he replied: "What did I have to organize it with? What could I offer? I had neither coal, goods, nor credit, I was not in the same position as my predecessors at the end of the Napoleonic Wars, who devised the policy, for nearly 20 years, of spending our surplus exports to rehabilitate the world. It was a case of our exports then. I did not have them. Therefore, I cannot be accused now of not taking a line to help Western Europe. I have nothing with which to do it. I have not had one ton of spare coal to ship to Western Europe to help in the rehabilitation. I have had nothing with which to negotiate."[36]

2) *That hopes for radical departures in international politics not be inordinately aroused.* Otherwise, there would be the danger of a quick plunge into disenchantment and pessimism lest what was hoped for did not materialize—something that the British people, with years of painful recovery from the war ahead, could ill afford to risk. Hopes for harmonious postwar Anglo-Soviet cooperation represented an obvious danger of this sort, as the Cabinet clearly recognized. Another danger was potentially connected with the United Nations. For those Labour partisans who saw the world in 1945 on the verge of an era of permanent peace, the new international organization loomed as the embodiment of socialist foreign policy's principle of internationalism—the new focus of international politics, a universal policeman and

judge, in brief, a would-be world government. How rapidly such optimism could turn into sour disillusionment was exhibited in the *New Statesman* scarcely two months after Labour had taken office. Commenting on the deadlock at the London Foreign Ministers' Conference, the journal singled out Bevin as an especially guilty party because of his failure to date to repudiate traditional foreign policy; it demanded that he either disavow any future interest in maneuvering for positions of power, or else—"a poor alternative—let us end this *United Nations'* sham, accept the splitting of the world into spheres, and agree to live unaggressively, though disunited inside our own back-yards."[37]

This was precisely the kind of either/or formulation that the Labour government apparently wanted to avoid. As its cautious policy makers saw things, the reduction of alternatives to stark polar choices was dangerous and reflected a doctrinaire predisposition. In the case of the UN, they therefore adopted a policy that, while shying away from all notions of supranationalism, let alone world government, assigned the body a useful if secondary role in maintaining international order. As Attlee told the Commons, Britain wanted to make the UN a place "where the policies of the states, and especially the greater states, could be discussed and reconsidered."[38] From this standpoint, the UN was thus seen as a forum, a convenient complement to the normal processes of diplomacy. There was nothing socialist in this view. In fact it was almost indistinguishable from the Tory view of the League of Nations during the interwar period.

3) *That unnecessary risks be shunned, however noisily Labour partisans clamored for taking them.* The most illuminating episode involved Francoist Spain. Labour propaganda during the war and then almost incessantly afterward agitated for the ouster of Franco from power. Presumably, a British move in that direction would have represented a concrete application of socialist foreign policy; and an anti-Franco movement became a kind of mass passion in party circles, the one subject in foreign affairs on which Left and Right, intellectuals and uneducated trade unionists, rank-and-filers and backbenchers, were able to find themselves in enthusiastic agreement. They all demanded sanctions against Spain, urged United Nations intervention, called for rupture of diplomatic relations, and even, in some cases, pleaded for an

armed socialist crusade.[39] But the clamor left the government undaunted. Aware that British diplomacy had more important matters to deal with, it was not ready to spend precious resources on an anti-Franco adventure even if it had desired to topple Franco from power. And probably, in true traditionalist fashion, it did not desire to do so because of the drawbacks that this might produce in the power struggle with the Soviets. For instance, the Chiefs of Staff in 1948 seriously entertained a "semi-Continental strategy" whereby an attack by the Soviet Union would result in a British fallback to Spain and Portugal and a subsequent offensive through the Pyrenees.[40] Throughout the entire intra-party dispute, the furthest the government was willing to go in appeasing the demands for action against Franco was to associate Britain with a UN resolution expressing disapproval of Spanish fascism.[41] Beyond that painless concession, Bevin did not stray from the course that he had plotted in August 1945 when he insisted that the question of the existing Spanish regime was something for the Spanish people, and for them alone, to settle.[42]

4) *That overseas commitments be reduced in order to make them more commensurate with the reduction in British power.* The alternative of trying to maintain all inherited British positions involved the towering risk of overextension: with British power spread too thin, dissipated at the periphery in fruitless gestures, the government might have then had no choice but to make unfortunate concessions to Soviet pressure. The holding operation in Greece, to take a pivotal example, might have been abandoned at a far earlier and more inopportune moment than turned out to be the case. In reality, however, there was never much danger that the government would be shortsighted about its commitments, regarding them as all equally sacred and inviolable. Both its actions and its declarations evidenced a sharp appreciation that Britain's reach exceeded its grasp, that its ends of policy had to be carefully arranged in order of priorities, thereby budgeting resources, energy, and worry time. Once the government had an operative system of priorities, it was willing to tolerate setbacks with respect to lesser objectives in order to gain ground on objectives deemed more important. Of course, no nation can state unequivocally in advance what ought to be the priorities of its policy, for what is of lesser or greater importance varies with the actions of other nations. To

return to the case of Greece, the Labour government braved criticism at home and scorn abroad from its nominal friends while doggedly pursuing the Coalition's policy there for over eighteen months, yet by February 1947 economic trouble at home and greater understanding from America made possible a reassessment of the priority hitherto attached to the area. In one cardinal respect the government's operative system of priorities never changed. As Attlee later observed, the government always applied the yardstick that its balancing policy in Europe had preeminent claim on its resources.[43]

The critics in the Labour Party also favored retrenchment but for entirely different reasons. They welcomed a withdrawal nearly anywhere, under any conditions, as a sign that Britain was at long last renouncing the sordid practice of power-jockeying. We have seen, for instance, how popular the demand was in certain circles for a unilateral pullout from the Mediterranean. These were notions far removed from the government's own calculations. If one general principle guided Bevin in deciding whether to pare a commitment or not, it was apparently the consideration of how this would affect the nation's overall power position; his primary concern was first to avoid creating a dangerous power vacuum somewhere and second, if a vacuum proved inescapable, at least to avoid making the Soviet Union the direct beneficiary. As Francis Williams noted about his friend, Bevin recognized at the outset that, while "Britain should reduce her foreign commitments and adjust her responsibilities to meet her diminished resources . . . she must avoid reducing them in such a way as to create power vacuums likely to produce new conflict.[44] Thus in Southeast Asia, the area British Foreign Secretaries have traditionally viewed as least strategically vital, the Labour government came quickly to terms with the new Asian nationalisms and withdrew completely at several points. But in the Middle East, an area of prime importance impinging decisively on British defense, communications, investments, and sources of petroleum, the government weighed with extreme care all choices concerning possible reductions in the British presence. Appealing to elementary nationalist instincts, Bevin was not averse to defending his Middle Eastern policy with the argument that the living standards of British workers hinged on successful defense of Britain's interests there.[45]

In all of this, there was but one facet of the government's policy that could not be reduced to traditionalist principles. I refer to its anti-imperialist convictions, socialist in inspiration. Labour entered power pledged to work for self-determination for the colonies, and there is no reason to doubt the genuineness of the government's anti-imperialism. It would, however, probably be wrong to lay too much stress on this as a factor in the government's behavior. As the British record in Indonesia and Vietnam suggests, the Labour government had no compunctions about siding with the colonial powers there and even in using captured Japanese troops to suppress local nationalist uprisings. And its record in the Middle East also suggests what we have just argued: that where anti-imperialist sentiment conflicted with crucial British interests, the government always let the latter consideration prevail. It is doubtful if a government headed by Churchill, for all his blood-curdling imperial oratory, would have behaved much differently.[46]

### PARTY REACTION

#### The Critics' Explanation

At first, the government's critics refused to believe that a Labour Foreign Secretary would willingly implement any except a socialist foreign policy. If the government's policy early assumed a traditional character, this had to be due to something highly improper, perhaps furtive, possibly even devious. The belief that Bevin had permitted himself to become unduly influenced by the moss-backed permanent officials at the Foreign Office soon presented itself as a satisfactory explanation.

Left-wing intellectuals in particular had never thought much of Bevin's intelligence in political matters. During the 1930's they had resented his growing importance in party councils, viewing him as a crude and bullying trade union martinet with an uneducated mind incapable of grasping subtle socialist truths. Nothing that he did while Minister of Labour in the Coalition government reassured them in this connection—quite the contrary.[47] After the war, accordingly, they had little difficulty in persuading themselves that he had fallen victim to sinister civil servants, themselves stuffy public school graduates and narrow-minded proponents of traditional ways. Accusations to this effect were aired as early as

February 1946 and then elaborated and discussed throughout the spring, the whole affair culminating in a composite resolution presented to the annual conference in July. The resolution did not explicitly charge that there was a Foreign Office conspiracy. What it did say was that the permanent officials were unsuited by background and temperament to sympathize with socialist principles; that they should therefore be removed and the existing methods of recruitment drastically overhauled; and that the Labour government ought to ensure that any new officials had sufficiently progressive views of their own.[48] The resolution, needless to say, was easily turned back, with Bevin making a skillful defense not only of the unimpeachable loyalty of his officials but of his entire policy.

Was there anything to the charge? Misgivings about the Foreign Office had a long history in Labour's ranks, stretching back to the days of E. D. Morel and the Union of Democratic Control. Against this background, it was therefore not surprising—particularly since the Labour government's traditionalist foreign policy caught the party unawares after 1945—that intense suspicion of bureaucratic machinations flared up. Ministers, both at the time and later out of office, dismissed the suspicion as unfounded, a fantasy. They repeatedly insisted on the complete loyalty and cooperation of the civil service; they repeatedly offered assurance that their advisers were all nonpartisan, impartial, and indispensable in the performance of their tasks. There is no reason to doubt this testimony; and yet for all of that, the government's critics must be said to have come close to making a valid and important point. For in every system of party government, whether parliamentary, presidential, or for that matter Communist, there is a major problem of ensuring party control of the permanent bureaucracy and party predominance in policy making. Whether such control is obtained as effectively as it could be in the British system is at least open to question, as more and more Britons themselves have begun to recognize (witness the flurry caused by the recent Fulton Committee). After all, when a new government moves into Whitehall, only about 80 posts change occupants. Many of these 80 senior and junior ministers may lack administrative experience, have little independent access to vital information (especially in foreign and defense policy) owing to poor parliamentary scrutiny, and are unable to make lavish use of political appointees to impose partisan views on the permanent civil servants.* Meanwhile the massive bureaucratic machine remains, its talented members—at any rate in the upper reaches of the administrative branch—gifted in the arts of adjustment, aged and worldly-wise, not particularly suited by temperament, formal education, and training to bold innovation.† None of this is a question of loyalty or cooperation, let alone deliberate conservative inertia. It is a matter rather of recruitment practices, enthusiasm for innovation, parliamentary and public access to vital information (especially in defense and foreign policy), and traditional executive arrangements.

Hence, pruned of its conspiratorial overtones, the charge raised by the Labour government's critics deserves to be taken seriously. Not only between 1945 and 1951 but for any Labour government looking for far-reaching legislative and administrative changes, there is a danger that its accession to office may do little more than change the names on a few desks in Whitehall.

It needs to be immediately added, however, that if the critics were right to the extent just mentioned, they were wrong in another and no less important sense. This is because the problem of party control did not present itself after 1945 in quite the way they assumed. As we saw in Chapter 3, the Labour ministers had abandoned socialist principles before Labour took office. The time to raise the question of administrative dilution of partisan enthusi-

---

* To cite just two instances of how party control may be difficult under these arrangements: In 1924 the Foreign Office awaited MacDonald's arrival with a certain foreboding, given his radical background. Within weeks a sigh of relief spread throughout the department. Lord D'Abernon, a key British ambassador, jotted down in his diary on 20 February 1924: "The Foreign Office people appear delighted with their new Chief.... He is much inclined to fall in with their views." Viscount D'Abernon, p. 55.

That this was not just a matter of a kink in MacDonald's makeup was shown by the experience of Hugh Dalton, when he became Parliamentary Under-Secretary to Henderson at the Foreign Office in 1929. He discovered that none of the officials had even bothered to read Labour's election manifesto "Labour and the Nation," and had to circulate copies in order to familiarize them with the party's views. He later complained of the Whitehall obstacle race, the subtle and seemingly endless barriers encountered when trying to push a new policy through the machine. See Dalton, *Memoirs, 1887–1931*, pp. 223, 237–38.

† It would be too laborious to cite all of the relevant writings of Brian Chapman, Bernard Crick, Richard Rose, Kenneth Waltz, and a score of others in support of these points.

asm was when Labour entered the Coalition, not when it won the 1945 General Election; and far from there being any need for Foreign Office officials to raise their eyebrows at suggestions of bold departure after the election, no bold departures were ever contemplated. Talk of Foreign Office machinations was therefore as misplaced as the defense by ministers of their advisers' loyalty was superfluous. It would have been more than peculiar, after all, if the Foreign Office had not given complete cooperation to a Foreign Secretary whose views so closely matched those of its permanent staff and of the Conservative Opposition as well.

## Ministerial Solidarity

Following the 1946 annual conference, many of Bevin's critics came to see that their grievances could no longer be adequately accounted for by a Foreign Office plot. Reluctantly they concluded that Bevin himself was a willful conniver in the glaring failure to repudiate continuity in foreign policy. As the *New Statesman* observed in a series of four articles entitled "Reorientations," "during Mr. Bevin's first year at the Foreign Office, we have witnessed a complete reversal of Labour's foreign policy."[49] The series charged that Bevin had become a convert to fanatical anti-communism since the General Election and that British foreign policy was therefore being conducted according to his own reactionary quirks as well as the prejudices of the officials serving under him. The *New Statesman*, however, did not abandon hope for an eventual socialist turnabout. Its strictures were directed almost exclusively at Bevin himself; by implication, the other leading ministers were free from the taint of atavistic traditionalist sentiments. If accordingly the absurdity of Bevin's views could be graphically demonstrated, would he not become isolated from his colleagues, who would then have no choice but to repudiate him as a grave liability?

This, at any rate, was the question that Bevin's critics within the PLP seemed to pose to themselves during the early autumn months. Its logic apparently struck them as overwhelming, because by November they were willing to defy party authority and to risk severe disciplinary sanctions by denouncing Bevin's policy on the floor of the House of Commons. This stage of the mounting intraparty conflict has aptly been called "the revolt in Parliament."[50]

The revolt began with a critical Amendment that 57 rebels attached to the Reply to the Throne Address, in an effort to drive a
wedge between Bevin and the rest of the Cabinet. That this is what
the rebels were aiming at was made abundantly clear by their
choice of timing, Bevin being out of the country and so unable to
defend himself and his policy in person. That they also calculated
wrongly was made no less abundantly clear. For Attlee, replying
in Bevin's place, not only delivered a stinging reproach to his de-
tractors; he went on and unfolded one of the better-reasoned defenses of the government's foreign policy. The net effect was to
shatter all lingering hope that Bevin, and Bevin alone, was motivated by traditionalist principles.

It was naïve, Attlee insisted, to demand that the nation's foreign
policy reflect a domestic party's ideology. Any groping in that direction would be foredoomed because there abounded hard and inescapable facts of international life—for instance, geography and
natural resources—which were impervious to ideological treatment. Accordingly, no matter how committed to a doctrine any
Foreign Secretary might be, he could not merely proceed to translate general principles into concrete policy. Not only would he
bump against the hard facts in doing so, but, what was more, because Britain had to operate in an environment not very amenable
to its own control, he would also find that other nations might
offer resistance. These other nations had their own views, perhaps
even their own doctrines, and yet they all had to be taken into
consideration in framing a responsible British policy. It followed
that the only reliable guide to policy makers was not some hazy
"ideological abstraction," but rather national interests—which,
so Attlee insisted, did not vary according to the political hue of
the party in power. Given all these complexities, a Foreign Secretary had always to be ready to ask the question when confronted
by the demands of other nations: "Shall I compromise on this
point or shall I refuse cooperation and break?"[51]

Attlee's argument was lucid and forceful. Whether it was persuasive is another matter. Much more was at stake in the words he
used than just a rebuke to Bevin's irked critics. In effect he was
asking the Labour Party to adapt its historical vision to the realities of governing as ministers themselves perceived them. This was
the first time that the Labour leadership had spoken in this mode,

and if party behavior over the previous sixteen months was anything to go on, the response that the leadership hoped for would not be easily produced.

### The Government's Counterthrust

Nevertheless the situation did not remain immobile, fixed in intellectual deadlock. By spring 1947, signs were turning up that suggested an unambiguous shift in prevailing party opinion. The leadership itself was in large part responsible for the discernible change, showing sufficient confidence, for almost the first time, to adopt an unsparing hard line against its critics. Instead of contriving, as it had through most of 1946, to find all manner of connection between Bevin's policy and socialist principles, it followed where Attlee had pioneered and set out to disabuse party members of their lingering illusions about socialist prospects.

What accounted for the government's new self-confidence? This is hard to say with any finality, but most likely it was beginning to take heart from recent developments on the international scene. For one thing, public opinion on both sides of the Atlantic was at last hardening in the face of continued Soviet intransigence, while for another thing the Truman Administration, which was undertaking a series of decisions leading to a revolution in American foreign policy, showed itself at long last ready to relieve certain British burdens. The growth in the Labour government's confidence was signalized, among other things, by a visible stiffening of commentary in party pronouncements issued from Transport House. "Cards on the Table," the official rejoinder to "Keep Left," serves as an illuminating example. Whereas previous Transport House statements on foreign policy had been intended, it seemed, to make the government's actions more palatable to an unhappy rank and file, "Cards on the Table" was almost brutal in its clobbering treatment of socialist criticism, and like Attlee's recent blast at the rebels in Parliament, it came close to repudiating almost everything the party had held sacrosanct for decades. Ridiculing those who equated anti-communism with fascism, it argued how ill-founded, even during the war, pro-Soviet sentiment had been; denouncing the policy of the third force (a dominant theme of "Keep Left"), it bluntly stated that Britain was too weak to take independent action; pouncing on anti-Americanism as fatuous, it went on in this connection to point out that until very recently Britain, not the United States, had served as the principal target for Soviet hostility. It agreed that the Labour government should aim at promoting international cooperation, a strong UN, and general peace, but it emphasized that until now the government had had to conduct foreign affairs under the shadow of recurrent noncooperation on the part of the Soviet Union. In view of these considerations, "Cards on the Table" exhorted the Labour partisans to take a fresh and sober look at the existing international situation and their conceptual understanding of it: "Many of us expect Britain to act as if she were still in the nineteenth century, the only world power in existence, a mighty empire unchallenged either in the military or economic spheres. Even more seem to imagine that in 1945 the Labour Government could survey the world scene from any immediate problems or commitments and choose the precise policy best calculated to achieve a Socialist millenium."*

Scarcely had Transport House's strong words been published than events, too, came increasingly to the aid of the government in its efforts to confound its critics. The first of these was the brusque Soviet refusal to participate in Marshall Aid, followed by its virtual declaration of war against the program, including the formation of the Cominform and the intensification of its pressure on the occupied countries of Eastern Europe. If these harsh actions did not suffice to explode most of the illusions still lingering in the West in connection with Soviet intentions, the Czechoslovakian coup d'état which was staged in early 1948 almost certainly did.[52] In Labour circles, there was a decisive hardening of opinion toward the Soviet Union. By mid-1948 only a hard core of left-wing critics continued with the struggle to explain these recent events according to the proper socialist critique of things. The vast majority of critics, in contrast, had apparently had enough.

* "Cards on the Table" (Labour Party: London, 1947), p. 4. The pamphlet was written by Hugh Dalton, the head of the NEC international subcommittee, and Denis Healey, the secretary of the international department of the party head office at Transport House. At the annual party conference shortly afterward, Konni Zilliacus and R. H. S. Crossman demanded to know whether Dalton and Healey alone had written it, whether Ernest Bevin had seen it and extended his approval, and whether the NEC had approved its publication. Dalton had to admit that he and Healey had published the pamphlet without securing the prior consent of the NEC. *LPCR*, 1947, pp. 106, 156.

The leadership, sensitive as ever to the evolution in party sentiment, capitalized on these developments by delivering a number
of swift, sharp blows to the dwindling lot of its critics. In an outspoken statement, the NEC condemned the Czech coup as a brutal
affront to justice and then pointedly added that it should serve as
an object lesson of the way "individual Socialists, by permitting or
abetting attacks on democracy, have connived at their own destruction."[53] Soon afterward the Cabinet announced the removal
of suspected Communists from posts relating to national security
—a measure Attlee indirectly justified later in a May Day address
that likened communism to fascism as enemies to democracy.[54] (It
was about this time, moreover, that the government was moving
boldly on several fronts abroad: it signed the Brussels Pact in
March, agreed shortly afterward to station American bombers on
British soil, and began nerving itself for opposition to the Soviet
campaign against Berlin.) No less than a year beforehand it would
have been difficult to foresee the government acting so assertively
in intra-party affairs. Yet so anti-Communist did the party mood
become, during the remainder of 1948, that the NEC encountered
no significant resistance at the 1949 annual conference for having
recently expelled Konni Zilliacus on the charge that his sympathies were more attuned to the Communist than to the Labour
Party.[55]

Nor was this all. The hardening of party opinion eventually
touched even the left itself, splitting it apart during the Berlin
crisis. A tiny band, numbering among its ranks some 45 backbench
members of the PLP[56] and employing the *New Statesman* as an
extra-parliamentary forum, maintained steadfast opposition to the
government and urged, among other things, that Britain avoid an
otherwise inevitable war by quickly meeting all Soviet demands
on the city. By way of contrast, several Labour partisans of impeccable left-wing reputation supported the government's position
throughout the dispute; among them figured many prominent
members of "Keep Left," who now broke with the group and were
in fact to remain outside its successor, "Keeping Left," when the
latter was founded a few months afterward. A similar division on
the left was also noticeable in the critics' extra-parliamentary or-
gans of opinion: if the *New Statesman* continued to champion the
dissenters' views, the *Tribune* shifted its direction and began to
function as a spokesman for the government's policy.

In brief, both events abroad and the leadership's actions at home combined by late 1948 to reduce the Labour government's critics to a small, die-hard assemblage. The effect was to decrease severely the scope of party conflict and even to stimulate hope for a new consensus in foreign policy.

### NATIONALIST DIPLOMACY:
### LABOUR AND EUROPEAN UNITY

So far the analysis has focused on the Labour government's policy in Europe mainly as it related to the Soviet Union. But Europe impinged on Britain in another sense as well, and looked at from the different angle of European unity, the government appears to have acted with equally traditionalist motivation. At the time its spokesmen denied this and tried to construct a socialist case for its behavior. Even today one can detect a good deal of lingering confusion in Labour circles regarding this initial period of European integration. But here as elsewhere we need to push through the cloud of phrases to the realities beneath. What we find only highlights the patterns uncovered earlier.

The semantic knot needs to be cut from the outset. By nationalist diplomacy I mean that a government, when faced with ripe opportunities for regional integration, prefers for reasons of national sovereignty either not to participate at all or (should that prove too impractical) to participate in only the most cautious and limited ways. In the case of the Labour government, these opportunities arose after 1947 in the form of three movements toward European union. One of these movements—military integration—was endorsed provided it did not advance beyond the limits carefully established by the Brussels Treaty and later the North Atlantic Pact. Another was joined in a noncommittal and unadventurous mood: economic integration insofar as its momentum was contained within the OEEC and European Payments Union and did not threaten to become more ambitious, as it did at the time of the Schuman Plan. Beyond intergovernmental cooperation of the sort represented by NATO and OEEC, the Labour government would not venture. Cooperation was fine, consultation was splendid, international secretariats were desirable; but as soon as the issue of supranational authority arose—that is, voting procedures other than unanimity and councils with at least some autonomous powers—the Labour government quickly boggled and refused to contemplate the slightest surrender of formal British sovereignty. Thus its ministers fought off French efforts to inject supranational vigor into OEEC with the same dogged persistence that they later evinced, returned to Opposition, in connection with the European Defense Community. Against this background, the third and most ambitious movement toward European union—political federation—never had a chance; the Statute of the Council of Europe, for instance, which was signed in May 1949, bore "in every phase the marks of the British resistance to federalism of the previous year."[57] No doubt outright political union was impractical on several counts and would not have made much headway even without British opposition. The French themselves, its most ardent proponents, soon recognized this. Yet even the Schuman Plan, which abandoned the federalist approach for the supposedly British-favored functional method of integration, did nothing to alter the Labour government's established attitude despite its socialist allure of economic *dirigisme*.

Plainly, by so jealously husbanding British sovereignty, the Labour government was affronting one of the party's fundamental principles—internationalism. With its contempt for national interests and its insistence that national sovereignty was evil, the underlying cause of international anarchy, socialist policy would presumably have dictated a warm embrace of all efforts calculated to promote a new international community: especially so, moreover, when these same efforts promised extensive collaboration with Continental socialists.* Yet socialist principles no more animated the government's behavior here than they did elsewhere. What marked its outlook was the most instinctive and unimaginative traditionalism. Its official position as politely stated by Bevin was that the "solid work of European unity" should proceed strictly by way of intergovernmental cooperation in economics and in defense.[58] Unofficially, the attitude prevailing in government circles at the time seemed a great deal more unseemly and, like the Tory view of the League of Nations before 1939, tainted by feelings

---

* The major socialist parties in Western Europe overcame their initial misgivings about the Schuman Plan and eventually supported its adoption. The West German Socialists took longer to become converted, though their objections had almost nothing to do with socialism and almost everything to do with their attempt, under Schumacher, to represent themselves to the German electorate as the guardians of nationalist purity. See Haas, pp. 132–33, 136–37.

of national superiority and highhandedness. The Europeans, it was assumed, could not possibly unite without British leadership; therefore let them talk their idle chatter, for nothing would ever come of it. Too harsh a judgment? Many Continentals, including and perhaps (as we shall see) especially socialists, would not think so. As one Continental critic recently observed, the British reception to the Schuman Plan was compounded of "superficial, emotional and short-term considerations."* Worse things, to be sure, have been said for years on the Continent, but when the Minister of State for Foreign Affairs in 1950 grants that this particular criticism is a "fair" account, it deserves to be taken seriously.[59]

That socialist principles would have dictated a far different course was in fact shown when several socialist critics, dismayed at the government's noncommittal conservatism, began agitating in early 1948 for political union. In January G. D. H. Cole, vociferous exponent of a third force, warned that time was running out for any initiative by Britain.[60] Then Bevin delivered his discourse on West European unity, and for a brief spell criticism slackened in the expectation that the government was at long last moving toward genuine political integration. When it turned out, however, that the Brussels Treaty, a traditional military pact, was the sole fruit of the recent British initiative, the critics grew alarmed and tabled a motion in the Commons urging the government to move forward with utmost dispatch toward "a political union strong enough to save European democracy and the values of Western civilisation."[61] Their concern manifested itself in other ways as well. Many prominent Labour backbenchers attended the May meeting of the Hague Congress of the Movement for European Unity, even though the NEC had publicly warned them against doing so, arguing that the question of European unification was a matter to be dealt with solely by governments.[62] Later in the same

---

* Sahm, p. 22. The Labour government, it is true, publicly rested much of Britain's objection to the Schuman Plan on the ground that it required nations to declare themselves in favor of the principle of a coal and steel community "prior to, rather than as a result of, inter-governmental decisions." (Miscellaneous No. 9 [1959]. *Anglo-French discussion regarding French proposals for the Western European Coal, Iron and Steel Industries*, Cmd. 7970, p. 11.) But Sahm and most Continental observers regard this technical point as little more than a smoke screen, and one major American study backs up their view: Diebold, p. 59.

month the critics moved their case to the floor of the annual conference. Presenting a resolution on European union, Fenner Brockway exhorted the leadership to give utmost priority to forming a European bloc "in complete military and political independence of the USA and the USSR."[63] The issue, Brockway argued, was no longer whether there ought to be a union or not, but only what kind it would be—socialist and third force or reactionary and Churchillian (Churchill being active in the Movement for European Unity at the time).

In reply the NEC had to proceed gingerly, since the mood at the conference hall was reported in the press to be favorable to Brockway's stand. Consequently, instead of outrightly opposing the resolution, the Executive chose a more prudent course of action: it agreed to accept the resolution while at the same time belittling it and all other schemes for European union as utopian, foolhardy, and altogether contrary to Britain's and Labour's best interests. Such is the impression, at any rate, that emerges from a study of Hugh Dalton's speech accepting the resolution on behalf of the Executive. The speech was full of artful doubletalk and tricky evasions. Professing to endorse the idea of a united Europe, it began by running over the Labour government's impressive record in domestic policy: full employment, fair shares, nationalization, and so on. Now all of this was in grave danger of being sacrificed on the "doctrinal altar of a federal Western Europe." Should Britain be reckless enough to throw in its lot with the Continentals, British workers might well awaken one day only to discover that the perennial constitution makers in Europe had "decreed" that the nation must return to presocialist conditions. The inevitable effect would be "trade depressions and all the rest." Dalton granted that Labour could not remain altogether aloof from the various movements promoting European integration; but its participation had to be realistic, limited strictly to the "functional approaches of inter-governmental cooperation," the federal approach amounting to mere "conclaves of chatter-boxes."[64]

Dalton's speech, for all its brutal language, seems to have been a fairly accurate reflection of prevailing feelings within government circles at the time. Even its ambivalent reference to functional approaches was an accurate rendering, for though implying that functional cooperation was desirable, it excluded any refer-

ence to supranational integration. Any lingering illusions of the
Labour government's true position were almost certainly shattered
soon afterward by the appointment of none other than Hugh Dalton as head of the British delegation to the negotiations on the
Council of Europe. Certain members of the delegation, mostly
left-wing in outlook, pressed for an ambitious pro-European policy.[65] But Dalton and the others apparently saw it as their duty
to dilute ambitious proposals to the point where they lost all
meaning. This was so, it needs to be added, even though the Continental socialists, especially the French, were themselves favorable
to those proposals and indeed initiated many of them.[66]

The socialist critics within the Labour Party watched these developments with dismay and bewilderment. Yet, in retrospect at
any rate, there was nothing very surprising about the Labour government's deep-dyed inhibitions about European unity; the surprise indeed would have been a decision to participate vigorously
in the movements toward that goal. For, as was already made
amply clear even by 1947, the Labour Party's commitment to internationalism had evolved under a unique set of circumstances:
namely, electoral weakness of the prewar sort, when Labour had
never enjoyed full control of the British government and when
its natural posture seemed to consist in unremitting opposition to
those who did have control. In this sense, the party could be said
to have not really risked much in denigrating the idea of national
sovereignty. But after 1945 circumstances had thoroughly changed.
The leadership now possessed complete command of state authority; it therefore had an infinitely greater stake in defending and
preserving that authority. In fact it had an overriding interest in
increasing the powers of the state, given the ambitious scope of its
proclaimed economic and social programs. Under these new conditions, the Labour government was quite obviously not prepared
to surrender British sovereignty to any supranational organization.

No doubt this line of reasoning could be construed as socialist
in one way or another, in which case it would be wrong to regard
the government's European policy as wholly traditional in inspiration. For that matter the government's supporters made out a defense in precisely these terms—domestic welfare, nationalization,
and control of industry; and there is no reason to question their

sincerity, in that the government's motives were most likely complicated and mixed. Still, it seems unwise to emphasize this side of things too much. In the first place, socialist foreign policy had never been conceived of as a doctrine that might someday necessitate a choice between socialism at home and internationalism; just the reverse had been the case: prior to 1945, Labour partisans had assumed that the domestic and international strands were not contradictory but complementary. Hence, regardless of motivation, the government's snub of European unification constituted no less a snub of a key socialist principle on the basis of accepted socialist logic. In the second place, moreover, there were two additional considerations that seemed to prompt the decision to ignore Europe, and neither had anything to do with socialism. In fact they had nothing to do with partisan politics at all, because both were embedded in the general political culture of the nation. One related to the role of the Commonwealth and the Empire, a subject whose impact on Britain's subsequent relations with Europe is too well known to require elaboration here. The other was an emotional and cultural gulf dividing the British Isles and the Continent, a gulf that had perceptibly widened as a result of the war. All of the Continental nations had been occupied and defeated, suffering untold devastation in the process, and the experience had been sufficiently traumatic to rob sovereignty of much of its meaning. But the British experience had been the diametric opposite. Britain had remained independent and ended up a victor, and in no small measure because of a quickening in national pride and faith; it thus emerged from the war completely confident in its ability to handle its destiny in the future exactly as in the past.

How nationalistic Labour's behavior toward Europe shaped up can be gauged by a glance at "European Unity," an NEC statement that constituted the most elaborate defense to date of the government's policy. Issued in 1950, "European Unity" was in effect a retort to the Schuman proposal, and its message was shot through with scorn for the whole idea of European unification. Not only did it flatly contradict the principle of internationalism by asserting that Labour could "never accept any commitment which limited its own or others' freedom to pursue democratic Socialism and to apply the economic controls necessary to achieve it"; it also went on to dismiss the West European regimes as hopelessly reactionary, thoroughly unfit to become partners in Labour's pursuit of justice. In saying this, "European Unity" was not referring simply to the contemporary West European political scene; without the least qualification, it proclaimed that any European supranational authority would have a "permanent anti-Socialist majority and would arouse the hostility of European workers."[67]

Such boisterous nationalism outraged many European socialists. Until even this late date and despite all previous British rebuffs, most Continental socialists had remained hopeful that the Labour government would place its prestige and influence at the disposal of the unification movements. But "European Unity" disabused them of their illusions, and the fact that it had been unveiled at a press conference in a haughty manner by Hugh Dalton only added to the shock. One French socialist leader commented shortly afterward: "The doctrine of Socialism in one country, whose inevitable misdeeds in Russia were already denounced by Trotsky, becomes a total absurdity in the small nations of the West. Those who cling to it, with the laudable aim of protecting social gains, are brought by the force of things to take in foreign policy more and more conservative positions contrary to the socialist spirit and the democratic ideal."[68]

IN CONCLUSION

Hence the Labour government's conduct of foreign policy can be seen to have proceeded almost entirely along traditional lines of inspiration. The question of a socialist policy arose, only to be rejected by the policy makers as irrelevant—not to mention bothersome and embarrassing. To the extent they can be said to have applied any overall guiding axiom at all, this did not derive from socialist principles but rather from a prudent empiricism, a cautious pragmatism, directed at adjusting and adapting the nation to an unfavorable international situation and, in so doing, at extracting the maximum possible advantage out of implacable necessities.

So characterized, British foreign policy between 1945 and 1951 enjoyed no small measure of success. Undoubtedly its supreme merit was to win enough time, during a period of unsettled turbulence and widespread dislocation, for Britain to complete the exacting process of reconstruction at home and to aid materially in establishing a tolerable equilibrium abroad, in Europe especially.

The immense progress on these counts was already striking by 1951. In 1945 Britain's status on the scale of world power had appreciably slipped as compared with its past position; its future was uncertain and its very security in doubt. By the time Labour left office, however, its policy had ensured that the nation retained an influential and responsible voice in world affairs, that its security was no longer in jeopardy but tolerably anchored; and that a new balance in Europe, underpinned by a working cooperation among Americans, West Europeans, and Britons themselves, was becoming firmly fixed. These were no mean achievements, and the quality of Labour's statesmanship deserves to be fully acknowledged.

All this on the one hand. On the other hand—and there is nearly always an other hand in such complicated matters—the government's record was not one of success alone, and an evaluation would be incomplete unless it weighed the defects no less than the merits.

Somewhat paradoxically, the most glaring defects seem to have derived from the same source as the merits themselves: from the policy's thoroughgoing traditionalism, its cautious and pragmatic goals of immediate adaptation and adjustment to the exclusion of long-range planning. On more than one occasion, the government appeared so earnestly bent on coming to terms with existing facts that it let slip by precious opportunities for creatively altering the facts for the nation's long-run benefit. For all the courage and determination evinced by Bevin and his colleagues in their struggle to cut back overextended commitments and to establish a tolerable European balance, they seemed to lack the incentive, the willpower, and the imagination to go beyond that goal, to define and to forge a new national destiny that would stir public opinion and sink into public consciousness. Certainly a concrete opportunity arose for doing so in connection with European unity. Until 1951 Britain could have had the leadership of a new Europe for the asking; after 1951 not only did the opportunity vanish but in its place was left a thick residue of mistrust among the Continentals.* Labour's failure of imagination is something that will not

* To a large extent, no doubt, the lack of creativity in Labour's policy making—which became pronounced beginning in 1949—was due to the worsening physical condition of Ernest Bevin. His condition became so serious that the

be treated lightly by the judgment of history: indeed the confused and still unresolved British relationship with European unity—its debacle in trying to join the European Economic Community in the early 1960's and its uncertain efforts in that direction at the present moment—already establish this point beyond doubt. Even apart from its timid lack of vision and daring, moreover, the Labour government's attitude betrayed the most stuffy and complacent sort of nationalism. No doubt the Conservatives would not have acted any differently if they had been in power, but this is beside the point. The Conservative Party, after all, had never concealed its nationalism, never tried to repress its haughty disdain and scorn of the Continentals. But Labour had prided itself exactly on its freedom from such parochialism: it claimed to be in possession of greater insight into the nature of world politics and on this basis had denounced traditional foreign policy as narrow-minded, insular, and regrettably chauvinistic. And yet when it came to power and had to make good its claim to greater insight and freedom from parochialism, its policy turned out to betray the same sort of defects. It was cautious, careful, overly wary of new departures from familiar and comfortable modes of thinking. If, in short, the Labour government deftly avoided one pitfall of the party's socialism, namely the illusion that foreign policy could be neatly and happily conducted in accordance with a set of doctrinaire principles, it seemed to have stumbled in the process into another pitfall, no less serious: it ignored altogether a ripe opportunity for a radical breakthrough in the traditional system of international relations.

All in all, both in its defects and in its merits, the Labour government's foreign policy was probably very similar to the kind of policy that would have been conducted by Churchill and Eden. The one major exception might have been the withdrawal from India, though even here it is difficult to believe that Churchill would have proved as oblivious, in office, of certain hard facts as his statements made in Opposition suggested. In nearly every other respect, Labour's policy developed in the manner foreshad-

conduct of foreign affairs was left in an uncertain and rather bewildering state. Attlee's reluctance to appoint a new Foreign Secretary, indeed his belief that there was no worthy successor to be found among Labour's ranks, amounts to a grave indictment of the leadership for not having nurtured a new generation of leaders in whom it could repose its confidence.

owed in the Fulton Address. Churchill himself often likened Bevin's work to his own ideas. In doing so, of course, he was motivated by political considerations, for he well knew how much the analogy enraged Labour supporters; but this does not make the analogy any less suggestive. Besides, on at least one occasion Churchill invoked it in such a way as to dispel any doubt that he intended his remarks as a genuine tribute. This was in February 1952, when Bevin was dead and the Conservatives were in office. According to Churchill: "The policy which I outlined at Fulton five [*sic*] years ago has since been effectively adopted both by the United States and by the Socialist Party. Two years later by the Brussels Pact and in the following year by the North Atlantic Treaty, the whole substance and purpose of what I said was adopted and enforced by the Socialist Government, and today we all respect the foresight and wise courage of the late Ernest Bevin in helping to bring those great changes about."* It should be added here that Churchill, while in Opposition, drew some satisfaction from seeing Bevin at the Foreign Office. As he told Secretary of Defense Forrestal, Bevin as a Labour Minister was able to talk more firmly to Russia than he himself could have if the Tories had been in office.[69]

The enormous distance in policy that Labour had traveled from the heady enthusiasm and optimism of early 1945 was strikingly shown during the next election campaign in February 1950.[70] At one point Churchill called for a "summit" conference between the great powers as the most useful means of settling their differences. The heads of state of these powers had not met since Potsdam, and the proposal apparently touched a responsive chord in many men's minds. Adding that he himself would be the best-qualified Briton to speak with the Soviets, Churchill contrasted the enmity of current Anglo-Soviet relations with the wartime "friendship" that he had established with Stalin.[71] Bevin rejoined the next day. He hardly thought Churchill's proposal merited serious consideration and dubbed it an electioneering stunt. The Labour government, he said, was prepared to sit down with the leaders of the Soviet Union in an attempt to thrash out their

---

* *The Times*, 20 February 1952. Anthony Eden also noted in retrospect the extent to which he "was in agreement with the aims of his [Bevin's] foreign policy and with most that he did." (See Eden, p. 5.)

differences—but only after the Soviets themselves had first given clear evidence of a change of heart.[72]

Here was the most startling of ironies. In less than five years, "left understands left" sloganeering had been turned on its head, and it was now the British right that claimed to be best qualified to elicit cooperation from the Soviet Union!

# Chapter six

# The Interplay of the Two Foreign Policies:
# The Level of Argument

The conflict raging within the Labour Party after 1945 can be most profitably studied on two levels. The first is that of intra-party politics, which deals with the conflict in terms of the positions adopted by various groups and factions and the ways they then interacted with Labour's diverse centers of leadership. The subject will be treated on this level in the next chapter. Here we will examine the conflict from the standpoint of its impact on the balance of internal party argument. Out of the clash between socialist and traditional principles, what changes were worked on party members' thinking? Did the government's policy force a reevaluation of socialist principles, and was this reevaluation of a long-term or merely ephemeral nature? Conversely, did the critics' heavy blasts affect the government's behavior in any substantial way, compelling it to alter its policy to suit their demands? What, finally, was the degree of consensus prevailing within the party when Labour reverted to opposition in 1951?

Obviously, questions of this sort impinge on a host of complex problems regarding the interplay of attitudinal variables (social orientations, opinions, images, beliefs, values, and the like) and the behavior of those holding them. Social psychologists have been working in this misty area for years now, and their general findings can be usefully employed here. For instance, an individual's *images* have been found to be tenaciously rooted in both personality needs and group affiliation and thus to be stubbornly resistant to environmental pressures directed at altering them; this is so ir-

respective of whether the pressures arise as spectacular events con-
tradicting the images in question or as deliberate attempts by
media and governments at persuasion and manipulation.* As
Deutsch and Merritt conclude after studying image "tenacity" in
international relations: "Our findings . . . attest to the resistance
of human thinking and imagining to sudden environmental pressures. Men cling to their earlier memories and character. They
call upon the support of their social groups to defend their images and beliefs. They distort many of their perceptions and deny
much of reality, in order to call their prejudiced souls their own."[1]
If we apply these findings to the questions raised above, we would
not, for example, expect the mass of Labour supporters to have
been easily coaxed into abandoning their ardent faith in socialist
principles—this regardless of the existence of spectacular events
like the Soviet thrust in Iran which conflicted with socialist images, or of the efforts of the Labour government at reeducation.

None of this should be taken to mean, however, that images are
completely resistant to external influences. They obviously can
and do alter, though the overriding question is the *degree* and
*durability* of any change. Generally speaking, a major reorganization of important images may be almost impossible to accomplish
short of intense pressures being applied continually over many
months and perhaps years; but even in the short run these same
pressures may cause shifts in some aspects of the images: for instance, in their relations to one another and to their surrounding
cues and contexts.[2] At the same time, change of any sort—whether
minor shifts or more ambitious reorganization—is more likely to
occur the greater the variance or inconsistency already characterizing the existing pattern of images. To take an example relevant
here, images are known to be anchored in, among other things,
group affiliations—in the powerful loyalties, mutual support, and
internalized norms that such affiliations normally generate.[3] If,

---

* The concept of image in social-psychological literature resembles our depiction of socialist foreign policy as a set of principles or attitudes, conjointly
held to form a distinctive mental outlook. Herbert Kelman, for instance, defines
an image as a combinatorial construct lodged in an individual's cognitive system, built up of "various specific memories and expectations, various generalized beliefs and opinions" (pp. 24–26). Finer and his colleagues are in effect
employing the same concept when they refer to the *syndrone* of socialist attitudes and propositions (pp. 48–59). As long as the reader grasps the common
underlying ideas, he will not trip over the particular term—image, principles,
syndrone—that happens to be used at any one point.

then, for some reason there is a rupture in the group's solidarity, and if this leads certain members to begin deviating from accepted beliefs and attitudes, the disruptive effect on the images held in common by the group may well be contagious.* Something akin to this happened in the case of the Labour Party. Group solidarity was broken when the leadership began acting contrary to socialist images and principles;† the result was to engender ambiguity in the minds of party followers, who were torn between conformity to socialist doctrine and loyalty to their leaders; sustained efforts by the government at persuasion and manipulation then heightened the ambiguity, and of course the greater the ambiguity the freer the government's hand in deviating from official norms.‡ Whether or not a shift in party images would actually ensue depended then on the *cumulative* impact of events over a long period. Here is where continuous belligerent Soviet behavior from 1945 on would have exercised its influence, and the same can be said about the impact of continuous friendly American behavior. The net effect was the change in party outlook by 1948.§

But to repeat: the principal question that needs to be investigated is the degree and the permanence characterizing the change in Labour's major socialist images (principles). Were the obvious shifts that took place sufficiently cumulative and important to result in a major reorganization of the images, or was the pattern of change less significant? In connection with the latter question, it is worth mentioning in passing another general finding uncovered by social psychologists: shifts in images often may only be temporary, followed by a return to earlier levels. As Deutsch and Merritt report: "Many attitudes and images persist, or return at least part of the way toward their previous state, once the immedi-

---

* "Although any norm that is sustained by unanimity possesses a unique source of power, it also suffers from a unique source of potential weakness. Such norms are especially vulnerable to those communications that present irrefutable evidence of a break in the solidly unanimous front." Janis and Smith, p. 200.

† It is worth noting that, in general, the leaders of any group often enjoy greater flexibility in deviating from official norms than the rank and file does, because "they have less to fear from the application of group sanctions." *Ibid.*

‡ Recall Churchill's aforementioned remark to Forrestal that an anti-Soviet policy conducted by a Tory government could not have rallied the kind of support in the country that the Labour government's policy actually managed to enjoy.

§ See below, pp. 219–21.

ate external pressures slacken and so long as the main individual personality structures and supporting social networks have remained intact."[4]

### LABOUR AND THE SOVIET UNION

After initial and heavy resistance in the ranks, the pattern of Labour images of the Soviet Union from 1945 on was marked by a fairly continual qualification of the strongly favorable orientation that had been built up over the previous quarter of a century and intensified during the war. Whether the Soviet images became so tarnished as to discredit all pro-Soviet sentiment is, however, another matter. For purposes of analysis, the changes that the opinion underwent can be profitably regarded as having progressed through five different stages.

\ *Stage I. Enthusiasm*

From mid-1945 until roughly the following spring, most Labour commentary on the Soviet Union was heavily laudatory, reflecting not only the predispositions built into socialist principles but also the optimism aroused during the recent electoral campaign. This was the stage when the party's more prominent left-wing stalwarts tended to set the tone of discussion: when the Soviet Union was eulogized as a new economic democracy, the natural ally of socialist Britain, and the ultimate guarantor of the European Revolution. Labour supporters who might openly express reservations were almost certain to draw sharp rebukes from their more vociferous colleagues. A theme that was particularly popular at the time urged the government to free itself of Western stereotypes when making policy that touched the Soviet Union. As the *New Statesman* asserted: "When the Russians say 'democracy' they do not mean what the Americans mean or what Mr. Churchill means. It is, for them, not a merely parliamentary word; it means a far-reaching change in the economic basis of society. . . . But according to the Soviet view, no democratic political government is possible *until the economic changes have been made*."* How repre-

---

* 27 June 1946. (Italics in original.) The *New Statesman* was the staunchest champion of the Soviet Union among pro-Labour publications. Kingsley Martin, its editor, freely admitted his belief that collectivism was inevitable and that Soviet Communism was one form of a generally desirable socialist evolution. See his article "Marxism Reviewed."

sentative such statements were of predominant party feeling can be seen in the wary pronouncements of the leadership. It will be recalled that Bevin, in his very first speech to the Commons as Foreign Secretary, had unburdened himself of some outspoken anti-Soviet feelings; the barrage of criticism that ensued seemed to have a decidedly sobering effect on subsequent government behavior. Even Bevin himself, never one to mince his words, appeared to measure his language carefully, and not until he and Vyshinsky exchanged insults, at the UN in February 1946, did he openly denounce the Soviet Union as a threat to peace.

One Labour theorist who was most influential in giving the notion of "economic democracy" intellectual respectability was Harold Laski, party chairman during this stage. Laski's prolific writings abounded with quasi-Marxist interpretations intending to show that the Soviet Union, while suppressing "bourgeois" civil liberties, had nonetheless created a new and exemplary sort of democratic society—one in which the average Soviet citizen supposedly led a fuller life than his counterparts in "formal" democracies.[5] It followed, in his estimation, that socialist Britain had a natural ally in the Soviet Union: that, indeed, an alliance between the two was mandatory if democratic socialism were to survive the inevitable counterattack of international capitalism in the postwar period. As he told the annual conference from the chair in 1946: "the achievements of their [the Soviets'] Revolution are one of the pillars of our own strength."[6] Laski continued to champion the Soviet cause, it is worth noting, long after most other Labour left-wing intellectuals were at least willing to grant that the evolution of Russian Communism had not worked out as they had once hoped—although, to be sure, they were often quick to blame the Western world for having caused this misfortune.[7] Laski maintained a formidable reputation in Labour circles all the same and, with the exception of the *Tribune* and the *New Statesman*, probably did more than anyone else to create a frame of mind on the left that recoiled from the government's policy of containing Soviet power.

## Stage II. Rationalization

As 1945 went by, Labour commentary on the Soviet Union shifted somewhat, concentrating less on the alleged merits of its socialism and more on the reasons for its uncooperative behavior in foreign affairs. The two subjects were often linked, though, by many commentators, who dismissed as far-fetched the possibility that the Soviet regime might be harboring aggressive designs; it simply was incapable of doing so because it lacked any economic impulse to imperialism. This belief, it will be recalled, was deeply embedded in the principle of working-class solidarity. Attlee himself had written in the 1930's that imperialism was nothing other than capitalism in its external relations. Someone like Laski was thus only elaborating the logic of the principle when he insisted after 1945 that "the Russian way of life . . . seeks as clearly to prevent external economic exploitation as the American way of life inherently drives its business leaders at once to seek for that exploitation."[8] What, then, accounted for current Soviet belligerence and noncooperation?

On the one hand, the answer was given—"fear": fear of the West arising out of pre-1939 Western behavior, fear of American capitalism, above all fear of the American nuclear monopoly. As a number of examples illustrating this line of thought have already been cited in Chapter 4, it suffices to recall here that the thesis relating to Soviet fear commanded appreciable respect in Labour circles during this stage. Well into 1947, "Keep Left" insisted that Soviet suspicion of the outside world could be traced back to the brutal deal concluded by the West at Munich.

On the other hand, the answer was also given—error and miscalculation: intellectual shortcomings were what was responsible for the strained relations between East and West. As the *New Statesman* observed, Soviet policy did indeed evince a certain hostility, but this did not at all mean that the Soviet Union thus aimed at conquest in the way Western reactionaries insisted it did. Rather, Soviet enmity had to be understood as fundamentally motivated by a desire "for complete intellectual and physical isolation from the West." This might be a mistaken (albeit understandable) objective, but at least it was no cause for alarm. On the contrary, to win the Soviets around to a more reasonable frame of mind, all that the West had to do was redouble its efforts to convince them of the benefits to be had from close cooperation.[9]

The thesis relating to error and miscalculation seemed on balance to be less popular than the thesis relating to fear. Usually it was employed only on those occasions when Soviet diplomacy proved too intransigent to be argued away on grounds of fear alone. Miscalculation supposedly explained, for instance, why socialist Britain, not capitalist America, was the target at this date of unremitting Soviet ill will. According to one left-wing commentator: "We are convinced that Russia's chief fear is of American dollar imperialism. In attacking us diplomatically, she considers she is 'going for' the weaker of the two Anglo-Saxon imperialisms. Unfortunately Bevin's words and deeds give her some justification for her false assumptions that we are in the American camp."*

That party opinion at this stage still reflected strong emotional attachment to the Soviet Union was illustrated in a different way by one of Bevin's speeches, delivered at the annual conference in June 1946. Laski, who was in the chair, opened the conference with a statement that "no small part of the responsibility for Russian suspicions must be borne by those who have decided upon secrecy in relation to the atomic bomb." Subsequently a lengthy composite resolution was moved urging that British policy be based "on firm friendship and cooperation with the progressive forces throughout the world, and in particular with the USSR, and that such a policy should override British imperial interests."[10] Bevin, in reply, denied that the government was conducting an anti-Soviet policy, and under the prevailing circumstances the denial was no doubt politic; but then he went on to demand, in a hurt voice, whether there was anyone in the conference "who historically did more to defend the Russian Revolution than I did?"[11] The question, besides being misleading, was gratuitous—and to that extent illustrative of the weight of party opinion, Bevin being led to posture as an enthusiast for the very country that he happened to perceive as a looming threat to British interests.

### Stage III. Disillusion

During this stage, which lasted roughly from late 1946 to late 1947, Labour opinion began to split. A shift in Soviet images was quite plainly taking place. Under the pressure both of govern-

* See footnote on p. 115.

ment efforts at persuasion and of cumulative events, a majority of party members seemed gradually to realize how ill-founded their lavish optimism of mid-1945 had been, and the result was that they now began to edge toward a more realistic appraisal of the existing situation.* Even then, however, outright criticism of Soviet policy was still too unpopular to be lightly hazarded. There were exceptions, and in some instances criticism amounted to outspoken denunciation, but even Bevin still apparently found it advisable to choose his words with care. Typical of his calculated restraint was a series of utterances that he made in late 1946 and early 1947 on the subject of Anglo-Soviet relations. In a broadcast speech of 22 December, he told the nation that Britain was still pursuing a "middle way" in foreign policy and considered itself tied to neither camp, the Soviet or the American. It seems fair to say that this statement was mainly intended to reassure disturbed Labour partisans, the "revolt" in parliament having just taken place. The Soviets for their part chose to regard the speech as a means of embarrassing Bevin with the Labour rank and file, for they insisted soon afterward that his professions of British neutrality conflicted with the Anglo-Soviet Treaty of 1942. Bevin rejoined by offering to extend the treaty for an indefinite period. On 29 March it was announced that talks to this end were being held in Moscow. For all practical purposes, this announcement was the sole outcome of Bevin's public "initiative." In May the talks petered out and the subject vanished into history.[12]

It remained for the more vocal radical sections on the left to carry the major burden of championing the Soviet cause. Yet even among left-wing groups a change in argument was discernible—clear sign that they were alert to the shifts taking place in party images of the Soviet Union. By about late 1946 the *fact* of Soviet uncooperativeness, whatever its origins, was irrefutable. This being so, the left ceased urging upon the government a "progressive" partnership with the Soviet Union and began instead pressing for a third-force policy. To the extent that the left still concerned themselves with the Soviet Union, they did so mainly in the form of

---

* The trend was captured by the very few useful surveys of opinion that were taken. Thus Mass Observation reported after a sounding in late 1947: "There are certainly many signs that anti-Russian feeling is hardening to-day, slowly and painfully, but steadily." Willcock, p. 72.

trying to establish that Soviet behavior, even if demonstrably un-friendly, was nonetheless not so unfriendly as to make neutrality an untenable policy. As Michael Foot argued, "the campaign which the Soviet Union conducts against us is not a reason for abandoning our Socialist objectives [read: third-force policy]; it is rather a reason for pursuing them all the more boldly."[13] Plainly, the more radical wing of the Labour Party found it exceedingly difficult to change their image of the Soviet Union beyond the barest minimum in response to the cumulative impact of events. After almost two years of continual Soviet belligerence, about the most many Labour partisans could bring themselves around to admit was that the Soviets were for the moment not acting so friendly as had been hoped for at the end of the war. Woodrow Wyatt attested to the tenacity of Labour's pro-Soviet images, par-ticularly on the left, when he wrote years later: "Our case was that the world was drifting into two great power blocs and that we were drifting into the American orbit through lack of deter-mination to keep out of it. Our distrust of Russia was still so weak that we thought it possible to maintain a neutral, third force posi-tion between America and Russia.... It was a return to the La-bour Party attitudes of the 1930's toward Russia. It was a recur-rence of the old feeling that Russia really was a Socialist country, and that, given a chance, she might develop toward democracy. We felt that she was not being given that chance, and America and Britain were unnecessarily building military alliances against her which were bound to make her afraid and were bound to make the international situation worse.... In short, we thought collec-tive security against Russia was more dangerous than the menace of Russia herself."[14]

## Stage IV. *Hardening*

The period beginning in late 1947 and continuing for about the next 20 months was decisive in determining the extent to which Labour's main images of the Soviet Union were altered and rear-ranged. This was the period during which Marshall Aid began arriving, the Soviets assaulted the program, and the OEEC and Western European Union were formed. It was also the period dur-ing which the government decided to intensify its efforts at reedu-cating party opinion. Together, the cumulative impact of events and persuasion represented formidable pressure bearing down on party attitudes and opinion; and the degree to which this pressure was forcing a shift in images was more than just hinted at by the impressive support afforded the government during the Berlin crisis in 1948. Even the left wing, it will be recalled, split at this point, with a sizable number of prominent radical mainstays rallying to the government's position. Three years after the war, in short, Soviet behavior was now so demonstrably belligerent as to make attempts at a charitable interpretation an increasingly awkward exercise.[15]

The most striking evidence of a shift in images concerned Labour's support of the North Atlantic Pact. As we have seen, there are dangers in construing the party's action to signify much enthusiasm for NATO, for the motives that prompted Labour members to acknowledge the necessity of an alliance were very mixed.* Nonetheless, the alliance was plainly anti-Soviet in certain unmistakable respects, and the fact of support for whatever reasons was in itself impressive. At the same time as Labour opinion of the Soviet Union was hardening, moreover, there was also a parallel change in the party's attitude toward Communism at home. At the 1945 conference a resolution urging affiliation of the Communist Party had been barely turned back, the margin of defeat a mere 95,000 votes. Heavy enthusiasm for affiliation had again surfaced at the 1946 conference. But those developments in the cold war over the next year which led to a shift in party images of the Soviet Union exercised a similar effect in relation to the Communist issue. Anti-Communism now tended to grow in proportion to the decline in pro-Soviet feeling, and by 1949 it became sufficiently intense that the NEC had little opposition in expelling

---

* In a poll taken in late summer, 1949, it was found that whereas 81 per cent of Conservative voters favored an alliance with the United States, the corresponding figure for Labour voters was only 69 per cent (*International Journal of Opinion and Attitude Research* [summer, 1949], pp. 288–89). Note that these figures are for party voters, not just active party members. Since the active Labour rank-and-file membership is more ideological than the larger Labour electorate, it can therefore be assumed that party members were even less enthusiastic for an alliance.

Further evidence attesting to the lack of enthusiasm is found in the high number of PLP abstentions when the North Atlantic Pact came before the House of Commons in May 1949. Despite a three-line whip, the abstentions numbered over 100.

three MP's whose activity was deemed to betray too many traces of the older, more permissive climate of opinion.

## Stage V. The Balance of Internal Argument: 1950 and After

Despite these visible changes in Labour's images, however, pro-Soviet sentiment cannot be said to have been entirely surmounted. Influential residues remained after 1949, though the sentiment now found expression in less conspicuous and more oblique ways than in the past. If, for instance, it was no longer fashionable to dwell on the peace-loving socialism of the Soviet state, it was still possible to deny or at any rate to downplay seriously the existence of any Soviet military threat. Until the Korean War, expressed views of this sort did not exercise much influence, and the reason had probably to do with the fairly stable international environment and the consequent condition of NATO at the time. NATO represented an anti-Soviet posture, but before 1950 it existed largely on paper as a multilateral guaranty pact; its tangible obligations, particularly with respect to rearmament, were few—or rather nonexistent.[16] Not even the more strident left-wing sections of the Labour Party could find much to complain about in such a painless military arrangement; as the *New Statesman* observed, NATO was tolerable and would not cause trouble so long as British and American taxpayers refused to be cajoled into dispensing large sums of money for defense.[17] But war in Korea changed all this overnight. Labour's choice was now more clear-cut than at any time since 1945: the party would have to decide between its long-standing antipathy to power politics and continued support of a government policy that was currently embarking on a vast program of rearmament—a program, of course, that made sense only on the supposition of a concrete Soviet menace. For many, as it turned out, the government was going too far; almost instinctively there was a revival of concern for socialist doctrine. Chapter 8 will show, for instance, that no small measure of the Bevanite appeal derived from Labour's inveterate reluctance to regard the Soviet Union as capable of endangering the peace—at any rate to the point necessitating vigorous counteraction by Britain. The leading Bevanite spokesmen touched a sensitive nerve of the party when they insisted, again and again, that the Soviet threat was being wildly exaggerated, that it was largely the figment of an anti-Communist hysteria.[18] Plainly, in their case there had not been a very extensive reorganization of Soviet images since 1945.

Another channel through which pro-Soviet sentiment continued to find expression was in the form of support for grandiose Soviet peace gestures, such as the Stockholm Peace Movement. These gestures proved especially attractive about the time of the government's decision to rearm West Germany. At the 1950 conference a pro-Soviet resolution managed to receive nearly 900,000 votes: still a distinct minority, but nonetheless indicative of a visible upsurge of Labour interest in the new Soviet strategy.[19] Shortly afterward 83 restive Labour backbenchers signed a Parliamentary motion urging the government to reconsider its rejection of a Soviet proposal for an East-West meeting.

No doubt it would be wrong to harp too much on these and other residues of pro-Soviet feeling. But equally it would be wrong to dismiss them as continuing to influence only a radical fringe of the party after 1949. The truth is that the emotional ties linking Labour to the Soviet cause were apparently never severed, only loosened. Bryan Magee, a young Gaitskellite at the time, has related a revealing example of how Labour partisans could *en masse* shut their eyes to even blatant evidence of Soviet belligerence. Attending a local Labour meeting shortly after the Hungarian Revolution in 1956, Magee found not only that the great majority of those present refused categorically to believe the reports of eyewitnesses attesting to the brutal role of the Red Army in the revolution, but that in addition the auditors felt compelled one after another to rise from the floor and defend the good name of the Soviet Union.[20]

### LABOUR AND THE UNITED STATES

Not too surprisingly, party images of America were conditioned in large part by the aforementioned changes in images of the Soviet Union.* There was, however, a difference between the two patterns of images from the perspective of their interplay with the government's policy, and this difference is sufficiently impor-

---

* This is to be expected because, as we have already seen, the four principles of socialist foreign policy were all of a piece and so interdependent: changes in one would thus inevitably produce changes in the others.

tant to merit emphasizing at the outset. The previous section sought to establish that the government's policy toward the Soviet Union was not greatly affected by party opinion, except insofar as the policy was probably more restrained during the first year or two than Bevin might have preferred: it was the critics', rather than the government's, attitudes and opinions that were forced to undergo adjustment as time passed. But this pattern was not entirely repeated in the case of party images of the United States. The interplay of attitudes and opinion, of pressures and persuasion, was much greater. As a result, though the critics were once again obliged to accommodate their initial images so as to bring them more in line with the government's policy and with the cumulative development of events, the government itself will be seen to have also found it prudent to adjust its behavior somewhat: to adopt a somewhat more socialist attitude toward the United States, one that became embedded in Labour's peculiar interpretation of Britain's "special relationship" with its Atlantic ally.

## Stage I. 1945: Anxiousness

By the end of the war Labour's traditional suspicion of American capitalism had grown acute in many sections of the party.* Since it was widely believed that henceforth American capitalists would spare no effort to obstruct British socialism, it was also widely believed that the last thing the Labour government should do was to seek intimate ties with the United States. As one backbench member of the PLP gravely warned, in that direction lurked dangers that would "destroy a chance of socialism at home or abroad."

Aside from the socialist principle of anti-capitalism, though not entirely disconnected with it, there appeared to be at least three additional reasons for Labour's pronounced uneasiness about the United States at the time. The first was pro-Soviet sentiment, and in this connection, so long as the majority of the party continued to hanker after extensive Anglo-Soviet cooperation, so long would they naturally object to close ties with the United States. Of the two other reasons, one was psychological in nature, the other pertained to economic matters.

* See above, pp. 114–15.

That psychological pressures were at work in conditioning Labour opinion is suggested by the very vague and highly elusive manner in which party members articulated their mistrust of the United States. For all of the charges they leveled, they never really made it clear why the Truman Administration should harbor ill will toward America's highly regarded wartime ally, still less what specific measures the ill will would take in order to nip British socialism in the bud. The question of socialism, for instance, had been automatically assumed by much of the Labour Party to have influenced the 1945 negotiations for the Anglo-American loan; yet none of the British negotiators themselves took this view—on the contrary.[21] As a result of the ill-defined and indeterminate nature of this mistrust, Leon Epstein has likened Labour's prevailing state of mind at the time to the long-standing American myth regarding a British imperial plot against American independence.[22] The analogy is suggestive. In fact, just as the origin and functions of the American myth could be profitably studied in terms of projection mechanisms, so too could Labour's anti-Americanism after 1945. Certainly many Labour pronouncements suggested that Labour partisans *wanted* to see themselves as under attack by an implacable capitalist foe; and now that the traditional enemy had been apparently vanquished at home in the recent general election, what better substitute was there than the United States? Not only was American capitalism bigger, tougher, and more resolute than the British variety, but the proclaimed determination of the Truman Administration to dismantle wartime economic controls appeared intolerable, almost an affront, to those who assumed as a matter of doctrinal faith that only centralized socialist regulation could adequately cope with the economic problems thrown up by the war. After 1945, in brief, many Labour enthusiasts found it convenient to transfer the focus of their traditional anti-capitalist fears across the ocean.

As for the economic cause of Labour's uneasiness, it derived directly from the belief that Washington's reckless willingness to give free rein to capitalism would inevitably provoke a huge slump, and that this would in turn drag socialist Britain into ruin. Scarcely had the war ended than certain Labour partisans began to foretell the imminent collapse of the unregulated American economy. When the American economy turned out to be enjoying its fastest growth in a generation and with little inflation to boot, this did nothing to ease the party's fears of the predicted collapse. On the contrary, in a determined attempt to make reality conform to their own preconceptions, these same Labour supporters announced their forecasts in increasingly strident terms. The 1946 annual conference was told, for instance, that the American economy was "hysterically chaotic," "absolutely wild," and in general beyond all redemption short of complete socialism.[23] Naturally, a British socialist government would be mad to ally itself with such a dangerous bulwark of archaic capitalism.[24]

Fears of this sort maintained themselves in intense circulation until the European Recovery Program was established. Thereafter less and less was heard in this vein. With the arrival of billions of dollars of Marshall Aid, it was difficult, after all, to snap at the hand that was subsidizing Labour's ambitious social and economic programs. Ministers, happy to disconcert their socialist critics, extolled such American support for British welfarism;* Conservatives, unhappy for their own reasons, deplored the "continued underwriting by the United States of British Labour political objectives."† All the same, many Labour partisans never really got over their initial jitteriness about American capitalism, and during the rearmament crisis of 1950–51, fears concerning the wild American economy made a sudden and noisy public reappearance. This resurgent alarm was not confined to left-wing circles alone. According to press reports, the whole of the 1952 conference cheered loud and strong on hearing from Aneurin Bevan that American economic achievements were illusory, the glittering surface of a basically corrupt social structure dependent for its success on a vast military program.[25]

*Stage II. 1946 to late 1947: Resistance to an American Alliance*

For these reasons, then, much of the mass party pulled in different ways from the government on the desirability of an American

---

* According to Cripps, then Chancellor of the Exchequer: "Without Marshall Aid something like 1½ million men might have been thrown out of work for lack of raw materials, unless we had all accepted a very much lower standard of living, too low to allow us to produce efficiently." *Daily Telegraph*, 15 July 1948.

† Millis, p. 488. See, too, Ernest Watkins, pp. 366–67, where it is argued that "because the men in Washington did not believe that they should interfere [with Britain's Socialist experiment], they allowed the experiment to be worked out where it should have been worked out—in Britain."

alliance. The average rank-and-filer—not just the left—remained suspicious about American policy until well into 1947, psychologically prepared as he was to cast not the Soviet Union but the United States in the role of the likeliest villain in world politics. From the socialist standpoint, the United States alone appeared to possess that unique combination of military power, economic strength, and capitalist social structure needed to make an aggressor.*

The overlap in viewpoint at this stage of the left and other sections of the party is worth elaborating. Whenever the topic of a possible Anglo-American alliance arose, even inveterate moderates might expose nervous reservations. Some simply opposed it on the ground that such a hookup was unnecessary because the developing cold war did not really concern Britain. Others, while conceding that British neutrality was chimerical, nonetheless looked askant at an alliance in the belief that the United States was less dedicated to peace than Britain itself and so would convert any Anglo-American collaboration into a wild anti-Communist crusade. If there was any difference between the moderates and the militants on these scores, it was one of degree, not of kind. On the other hand, it was only to be expected that Bevin's most radical and vociferous critics would exploit these generalized misgivings for their own purpose, playing on the moderates' unease so as to further the socialist offensive against the whole of the government's foreign policy. Thus R. H. S. Crossman warned that Washington's true aim was to form a pact against Communism "whereby Britain provides the soldiers and America the guns."[26] Varying the image, "Keep Left" warned that the government, in working for close American ties, threatened to turn

---

* This belief formed another prominent part in the rebels' case of November 1946. But that anti-American sentiment was intense throughout *every* section of the party is attested by several other pieces of evidence. At the 1946 conference, for instance, a resolution strongly opposed to "tying the economy of Britain with that of capitalist America" mustered 2.5 million votes. And public opinion surveys found an "alarming increase in anti-Americanism" throughout the entire British public at the time. The surveys were not very carefully conducted, responses frequently not being stratified in terms of party affiliation, but it can be safely assumed that the degree of anti-American feeling was significantly greater among Labour as opposed to Conservative supporters. As Mass Observation, a survey organization, found, favorable comment regarding the United States "now comes mainly from Conservatives." Willcock, p. 65.

Britain into "a pensioner of America earning its living by fighting America's war overseas."[27]

Another point worth elaborating is that just as misgivings concerning America were not restricted to the left but instead pervaded the entire Labour Party, neither were they confined to Labour circles only. In reality, such misgivings formed part of the prevailing climate of opinion in Britain at the time.* When the Bevanite publication "One Way Only" asserted that "it is not unknown for a giant to wish to use his strength, even though he is not attacked,"[28] it was not venting simply a radical opinion of the far left. Most Britons, whether Labour, Conservative, or Liberal, worried that the wisdom of American policy would fall far short of its immense power.[29] It is important to appreciate how widespread doubts about the United States were at the time. Coloring the way most Britons came to understand the "special relationship," they drove Labour, legatee of an anti-capitalist tradition, to impart a slight socialist twist to the notion.

We can get at this from a different angle by noting what it was that underlay the contagious uneasiness. Numerous and varied as the causes were, quite clearly resentment of American power and fortunes bulked large. The sentiment was natural enough in the prevailing circumstances. Britain, after all, had fought valiantly during the war, it had emerged a lauded victor, but it also emerged a second-rate power that was temporarily down and out. On the right, among certain Conservative elites schooled to regard their nation as uniquely qualified to rule others, the resentment crystallized as a nagging suspicion that Roosevelt's and Truman's anticolonialism cloaked schemes for making America top dog at Brittain's expense.[30] In the center and on the left, misgivings of this sort naturally exercised the imagination to a lesser extent. But if Labour partisans did not begrudge American power either so openly or so cavalierly as did right-wing Tories, nonetheless they, too, evidenced a longing for greater independence of policy than national resources permitted. In this regard, they and other British progressives were caught in a peculiar dilemma. On the one hand, they regarded dissolution of the Empire (with American prodding) as desirable, the triumph of liberal and socialist ideals.

* The title of Leon Epstein's *Britain, Uneasy Ally*, the best study of the subject, is itself suggestive.

On the other hand, they regretted the undermining of British power that withdrawal apparently signified; for just when they had a government in office that seemed full of good intentions, they saw its ability to act on those intentions gradually vanish. Only the United States had the necessary resources, the necessary capacity, to perform many of the virtuous tasks that Liberals and Labourites set for their own nation. This was often acknowledged by them, and many defended American policy in the face of strident strictures from the extreme left or right—the *Economist* even came to make something of a specialty of this. At the same time, however, they instinctively seemed to assume that Britain itself would have done a better job of things if only it had possessed the means available to America. If only America had dealt with China as wisely as Britain had handled India. If only America had taken the tolerant view of neutral states that Britain did. If only . . . In brief, whatever their political temperament, many Britons found it hard to repress an ambition to act as schoolmaster to the youthful nation across the ocean.[31]

### Stage III. *1948 On: Acceptance of an American Alliance*

By early 1948, the Labour Party was rapidly ridding itself of its initial doubts regarding the value of an Anglo-American alliance. Soviet belligerence over the past few months left its mark here. But it was above all Marshall Aid that was leading to a more favorable attitude toward the United States in Labour circles.

The impact of Marshall Aid can be graphically traced in terms of left-wing behavior at the time. Initially, Marshall's offer had intensified, not lessened, the left's fears of close association with the United States; for it was automatically assumed that the offer could not be genuine, that it concealed a devious plot by means of which Wall Street hoped to escape the inevitable contradictions of a capitalist economy. But faced with obvious American willingness not to attach political conditions to the Economic Recovery Program, the left began subsequently to revise its judgment and to perceive the whole of American policy in an entirely new light. Within months there had occurred a notable shift in images.[32] Gone was the erstwhile socialist thesis concerning a predatory American foreign policy aimed at exporting capitalist surplus and undermining British socialism; in its place appeared a new thesis—one that was still socialist but adapted and adjusted to the improving image of the United States. It was now claimed that American capitalism was not in control of Washington, after all; that rather the "progressive elements" in American life were, as shown by the recent Marshall Aid offer; and that Truman was possibly a bit of a socialist sympathizer himself—or at any rate a firm radical who, in spite of his mid-Western garb and style, at bottom shared the same "moral values as Labour" and had "the same enemies."[33] Enthusiasm for associating socialist Britain with this newly discovered progressive America climbed rapidly among left-wing circles; and by the spring of 1948, socialist stalwarts who had once denounced American policy in uncompromising terms began converting in large numbers to the Anglo-American faith. One of the first to announce his conversion was R. H. S. Crossman. In January 1948 he told the Commons that he "wanted to be frank," that his views of America had changed "a great deal" over the last six months; as late as a mere half-year previous, he "could not have believed" it possible for Washington to offer enormous aid "with as few political conditions."[34] So complete did the identification of Labour's socialist cause with the Truman Administration become, during the following months, that Truman's November electoral victory was hailed as a Labour triumph and a Tory defeat. And when, shortly afterward, the Administration introduced the Point Four program of technical assistance, the Labour Party including the left wing seemed convinced beyond a doubt that they had their own man in the White House.

As these examples suggest, the left—once its image of the United States rapidly improved, owing to the powerful impact of successive events during 1947 and 1948—was essentially straining to make that image as socialist as possible. The reason seems clear enough: the left was explaining to itself why a capitalist nation was behaving cooperatively, indeed most amicably, toward socialist Britain when from the socialist viewpoint it should have been doing the contrary. The explanation was that the United States was not really capitalist after all. Hence, not only could British socialists put up with an American alliance in good faith; what is more, socialist principles could continue to command their allegiance.

The image of covert socialism in the Truman Administration had its advantages: not least that it made an Anglo-American alliance more palatable to the average Labour partisan. But it suffered at the same time from a potentially serious drawback. For it made acceptance of the alliance more or less conditional on poorly understood trends in American politics. The *New States-man* argued that "Mr. Churchill's political future was bound up with Senator Taft's." What then would happen if the Republicans were voted into power? Would the alliance suddenly become anathema again, as it had been prior to June 1947? At the very least, there was the danger that the socialist interpretation of American politics would exaggerate the changes in foreign policy that might accompany a Republican victory.[35]

## Labour and the Special Relationship

In spite of this danger, the party leaders, both in Parliament and at Transport House, nonetheless took pains to cater to their followers' hankering to have the Anglo-American alliance depicted as ideologically desirable. The leadership realized that it was only prudent to do so, because outright appeals to British interests would not themselves suffice to make the alliance respectable, let alone popular. Thus it happened that the Labour government's cooperation with capitalist America came to be justified in no small measure by reference to arguments that accorded, however loosely, with socialist principles.

There were a number of intellectual contrivances to which the leadership had recourse for presenting Anglo-American collaboration in such terms. One of them, touched on earlier, was to portray the Atlantic Pact as a system of collective security, an argument that appealed to Labour biases far more effectively than could talk about a defensive coalition. A variation of this theme was to counter criticism with reminders that the United States fully supported the United Nations, thereby creating the impression that Britain was bound to the United States more by common membership in the international organization than by alliance ties. Yet a third contrivance was to ease rank-and-file doubts concerning predatory American capitalism by arguing away the capitalism of American society. To be sure, once Marshall Aid began leading to an improved image of the United States, it was less and less necessary to argue so; yet even then members of the government could be found reassuring their followers in terms such as that "the United States is as much a welfare state as we are only in a different form."[36]

But far and away the most popular means of rendering the alliance acceptable was to disguise the degree of British dependence on American power. That is, the power relationship of the two nations was either discarded as unimportant or simply ignored. Britons of every political outlook, not just Labour partisans alone, were naturally pleased to have the alliance depicted as a "partnership" wherein Britain, even if materially weaker, was thought to more than compensate for this by virtue of nonmaterial assets such as greater experience in world affairs. The effect of representing the alliance in these terms was to enshroud the notion of Anglo-American cooperation in equivocation and thereby to lead Labour into its peculiar interpretation of the "special relationship."

The latter is an important point, a major way station on the line of our argument. In order to avoid misunderstanding of the remainder, some elementary observations regarding alliance systems deserve to be noted.

Any operative alliance requires its various members to modify their policy and their behavior in deference to each other's views, and an alliance like NATO in which power is very unevenly distributed is no exception. Indeed, if anything, the most powerful member would do well to go out of its way to reassure its weaker allies, for otherwise the alliance risks degenerating in their eyes into a mere relationship of hegemony-dependence. No one in Britain, of course, wanted his country to be treated as a mere dependent; and the Labour government was thus only doing what any British government would have done when it insisted that Britain's voice in matters of common concern be attentively listened to in American councils. As Clement Attlee said, Britain would never tolerate being "regarded as a mere tool of any other country."[37] It was no less proper for Britons, if they so desired, to look upon the alliance as a partnership that was the more valuable in that it afforded their government the opportunity to hand advice to supposedly inexperienced American policy makers.* The latter view was, to be sure, seldom expressed in these terms.

---

* As Epstein shrewdly notes (*Britain, Uneasy Ally*, p. 34): "it was not merely paradoxical that the realistic appraisers of Britain's postwar dependence on American power ... should be the most eager to have the relationship as near to equality as possible," for this would make the exercise of the British "tutorial role ... more credible and more satisfying."

Both prudence and politeness required a more politic course, and this was to insist upon the need for extensive "consultation." In the quasi-official opinion of *The Times*: "Britain has much to give, by way of counsel and initiative, to the shaping, still tentative and uncertain, of a world policy, political and economic, "at the summit" in America; and it is today as always the special feature of their special bond that, whatever the balance of power between them they can, and should, talk together as free men."[38] These simple and banal observations, to repeat, are intended to prevent any misunderstanding of what follows. For the fact of the matter is that the demand on the British side to influence American policy as a condition of the alliance went far beyond a mere asking for consultation.

At first the demand was carefully framed. Britain, it was widely said, should and must be treated as a partner of the United States, not its dependent. But as time passed, and Britons worried when it was realized how little leverage their nation actually had over American policy, the demand for consultation and equal treatment was less and less interpreted to mean simply that American policy should be adjusted to allow for British views. Instead, the demand came seemingly to mean that, on divisive issues of alliance policy, the British voice should *always* be listened to as automatically both wisest and most prudent. What accounted for this somewhat immodest translation in the British view of the special relationship?

On the right of the political spectrum, the answer is pretty straightforward: the alliance was valued in Tory circles because of the opportunities it might afford for harnessing British diplomatic skill to raw American power. To say this is not to deny that Conservatives also valued the alliance because it enhanced British security. Indeed, from the perspective of traditional policy, no other justification would have been needed. Still, the statements of many prominent Conservative spokesmen made it plain that they also had more ambitious objectives in mind—objectives that assumed far greater British influence in alliance policy than British power alone would have suggested. Typical was the remark of Viscount Hinchingbrooke when he wrote: "The Americans provide the hustle, the resilience, and strength of their capitalist economy, and we provide diplomacy, interpretation, conciliation, wisdom and poise."[39] This outpouring of national pride was not confined to the right. The left wing of the Labour Party championed its own version: Britain's moral influence. "Moral influence alone can save the world," R. H. S. Crossman told the Commons, and he was not noticeably modest in discussing Britain's claim to it.* In short, left-wingers no more doubted that men of good will would hasten to heed their moral counsel than did many Tories that the young novices in Washington were eager for their worldly advice on statecraft.

Predominant Labour opinion, for its part, was more modest. Nonetheless it, too, interpreted the special relationship in a manner that overstated British influence in the alliance. In particular, the demand that the British voice must always prevail in disputes was advanced because most Labour partisans assumed, as a matter of course, that the British role would invariably be one of moderating American policy. This was not necessarily a question of American intentions. In the immediate postwar aftermath, it is true, even Labour moderates had nursed doubts on this score; but by 1948 nearly everyone except certain left-wing diehards was willing to grant that the United States was probably peace-loving. The question was rather one relating to the degree of the American commitment to peace. And in this connection Labour *en masse* seemed convinced that the United States was less determined than Britain itself. The party feared that American policy makers did not have a sufficiently prudent fear of the dangers of war and consequently that they might be willing to risk bold measures which could only provoke the Soviet Union. For this reason, therefore, the cautious hand of British statesmanship supposedly would be needed to keep American policy firmly under leash.

The causes of Labour's apprehension are easy enough to isolate. Three in particular are worth attention, two of them being directly bound up with socialist principles. The cause that has nothing to do with socialism was not in fact restricted in its influence to Labour circles—the different wartime experience of the two countries. Britons, having been exposed to German aerial attack at a

* 430 *H.C.Deb.* 538 (18 November 1946). Five years later Aneurin Bevan was so certain that Britain had the "moral leadership of the world" that all mankind was told "where to go and how to go there" by the British example. 487 *H.C.Deb.* 39 (23 April 1951).

time when the American continent had remained invulnerable, were convinced that they were more alert to the dangers of war in the nuclear age than Americans themselves. But beyond that, it seems that the average Labour partisan was never able to shed his strongly rooted feeling that capitalism and war were somehow all of a piece. During the interwar period especially, the anti-capitalist principle had dominated Labour thinking; and it was thus not altogether surprising that even when the party's image of America measurably improved, beginning in 1947, a thick residue of unease remained—how much, indeed, the Bevanites were to discover to their benefit after 1950. In the third place, finally, most prominent Labour spokesmen recoiled from the outspoken American tendency to regard Communism *per se* as the major threat of the time. The behavior of the American public in this connection naturally added to the belief that Americans as a whole were self-righteous, impetuous, and immoderate. The belief, to be sure, was not just a Labour preoccupation, but the principle of anti-capitalism gave it a sense of urgency that it lacked in non-Labour circles.

The argument has now brought us full circle. The Labour leadership found it profitable to cater to the party's desire for an ideologically respectable Anglo-American relationship; obviously, then, the easiest way to sustain the desired impression was for the government to act out the special relationship as the party understood it. Of course, the government would probably have sought to maximize its influence over American policy in any case. That was only reasonable and to be expected. At the same time, the government's actions suggest that its motives went beyond considerations of foreign policy proper: that, in truth, its actions were also intended in large part to influence not American policy makers but rather domestic opinion and above all to keep the Labour Party satisfied. Again, the government's motives in doing the latter were not unreasonable; it was faced with a mass of restive followers, and it naturally had to do what it could to quiet their fears and objections. But the trouble was that the government's behavior also entailed certain unanticipated drawbacks.

For instance, the world "consultation" came to acquire somewhat peculiar overtones. Ministers might intone it whenever Labour backbenchers gave signs of growing particularly restive over some new departure in American policy. On such occasions it turned out that the line of least resistance was to express public concern about the new American course and to promise to do what was needed in the way of modifying it. In this way, the government reassured Labour partisans that it was performing the proper British role in the special relationship.

In themselves, there was nothing improper about the Labour government's efforts to influence American policy, particularly when that policy seemed imprudent. As a major ally of the United States, Britain had every right to ask for consultation and to use it for the purpose of modifying American aims; and for its part the American government had a no less tangible obligation to give its closest ally a fair hearing. But the question is: on divisive issues whose view would normally prevail, the American or the British? Quite obviously the American would, for the reason that the British were more dependent on American power for their security than vice versa (which is only another way of saying, of course, that the maintenance of the Anglo-American alliance was more in the British than the American interest). This hard fact of the power relationship between the two nations seems almost self-evident. Yet it appears to have escaped Labour's grasp. The power factor was obscured, apparently, because it conflicted directly with the party's conception of the special relationship.

The conception was thus self-deceptive. And as such it involved the danger that the Labour Party, once its initial optimism about the degree of British influence became frustrated, might despair and in its despair sour on the whole idea of an Anglo-American alliance. In fact, this is more or less what happened during the 1950's. A large body of the party, including part of the leadership, began openly regretting the alliance, protesting that it had reduced Great Britain to nothing less than an American vassal.

Arguably, had the party been forced to a more realistic view of the alliance from the outset—had, that is, the leadership not so carefully ministered to its followers' wish to ignore the power relationship between Britain and America—then much of the trouble over foreign policy that the party experienced in the 1950's might have been avoided. No doubt it is too easy to say this in retrospect, more than a decade after the events in question. No doubt the leadership spared as much effort as it thought wise at the time in ladling nonsocialist policies down socialist throats—and if there were means at hand for making the policies more palatable, then it was obviously going to have recourse to them. It may even be unreasonable to ask that harried policy makers so modify their calculations as always to consider the long-run repercussions that will affect only a section of the community. But it may not be entirely unreasonable. There are, after all, degrees of realism, and the point that the previous paragraphs have tried to establish is that the Labour Party's conception of the special relationship was very low on the scale. At the very least, a more realistic view of the alliance might have had the merit of publicly airing where and to what extent British and American interests did not converge, as a result of which each side might have had a better appreciation of the other's objectives.* Labour's conception of the special relationship lacked this merit because it generated an attitude whereby the party simply assumed that if the interests of the two nations did not mesh, this was inevitably due to American rashness.

### The Far East

The most striking example of the confusion and misunderstanding that could ensue concerned the Far East, as events during the fall of 1950 demonstrated.

This was the one area where American and British interests not only did not converge but openly conflicted to a certain extent. Different historical involvement, sharply divergent geographical and strategic considerations, dissimilar commercial and colonial stakes, the problems of India, Japan, and especially China—all of this tended to prevent a full coincidence of interests on the part of the two nations.[40] Naturally then American policy in the area was bound to generate at least some criticism in Britain. On balance the policy may even have been unwise, but the point is that neither its defects nor its merits were discussed in concrete terms against the background of the different interests of the two nations. That background was scarcely noticed in Labour circles (or, for that

---

* For that matter, one might further argue that a more realistic view would also have had the merit of disclosing that the interests of Britain and the United States did not differ fundamentally anywhere save in one area (discussed in the next section), and that therefore most of the disputes between Britain and the United States after 1950 were connected more with different national styles than with the substance of particular issues. As a recent British observer has noted, "Even under the most explicit apologist for the moral line, John Foster Dulles, it is doubtful whether the substance of American policy toward the U.S.S.R. was significantly different from that of Britain." (H. G. Nicholas, p. 169.)

matter, in other British circles).⁴¹ Instead, prompted by its feeling that where British and American policy differed this had to be due to American rashness, the Labour Party resorted to commentary that automatically condemned American behavior as naïve, self-righteous, and immoderate.⁴² And this being the case, it followed no less automatically that the Labour government was urged to uphold the party's conception of the Anglo-American alliance by moderating American policy. Not too surprisingly, the Korean War further intensified the party's concern. For despite the fact that Labour had originally welcomed the American intervention, the entrance of massive Chinese forces in the autumn led to fears that Washington would sooner or later recklessly touch off a general Asian conflagration.⁴³

It was in this nervous atmosphere that news arrived regarding a 30 November press conference in which Truman stated that his Administration was "considering" the use of nuclear weapons in Korea. That it was an unfortunately ambiguous statement, made in hasty response to an unexpected question, was recognized by Truman himself; he immediately had his press secretary issue a clarification to the effect that "consideration of the use of any weapon is always implicit in the very possession of that weapon," but that the aim of American policy to keep the war limited remained unaltered.⁴⁴ The damage was done, however. In the Commons, the subject was debated with considerable apprehension voiced on all sides, but particularly by Labour backbenchers worked up about the wild men in Washington.⁴⁵ It was at this point that Attlee rose to announce, dramatically and unexpectedly, that the Cabinet had decided on the wisdom of his journeying to Washington. The role of the British moderator was to be played to the full.

No doubt the Cabinet, if not necessarily fearful of the wild men, was anxious about current American policy. No doubt it was disturbed lest Washington attach greater priority to Asia than to Europe. By itself, then, Attlee's decision to journey to Washington to represent the British viewpoint in person was understandable. Yet if the decision itself was not unreasonable, the same cannot be altogether said about the dramatic manner in which it was sprung on the nation. Not only did Attlee convey an impression that the government shared the worst apprehension concerning American policy, but even more it seemed as if the principal objective of his trip was to save the world from incredible American folly. In this regard, the chapter heading in Francis Williams's book that relates Attlee's memoirs of the trip—"To Stop A Third World War"—seems no accident. Yet at the time neither Attlee's letter to Truman requesting a meeting nor his letter to the King explaining the reasons for the trip touched more than very obliquely on the matter of Truman's statement.[46] For that matter, the trip, as Attlee himself confided to the King, had "been under consideration for some time." Nonetheless, as well as doing nothing to contradict the public belief that his trip was primarily to deter the Americans, Attlee informed the Commons, upon his return, that he was now "satisfied" that the Truman Administration would henceforth comport itself with restraint.[47]

The implication, as well noted at the time, was obvious. If no atomic bomb was dropped, was this not due to the firm hand of British diplomacy? Most Labour partisans had no reason to doubt that the answer should be decidedly affirmative. Nor was the trip of December 1950 an isolated instance of the confusion that could arise. Other ministers as well as prominent Labour spokesmen outside Parliament were not beyond claiming credit that (to quote a recent British study) "British pressure and reasoning was ... behind all the sound decisions of the Administration not only in the case of Attlee restraining Truman from using the atomic bomb on North Korea and from going to war with China, but also in the relief of MacArthur, an operation for which Shinwell was later to claim partial responsibility."[48] In short, Labour's conception of the special relationship was universally believed to have fully justified itself. The Labour government had played its crucial role in the alliance and in doing so had moderated American policy and saved the peace.

That the Labour Party was deceiving itself, and in part because of the leadership's behavior, was disclosed a few years later with the publication of Truman's *Memoirs*. Attlee, according to Truman's account, far from having saved the world, had in fact scarcely touched on the topic of the atomic bomb during the course of his four-day talks with the President. Moreover, the only time he did broach the subject was by way of an aside—after the formal talks had been concluded and while the communiqué was already in the process of being drafted. In reply Truman assured Attlee that he had never intended to employ the bomb, and briefly explained how his press conference statement had been misunderstood. And this, evidently, was the full extent of the exchange. Attlee quickly let the topic pass after he and Truman agreed to insert in the communiqué a short passage clarifying their joint position on the use of atomic weapons.[49]

Such, then, was the impact that the Labour government apparently had in boldly modifying American recklessness. Attlee's subsequent account in Francis Williams's book, it should be added, does nothing to discredit Truman's version. The chapter heading "To Stop A Third World War" thus seems out of place, if not ostentatious. Significantly, at least one prominent left-wing critic of the government's foreign policy arrived at precisely this conclusion years later. Reviewing Truman's second volume of memoirs in the *New Statesman*, R. H. S. Crossman was sufficiently surprised to discover that Labour had not actually saved the world in the manner claimed by Labour Party lore that he was moved to urge his fellows to reexamine the whole notion of Labour's "moral influence." As he said: "We have all made speeches about the Labour Government's moral influence in Washington and the restraint it exerted on America's wild men. In fact these claims fail to do credit to the courage and will-power of Harry Truman. The President, on his own initiative, exercised both the moral influence and the restraint. No doubt it sustained him to know that his major ally either backed his policies or—as in the case of Communist China's admission to the UN—was content to register a formal protest. But the fact remains that the Labour government was so nervous of losing American support that it conceded the Americans bomber bases in Norfolk without demanding any *quid pro quo*, and then reversed its publicly declared opposition to Germany as soon as Mr. Acheson insisted on it."[50]

In the short run, Labour's notion of a special relationship probably had a salutary effect. It offered reassurance, in the face of considerable unease throughout the ranks, that the Labour government was more than holding its own in the alliance—that it was exercising massive restraint on the policy makers in Washington and preserving peace accordingly. The long-run impact of the notion was less benign. For it only encouraged those in the party who were all too ready as things stood to downplay considerations of power, and who, for instance, argued during the conflicts of the 1950's that Britain's influence and authority in the world had nothing to do with such mundane matters as membership in an alliance resting on a threat of nuclear retaliation.

### LABOUR AND THIRD FORCE NEUTRALISM

"[The Labour government's foreign policy] should provide a democratic and constructive Socialist alternative to the otherwise inevitable conflict between American capitalism and Soviet Communism in which all hope of world government would be destroyed [1946]."[51]

"This great nation has a message for the world which is distinct from that of America and that of the Soviet Union [1951]."[52]

"We [the Labour Party] can best serve the cause of peace by sticking to our distinctive Socialist principles, and refusing to subordinate them to American, Russian or other pressures [1952]."[53]

The third force was the alternative to the government's foreign policy which its critics in the Labour Party vigorously espoused from mid-1946 to about late 1948. It originated in the recognition by all except a few diehard socialists that Anglo-Soviet cordiality was improbable for the time being and that, accordingly, socialist foreign policy as initially conceived at the war's end had to be shelved for the time being too. With that revelation, there remained but two alternatives for British policy. One, the course already chosen by the government, pointed to alliance with the United States. Until the party's major images shifted to the American favor in 1948, this course, naturally, did not recommend itself to Bevin's numerous critics; in its direction lurked dead certain subservience to American capitalism, subsequent subversion of British socialism, and sure-fire aggravation of East-West tension. The second alternative, the one more acceptable from the socialist viewpoint, pointed toward a "middle" road. Breaking with traditional practices, Britain would spurn power jockeying and pursue a different, a radical, a socialist course in world politics: in short, a third force policy.

In concrete terms, the policy reduced to the demand that Britain should form and lead a bloc of nations in Western Europe.

This bloc would be neutralist, social-democratic, and strong enough to guarantee its integrity and security; as such, it would be in the position to mediate between East and West and so save the world from an otherwise inevitable war. To the Labour spokesmen who championed the policy, Britain was uniquely suited for leadership of the third force: being socialist, it had no reason to take sides in a conflict between Communism and capitalism; being incomparably experienced in world affairs, a world power in its own right, and highly regarded by others, it would be the leader by default. To the same spokesmen, Britain even had a solemn *moral* obligation to take the middle course. According to "Keep Left," for example, the world deserved an alternative to a sterile choice between anti-Communism and Communism.[54] Just as the Labour government was wisely steering "a middle way between capitalism and Communist planning" at home, so it should apply the same logic to foreign affairs and carefully steer between "the sharp alternatives of a world rule by America and a world rule by Russia."[55]

At the bottom of the third force idea can be discerned a powerful longing, a passionate yearning, to contract out of the developing East-West struggle. In turn, this emotional state of mind was largely the outgrowth of socialist principles.[56] Labour partisans had been conditioned by socialist policy to assume that peace and cooperation were the natural order of things and that conflict was illusory, a grievous mistake owing to misunderstanding and miscalculation. The notion that nations might come into conflict because of *incompatible aims* was thus alien to this socialist view— so much so, indeed, that the party could flatly state in 1944 that "we are confident that the vital interests of all nations are the same. They all need peace."[57] Consequently, did it not follow that the developing cold war was all a mistake? If the two superpowers could not get along amicably, was this not due in large measure to their lack of experience in world affairs, their unbalanced social systems, their self-righteousness and immoderation? And why then should Britain involve itself in their needless, meaningless conflict? Would not the wiser course be one of vigorous neutralism, Britain remaining carefully aloof from the conflict the better to isolate it and to bring the two disputants to their senses? Such, in brief, were the principal socialist assumptions behind the logic of the third force policy, which was intended to point the way toward British disengagement.\*

### The Origins of the Third Force Policy

Although the third force policy was not actively espoused until mid-1946, it was rooted in the hope, widely held in Labour circles during the war, of general European revolution. At the 1945 conference, convened in May, a number of speakers made lavish reference to the anticipated revolution and demanded that the party construct its entire foreign policy in support of it. As called upon by Denis Healey, for instance, Labour was not to hesitate in giving both "protection and assistance" to the revolution; Healey added that violence and bloodshed might ensue, but insisted that this possibility must not deter the party from remaining faithful to its socialist commitment.†

At that date, the eventual third force enthusiasts foresaw no incompatibility between promoting European revolution and cooperating with the Soviet Union. It was assumed, amidst the euphoria of "left understands left" thinking, that the Soviet leaders automatically favored the same sort of revolution that Labour itself anticipated. At the September London Conference of Foreign Ministers, where deadlock ensued, this assumption received its first hard knock. The revelation of East-West disunity came as a shock to socialist mainstays, and some of the more imaginative appreciated the need to rethink the party's foreign policy. For all practical purposes the alternative they hit upon, in their discussions during September and October, was third force neutralism, though at this early stage its rationale remained ill-defined and its implications uncertain.[58] Before this new socialist alternative would be more fully thought out, it was necessary that the still widespread and lively hope of collaboration with the Soviet Union be further overtaken by East-West events.

---

\* Just how powerfully these assumptions were felt can be gauged from the way in which they have continued to sway the thinking of certain Labour partisans. Thus A. J. P. Taylor, in a recent review of a book dealing with the cold war, writes: "The 'cold war' was an American invention from start to finish and is dying away, or so they say, because the Americans themselves are ceasing to believe in it." *The Observer Review*, 26 February 1967, p. 27.

† See above, pp. 90–91.

## The Third Force Policy Matured

In the eyes of its advocates, the third force policy required socialist neighbors in Europe. Until mid-1946 or so, this requirement was roughly satisfied because the Continental socialist parties were significant forces in the politics of several West European nations. Then came the various elections of 1946, and the government's critics watched in dismay as one socialist party after another suffered setbacks. The prospects of a third force policy were now widely assumed, in left-wing ranks, to be rapidly vanishing and in danger of complete disappearance unless the Labour government stopped its shilly-shallying and gave a bold lead to the European left. The *Tribune*, for instance, noting that the "Revolutionary Spring of European Liberation" was fizzling out, warned that a socialist departure in British foreign policy had to be made now or never.[59] How desperate the Labour third-forcers were growing may be gauged from the acrid, almost abusive manner in which the *New Statesman*'s "Re-orientation" series attacked Bevin personally. Among other things, he was accused of having become a secret convert to anti-Communism following the General Election, of acting like a trade union tyrant in party councils, and of letting himself be made the docile tool of the anti-socialist staff in the Foreign Office.*

It was against this tense background that dozens of Labour MP's gambled on staging what was earlier termed an open "rebellion" on the floor of the Commons. In late October, the group (estimates of whose size vary from a low of 52 all the way to 100[60]) gave a forewarning of its intent by sending Attlee a letter enumerating its major grievances.[61] In essence they reduced to one paramount charge: the government had so far failed to live up to the expectations it had aroused during the recent General Elections. The voters were said to have plumped for "the middle way" in foreign policy; they expected both a British lead to the socialists on the Continent and concrete measures on behalf of world government. Yet far from having done either, the government had by its actions in office only "brought discouragement to Democratic Socialists"; whether by design or default, the effect of its

---

* See above, pp. 137–38.

actions was driving Britain into the American orbit. The rebels, failing to get satisfaction, decided to move their case to the floor of the Commons.

The debate that ensued was used to air standard socialist criticisms and to try isolating Bevin from the rest of the Cabinet.[62] But the rebels did not limit themselves to strictures only. Crossman, who introduced the amendment, proceeded to unpack an able argument in favor of a third force policy, the only policy that accorded with Labour's venerable socialistic principles and offered a realistic hope for peace. He exhorted at one point, in good socialist logic, that "the aim of our foreign policy" should be "to carry out in foreign affairs what we are doing in domestic affairs."[63] To date, however, the government had not given the slightest hint of its intention to bring foreign and domestic policy in line; as yet, it had not provided any meaningful alternative to "the Fulton Policy which regards Russia like Nazi Germany." There might be a question, Crossman conceded, of Britain's capacity to pursue a successful socialist middle course, but the answer in his estimation was that it obviously could. For much as British power was overshadowed by the material resources of both America and Russia, the nation nonetheless enjoyed one priceless asset, its moral influence—and moral influence "alone" could save the world.

Much of Attlee's skillful rejoinder has already been dealt with, in the context of the rebels' effort to isolate Bevin.* What is worth recalling is that Attlee directly replied to the demand for a third force policy, which he dismissed as absurd—a figment of vivid imagination which had "to stretch out for facts to support it[self]." Both the tenor and substance of Attlee's remarks made it evident that the rebels were not going to get as much as a scrap of satisfaction from the frontbench. Indeed they themselves turned out to be embarrassed by their gambit, and asked that their amendment not be pressed to a division.†

This did not mean, however, that the third force advocates were ready to give up. The exact opposite was the case, for the publicity given to third force ideas during the rebellion led to noticeably

---

* See above, pp. 138–39.

† Nonetheless it was pressed to a division at the insistence of two former members of the Independent Labour Party. Crossman and his fellow rebels abstained.

increased interest in party circles around the nation. If Parliament itself was not a serviceable vehicle for further discussion, other means were available, and there ensued over the next few months a spate of writing and oratory that simultaneously denounced the government's betrayal of socialist principles and urged the leadership to repent by introducing a third force policy. The *Tribune* was particularly vigorous in championing the cause, noting in its first issue following the rebels' abortive efforts that the government had not made the slightest socialist gesture in foreign policy during its fifteen months in office.[64] Several pamphlets and essays emphasizing third force ideas, such as Leonard Woolf's "Foreign Policy: The Labour Party's Dilemma," also blossomed during this interval, culminating in the spring 1947 publication of "Keep Left," the most influential of the lot ever written.

### The Third Force and Power Politics

One of the more curious features of the third force policy was its ambivalent stand on power politics. For enthusiastic as most of its advocates were about the efficacy of moral influence, not all of them advanced the policy out of pacifist convictions only. Britain was not to pursue the middle way in world affairs from a position of military weakness.[65] If the envisaged British-led bloc were to intervene in world affairs on behalf of peace and socialism, it had to be "strong enough to deter an aggressor."[66] More specifically, for it to be strong enough to deter a Soviet-American conflagration, it had somehow to wield military power approaching that of either Russia or the United States.[67]

For this reason, accordingly, most of the November 1946 rebels decided to support the Labour government's controversial Conscription Bill in March 1947. The bill, which proposed to establish the first peacetime draft in British history, encountered enormous opposition from Labour's own ranks, even among otherwise loyal trade union backbenchers. Yet few of the party's prominent third force proponents were among the dissenters. In their view, the Labour government had to have sufficient military resources at its disposal so that a third force policy, when initiated, could operate from a base of tangible strength. As the *Tribune* later explained: pending world government, the Labour government armed would be a "far greater factor for peace" than if it remained unarmed and had "only pious resolutions at its dispos-al."[68] Plainly, for all their attacks on the government's traditional foreign policy, the third force critics were not really opposed to power politics *per se*. Power was all right, provided it promised to serve the correct ideological objectives. In this respect, the third force policy represented a break of sorts with the Labour Party's pre-1939 anti-militarism.

But only "of sorts." For to the degree that the third force champions rested their approval of power on strictly ideological grounds, they were in effect reviving the argument that had been employed by Cripps and the Socialist League. The latter had objected to British rearmament, not on traditional pacifist grounds, but rather because of their class-biased distrust of the National government; they had not disapproved of armaments that promised to strengthen the working class vis-à-vis its class enemies.* The attitude of the third-forcers of 1946–48 was not very different. They objected to large defense expenditures only if these expenditures would strengthen the government's hand in conducting a traditional balance-of-power policy; but they were willing to support a measure like conscription so long as there remained a flicker of hope that it could eventually be used to serve their own ideological purposes.

### The Decline of the Third Force

Enthusiasm for the third force policy reached a peak at about the same time "Keep Left" appeared, in the late spring of 1947. Shortly afterward opinion within the party shifted markedly, and within a year the policy had lost most of its appeal, even to those who had appended their names to "Keep Left" itself. There were above all two principal reasons for this evolution of opinion.

The first was a major theme of earlier sections: the discovery by the Labour Party, including the left wing, of "socialist" allies in Washington. As the *Tribune* observed in early 1948, the important question was no longer how to find a middle way in foreign policy, but only how to continue the socialization of the Anglo-American relationship.[69] The more the government's erstwhile socialist critics became preoccupied with the supposed ideological possibilities of the alliance, the more they lost interest in third

* See above, pp. 25–26.

force notions. Many even came to express publicly their repudiation of the third force policy. Thus Crossman, in one of his recurrent professions of personal beliefs to the House of Commons,
admitted on one occasion that he had once been a third-forcer,
only to add that he had clearly been wrong in not foreseeing at
the time "the great expansion of American foreign policy and
possibilities."[70] While Crossman's personal vision of a socialist
Anglo-American bloc was suffused with heady enthusiasm,* it did
not differ too much in substance from what other sometime third-
forcers came to say. The "Keeping Left" group proclaimed in 1950,
for instance, that the foreign policy of the old "Keep Left" days
had to be "scrapped" now that better socialist prospects in the
form of the American alliance had arrived.[71] Even the Bevanites
were not entirely removed from this kind of thinking. Thus "One
Way Only," the most important elaboration of their viewpoint,
claimed as late as June 1951 that there still remained a chance to
make the Anglo-American alliance genuinely socialist if only the
Labour government would exploit its influence in Washington.[72]

This brings us to the second reason for the declining attraction
of the third force policy: the party's recognition, by the end of
1947, that Western Europe was no longer ripe for revolution. By
1948 nearly every section, the center and the right no less than the
left, was dismissing European politics as hopelessly reactionary—
poor soil for socialist cultivation. Even prominent third force advocates were obliged to grant this. Thus, for instance, only a few
months after "Keep Left" had designated an Anglo-French alliance as socialism's sole hope of salvation, the *New Statesman* came
full circle and warned that the French Cabinet was now "dominated by bankers and men of affairs."[73] The more the Labour
party flinched from involvement in European integration, the faster third-forcers abandoned the "middle way" in foreign policy.
Where once socialists had, in 1946–47, detected economic disaster
in close ties with America, in 1949–50 they detected no less a disaster in close relations with Europe. As the *Tribune* emphasized
at one point, "to plunge into European integration [was] to fall in

---

* For instance: "Accept the Cold War as the challenge of this century and the
Fair Deal as a potential ally, and you have the beginnings of a socialist foreign
policy which can achieve that 'agreement to disagree' between East and West
which is the only alternative to war." Crossman, "Reflections on the Cold War,"
pp. 14–15.

with methods of ruthless deflation and *laissez-faire* now prevalent on the Continent."[74]

These grave notes sounded similar to the strong reservations that Hugh Dalton had expressed the previous year at the 1948 conference. Thus even if belatedly the critics in the party joined with the government in dismissing European ties in foreign policy. By 1950 third force champions were few and far between, not to mention somewhat reticent in espousing their views; and the way was clear for the kind of nationalist abuse with which "European Unity" greeted the Schuman proposal.

## Neutralist Residues

Nonetheless neutralist notions did not entirely fade, any more than pro-Soviet sentiment ever did. If the third force policy fell into disfavor beginning in 1948, the neutralist impulse behind it was not so much banished as repressed in the upsurge of excitement that led socialist critics to devote themselves to Anglo-American ties. As a result, there lingered a distinct danger that once the illusions surrounding those ties were punctured, socialist exuberance would sour and neutralist longings be reawakened in the ensuing disenchantment. In fact, something like this swept through party ranks following the outbreak of the Korean War.

The reaction can be traced, for instance, in the behavior of R. H. S. Crossman, usually a good barometer of the ups and downs of sentiment among the government's critics. It will be recalled that, as late as the winter of 1950–51, Crossman assured his fellows that the cold war was the socialist challenge of the century. At almost this very moment, however, the Labour government introduced its third and biggest increase in British rearmament, and suddenly Crossman and most other former third-forcers discovered that their foreign policy of 1946–47 had been generally correct after all. By autumn 1951 Crossman was discussing American policy in terms of unqualified gloom.[75] At the 1952 conference he made reference to the "hysterical fear in Washington and in the Kremlin" and warned that, in the event of war, socialists should cultivate a diligent neutralism.[76]

Once again, moreover, British neutralism was taken to mean, not a policy of quietude, but rather an active, an energetic alternative; in short, the leadership of some powerful third force bloc. A problem now arose, however, that had not been present during the 1946–47 period: since Western Europe was no longer viewed as a suitable ally, with which nations was a neutral bloc to be established?

Crossman himself made one proposal. This was with Tito's Yugoslavia, or more precisely the "national Communism" it represented, since even the most anti-militaristic Labour socialist realized that Yugoslavia itself was too weak to figure as a potential mainstay of the new British-led force.[77] Another possibility—one that became very popular among Bevanite ranks—was to advocate that Britain throw in its lot with the neutralist underdeveloped nations. In doing so Britain could, at a stroke, shake loose from the American alliance, unilaterally renounce nuclear weapons, and join the ranks of Nehru, Nasser, and (eventually) Nkrumah. The prospect was all the more attractive because of its apparent opportunities for British leadership: as the original third-forcers had seen their socialist European bloc as British-led, so the Bevanites saw the new neutralist bloc as eager for British tutelage. Bevan himself asserted again and again that the underdeveloped nations were anxiously awaiting the "uncompromising lead" that a morally invigorated socialist Britain could offer.[78] Neither Bevan nor his followers ever spelled out their reasons why the ex-colonials should welcome such a lead. Perhaps it was a question of their exaggerated notion of Britain's moral stature. Perhaps it was an inverted imperialism. Maybe it was merely talking to the wrong people in the underdeveloped areas. In any case, whatever the reasons, there was no denying that leadership of the third world was assumed to be a concrete means of translating socialist principles into policy during the 1950's.

The most striking instance took place in 1953, on the occasion of an address that Bevan made to the Indian Parliament. Urging the creation of a third force, he dwelt on the enormous influence it could exert in world affairs: the new bloc would encompass the entire spectrum of underdeveloped nations, eventually effect a realignment of world power, and thereby compel the "two giants —Russia and America—to see wisdom."[79] Nehru lost no time in repudiating the entire scheme as both fanciful and dangerous. Talk of a third bloc, he warned, only "frightens and embarrasses" people; he further observed that the cause of peace was best served "without too much shouting."[80] Bevan was evidently not too dampened in spirit by this reproach. Upon his return to England he was once more entreating the Labour Party "to put itself at the head of those forces which are genuinely concerned to mediate between the two great Power blocs into which the world is perilously divided."[81]

### LABOUR AND POWER POLITICS

"I believe the way to meet Fascism is not by force of arms, but by showing that with co-operation in the economic sphere far better conditions are obtainable than by pursuing a policy of aggression [1937]."[82]

"Soviet Communism cannot conquer the world except as a result of social and economic collapse in the non-communist world, and the first line of democracy's defense must be a policy of full employment and fair shares [1950]."[83]

Historically, nothing about traditional policy struck Labour partisans as more objectionable than its use of force as a major instrument. Reliance on force ran counter to all four socialist principles. It contradicted internationalism, becoming the *ultima ratio* in the defense of selfish national interests; it clashed with class consciousness because it reduced the workers to mere cannon fodder in times of war; it conflicted with anti-capitalism by enabling the imperialist powers to maintain control over backward nations. Finally, of course, it flew in the face of the anti-militarist principle itself. As Attlee said in 1937, "the Party is agreed in its rejection of the policy of the Balance of Power and of the use of force as an instrument of policy."[84]

Naturally, then, it followed that Labour was also historically opposed to armaments, the instruments of force. Arms were regarded by the party as evil in themselves: they tempted leaders, bred a war mentality, ultimately made war inevitable. Once again an able statement of the party's feeling can be found in the utterances of Attlee, who proclaimed in 1935, shortly before attaining the PLP leadership: "It is impossible for us to get any kind of security through rearmament. The only way we can have it is by trusting each other, and armaments breed distrust."[85]

After 1945 matters became more complicated. On the one hand, the Labour government maintained a consistently high level of defense expenditures—the highest of any non-Communist nation till 1950. From the government standpoint, such massive defense efforts were entirely reasonable; they followed directly from its choice of foreign policy and were indispensable to the policy's execution. On the other hand, whatever the rationale, the government's military efforts could hardly be squared with socialist principles. To many Labour partisans, such militarism loomed as the most blatant betrayal of all, and they assailed defense budgets and force allocations with no less vigor than they did British behavior in Greece, or in Iran, or in Germany. In essence their criticism was three-pronged.

### 1. The Moral Argument

Almost as a reflex action, the government's critics resorted to moral arguments first. Their case, stripped to the bones, was that hefty arms expenditures did not add to the nation's influence but actually detracted from it—instead, Britain's real strength derived predominantly from its moral reputation, a compound of its war-time prestige and postwar socialism, and in this regard arms were only counterproductive. Some such conviction as this ran as a moral thread through much of the hostile commentary on the government's policies, foreign and defense alike. It appeared in R. H. S. Crossman's speech during the November 1946 rebellion, when he insisted that moral strength could "alone" save the world. It reappeared five years later in Aneurin Bevan's resignation speech, when, as justification of his stand against the government's huge rearmament program, he observed that Britain enjoyed "the moral leadership of the world" and could by virtue of that influence alone persuade other nations "where to go and how to go there."* The logic was impeccably socialist; the symbolic message was predictably stirring.

In pressing their case, the critics had general influence in mind. But a corollary of their outlook was their faith in moral gestures as a solution to specific diplomatic crises. One such gesture was embodied in the demand that Britain unilaterally withdraw from

* Quoted above, p. 175.

sensitive regions as a means of proving its goodwill to the Soviet Union.* Another moral gesture that enjoyed a vogue called upon Britain to shun close ties with America: by this course of action, the Labour government would show what it thought of the whole notion of power blocs. But far and away the most dramatic gesture would be a unilateral renunciation of nuclear weapons. The capacity for such self-denial was counted, in fact, a major corollary benefit of a third force policy: by disowning any and all intent to develop nuclear weapons, the British-led bloc could set an example that would break the existing East-West deadlock over the problem of international control and prepare the way for subsequent disarmament.†

### 2. *The Argument of Intolerable Economic Burdens*

Toward the end of 1946, the critics of the government began pursuing a second line of attack on its defense programs, one crossing from the moral into the economic sphere. The objection was now increasingly raised that the high level of defense spending was a major cause of Britain's economic troubles. The government, by reason of its efforts to maintain large forces, was held to be diverting scarce resources like labor power from domestic industry, thereby hampering materially the recovery of productivity.

Unfortunately for the critics, hard figures did not bear their argument out: productivity by the end of 1947 was actually 15 per cent higher than in 1938.‡ Instead of abandoning the economic line of attack, however, the critics resorted to refining their argument in an effort to sustain its credibility. For instance, they could and did contend that even if productivity were on the rise, it would be rising all the faster save for inordinate defense burdens. But far and away the most popular refinement was to charge that the level of defense spending was bad because it posed a threat to expenditures on the social services—the backbone of the new welfare state.

So stated, the economic argument neatly supplemented the mor-

* It will be recalled, for instance, that "Keep Left" urged a speedy withdrawal from the whole Mediterranean area.

† "Keep Left," p. 38. A similar scheme was unfolded almost three years later in "Keeping Left."

‡ Worswick and Ady, p. 10. By the end of 1950, productivity was up 50 per cent from the 1938 level.

al argument. Britain's influence in the world was held to lie in its moral strength; its moral strength in turn derived from socialist programs at home. But then this only meant the most effective instruments of foreign policy were not armaments but rather such things as fair shares, redistribution of income, and nationalization: increase efforts in the latter areas and you would automatically find British influence to have climbed. Hence it followed that armaments were doubly bad: not only ineffective in their own right, but, what was worse, wasteful of precious resources that could be better and more wisely spent on the really potent socialist instruments.

Though this line of criticism was adhered to throughout the tenure of the Labour government, it reached perhaps its peak of popularity during the months after the abortive rebellion of November 1946. The economic crisis of winter 1946–47 acted as a particularly strong catalyst here. Article after article in the left-wing press, speaker after speaker at local party meetings, one angry backbencher after another, all became absorbed in such issues as the availability of manpower resources, the size of the armed forces and its impact on domestic industry, the intolerable costs of British commitments, and the lag in export recovery. In March 1947 the government's proposed defense expenditure of 899 million pounds was denounced by members of the PLP as economically reckless. Two months later "Keep Left" charged that the government's foreign policy was necessitating a level of defense spending that would sooner or later drive the nation into bankruptcy. To make matters worse, such spending was found to be not just economically irrational but also altogether futile; for "however many men we maintain in the armed forces, and however many millions we spend on the service budgets, the British Isles are no longer defensible in a major war."[86]

### 3. Further Refinement: The Argument over Priorities

The argument against arms in favor of socialist programs did not, by itself, complete the socialist case. There remained a hitch that the critics recognized had to be dealt with on its own terms—namely, that as long as a Soviet threat loomed beyond contention, the government would naturally nurse grave doubts about meeting this threat through moral strength only. To erase these doubts, the critics were therefore moved to one further series of refinements, all aimed at putting the East-West conflict in proper socialist perspective.

It will be recalled that early in the postwar period a staple of the socialist attack on the government had been the flat denial of any Soviet threat. In good socialist fashion, the argument had been advanced that the Soviet Union could not possibly be a threat because it lacked all economic impulse to imperialism. But when, by late 1946, the fact of Soviet hostility could itself no longer be denied, the government's critics shifted ground and conceded that there was a danger from the East after all. But that danger was decidedly not military; to suppose that was to fall into the same trap as Bevin and the Cabinet. Socialist analysis disclosed, instead, that the threat was essentially ideological, the East-West struggle being, at bottom, nothing more nor less than a protracted conflict to determine whether the Communist or the democratic creed would win the hearts of the people. Obviously, by interpreting the struggle in these terms, the opponents of the government's defense programs were intent on showing how futile it was to try halting the spread of Communism—of rival ideas—by arms. There was only one way to meet the Communist challenge, and that was by means of a vigorous social and economic alternative that could win the gratitude and allegiance of mankind. Capitalism of course would not do, no matter how reformed it might be; only socialism would, and in particular the kind that a left-wing Labour partisan wanted the Labour government to espouse in Britain itself.

Thus, with the addition of the above refinement, defense expenditures stood condemned for three related reasons. Not only were they morally harmful and economically disastrous, but what was more, they created the dangerous illusion that the spread of Communist ideas could be halted by means of bullets.

In this regard, as in so many others, R. H. S. Crossman proved an able source of argument. Denying that Communism followed the Red Army, he told the 1949 conference that the exact opposite was really the case: Communism could take root only after the social and economic soil had been well prepared in advance, meaning that democratic socialism had not been able to take root first. Not even the recent Czechoslovakian coup had been materially influenced by the presence of the Red Army, Crossman noted, adding that he ought to know since he had been in Prague immediately afterward. The moral to be drawn from this was clear and compelling: a wise foreign policy had to aim above all at promoting the attraction of a socialist alternative to the working class. Unhappily Bevin and the government had not yet seen the light, but hope could not be given up that eventually they would. All really they had to do was to start getting their budgetary priorities straight, which meant—Crossman explained—nothing more than that the social services had to take precedence over defense expenditures in allocating resources. For "whenever, in the last four years, we have put our faith in socialist domestic policy we have won, and whenever we have put our faith in armaments we have not done so well."[87]

This line of reasoning, which may be called the argument over priorities, struck a noticeably responsive chord in Labour quarters. Aneurin Bevan, for instance, electrified the same conference with the striking slogan "priorities is the religion of socialism." The argument quickly became the meeting ground for the several crosscurrents of dissatisfaction with the government's defense programs and foreign policy that still existed in the period after 1948 but before the Korean War. Its most elaborate amplification was undertaken by "Keeping Left," which appeared several months later, in early 1950, and the manifesto would deserve attention for this if for no other reason. But there is also another reason for examining its argument: it turned out that many of the themes that subsequently became identified with the Bevanite cause were foreshadowed in the pages of "Keeping Left."[88]

"Keeping Left" delivered its message with a sense of urgency, largely owing perhaps to the widespread suspicion that the West German Republic, which had only recently been established, might be asked to contribute to Western defense. Now more than ever, therefore, the Labour government had to be enlightened, had to be prodded into getting its priorities straight before it committed the most serious mistake of its militaristic policy to date. The manifesto went straight to the crux of the matter, raising the whole question of Western armament and querying what possible purpose large-scale defense preparations might serve. There was no likelihood of a Soviet attack; the existence of the North Atlantic Pact provided a sure deterrent to that. If the West desired more security, then this had to be obtained by measures designed to cope with the challenge from the East in social and economic terms. As the text read at one point: "Our military commitments are not, as the Tories affirm, a first call on our resources: economic commitments at home and abroad must have priority over them." Indeed a policy of armament, precisely by reversing these priorities, "actually accentuates the social crisis, actually increases our insecurity." Two related tasks awaited a vigorous response if priorities were to be put right. First, the Labour government should implement bold and uncompromising socialist programs so as to strengthen the social fabric of the democratic nations, with Britain, of course, placed at the top of the list. Second, at the same time it should sponsor a "World Fair Deal," a massive project of economic assistance to the underdeveloped nations—the area where the East-West ideological conflict would ultimately be decided. While "Keeping Left" recognized that the United States alone had the resources for such a project, it was hopeful that the Labour government could rally the necessary support of America's progressive forces. It was no less hopeful, with these two tasks being executed, that the Labour government would retain "the moral leadership which is her real power in the world today."[89]

### Another Motive

Thus the elaborate critique which the opponents of the government's defense programs developed and amplified over the years. It was a critique, of course, that accorded in all its essentials with socialist principles; it was also a critique that did not lack merit or insight in many of its observations, such as "Keeping Left's" prescient appreciation of the pivotal significance of the third world to the East-West conflict. Whatever its obvious virtues (and no less obvious defects), however, the critique cannot be seen apart and in isolation from an additional motive of the critics that had scarcely anything to do with foreign or defense policy *per se*, but nearly everything to do with serving the left's domestic objectives.

After 1948 the Labour government did little to gladden ardent socialists. By that date, most of the Cabinet seemed disposed to soft-pedal the rate of innovation in order to consolidate present achievements and to increase the efficiency of the new mixed capitalist economy.[90] The decision to proceed with caution meant, among other things, less and less nationalization of industry; for instance, "Let Us Win Through Together," the 1950 election manifesto written largely by Morrison, the leading go-slower, stipulated only a handful of industries for public ownership. Naturally all this left the socialist mainstays in the party baffled and distraught. Believing that nationalization alone spelled the difference between genuine socialism and mere tepid reformist capitalism, they began to suspect that the entire socialist fervor of the Labour movement—and not just the devotion to socialist foreign policy alone—had all but burned itself out. Time seemed to be desperately slipping by. If the party was to be saved from the sclerosis of malignant reformism, then it had to be liberated from the timid grip of overprudent ministers; it had to be shocked and jolted into rededication to the socialist cause both at home and abroad. On this score, the severe setback administered to Labour's majority in the 1950 general election only fortified the critics' conviction. They were certain past all doubt that the setback was a direct consequence of the leadership's failure to attract the electorate with a sufficiently radical program.[91]

What, accordingly, could have been better suited to rekindle Labour's waning socialism than all-out espousal of the sort of measures recommended by "Keeping Left"? In implementing them, the Labour government and its supporters would enjoy in effect the best of two worlds. At the very time that they were reviving their faith in socialist policy abroad, they would be effecting a new, bold socialist breakthrough in Britain itself.

# Chapter seven

# The Interplay of the Two Foreign Policies:
# The Impact on Intra-Party Politics

The extent and volume of opposition to the government's foreign policy confronts us, at this point, with a question of pivotal significance. How did the leadership manage to maintain control of a discordant Labour Party, asserting authority over it and so preserving the discipline indispensable to Cabinet government?

Any Prime Minister is simultaneously a party manager and he must, in fact, be a skillful manager if he is to be a successful leader of the nation. This dual role is readily enough perceived, but its implications for the political system often go unappreciated. Focusing one's gaze on party voting alone, it is easy to see only disciplined armies parading loyally at their masters' beck and to conclude from the consequent eclipse of Parliament that "nowhere else is a Government normally so free to act decisively."[1] Yet to affirm this is to confuse the formal authority to make decisions with the actual possession of effective means of power and the will to use it, though no doubt the conclusion follows reasonably from casting one's gaze so narrowly. The truth is, however, that division lobbies are only the last stage in a complicated sequence in intra-party politics. Parties are not monoliths but are comprised of—or, depending on your view, riddled with—factions, tendencies, independents, and leadership cadres; and it requires unremitting attention and deft calculation and no small amount of bargaining and manipulation to achieve cohesion in voting.[2] The need to manage the party in this manner thus amounts to an often formidable restraint upon the power of a Prime Minister.[3] The leadership problem, to use Kenneth Waltz's apt phrase, is inescapable and goes far toward explaining the curious paradox why British governments enjoying unchallenged control over Parliament are frequently unable to translate much of their formal authority into effective power. It is true that a Prime Minister nearly always gets his party, in the end, to follow the government line, "but within limits that are set in part by the party members collectively." That is, he must in his role as manager first ascertain what it is that the members will be willing to follow.[4]

The question posed at the beginning, then, is as crucial as its wording suggests. To assume that the leadership coped successfully with the opposition because British parties are well disciplined, their discipline attested to by their voting record, comes close to being a tautology and begs the question of how the discipline is derived and then maintained. True, there are always a number of pressures on MP's to keep in step; but not all are self-evident, and in the case of the Labour Party between 1945 and 1951 they need to be carefully probed. In general, two sets of counteracting pressures determined the outcome of the leadership problem at the time. One set benefited the critics, relaxing discipline and encouraging the emergence of factions and tendencies opposed to the government's foreign policy. The other set, deriving in part from the internal structure of the Labour Party, but also from certain factors unique to the period, favored the government and eased its problem of control.

### THE PLP

*Pressures favoring opposition.* A major pressure was inherent in the enormous electoral victory of 1945. For, paradoxically, the effect of the huge Labour majority was to dilute discipline within the PLP on the floor of the Commons. With the government's overall superiority of 149 over the Opposition, backbench Labour MP's might have been disinclined to toe the official line; they could have argued that their own view of things ought to be publicly aired, however much it differed from the government's own views, because their opposition could not possibly jeopardize Labour's hold on office. The use of the subjunctive mood here is intentional. For the fact is that backbenchers never had much opportunity to develop this particular argument. The leadership, perhaps anticipating it, took the initiative in the matter by introducing several reforms into the traditional organization of the PLP which seemed, on the surface, to meet the demands for greater backbench influence and freer discussion. The leadership established a small liaison committee, whose primary responsibility, according to the Parliamentary Report, was to maintain "a close contact between the Government and the backbenchers"; it also established a number of party groups that, between them, covered the whole field of government activity and were chaired by backbenchers; and, most important of all, in 1946 it suspended Standing Orders. The party was asked to regard the latter reform as an "experiment," motivated by the belief that "the building of a tradition of free discussion combined with a true spirit of good fellowship, co-operation and comradeship in a great cause is to be preferred to written Standing Orders."*

Freer discussion was indeed the result. It was in no small measure owing to this reform that many of the Labour MP's, discontented with the government's foreign policy, were emboldened to make their opposition public: to table motions denouncing government proposals or move amendments critical of them, to speak out and condemn innumerable British actions abroad, and to abstain and even vote contrary to party policy in divisions when matters of conscience themselves were plainly not involved.† The rebellion of November 1946 was a striking manifestation of the degree to which discipline was relaxed. So, too, was the protracted backbiting and bickering relating to the 1947 Conscription Bill. In one division on the proposal, for instance, 72 Labour MP's voted against the government and another 76 abstained—which

---

* *LPCR*, 1946, pp. 56–57. Standing Orders, which had first been imposed in 1929, were not reimposed until 1952 at the height of the Bevanite controversy. A further modification of the Orders was undertaken in January 1946 (see Alderman, "Discipline in the Parliamentary Labour Party, 1945–51," p. 297).

It is worth noting that the initiative for the reforms was taken by Herbert Morrison, who later claimed that the internecine warfare of the 1929–31 period had convinced him of the need for new measures to improve relations between backbenchers and the leadership. (See Morrison, *Government and Parliament*, pp. 121–24.) A former Labour MP at the time, critical of the leadership from a right-wing viewpoint, charges that Standing Orders were suspended because they couldn't be enforced anyhow. (See Bulmer-Thomas, p. 128.)

† The PLP traditionally permits *abstention* in the case of members who have "good grounds for conscientious scruples."

meant that out of a total of 390 Labour members, only 242 rallied to the leadership's support.*

That the leadership would not have so casually tolerated such open dissent if Labour had not enjoyed a huge overall Parliamentary majority was more than just hinted at by the behavior of the

---

* Since the 18-month Conscription Bill aroused more public opposition than any other measure, it is worth briefly describing what was involved in it. Traditionally, no issue was likely to excite Labour passions more than conscription, and it had been regarded as repugnant by all sections of the party, left or right. Pacifists disliked it for obvious reasons; radicals opposed it on the ground that it served only to increase the power of the workers' enemies; middle-class parliamentarians objected to it because it seemed un-English and to smack of Prussianism. Even trade unionists, otherwise more appreciative of the role of force in international politics, opposed conscription because they believed (rightly so, given the experience of World Wars I and II) that compulsory military service was inevitably followed by industrial conscription. In 1939 all these elements had joined together to protest the Conscription Bill that the National government introduced during the spring.

In early November 1946, Attlee told a meeting of the PLP that the low level of enlistments had forced the government to draw up a Conscription Bill that would extend wartime conscription into peacetime. The period of service was to be for 18 months, and the bill asked that conscription be extended for an *unspecified* period of time after January 1949. The PLP was thus requested to endorse a revolutionary bill, establishing the first peacetime conscription in British history and, what was more, on an apparently permanent basis. The response was predictably stormy, and though a majority was mustered in support of the leadership, 54 backbenchers voted against the bill's introduction and an even larger number abstained. Shortly afterward, an Amendment signed by 70 Labour MP's was tabled to the King's Speech urging that the government refrain from embarking "upon a peace-time policy of military conscription." The Amendment was debated and voted on in mid-November, and received the support of 53 members of the PLP. (430 *H.C.Deb.* 640, 18 November 1946.)

In March 1947, the government brought the bill before the Commons. By now the PLP was badly split; 75 members signed a motion urging the bill's rejection, and it was in the subsequent division that the 72 votes against the government and the 76 abstentions were registered. Faced with opposition of this magnitude, the government decided that its most prudent course was to compromise: two days afterward, it agreed to reduce the period of compulsory service by one-third, from 18 to 12 months. The concession satisfied many of the dissenters, with the result that the Conscription Bill was eventually adopted, on its third reading, with only 36—mostly well-known pacifists—still in opposition.

The concession, it should be added, did not cost the government very much. The important thing was that, in the teeth of impassioned resistance, it had managed to have the principle of peacetime conscription vindicated. Only a year and a half later, moreover, the government proceeded to retract the concession altogether, introducing a measure that extended the period of compulsory military service to 18 months again.

Bevanite rebels in 1951. The party's overall majority by then had shrunk drastically to a mere five seats, and any opposition from the backbenches might have seriously jeopardized the government's hold on office; therefore, even though Standing Orders were still formally suspended, Bevan, Harold Wilson, and John Freeman—the three members who resigned from the government at the time—promised that they would remain loyal to the party line in the House of Commons.* They offered this assurance, it should be noted, even though they had not only a more concrete grievance than did (say) the rebels of November 1946, but one that clearly was shared to a great degree by the rank and file too. Obviously, dissenters were well aware of the need to proceed with caution if the circumstances of governing required it.

There was a second pressure inherent in Labour's huge majority that helped to relax PLP discipline. In consequence of the electoral landslide, Labour's representation in the House of Commons swelled nearly threefold; most of the new Labour MP's were young, without political experience, eager for radical change both at home and abroad. They were especially optimistic regarding the degree of initiative that would be open to the Labour government in foreign policy. Not too surprisingly, Bevin's cautious policy made them chafe and grow restless. The life of a backbencher in any government party is frustrating enough in any case, consisting in the main of acting as a rubber stamp for frontbench measures; he normally has little direct impact on their conception, and no or hardly any material scrutiny of their implementation by the civil service.† To escape this frustration, then, many of the more restless Labour MP's gathered together in the various unofficial factions, offbeat groups, and irregular cliques that cut across formal lines of organization and authority within the PLP at the time. "Keep Left" was only the most prominent of a host of such groups that flourished between 1945 and 1951.[5] Many of these groups were preoccupied with foreign policy, and it was no coincidence that they were; historically, foreign affairs has been

---

* Butler, p. 15. As Alderman ("Discipline in the Parliamentary Labour Party 1945–51," p. 303) notes, "backbench critics during the brief 1950–51 Parliament were, for the most part, very restrained."

† For one recent Labour backbencher's views on this subject, see Mackintosh, "The Reform of Parliament," pp. 38–55.

the area of policy most vulnerable to the criticism of impatient backbenchers. Of the several reasons why, perhaps the most important is that since information about foreign events is nearly always harder to come by than information about domestic issues, those who discuss the former find it an easy task to keep the discussion on an elusive, if indeed not evasive, level.[6] In other words, dissatisfied backbenchers discover that they can raise objections to a government's foreign policy which are by no means easy to refute, whereas similar opportunity is much rarer in domestic matters. From 1945 on, for instance, Bevin was frequently criticized in the following manner: "Our complaint is that the Government's conduct of foreign affairs during the past thirteen to fifteen months has been merely a continuance of Tory foreign policy, and that the enthusiastic support which the Foreign Secretary gets, in the absence of any repudiation from the Government front bench, is a confirmation that this is so. I am sure that no one on the Government Front Bench believes that there ought to be no difference between a Socialist foreign policy and a Tory foreign policy."[7] It is difficult to conceive that critics of domestic policy would have so easily got away with voicing grievances in terms as devoid of concrete references as this.*

For all the recurring outbursts of this sort, backbench influence, such as it was, operated almost exclusively through party and informal channels rather than on the floor of the Commons. Sniping from the Labour benches was invariably brushed aside with typical flair and evasiveness by frontbench spokesmen. As for open rebellions, the failure of the Crossman-led November 1946 revolt underscored the futility of this mode of protest; if the anti-conscriptionists met with more success, this was because of the wholly exceptional nature of the controversial issue involved. Where party channels were concerned, however, it might seem as if the government's critics had more promising opportunities to make their weight felt. Dissenting views could be conveyed by letters to

---

* In line with this argument, W. L. Guttsman found in a study of backbench dissent within the PLP from 1945 to 1951 that, of the nine major acts of opposition that took place, seven pertained to either defense or foreign policy (p. 269). A similar conclusion is arrived at by Alderman, who says that "foreign policy and defense were, as might be expected, the issues on which serious rifts between Government and backbenchers most frequently occurred" ("Discipline in the Parliamentary Labour Party, 1945–51," p. 249).

ministers or by chance encounters in the House; they could also be passed on through the Whips, at full-scale party meetings, and in the official external affairs group (discussed below). In addition, there were the unofficial groups of the "Keep Left" sort available as vehicles of protest. Why then, with PLP discipline relaxed and much of the party plainly unhappy about foreign policy, did the critics not actually enjoy a greater impact than they did?

*Pressures favoring discipline.* The short answer is that the leadership had advantages of its own that more than offset any pressures, weakening party discipline. Hence, chip away though they might, the critics never managed to jeopardize seriously the leadership's authority.

In the first place, even though formal Standing Orders were suspended, there were other, more subtle controls at the leadership's disposal to promote its supremacy over backbenchers. These were nothing more—but also nothing less—than those customary obligations, traditional procedures, and in general implicit norms that are attached to the role of PLP membership and normally regulate the behavior of the individual members. Together, these unwritten but powerful and inescapable norms amount in effect to special Standing Orders. Not that they are totally rigid and preclude any latitude of behavior. No role can be wholly inflexible in its standards of performance, and the role of a Labour MP is no exception; precisely for this reason the PLP is not a solid monolith, uniform and undifferentiated, but a complex group divided into factions and tendencies. Still, there are definite boundaries beyond which deviation from a role's norms becomes punishable, and again the role of a Labour MP is no exception. The correct standards of performance by members are implicitly known and agreed upon by the membership as a unit. Making above all for a well-defined sense of esprit and teamwork,* the norms in question elevate cooperation to a principal duty and thereby underpin the leadership's authority. At no time is this more obvious than when the PLP is in office; in such periods, the party has not

---

* "We made it clear that the party would expect its members to practice good comradeship and work as a team," Herbert Morrison later said in commenting on the suspension of Standing Orders. (*Government and Parliament*, p. 29. See too Morrison, *An Autobiography*, p. 254.)

functioned much differently from the more hierarchical Conservative Party.[8]

The years 1945–51 were decidedly no exception. Dissent within the PLP was tolerated, but only if it was reasonable; and what was reasonable was supposed to be readily understood even if not explicitly prescribed. Hence, backbenchers who refused to swallow the minimum necessary dose of team spirit were soon made aware that they were courting trouble. The very declaration proclaiming the suspension of formal Standing Orders stipulated that the experiment was not to "prejudice the right of the Party to withdraw the Whip from Members, should occasion require."[9] That nearly all of the Government's critics well understood the meaning of this proviso, and exercised restraint accordingly, was shown again and again by their wary behavior on occasions of open defiance. Thus, as a typical instance, the rebels of November 1946 proclaimed in advance their intention not to divide the House on their amendment. Critics still bold enough to risk dramatic dissent anyhow also risked instantaneous reprisals; the only question was how severe. In this connection, the case of the 37 Labour MP's who signed the April 1948 "Nenni Telegram," a cabled encouragement to the extreme left wing of the Italian socialist party, was instructive: Immediately and severely reprimanded for defying policy toward Italy, sixteen of the signatories disowned the telegram and apologized forthwith, while the remaining 21 offered formal assurance of future good behavior; as for John Platts-Mills, the ostensible leader, he found himself deprived of the whip and subsequently expelled from the party altogether.[10] Running as an independent in the 1950 General Election, Platts-Mills along with three other expellees suffered the expected fate: crushing defeat.

In the second place, the leadership of the PLP enjoys immense influence and authority simply by virtue of the enormous privileges that automatically accompany that role. The power of patronage in the hands of the Prime Minister is a potent force, possibly exceeding the corresponding power of the American President, who must operate in a system of executive-legislative separation.[11] Obviously the suspension of Standing Orders did not restrain the exercise of the Prime Minister's power in one way or another. As one backbencher observed in 1947: "The authority of the Whips lies not in their power of imposing public penalties but in their private condemnation. They hold the political careers of Members in their hands."[12] Naturally, then, any ambitious backbencher was usually careful to keep his criticism of the government's foreign policy within distinct boundaries; and this was the probable case however strongly opposed to the policy he might have been.* As might be expected, most backbenchers were ambitious and hungered for promotion; hence most trimmed their critical remarks accordingly. The exceptions—the more notorious dissenters—enjoyed prominent reputations as journalists and publicists, and were handsomely paid by the press precisely for criticizing the government and party policy.[13] Dissent, from their viewpoint, carried its own rewards. In comparison with the excitement, psychological satisfaction, monetary gain, and prestige to be had as outsiders, the financial and other inducements of conformity, of dutifully awaiting minor office and then working diligently upward, seemed decidedly unappealing.

In the third place, the leadership was powerful vis-à-vis its backbench critics by virtue of sheer numbers. To take a pretty typical year—1950—there were 68 senior and junior ministers in the government, plus some 27 parliamentary secretaries and chief Whips (these regarded as Junior Lords of the Treasury). If assistant Whips are added to this number, it follows that the leadership could always count on a solid phalanx of over 100 MP's to back its measures in the Commons regardless of circumstances.[14] This figure alone represented about one-quarter of the total PLP strength at the time, and about one-half the votes needed to sustain the government in any division. Moreover, add to this lot the indeterminate but large number of backbenchers who, though not in the government, aspired to be and tempered their criticisms accordingly; add, too, nearly all of the 120-odd trade union MP's, whose previous experience in the trade union movement had taught them to regard loyalty as the cardinal virtue of organizational behavior—add them all up and it is easy to see that there were not many backbenchers left to join the ranks of the persistent critics, no matter how much they might sympathize with the latter's views.[15]

* As one observer has concluded, "the orthodox career politician must nowadays be, in a parliamentary and ministerial context, more orthodox than ever if he wishes to reach the Cabinet." Willson, pp. 225–26.

In the fourth and final place, the government enjoyed an incalculable advantage deriving from its legislative achievements at home. Whatever the degree of hostility to its foreign policy, the leadership was no doubt fully aware that the party's support would hinge mainly on its domestic rather than international record. This was not simply because the average party partisan, whatever his allegiance to principles and ideals, was interested in matters that touched the quality of British life directly—in welfare measures, economic policy, advances on the social and educational front; it was also because sufficient success in these areas could, for obvious psychological reasons, more than offset the arid socialist record abroad.* A new Britain, a more just and equitable post-capitalist Britain, seemed just around the corner. Hence, as long as the Labour Government appeared to be moving vigorously in that direction, it could reasonably count on retaining the major part of the party's confidence regardless of the discontent over foreign policy itself. And the fact is that the government's achievements were impressive; by 1948 it had implemented nearly all the domestic promises embodied in the 1945 election manifesto. Along with the aforementioned three advantages, then, the government's success at home consolidated its authority in the eyes of its followers and produced a predominant outlook of awe and deference on their part.[16]

### Extent of Opposition

How large, then, was the opposition in the PLP? Any estimation must remain highly problematic on several grounds. For one thing, it is necessary to distinguish several categories of critics: *persistent* critics, who were unrepentant socialists in foreign policy and defied the government repeatedly and almost without respite; *occasional* critics, who also wanted a bold socialist policy but whose defiance, in the form of adverse votes against the government in Parliament or of adverse commentary in the media, was less regular; *hesitant* critics, who voted openly against the government on only one or two occasions but whose attitudes were plainly out of sympathy with at least much of the government's policy;

---

* Back in 1907 Keir Hardie observed that, significant as "questions of foreign affairs, the welfare of subject races, and militarism" were, they lacked the immediate urgency of bread-and-butter issues. *LPCR,* 1907, p. 38.

and finally what could be called *covert* critics, who, while never coming into public collision with the government line, were unhappy with it in one sense or another. Although the latter two categories of critics never posed a serious threat to the leadership's authority, it did not follow that they were therefore of no consequence; on the contrary, their lack of enthusiasm for many government measures meant that they were a force not to be ignored whenever the other two categories of more recalcitrant critics themselves threatened to bolt. For another thing, the mere adding of numbers does not provide a completely reliable indicator of opposition—in part because of several borderline cases in connection with the aforementioned categories, but also because of an intractable problem of incommensurability. In which category should one place a Labour MP who criticized the frontbench in Parliamentary debates and in the left-wing press, but who, for individual psychological reasons, did not pursue his opposition to the point of voting against the government in a division? Again, how is the problem of abstention to be handled, given the diverse motives that might be involved? Failure to vote might be due to sickness, for instance, but how is one to know when sickness was feigned in order to defy a three-line whip? Yet it is precisely on a measure like approval of the North Atlantic Pact, in connection with which only six negative votes but dozens of abstentions were visible, that we would like to resort to statistics.

In view of these obstacles, the best we can do is to estimate a range within which the magnitude of persistent opposition can be assumed, with some confidence, to lie. In this sense the number of persistent critics can be put somewhere between 50 and 75.* This is a fairly wide range, yet the attempt to be more precise is likely to remain self-defeating. At least the estimation as it stands is underpinned by considerable unambiguous evidence, as a study of several occasions of prominent dissent reveals. In the November 1946 rebellion, 44 Labour members originally signed the adverse

---

* Alderman estimates that 74 MP's voted against the government on five or more occasions, while at least 217 of the 393 MP's elected in 1945 did so at least once ("Discipline in the Parliamentary Labour Party, 1945–1951," p. 294). Unfortunately for our purposes, Alderman's estimate does not distinguish between domestic and foreign affairs. But Jackson's recently published work makes it crystal-clear that "external affairs problems and military issues dominated Labour's dissension" (pp. 45–86).

amendment, and subsequently at least a dozen more added their signatures and about 70 abstained when a vote was pressed; 72 members voted in March 1947 against the Conscription Bill; 63 members voted at least once against the government's 1949 Ireland Bill, whereas slightly fewer bolted over measures relating to Palestine in both 1948 and 1949.

Of course, even taking the upper limit of 75, those Labour members who persistently proved insubordinate represented less than 20 per cent of the total PLP. Does this mean that our recurring argument regarding the Labour Party's disenchantment with the government's foreign policy stands refuted? Not at all—on three grounds. In the first place, given the aforementioned pressures which maintained discipline and consolidated the leadership's authority, it seems fair to infer that the actual extent and volume of discontent never found their way to the surface. In the second place, the active opposition of the persistent sort was severely hampered in that it was fragmented into various groups and cliques lacking in cohesion: among them, pro-Soviet sympathizers and anti-Americans, third-forcers and pacifists, disillusioned idealists and frustrated office seekers. Of course, many of these groups had overlapping membership, but the fact remains that they added up to a tendency sharing socialist attitudes in common and not to a distinct faction with recognizable leadership, a well-defined program, and a measure of internal discipline. (The "Keep Left" and "Keeping Left" groups were somewhat of an exception, yet both remained small in number and anyway were prone to disruption.) Above all, this socialist tendency was handicapped by its lack of a leader of national stature, someone with definite chances for the leadership of the entire party round which the disparate groups could coalesce and crystallize into a potent faction—a gap, incidentally, not filled until Bevan's resignation in 1951. In the third place, finally, the government's domestic record is of sufficient importance to be worth singling out again. Its successes in welfare and economic policy simply cannot be overemphasized. Without them, not only is it possible that discontent with foreign policy would have been far harder to offset, but it is also likely that a large and distinctive faction would have materialized long before 1951.

As matters stood, the existence of 50 to 75 persistent critics is something not to be slighted; it more than hints, for the above three reasons, at how pervasive disenchantment must have been. Between 1945 and 1950 there were over three dozen backbench revolts, most of them involving foreign affairs and defense. The best overall evaluation belongs to Denis Healey, a firm supporter of the government, who observed in 1952 that the "bulk of the Party membership" did not really approve Bevin's foreign policy and continued to view the world in terms of socialist principles.*

### External Affairs Group

Before considering the extra-Parliamentary Labour Party, the influence of the group on External Affairs within the PLP may be worth describing. This can be brief because it was almost entirely without consequence.

The External Affairs group was one of 20 such bodies established in 1945 as part of the effort to give backbenchers a more active role in Parliamentary work and at the same time to provide the government with regular access to backbench opinion. The groups functioned in different ways: some spawned subcommittees, others did not; some elected their own chairman, others had theirs imposed by the frontbench. In principle, ministers were supposed to maintain close contact with the group whose subject area came within the purview of their departments, and in fact some did endeavor to acquaint themselves with the views of the members. On the whole, however, the groups never really gave backbenchers any more influence over policy making than they would have enjoyed in any case as Labour members.[17] Essentially there were two reasons why. First, ministers refused on constitutional grounds to submit proposals before announcing them publicly, which meant that the groups did nothing to ameliorate the problem of access to information.[18] And second, ministers were reluctant to use the groups on practical grounds because of the belief that the backbenchers most active in them were crusading militants and enthusiasts.

These general observations apply with particular appropriateness to the External Affairs group. Filled with many of the per-

---

* Healey, "Power Politics and the Labour Party," p. 164. Compare this with Roy Jenkins' similar observation (cited above, p. 94) that "the foreign policy of the Labour Government never bit deep into the consciousness of the party."

sistent critics of the government's policy, it alienated Bevin from the outset and he hardly deigned to attend more than a handful of its sessions. Dalton later observed in this connection (and despite his personal differences with Bevin, there is no reason to doubt his account): "Bevin . . . had a terrible group on Foreign Affairs. He did not pick it, as I did [mine]. He let it pick itself. And in came all the pacifists, and fellow-travelers, pro-Russians and anti-Americans, and every sort of freak harboured in our majority."[19] Though an overhaul of the committee system was undertaken in the spring of 1947, this did little to improve the functioning of the groups. By then, the critics who had entered the External Affairs group on a wave of high hope were already becoming bored with its ineffectuality, and many of them ceased attending its sessions in order to devote their energies to unofficial groups like "Keep Left" and "Keeping Left."[20]

## THE EXTRA-PARLIAMENTARY PARTY

*The NEC.* According to the party constitution, the NEC is both a policy-making body and the administrative authority of the Labour Party, subject to the superior control of the annual conference.[21] Although its actual powers in comparison with the other centers of the party have been a matter of controversy, it can be safely described as essentially an auxiliary of the PLP leadership. Certainly, as far as foreign policy is concerned, McKenzie's evaluation is incontestable: "Not once in the lifetime of the Labour Government of 1945 and 1950 did the NEC give any public indication that it disagreed with any item of government policy."[22]

There were, to be sure, members of the NEC who were generally hostile to the government's foreign policy. This even included Harold Laski, its head during 1945–46, but the critics were always a tiny minority during the period under consideration, probably never numbering more than four or five. Moreover, their criticisms were entirely without effect. By a skillful use of policy statements, disciplinary powers, and administrative authority at conferences, the remaining 22–23 members who comprised the majority saw to it that the NEC acted as a serviceable instrument of the government in overriding opposition.* In fact it proved to be

* The critics were particularly irked by the manner in which the NEC limited criticism at conferences. Movers of resolutions from the floor were restricted to

so docile that in 1948 Laski declined further nomination for membership, on the ground that a critic could operate more effectively as an individual party member.[23]

The international subcommittee of the NEC was also used to stifle criticism within the party at large, particularly by means of its educative functions. Working closely with the international department of the permanent bureaucracy at Transport House, it issued a number of policy statements and pamphlets supporting the government's foreign policy and contesting, often with skillful polemical effect, the views of the socialist critics. Cooperation between the two bodies was facilitated by the personal rapport between Dalton, head of the subcommittee during much of the 1945–51 period, and Denis Healey, secretary of the international department.[24] As mentioned before, they were responsible for two of the most important party statements—"Cards on the Table" and "European Unity."

The NEC, it should briefly be noted, had not always functioned in such a subordinate role. Its authority had been much greater during the 1930's, for instance, as a result of the catastrophe that overtook the PLP in the 1931 general election. But the emergence of a powerful PLP in 1945 led to its virtual monopoly of policy-making power. The decline in the NEC's status can be gauged from the reduced frequency of its meetings. Whereas in the 1930's it met on the average of over 35 times a year, after 1945 it averaged fewer than twelve sessions a year.[25]

For all these reasons, then, the following observation of Kenneth Younger, a Minister of State for Foreign Affairs in 1950–51, appears substantially correct: "My recollection of the function of Transport House when Labour was in power is that it was employed to convince the Movement that what Ernest Bevin had already decided was right rather than to tell Ernest Bevin what the Movement expected him to do."*

---

ten minutes, and successive speakers to five minutes. In contrast, the spokesmen chosen by the NEC to reply to the resolutions (most of them in the realm of foreign policy being critical of the government) were not subject to any time limit. The critics also objected to the manner in which the NEC brought together a number of resolutions into a frequently clumsily-worded composite resolution.

* Younger, "Public Opinion and Foreign Policy," p. 171. It should be pointed out, in this connection, that the Bevanites came to express a similar opinion—though they meant it, of course, as a rebuke.

*The Conference.* Labour's Constitution stipulates that "the work of the Party shall be under the direction and control of the Party Conference." Even more than in the case of the NEC, however, the actual authority exercised by the conference has been a matter of dispute, and it is not proposed to reopen the controversy at this point. All that need be said, for our purposes, is that just as the NEC enjoyed greater decision-making powers in the prewar period, so too did the conference and for roughly the same reason: the comparative electoral weakness of the PLP. After 1945 the PLP clearly grew in authority as compared with the conference, and if the PLP leadership did not come to dominate the latter in quite the sense or to the degree that McKenzie contends, it nevertheless wielded sufficient advantages to retain the upper hand between 1945 and 1951 with noticeable ease.

Not one conference during this period ever threatened seriously the PLP leadership's authority on a measure connected with the government's defense or foreign policy.[26] But this did not mean that the local constituency parties or all of the affiliated unions were therefore satisfied with that policy, contrary to what has been recurringly argued here. The fact is that the government's critics did strive to convert the conference into a vehicle of protest; the preliminary agenda for one year after another teemed with strongly adverse resolutions. But another fact of greater consequence was that because of the immense advantages in the hands of the leadership—its prestige, the pride and awe with which delegates viewed it,* its control of conference procedures through the NEC, and not least the domestic record of the government—none of the hostile resolutions ever managed to elicit widespread support. Either they were deftly turned aside by the NEC's spokesmen and withdrawn, or—if not too explicit regarding concrete commitments—they were accepted "for consideration" but never acted upon.†

* "If anything," McKenzie observes (p. 510), "Labour conferences have tended to View Labour Governments with even more awe and pride than characterizes the Conservative attitude to Governments."

† The NEC resorted to the latter stratagem, for instance, in regard to a resolution moved at the 1947 conference urging that the Ruhr industries be socialized. Bevin, speaking for the NEC, agreed to accept the resolution in the sense of giving it "full consideration" (*LPCR*, 1947, p. 163). Yet a year later backbench Labour MP's were jumping to their feet in the Commons to protest the government's announcement that it was no longer advocating public ownership in the Ruhr region.

The 1946 conference affords a fairly typical illustration of the adept manner in which the NEC disposed of opposition. Of the 46 resolutions relating to foreign and defense policy that appeared on the final agenda, 44 were critical of the government. At the request of the Conference Arrangements Committee (an NEC auxiliary), the affiliated organizations where the resolutions originated agreed to have them reduced to five composite resolutions under the general headings of "Government Policy," "Foreign Service Recruitment," "Palestine," "Spain," and "Relations with the USSR." Even this apparently simple administrative chore worked to the critics' disadvantage; for most of the composite resolutions were so clumsily worded, so prolix and discursive, that they amounted to ragbag collections that probably struck many delegates as either intemperate or inconsistent or altogether incoherent.* When the conference opened, the five composite resolutions were all moved by representatives from constituency parties, who were limited to ten minutes of speaking time. Successive speakers were limited to half that amount. In contrast, Bevin in responding for the NEC had as much time as he wanted to make his case; he ended by requesting that the resolutions be withdrawn. Two of them subsequently were, while the remaining three, when pressed to a vote, were overwhelmingly defeated. The fate of a sixth resolution, moved by an affiliated union and favorable to the government, was no less instructive. To no one's surprise, it

---

* The composite resolution on the USSR, for instance, rambled on in the following manner: "This Conference is of the opinion that world peace can only be based on a British policy directed to ensure firm friendship and co-operation with the progressive forces throughout the world, and in particular with the USSR, and that such a policy should over-ride British imperial interests. The Conference re-affirms the pledges made by Conferences of the Labour Party in the past to respect, co-operate with, and assist in every way possible the struggles of the working-class movements. . . .

"This Conference recognizes that to this end every endeavor should be made to eradicate the remnants of Fascism throughout the world. The Conference therefore calls upon the Government:

"*a*. To maintain and foster an attitude of sympathy and friendship toward the Soviet Union and do all in its power to establish the interchange of trade and cultural relations with the USSR . . .

"*b*. To repudiate Mr. Churchill's defeatist proposal to make the British Commonwealth a mere satellite of American Monopoly Capitalism which will inevitably lead to our being aligned in a partnership of hostility to Russia" (*LPCR*, 1946, p. 157).

was warmly received by Bevin and no less warmly adopted by the conference itself.

All in all, then, the conference did not prove to be a serviceable vehicle for the critics' purposes. Aside from affording them limited opportunity for airing their grievances, it remained obedient to the leadership and faithful to the government's policies. Whether the conference would prove as docile once the party reverted to opposition, is, however, another matter that we will deal with later.

### THE TRADE UNIONS

To complete the picture, something should be said about the role of the trade union movement. It is a commonplace that the power structure in the trade unions is oligarchical[27] and that, accordingly, the leadership enjoys enormous leeway in making policy, especially in connection with politics[28]—so much so, indeed, that the mere change of the general secretary can by itself effect a breathtaking reversal of the union's political stand. The most striking example of this was the turnabout in the policies of the Transport & General Workers' Union effected by Frank Cousins, following Arthur Deakin's death in 1955.

The vast latitude of arbitrary decision available to a union general secretary could pose severe problems for the Labour Party, given the crushing weight of the trade union vote at the conference. On the whole, however, despite allegations to the contrary, dominance by a clique of powerful union bosses has never really materialized. Of the several reasons why, perhaps the most important is that the more powerful trade unionists have normally preferred to avoid interfering extensively in party affairs relating to strictly political questions. Experience has taught them that their potential power in these matters is best employed prudently and discreetly if at the same time they want to prevail on those issues with which they are directly and professionally concerned, such as incomes policy, immigration, taxation, and welfarism. Aggressive behavior may even be counterproductive. The headstrong trade union mogul who tries to bully the political wing, flaunting his massive block vote and reminding the party of who pays most of the bills, may well end up not only outraging the constituency parties but also embarrassing and offending the NEC and the PLP leadership. The usual exception to this—the time when even normally circumspect trade unionists decide to begin throwing their weight around—occurs during periods of acute crisis, when the party is sorely split and the political leadership proves unable to act with decisiveness. Thus, for example, Bevin and Citrine took an active role because the party wavered for years on the crucial issue of rearmament. Similarly, the stormy incursions of first Deakin and later Cousins into politics during the 1950's were invited by the fierce struggle for the leadership and the consequent inability of the party to resolve pressing and fundamental matters of policy.[29]

But the problem of weak political leadership did not arise during the 1945–51 period. The same pressures that offset backbench unrest and produced compliant conferences also tended to keep the trade union movement loyal to the government. Then, too, the trade unions had traditionally been the section of the party least enthusiastic about socialist foreign policy. To the extent there was dissatisfaction with any government measure, many trade union leaders preferred to press their views quietly behind the scene rather than threaten to force a showdown at Labour conferences; indeed, they came to learn that they could most effectively bring pressure to bear on the government through channels formally outside the structure of the party—above all, through the TUC General Council as a powerful interest group.[30]

This is not to say that none of the major unions balked at the government's foreign policy or openly opposed parts of it. On the contrary, it turns out upon further inspection that the union movement did not behave uniformly at all. Three of the Big Six— the transport workers, the general and municipal workers, and the miners—were solidly behind the government. Together, they wielded a total voting strength of more than 1,900,000, which alone represented about 40 per cent of the total votes cast at conferences. The leaders of this trio, Arthur Deakin of the Transport Workers, Tom Williamson of the General and Municipal Workers, and Sam Watson and Will Lawther of the Miners, were tough, obstinate pillars of orthodoxy as well as militant anti-Communists.[31] Counteractively, however, two other members of the Big Six—the Shop Distributive and Allied Workers and the Railwaymen—frequently cast their 680,000 combined votes on the side of Bevin's most vociferous critics. The Engineers with 595,000 votes often joined them, as did several small unions like the militant Fire Brigades' Workers.

Thus the picture of a monolithic trade union movement docilely obedient to the government line is false. As much opposition to the government stemmed from hostile unions as from hostile constituency parties; and even though a larger portion of the trade union movement remained loyal, this fact of hefty trade union opposition remains important and suggestive—particularly considering that a trade unionist was in control of foreign policy. Indeed, one might argue that with less orthodox leadership even the three loyal giants might have betrayed more signs of dissatisfaction than they did—an argument that finds support in the behavior of the Transport Workers after 1955. Even as things stood, the amount of discontent that did exist within the unions was of sufficient consequence to be used to advantage by the Bevanites (which puts their subsequent theory of tyrannical trade union orthodoxy in a somewhat different light). At the 1951 Trades Union Congress, for instance, a Bevanite resolution condemning the Health Service charges that had prompted Bevan's recent resignation was only barely defeated by a vote of 3,775,000 to 3,272,000.[32]

### CONSENSUS VS. CONFLICT

By spring, 1949, the Labour Party was closer to a new consensus on foreign policy than at any date since the General Election of 1945. This new, though still uneasy and inchoate meeting of minds was the product of both events abroad and political interplay at home.

On the one hand, the whole evolution of the cold war since early 1948 had exploded most of the illusions regarding the postwar international environment that flourished so luxuriantly in Labour's ranks in 1945. The Soviet rejection of Marshall Aid, its organization of the Cominform and the subsequent expulsion of Yugoslavia, its furtive role in the Czechoslovakian coup and the fractious antics of West European Communists—all combined to erode the image of a socialist, cooperative, peaceful-minded Soviet Union. At the same time American prestige had been steadily rising. When, as a result of these parallel developments, the Berlin crisis finally blew by in the spring of 1949, even many of the once staunchest critics of the Labour Government were left with a different opinion of its existing foreign policy. Not that they were necessarily enthusiastic about it, though some in fact were; instead, their predominant attitude was an amalgam of greater tolerance of the policy and expressed hope for its socialist salvation through collaboration with the Truman Administration, Labour's ally in capitalist America. It must be remembered, moreover, that the international environment in 1949 and early 1950 was comparatively quiescent and stabilized, with the Kremlin already moving toward a strategy of peaceful coexistence. But the impact of events abroad was only part of the story. For, on the other hand, the vigorous educational campaign undertaken by the leadership, beginning with "Cards on the Table" in 1947, was no less a contributing factor to the emergence of an incipient consensus. The critics had gradually been put on the defensive and then isolated. Less and less was now heard about the sorrowful contrast between the government's policy and socialist principles, and more and more about the distinct socialist possibilities opened up by the Anglo-American alliance.

The emergence of at least a tenuous consensus can be traced by studying the flow of resolutions at conferences. The following tabulation summarizes the steady decline in hostile resolutions on both foreign and defense policy from 1947 through 1949:[33]

| Year | Favorable Resolutions | Unfavorable Resolutions |
|------|------|------|
| 1946 | 2 | 44 |
| 1947 | 3 | 42 |
| 1948 | 1 | 17 |
| 1949 | 0 | 6 |
| 1950 | 3 | 25 |
| 1951 | 2 | 64 |

As can be seen, the opposition to the government as measured in volume of resolutions declined by six-sevenths from 1947 to 1949. Even allowing for the reduction in resolutions that affiliated organizations could make, this suggests a definite downward swing. An examination of the substance of the resolutions submitted at the 1949 conference, as well as of the debate they generated, offers further substantiation of this trend. Those critical of the government spoke in tones decidedly lacking the usual bite of previous hostile commentary. Typical were the remarks of R. H.

S. Crossman, who observed that everyone in the party—everyone, whether on the "Left, Centre, or Right Wing"—could be "proud of four years of foreign policy."[34]

Further evidence of a developing agreement, however shaky and incomplete, was furnished by the publication of "Keeping Left" a few months afterward. The pamphlet was, to be sure, critical of the government's policy, but the point is that where "Keep Left" had cauterized all of Bevin's measures without exception, the language employed by "Keeping Left" was for the most part temperate. Again, where "Keep Left" had thought that the world stood on the brink of nuclear disaster in 1947, the later publication found reason for considerable hope. Perhaps the most striking indication of the trend in question was the admission that the critics' previous foreign policy—a socialist policy—now "had to be scrapped."

The 1950 general election campaign bore further witness to the trend. In marked contrast to the 1945 campaign, there was little difference between Tory and Labour pronouncements regarding foreign policy. The one notable exception was Churchill's dramatic appeal for a summit-like conference, and if this showed anything, it was that the Labour leadership seemed confident enough to adopt the more aggressive anti-Soviet posture in public.

The Labour Party emerged from the election with its once huge Parliamentary majority slashed to a mere five seats. In light of this slim margin, it no doubt seemed reasonable at the time to suppose that if the party was going to continue to govern effectively, its members would more than ever stress their incipient unity with respect to foreign policy. And yet, in less than a year, the spirit of consensus was once more shattered, and not even the protracted and confused endeavors of another decade would fully suffice to silence the renewal of bitter conflict.

# Chapter eight

# The Rearmament Crisis and the Renewal of Conflict

> *I believe that the putting up of the war machine in the absence of a sane social policy of itself makes war inevitable.*
>
> —ANEURIN BEVAN

> *Anyone who tries to persuade the public that in these times freedom can be defended without sacrifice and without hardships is deceiving himself and our people, and is doing a grave disservice to our nation.*
>
> —DEFENCE MINISTER EMANUEL SHINWELL

Two chains of events, the one following directly from the other, were responsible for shattering Labour's tenuous consensus on foreign policy. The first, in June 1950, was the Korean War; the second was the Labour government's consequent rearmament program. The war, by leading to a rapid deterioration in the international environment, alarmed the government's recently dormant critics; it reactivated all their doubts and uncertainties, their fears and anxieties that had receded into the background over the previous fifteen months. In this nervous atmosphere, the vast rearmament program amounted to an explosive issue, one on which the now aroused critics could challenge anew the whole of the government's foreign policy. The effect was disastrous for party unity. It replaced inchoate agreement with angry discord, promoted the disruptive emergence of the Bevanite faction, and reopened bitter doctrinal disputes lingering to this very day.

## THE BRITISH REARMAMENT PROGRAM

One month after the invasion of South Korea, the NATO allies received an appeal from Washington "to help to establish and to maintain the common strength of the United States and other free nations at an adequate level."[1] The response of the Labour government was predictable, entirely in accord with the principles underlying the traditional foreign policy that it had been conducting over the previous five years. The government agreed, without the least hesitation, to introduce massive rearmament measures.

Three pivotal reasons interacted to make this choice unavoidable. In the first place, Washington had just increased its own proposed defense budget fourfold; and since it was not prepared, in the anxious circumstances of the moment, to bear the major burdens of defense in Europe while fighting a war in the Far East, it resolutely expected its European allies to make sacrifices of a similar kind and magnitude.[2] The Labour Cabinet had no illusions concerning either the intensity of Washington's feeling or the issue at stake. It realized that to hesitate, to appear indecisive in the face of the requested sacrifices, would be to jeopardize the entire system of Atlantic security that it itself had worked unflaggingly to construct. In the second place, the fear gripped government circles that Korea might be only a diversion, a stratagem by means of which the Soviet Union was preparing for aggression elsewhere. Western Europe seemed the logical target, exposed as it was, in Defence Minister Shinwell's estimate, to 175 combat-ready Soviet divisions.[3] American protection thus loomed more indispensable than ever; yet now that the United States was being drawn to the Far East, its willingness to undertake large-scale military commitments in Europe could be taken even less for granted than before. The price of American security had suddenly risen, and no one had any doubt that it was decidedly a seller's market. In the third and final place, a huge British rearmament was all the more essential because of Britain's self-chosen role in the security system at the time, whereby it sought to mediate between American demands and European strategic concerns. On the one hand, Washington expected the Labour government to give a lead in rearming to the other European allies; on the other hand, the Europeans expected it to use its special influence to keep American attention riveted on the defense of the Continent. On both counts, the Labour government found itself obligated to respond firmly and quickly to the American appeal.

What would be the magnitude of the British effort? That, of course, was the critical question. Defense estimates for 1950–51 had been originally set at 780 million pounds, roughly 7.5 per cent of GNP,[4] and then raised in the summer by an additional 100 million pounds following a review of the British military establishment.[5] Since the review had been undertaken entirely outside the Korean War context, Shinwell warned the Commons that further expenditures would probably be required. On that very day the appeal from Washington arrived, and the result was indeed further expenditures: not on just one but on three separate occasions, each augmentation enmeshed in an overall defense program framed for a three-year period.

The first overall increase was announced within nine days.[6] The government now proposed to spend 3.4 billion pounds over the next three years, a rise in expenditures of almost 50 per cent per annum above the original 1950–51 estimates. It was also announced that this revised program was highly provisional, since the new estimates had been but hastily calculated, in rough fashion, so as to meet a ten-day deadline set by the American appeal. There was thus nothing to keep the program from being increased (or decreased); in fact the Commons, which was in adjournment at the time, no sooner reassembled in emergency session in September to consider the question of rearmament than it learned of a second general increase. According to government spokesmen, this was necessitated by certain changes in defense policy made during the August interval: among them, higher pay for the armed services, extended conscription from 18 to 24 months, and accelerated arms production. As a result of these additional costs, the proposed three-year program rose another 200 million pounds— to a total of 3.6 billion pounds. Attlee claimed that the new overall figure constituted the maximum that the country could undertake "without resorting to the drastic expedients of a war economy.[7] Other government speakers offered assurance that the program could be safely carried out without causing major economic damage; Hugh Gaitskell, Minister of State for Economic Affairs, was especially optimistic on this score.[8]

The third and final round of increased expenditures was announced by Attlee on 29 January 1951. It added 1.1 billion pounds to the September level, an increment of nearly one-third, which brought the total three-year program to an overall 4.7 billion pounds. With allowance made for predicted growth in productivity, this projected target represented an average of 14 per cent of GNP per annum. The program was to proceed at an uneven pace, arms production, for instance, running twice the pre-Korean rate during the first year, then picking up momentum and continuing at a still faster clip for the remaining two years.[9]

Hence, within the space of a mere six months, the Labour government responded to the deterioration in the international environment by more than doubling its pre-Korean defense effort.

The Bevanites were later to charge that the 4.7 billion pound program was reckless, utterly unsound—among other things—from an economic standpoint; and, as we shall see, there was merit in their argument. But the government's reasoning did not lack merit either. The question that prompts itself, then, is which side had the better case on balance.

This is not easy to say. The fact is that the question cannot really be seen apart and in isolation from the broader context of the recurring conflict between socialist and traditional foreign policy, for what essentially divided the two sides had far less to do with mere judgment in economic matters than with contrary perspectives and theoretical understanding of the existing international situation. The Bevanites did not rest their case on economic grounds but embedded it in a complex critique of the Korean War, Soviet intentions, the American alliance, and the conflicting claims of welfarism and rearmament; and this critique derived, of course, from socialist principles. The government, for its part, relegated economic considerations to a place of secondary import in its calculations. What preoccupied its attention were the strategic concerns of the moment as it perceived and understood them, and its understanding and perception were heavily conditioned by the traditional rationale underlying its entire foreign policy.

If these considerations are valid, it follows that the behavior and, more fundamentally, the motives of the two sides need to be probed and dissected. Only when this task is accomplished will an answer to the above question be possible.

### THE GOVERNMENT: IMAGE AND CALCULATIONS

That the government subordinated economic to strategic considerations is easily shown, if only because it ignored, in the course of all three rearmament programs, financial ceilings which it had earlier imposed. When Shinwell announced the 100 million pound increment on 26 July, for instance, he granted that "much larger sums" would probably be required, but insisted at the same time that "we can do no more from our own resources than make a *be-*

*ginning* on such a program." Yet this proviso was apparently dis-
regarded by the time Attlee unfolded plans for the 3.6 billion
pound program. Moreover, somewhat as Shinwell had earlier
done, Attlee on this occasion fixed an economic ceiling to the
program; the 3.6 billion pounds were said to represent the "maximum" that could be done short of "resorting to the drastic expedients of a war economy." The program seemed all the more
conclusive because of a second condition stipulated by Attlee,
which was that the program's fulfillment would be conditional
on large-scale American assistance. Yet both of these conditions
were brushed aside when Attlee made public the final 4.7 billion
pound program in January. Not only was the maximum stipulated in September abandoned, but nothing more was mentioned
regarding American assistance as a prerequisite (though assistance
was nonetheless still hoped for). Attlee, in justifying the upward
revision, struck an entirely different note. The new program was
to "be carried out . . . to the limit of the resources under our control."[10]

As for the government's strategic concerns which governed its
calculations, these can be pretty faithfully reconstructed. It is
clear, for instance, that the ominous lessons of the 1930's weighed
heavily on the minds of many ministers, which was not too surprising, of course, in view of their conviction that Labour vacillation and not just Tory folly alone had caused the disasters of
that period. Appeasement was something to be avoided at almost
any cost. "Naked aggression and it must be checked," Attlee told
the Commons shortly after the North Korean invasion, adding the
comment that "the salvation of all is dependent on prompt and
effective measures to arrest aggression wherever it may occur."[11]
The government's subsequent rearmament decisions were no
doubt facilitated by UN involvement in the war, but on two
counts its behavior would have probably remained unchanged in
either case. First, mere condemnation of aggression by an international organization had not sufficed in the past to elicit a firm Labour response, as the party's record during the Manchurian and
Ethiopian incidents had exhibited. It thus seems likely that the
cold war context and the desire to preserve the system of Atlantic
security figured more prominently in the government's calculations. And second, this seems all the more likely since the govern-

ment was less concerned with aggression in Asia than with possible aggression in Europe, a context covered by NATO, a traditional military alliance, rather than by the UN.

Another reason that economic considerations were subordinated to strategic concerns had to do with American pressure. No modern nation-state is completely sovereign with respect to the whole range of political decisions that it must constantly make; every national political system is *penetrated* on crucial occasions by influential actors from other national societies. As James Rosenau defines it, "a penetrated political system is one in which non-members of a national society participate directly and authoritatively, through actions taken jointly with the society's members, in either the allocation of its values or the mobilization of support on behalf of its goals."[12] In this sense, the British system in 1950 was unquestionably penetrated on the issue of rearmament. American actors participated in the processes of allocating values and attaining goals relating to the issue, and they did so authoritatively, in that the resulting decisions were no less legitimate than were other decisions in which they did not participate.* The reason for the American penetration is easy to specify: British military dependence on the United States. The point can also be put more positively: the Labour government set enormous store by its alliance with the United States, now rendered all the more important in its eyes by the Korean War, and it did so to the point that it was willing to alter the existing pattern of allocating values out of deference to American wishes. This was shown on more than one occasion, beginning with the appeal of July 26. More appeals, all of them urging a greater rearmament effort, followed in proportion to the worsening Korean situation. Washington, in effect, was steadily raising the price of its commitment to defend Western Europe, in large part because of domestic pressures from Congress and the military but also out of the Administration's conviction

---

* I want to stress that the decisions in question were authoritative and legitimate. As Rosenau, following Easton, observes (p. 64): "Such external penetration may not always be gladly accepted by the officials and citizens of a society, but what renders decisions legitimate and authoritative is that they are felt to be binding, irrespective of whether they are accepted regretfully or willingly." An example of regretful penetration is Soviet influence on Finnish elections, whereas American penetration into rearmament matters in Britain tends more toward the pole of willingness.

that the grave situation warranted abnormal sacrifices. Attlee, in his meeting with Truman in December, agreed that "the military capabilities of the United States and of the United Kingdom should be increased as rapidly as possible."[13] Translated into different terms, this signaled the Labour government's abandonment of the September 3.6 billion pound maximum. It abandoned this ceiling, moreover, without ever getting prior assurance of American aid; in fact the American position on the matter had hardened since the summer.[14] A few days later, the Labour government explicitly pledged itself at a meeting of the Atlantic Council to revise its 3.6 billion pound program upward.[15]

That a political system is penetrated, however, does not necessarily mean that it is fully penetrated—that its national decision makers are powerless. Penetration is a matter of degree, and in the case of the British system in 1950–51, there were limits to the Labour government's readiness to tolerate American participation. Washington, for instance, was known to have been dissatisfied with the final 4.7 billion pound program; it exerted pressure to raise the level to at least 6.0 billion pounds, and even managed to enlist the support of the United Kingdom military chiefs.[16] Nonetheless, despite its susceptibility to such pressure, the Cabinet refused to acquiesce and argued that a greater effort would be economically harmful. Short of Washington's applying sanctions to have its will prevail, the limits of its penetration had been reached.

### OCTOBER 1950–FEBRUARY 1951: PROLOGUE TO BEVANISM

If there was one area of the Labour government's policy to which its critics were never reconciled, not even during the period of tenuous consensus, this involved defense expenditures. Indeed, it was precisely during this period that the argument over priorities was forged into a serviceable socialist doctrine. At the 1949 conference, for instance, general harmony prevailed except on the defense issue, and Crossman and others congratulated the government on four years of foreign policy, only in the next breath to expostulate with it for sadly wasting money on armaments that could be better employed in further welfare activity. Given this persistent undercurrent of hostility to defense spending, it was only to be expected that many Labour partisans turned out to be shocked by the government's September rearmament program of 3.6 billion pounds. The while thing seemed to them to smack of mindless militarism, and they (rightly) suspected that American pressure had been involved. Over the next few months, more and more backbenchers as well as rank-and-filers became alarmed at what they referred to as hysteria in government circles.

How alarmed can be conveniently traced by following the reversal of the *Tribune*'s sympathies. The journal, it will be recalled, had broken with the ranks of the critics during the Berlin crisis, then subsequently endorsed the North Atlantic Pact; the Korean War thus found it predictably sympathetic to American intervention and in favor of British help. And yet within at most a mere three or four months' span, the *Tribune* was functioning as a vociferous voice of rank-and-file disgruntlement and apprehension.

Although the first note of uncertainty crept into the *Tribune*'s pages in early August, at the time the government announced its first (3.4 billion pound) rearmament program, its commentary manifested distinct uneasiness only following the September debate on the 3.6 billion pound program. An editorial in its 15 September issue doubted the ability of the nation to absorb economic burdens of this magnitude. Then in October appeared "Full Speed Ahead," a *Tribune* pamphlet that expressed the most agonizing qualms regarding the government's behavior. Asserting, in language reminiscent of "Keeping Left" (which, however, had been published six months before Korea), that there was no evidence whatever of any Soviet military threat, it warned that the primary task was still to keep budgetary priorities straight and that, therefore, the rearmament program should be drastically pared down. Otherwise, "exaggerated notions of Soviet strength" would irreparably dislocate the economy, thereby undermining Labour's hard-won social achievements and handing the Russians in effect a "bloodless victory." In addition, as if to signal the collapse of the party's inchoate consensus, "Full Speed Ahead" demanded that the government return to sanity and introduce a bold socialist foreign policy.[17] The subsequent deterioration of the Korean War following the entrance of Chinese troops led the *Tribune* to concentrate its barbs and strictures on the other member of the Anglo-

American tie. With increasingly ardent abandon, it lashed at American policy and policy makers, decrying their impulsiveness and recklessness, warning that their anti-Communist mania would provoke war with China, and urging therefore (as one issue put it) a "negotiated settlement at all costs." When the Truman Administration persisted nonetheless in fighting a limited war, the journal located the reason in the "total surrender of the American moderates, men like Acheson and Truman, to the Republican clamour."[18] By early February it was all but forecasting a holocaust to be visited on the world as a consequence of American hotheadedness. It insisted that "the danger of war no longer arises solely from Soviet policy. It arises also from the temper which has been aroused in the United States and the foolhardy policies on which the erstwhile progressive Government in Washington has been launched at the bidding of an ever more raucous and hysterical reaction."[19]

It needs to be immediately added that this was in nowise a unique sentiment in Labour circles at the time. The whole party was infected with chafing disquietude, as shown by the ever more severe attacks under which both American policy and the government's support of it were coming. Not one of the major left-wing publications actively championed the government's cause, which was perhaps predictable, but more unexpected sources also found ample cause for alarm. From the one side, the *New Statesman*—which like the *Tribune* had backed initial UN intervention in Korea—warned that what had started as resistance to aggression had "ended as an insane American gamble in the diplomacy of power politics."[20] From the other and less foretellable side, the pro-Labour but by no means pro-left *Daily Mirror* "provided headlines, day after day in January, 1951, which presented its millions of scanners with an almost entirely unrelieved, and unexplained, picture of American belligerence, only barely restrained by the efforts of British Labour statesmen."[21] The tempo of apprehension was also caught by opinion polls. One survey revealed that no less than 25 per cent of Labour *voters* thought America was more likely than Russia to start a general war (the corresponding Conservative figure was only 8 per cent).[22] Given the usual difference in ardor between ordinary Labour voters and party activists, the proportion of the latter holding this opinion was no doubt considerably higher still.

Clearly these anxious discontents were not mere transient distempers of the moment. They betokened something more deeprooted, something that had to do with a pervasive uncertainty regarding the soundness of the government's foreign policy. Labour, in short, was passing through one of its profound crises in confidence.

The force of this observation is made all the stronger by reference to another and equally gnawing source of unease at the time: impending German rearmament. "Keeping Left's" admonitions had been to no avail, for, in September 1950, Bevin joined Robert Schuman and Dean Acheson in agreeing to the principle of a German contribution to European defense. Perceived American recklessness and British rearmament aside, no issue could have been more inflammable from the predominant Labour point of view. To be sure, the issue was not particularly popular in the nation at large, but at any rate the Conservative leadership was sufficiently steeped in the rudiments of balance-of-power politics to appreciate the wisdom of a German build-up and the need to champion it within party ranks. With Labour, however, it was an entirely different matter, not least because of an intense hostility to postwar German capitalism. The latter seemed to many party members to be scarcely better than prewar fascism, and long before September 1950 a loud and insistent clamor had been raised against the "German-American financial condominium over the Western Continent."[23] Small wonder, then, that American-sponsored German rearmament seemed so sinister and stirred so many misgivings, and was taken to be another blatant sign of headlong American impetuosity; or that, once absorbed into the general socialist syndrome being reactivated at the time, it would lend itself so appropriately to the Bevanite cause. Under these circumstances, the government itself had second thoughts and sought relief in equivocation. In February, Attlee informed the Commons that Labour's commitment to German rearmament needed to be clarified—clarification meaning, as it turned out, an elaborate hedge in the form of prior conditions that would have to be satisfied before Labour could sanction German arms.*

---

* The three major conditions were (1) the prior rearmament of the Atlantic Pact nations, (2) West German agreement to their rearmament, and (3) the integration of German military unity with other national contingents. See Attlee in 484 *H.C.Deb.* 67 (12 February 1951).

Did this concession have any effect in appeasing the critics? Quite probably it did, though this is hard to document, since alarm within the party was still constantly on the upsurge in connection with American behavior in Korea and with the economic problems of rearmament at home. At any rate, what success the Attlee conditions did enjoy was decidedly of short duration. In the long run the ungovernable problem of interpreting them, in changed circumstances, furnished the Bevanites with a convenient issue on which to challenge anew the leadership's authority.

### BEVANITE REVOLT

By mid-February, then, the climate in the Labour Party was tense, shot through with unrest and uneasiness in most circles and with outright anxiety in others. It was in this charged atmosphere that Aneurin Bevan, now Minister of Labour, spoke in a Parliamentary debate on the 4.7 billion pound rearmament program. The speech is worth examining as a prelude to the subsequent party crisis.

As a minister, Bevan was ostensibly speaking in favor of the program, and on the surface his talk seemed to amount to that. The *Manchester Guardian* even commented that it was one of the best defenses of the government's policy to date.[24] Upon closer scrutiny, however, the speech can be construed in another light, too, in which it appears as much a case against *rapid* rearmament as a defense of the rearmament program; indeed, several points that Bevan subsequently elaborated on in his resignation speech, and that came to figure as part of the theoretical message of his faction, were foreshadowed here.[25] For purposes of analysis, they can be gathered into two broad categories. The first called into question the very ground for large-scale rearmament. Bevan resolutely disparaged any Soviet military danger and insisted that no nation with a steel capacity far inferior to that of its combined adversaries would coldly contemplate an attack on them.[26] At the same time, he dwelt on what he did think was a looming danger: the menace created by converting "the complicated machinery of modern industry to war preparation too quickly." Not only would priorities be wildly distorted and the economy irreparably harmed in consequence, but inevitably a campaign of hate and hysteria would be engendered as "in other places."[27] Thus, without naming America directly, Bevan joined the standard argument over priorities to the recently reinvigorated anti-Americanisms flourishing in the ranks.

One of these points is sufficiently intriguing to single out here: Bevan's ardent concern with the health of the economy in a period of military mobilization. This seems like a decidedly socialist concern, and in fact it follows directly from socialist principles; yet the interesting thing is the extent to which this concern paralleled right-wing fears in America at the time. Dozens of senators like Taft and Byrd and congressmen like Cannon and Mahon were also alarmed at the prospect of heavy defense expenditures, and they consistently criticized Truman's defense budgets (even the comparatively small ones before 1950) as though the American economy might go bankrupt as a result at any moment. The similarity in viewpoint of the two groups is uncanny. Like the Bevanites, the Congressional right located the primary security of their nation in the condition of the civilian economy, especially in the maintenance of prevailing consumption standards: Congressman Mahon, for instance, worried lest the Administration's spending were "to bankrupt the country or squander our dwindling resources; that would be the road to national insecurity and the possible loss of the next war if one should come."[28] Again, just as Bevan warned the Commons of the inevitable internal dangers accompanying rapid rearmament, so Senator McClellan proclaimed that "economic instability caused by deficit spending constitutes a much greater threat from within to both the security and survival of our liberties than does the military threat of communism from without."[29] Yet, again, in the same sort of way that Bevanites feared that large defense spending would at some point invariably undermine Labour's socialist experiment, their counterparts in Washington believed that "there is a point at which free enterprise must go on a downward path . . . and turn to a socialist form of government."[30] Most striking of all, the American right even developed a version of the socialist priorities argument. According to Senator Henry Cabot Lodge, "there should be a thoroughly scientific determination of what the point of public expenditures is at which we shall have to militarize our economy and go to allocation, priorities, rationing, and other controls."[31]

Bevan spoke on behalf of the government in mid-February; his resignation took effect two months later. This raises a question of of signal importance. What motives were at work during the interval in prompting Bevan's decision? Two different sets can be distinguished.

The first yields the explanation that Bevan was actuated primarily, if indeed not entirely, by strictly personal considerations. Interestingly, this has been the explanation preferred by many of the principal Cabinet ministers on whom Bevan walked out.[32] If it is correct, then socialist principles had little or nothing to do with his behavior; at most they furnished a convenient pretext and guise, a serviceable lever by means of which he could rationalize and further his personal aims within the political arena. But in fact this does not seem to be the whole story. Ambition, fervent desires for rank, power, and fame as well as the rancor arising from their frustration—these all played some part, no doubt, in Bevan's calculations, but the point is whether they constitute by themselves a sufficient explanation of what happened or whether it is also necessary to refer to matters of principle, policy, or ideology.

The personal considerations that obviously bulked large in Bevan's decision are easy enough to isolate, particularly the two that in retrospect seem strategic. The first involved a double jolt to his political aspirations. The initial blow was delivered in October 1950, when the Chancellorship of the Exchequer fell vacant and Attlee bypassed him by appointing Hugh Gaitskell to the post; the second blow came the following March, when Ernest Bevin resigned as Foreign Secretary and Herbert Morrison received the appointment. Bevan, as Dalton later observed, was "much vexed" by these developments; he let it be known that he himself was best qualified for the posts and deserved promotion by virtue of his record at the Ministry of Health.[33] Beyond this, moreover, Bevan sensed an obvious threat to his ambitions for the eventual leadership of the party. Until then, he might have been excused for thinking himself the likeliest successor at some future time; after all, not only had he performed deftly as Minister of Health, but in addition he was acknowledged to have "outstanding qualities" as an orator and debater[34] and to enjoy a sizable following in the party at large, having repeatedly received the highest poll for a constituency seat on the NEC. Not least among his assets was his age—only 53, which contrasted sharply with the ages of other prominent ministers who were all at least in their mid-sixties. All of them, that is, except Gaitskell, who was even younger (44) and who, so it might appear, was now being groomed by Attlee as a direct rival for the leadership. Bevan would have had to be more than human not to be vexed or to reconsider his future prospects in the light of these new and entirely unforeseen circumstances.

Besides, he was probably all the more impelled to a thorough reconsideration under pressure of a second, somewhat related danger: the longer he continued to defend the government's rearmament program, the likelier he would end up alienating his large following among the ranks. Despite the reservations he had expressed at the time, his February 15 discourse was, after all, still a defense of government policy and had been widely interpreted as such. Bevan could not have been very happy to take such a public stand. Throughout the whole of the first Attlee government, he had, in effect, been in a position to enjoy the best of two worlds, to operate as a member of the Cabinet yet simultaneously to maintain his reputation as a fulsome radical—and the reason was that as Minister of Health and Housing he only had to defend domestic policies, and popular policies at that. But defending measures like rearmament, which is what he had to do as Minister of Labour, was an entirely different matter. It placed him in an exposed position, where he risked incurring considerable unpopularity with backbench militants and rank-and-file enthusiasts, and the prospect must have struck him as not very appealing. As long as there remained a chance of promotion to a higher ministerial post, the advantages of remaining in the government might have outweighed all the irritating disadvantages. But his failure to succeed either Cripps or Bevin no doubt reversed this balance in his eyes.

Such were the obvious personal motives involved in Bevan's behavior. The question is whether these amount to a sufficient explanation of his behavior. As mentioned before, this does not seem to be the case. In fact, to assume that Bevan acted only on the strength of personal considerations is to make the same sort of error as to assume that policy disputes and questions of principle alone counted. There are at least three major reasons for assuming that issues relating to socialist foreign policy materially mattered. First, Bevan had very much the disposition of a political visionary, the kind of enthusiast to whom Labour's socialist principles would not only strongly appeal but loom as articles of fervent faith. He was in fact a self-confessed ideologue, writing in one place that "it is the practice of many publicists to sneer at the Labour party for clinging to what are called 'doctrinaire' principles. You would imagine from the manner of these attacks that lack of principle is a suitable political equipment. No statesman can stand the strain of modern political life without the inner serenity that comes from fidelity to a number of guiding convictions. Without their steadying influence he is blown about by every passing breeze.... Without [a general body of principles which make up one's philosophy] politics is merely a job like any other."* Except for saints, what a man professes and how he actually behaves are, normally, two different things; but by the prevailing standards within the British system, the gap in Bevan's case must be judged a narrow one. His whole political career until 1945 marked him as a genuine radical activist. Notorious class antagonist, Socialist League mainstay, (temporary) expellee from the Labour Party, unregenerate opponent of the Coalition government: such were the characteristics that distinguished his behavior and inspired his followers to believe in his doctrinal purity even after he was pitched straight from the backbenches into the Cabinet.

Second, Bevan's fierce dispute with the leadership in the spring of 1951 was only the latest eruption of his long-smoldering antagonism to its growing domestic moderation. He had been the foremost advocate in the Cabinet of iron and steel nationalization, even threatening to resign unless his colleagues went along.[35] Gaitskell, whose budget of the current spring was seized upon by Bevan as the immediate cause for falling out with the leadership, enjoyed, oppositely, a reputation as a firm "consolidator" and had taken a go-slow stand on further nationalization. The issue

---

* Bevan, *In Place of Fear*, pp. 95–96. Bevan's ideological bent is ably captured in Michael Foot's biography (*Aneurin Bevan*, p. 494): "Bevan's quarrels ... [with the Labour leadership] derived from profound differences of principle. He never saw them in any other light and he never ceased to rail against the habit of newspapers of 'personalizing' every dispute in which he engaged.... The argument, not the man, was the origin of his animosities. He himself was so convinced of this truth that he regarded the attribution of any other motive a scandalous malice."

at stake, then, was not just a matter of personal ambition and personal friction but also a question of doctrine and principle, though in the person of Gaitskell, an arch-revisionist, the two factors largely overlapped. Here was the link that enabled Bevan to join his ideological grievances in the domestic field to the mounting disquiet over rearmament and foreign policy; for he obviously saw the recent blows to his personal fortune as part and parcel of the developing conflict between revisionism and orthodoxy. No less than the "hysterical militarism" that he detected, his personal injuries apparently loomed in his eyes as a dreadful portent of an anti-socialist upsurge, and Gaitskell's budget—its challenge to the principle of a free health service—could only have hardened and cemented this impression. "It's 1931 all over again with Gaitskell playing the part of Snowden," he protested to a journalist: "He and Morrison are leading the Party to absolute disaster."[36]

Third and finally, whatever personal motives entered into Bevan's decision, the fact remains that his resignation was justified in terms of principles and policy issues.[37] Bevan could not and did not represent his challenge to the leadership as a purely personal matter, and those who rallied so enthusiastically to his cause did not do so simply because of his political charisma. They regarded the government's rearmament program, and the foreign policy from which it derived, as wrong, dead wrong; and fearing for the purpose of the party in the future, they and Bevan together fashioned an elaborate theoretical critique as a means of routing the existing leadership. In nearly every respect, that critique was a defense of socialist orthodoxy.

### THE BUDGET DISPUTE

When Attlee, in announcing the 4.7 billion pound rearmament program, added that it would be "carried out to the limit of the resources under our control," the government in effect served notice that reductions in its civilian expenditures might be required. In the preliminary discussions of the budget that went on in February and March, Gaitskell argued that one area where money could be saved would be the National Health Service if a charge of 50 per cent was placed on spectacles and dentures, hitherto provided free. Bevan objected strenuously, on grounds of principle. As he subsequently told a Labour gathering at Bermondsey in early April, he would "never" belong to a government that "proposed to put charges to patients on parts of the National Health Service."[38] Failing to get the satisfaction he demanded from the rest of the Cabinet, which stood by Gaitskell, Bevan resigned from the government two weeks later.

Bevan's supporters later blamed Gaitskell for causing the ensuing party split, charging that he had been pigheaded about the proposed spectacles and dentures fee. They pointed out that the consequent sum saved by the Treasury was ridiculously small, a mere 13 million pounds—this out of a total budget of some 3.5 billion pounds. In their view, Bevan and the two colleagues who resigned along with him were left no choice, driven to their desperate course out of exasperation with Gaitskell's perverse decision to rest acceptance of his budget on such a trivial issue. Trivial, that is, in terms of the sum involved: as for the principle at stake, Bevan and his supporters agreed that the budgetary dispute was a matter of utmost importance, involving nothing less than the whole future of the welfare state. If the principle of a free Health Service were scuttled, where, after all, would the line be drawn under the intense pressure of near-hysterical militarism, massive and unnecessary rearmament, and runaway inflation? This was the question that the Bevanites posed to themselves, and to others, again and again over the next several months.

In retrospect, the sum of money involved in the dispute was unquestionably trifling. Even so, this does not necessarily mean that Gaitskell was perverse and wrongheaded in imposing his will on a fiercely protesting colleague. From his viewpoint, and presumably the viewpoint of the Cabinet majority standing by him, there were other and more pressing matters to be considered.

One had to do with expenditures on the Health Service, which had recently exceeded all expectations and appeared to Gaitskell and his colleagues as threatening to get out of hand. In this sense, a charge on hitherto free services might not only be reasonable but commend itself as a deterrent to frivolous use of the Health Service and its facilities. Whether Gaitskell had a better case than Bevan in this connection is, however, something else again and does not particularly concern us.

A second and more relevant matter involved the way budgets are normally hammered together. Cabinet tussles over departmental allocations often concern only minor sums; what may be important is not so much the size of particular funds as the fact that somewhere, at some point, the Chancellor of the Exchequer has to draw a line in weighing and balancing the various departmental claims and then make it clear to his colleagues that, so far as he is concerned, this line is final.[39] Of course, the Chancellor may not always get his way; Cabinet government permits a disgruntled minister to appeal to the body as a whole, in which case it must collectively decide who is to prevail.[40] Bevan appealed in just this way and, finding himself overruled and Gaitskell upheld, had either to submit or to resign. Moreover, Gaitskell was probably more obstinate because he was a new Chancellor than he might otherwise have been; for prudence dictated that he assert his authority from the outset if he did not want to risk the prospect of seeing it challenged repeatedly in the future, of watching one minister after another imitate Bevan's tactics of resistance.* In the clash of wills between the two, Gaitskell anyway was not alone in being stubborn. Acccording to Dalton, Bevan was "truculent, arrogant, rhetorical, already hinting at resignation if he were thwarted, determined either to bend the Cabinet to his will or break it."[41] Doubtlessly, he was banking on the hope that his own prestige and following in the party were too much for Gaitskell—this, at any rate, would account for his making the dispute public in his Bermondsey speech, at a time when discussions of the budget were still going on.

Quite aside from these two matters, however, a question of principle was most basically at issue. This of course is what the Bevanites contended, but the question cannot be so easily disposed of as they were prone to believe. The truth is that not just one but rather two sets of principles were at stake—principles standing in direct contrast to each other. On the Bevanite side, the principles involved placed a far higher value on welfare expenditures than on rearmament; they did so, not because they slighted the needs of foreign policy as contrasted with domestic considerations, but because they manifested a profoundly anti-militarist bias and

---

* Shinwell reports (p. 224) that "many of my colleagues were doubtful about the wisdom of the cut [in Health Service expenditures]. They hoped for a compromise, but Gaitskell, in a difficult financial situation, was in no mood to compromise."

formulated the requirements of a good foreign policy in largely social, economic, and moral terms. On the government's side, the principles involved were those constituting the rationale behind its traditional foreign policy, and prominent among them was a firm emphasis on maintaining harmonious relations with America, on preserving the structure of Atlantic security, and on meeting a recognized common danger. Because the two sets of principles started from entirely different assumptions and postulates, because they yielded an entirely different perspective of the international environment, and not least because those who held them did so with utter conviction, there was little or no room for compromise.

### THE RESIGNATIONS

That fundamentally a clash of principles underlay the dispute is made all the more evident by inspection of Bevan's resignation speech of April 23.

Two days before that, he had informed Attlee of his decision in a letter cataloging four major disagreements with the rest of the Cabinet that made his continuance in the government "dishonourable." These were: (1) that the rearmament program was "physically unattainable" short of causing grave and irreparable structural damage to the economy; (2) that the program would inevitably provoke runaway inflation; (3) that the budget shifted the main burden of defense expenditures onto the working class; and (4) that the budget also signaled the "beginning of the destruction of those services ... which were giving to Britain the moral leadership of the world."* In reply, Attlee noted that Bevan had extended "the area of disagreement" with his colleagues far beyond his objection to charges on dentures and spectacles. This was Attlee's way of referring to the clash of principles, and any lingering doubts that he or others might have had on the basic issue at stake were shattered by Bevan's subsequent remarks to the

---

* The letter is quoted in full in Williams, *A Prime Minister Remembers*, pp. 247–48. Attlee, incidentally, had been in the hospital throughout the preliminary discussions on the budget, Morrison presiding over the Cabinet in his place; on p. 246 of Williams's book, he claims that had he been well enough to take charge, he might have prevented the resignations—something that is very dubious.

Commons. For the speech, though stopping short of the full-blown socialist critique that the Bevanites were to unpack in the months to come, was nonetheless a reflective and sustained attack on not just the rearmament program but the whole course of the government's present foreign policy.

The opening notes echoed the principal themes of his February discourse. Reminding the House how he had warned on that occasion against letting rearmament get out of hand, he now insisted that this was exactly what had happened in the interval—the demand for primary materials from abroad had soared, their prices had been dragged up in consequence, and the terms of trade were deteriorating without respite; as a result, the nation faced a spiraling rise in the cost of living, untold dislocation was being inflicted on its normal patterns of productivity, and, not least, there was a glaringly inadequate "supply of materials, components, and machine tools." Since, Bevan observed, the Prime Minister himself had conditioned the rearmament program on availability of the latter items, that program now had no further claim on Labour's loyalties; hence the reason for his own withdrawal of support.[42]

With these preliminary points out of the way, Bevan turned to a biting four-pronged attack on the government's foreign policy and related activities. First, reiterating in effect the fourth socialist principle, he struck a loud anti-militarist tone and asserted that the challenge of totalitarianism is "first social and economic, and only next military."[43] This led him, in the second place, to restate in detail the standard argument over priorities: these the government had hopelessly muddled in its new budget, and the result was jeopardizing the nation's standard of living, undermining its fair shares and other welfare accomplishments, adding through its scramble for raw materials to the dislocation of the international economy, and so creating in the upshot a "whole series of Trojan horses" within the gates of the Western world. Indeed, British liberties and parliamentary democracy were already moving under the shadow of sudden and unpredictable collapse.[44]

At this point Bevan then maneuvered about to link up all these menaces to the anti-American jitteriness in the party. There was no question but that capitalist America was principally to blame for the world's troubles, and whether the Americans realized it or not, their reckless militarism would end by inflicting more harm on mankind than could possibly be done by the Communists against whom they were so hysterically rearming. What was more, it was "perfectly clear" that the world's economic health would be imperiled so long as the huge American production machine remained unregulated, free of central control.[45] And finally Bevan revived the third force policy, of which little had been heard for the past two years, the erstwhile third-forcers having come to concentrate their efforts upon further "socializing" the Anglo-American alliance. Little had been heard, that is, until the last two or three months, when as a result of the upsurge in anti-Americanism a rapid change in outlook was discernible; neutralist sentiment was again reactivated, and it only took Bevan's remarks to crystallize it into a renewed and vigorous tendency within the party. Britain, he told the House, had managed since 1945 to seize the moral leadership of the world by virtue of its welfare achievements, to the point that everyone else automatically looked to it for a portent of what they themselves should be doing. There was nothing that could really compete with the message of *true* British socialism, a message that was and had to remain completely distinct from what either the Soviets or the Americans could offer. In fact—and here Bevan could well have been echoing the rebels of November 1946—that message was mankind's only hope for peace and salvation.*

ASSESSMENT

How valid was this Bevanite case? The answer must remain inconclusive. In a strictly economic sense, the case made a number of

---

* 487 *H.C.Deb.* 39 (23 April 1951). Bevan was joined in resigning by two younger members of the government: Harold Wilson, president of the Board of Trade, and John Freeman, a junior minister. Wilson addressed the Commons on the day following Bevan's speech, and he was briefer, less inclined to place his resignation in ideological perspective, and certainly less disputatious. The closest he came to affirming a socialist principle was a reference to the need for the government to get its budgetary priorities straight; even then, he did not doctrinally assert that the social services deserved first priority— only that they had "a contribution to world peace no less real than an unobtainable rearmament program." In line with this more cautious phraseology, he was also careful to grant that there were genuine strategic reasons that might justify large-scale rearming. For the rest, his speech dealt with his conviction that the 4.7 billion pound rearmament program was economically unsound. 487 *H.C.Deb.* 229–31 (24 April 1951).

telling points, above all, that the rearmament program was probably too ambitious, given in particular the unavailability of adequate materials, components, and machine tools. Yet even on
strictly economic grounds the case had certain drawbacks. In some
ways, in fact, it was decidedly erratic. Thus, the Bevanites predicted that the current economic crisis would be a protracted one,
lasting perhaps for years, whereas by as early as the autumn "most
prices must have been back to the levels which could be accounted for by the trend of production and consumption";[46] even the
drain on the gold and dollar reserves continued only into the
first quarter of 1952, after which it was halted and then reversed.[47]
Moreover, the charge that the budget was inequitable, shifting the
major burden of rearmament onto the working class through
planned inflation, seems unfair to Gaitskell and the rest of the
Cabinet; Gaitskell himself roundly dismissed the charge in a subsequent speech and pointed out that, far from the welfare state's
being subverted, he had made provision for raising overall expenditures on the social services by fifty million pounds.[48] All the same,
in strictly economic terms the Bevanite case must be judged to
have fared well. Rapid inflation did temporarily take place (the
cost of living index climbing by 8 per cent), the reserves were under
severe strain (an outflow of 2 billion dollars being needed to cover
the trade gap by the end of the year), the necessary materials were
not all available, and some industrial dislocation apparently resulted. Most telling of all, the Conservatives themselves vindicated the case in large part when, on entering office in late 1951,
Churchill observed that the existing rearmament schedule was
too ambitious and had to be "stretched out."[49]

On the other hand, an evaluation that stopped at this point
would leave a great deal unevaluated. For the heart of the matter
at stake between the Bevanites and the government was not economic in nature but political; and in a political sense, the Cabinet had good, sound reasons to proceed as it did despite the economic drawbacks involved. The point is significant and deserves
elaboration.

The reason political considerations predominated has already
been specified; the two sides approached the international situation out of which the pressures for rearmament arose with contrary perspectives, based on two incompatible images of the world

deriving in the one instance from socialist, and in the other from traditional, preconceptions and predispositions. They perceived the situation differently, defined their relation to it differently, understood the vital issues at stake differently. If perception of a threat were similar to perception of a tangible object, then the intrusion of such contrary preconceptions and predispositions would not have greatly mattered; in that case the question of whose perception was correct could have been easily settled. But, of course, threat perception is in another category. It is largely a matter of inference, of intuitively piecing together the evidence at hand relating to the capabilities and intentions of another actor; and in interpreting evidence of this sort, preconceptions and predispositions are bound to come into play. No wonder, then, that the government and its Bevanite critics disagreed so sharply and were so irritably impatient with each other. They literally saw the world through different eyes. Trust in the valuable American ally, concern for the system of Atlantic security, apprehension of Soviet intentions, and faith in power balancing swayed the perception of the one; distrust of American capitalism, half-trust in the Soviet system, antagonism to armaments, and concern for the domestic effects of rearmament swayed the perception of the other.

The same point can be put differently. Let us suppose that the Bevanites were right in insisting that the rearmament program was predominantly a question of priorities. The costs of defense should then be seen as consisting of sacrifices in civilian or nonsecurity values; and in any rational budgetary allocation, these costs must be weighed against the promised gains in security so that a balance is drawn between them. Yet precisely herein lay the crux of the dispute. *For the question of where to draw that balance, of whether to give priority to an increment of defense or nondefense values, is a matter of political judgment.* It is assuredly not dictated by objective economic indexes, and should the political authorities deem it necessary, defense can take such priority as to reduce civilian living standards to the minimum level compatible with public morale (which was the case in World War II). This is why the Bevanite accusation that the government failed to get its priorities straight is misleading. The question was clearly one of different political judgments in ordering priorities. On the one hand, the Bevanites insisted that social and economic policy should take precedence over defense policy, but they did this only after first arriving at the subjective judgment that the principal Communist challenge, even in 1950–51, was economic and social, not military. Conversely, if someone did not agree with this judgment, if he believed as the Cabinet majority apparently did that defense was now of primary importance, then his ordering of these matters was bound to be different.

The problem thus reduces to the question of whose judgment of the international situation was soundest. And yet this is a question that cannot be answered empirically, not even in retrospect. The essence of this matter was the conflicting estimations of Soviet intentions at the time. In the event, of course, no Soviet attack was launched; but whether this was because the attack was deterred by the vigorous Western rearmament, or whether it was simply that no such attack was ever seriously contemplated, is something impossible to determine short of the principal Soviet policy makers involved publishing detailed memoirs. Stalin has long been dead and those of his surviving associates who might have been privy to his thoughts remain, for obvious reasons, silent. In the absence of this, the only conclusive evidence, how then can one prove that what did not happen would have happened if only one circumstance had been different?

### THE TRIUMPH OF CONFLICT: BEVANISM AS A FACTION

The Bevanite view of the world developed rapidly after the April bout of resignations. So, too, did its attraction to the Labour Party. Bevan, in taking the step that he did, was able to bring all the miscellaneous discontent and disillusion in the ranks into sharp focus instantaneously. Until then, the critics had been unorganized, split into disparate and often *ad hoc* cliques, coteries, and cabals. Although there was a clear socialist identity running through their expressed attitudes, the critics lacked cohesion, their composition varying from issue to issue; they never arrived at a single well-defined program, their causes and concerns running the gamut from armed third force neutralism to outright pacifism; and they remained essentially a lot of second-string politicians, lacking an acknowledged leader of clear national stature. At most they formed, not a faction, but a tendency—that is, "a stable set of attitudes, rather than a stable group of politicians [with a measure of discipline and cohesion]."[50] But now Bevan's resignation transformed the situation. Suddenly and unexpectedly, this socialist tendency was joined company by one of Labour's most eminent members, a superb orator, a former outstanding Minister who enjoyed a sizable national following and had weighty claims to the party's leadership. No wonder the *Tribune* found immediate reason to celebrate "the dynamism . . . already carrying us forward to new positions of Socialist strength and Socialist unity."[51]

Here, obviously, lay all the makings of a coherent faction, self-consciously organized and able under the aegis of the leader to operate as a formidable and distinctive unit. What was more, those in the party opposed to the government now had at hand an extremely popular issue on which to rest their challenge: the health service charges and the detrimental economic effects of rearmament. A Gallup Poll suggested just how popular: 6o per cent of those interviewed, Labour or otherwise, expressed support for Bevan's position in the health service controversy.[52] A lively response was also stirred in the trade union movement. At the annual conference of the TUC in September, a Bevanite resolution on the health service was barely repulsed by a vote of 3,775,000 to 3,272,000.[53]

Still, as long as the Labour government depended on a precarious majority of six in the Commons, dissent was hard to organize, and a distinctive and coherent faction did not fully crystallize, therefore, until after the party's 1951 electoral defeat. Thereafter the Bevanite cause picked up impressive momentum, generating enthusiasm in every section of the party. Churchill's slowdown of the rearmament program in January 1952 did nothing, of course, to reverse this process. By March the Bevanites felt sufficiently confident of their strength to defy the leadership on the floor of Commons during the debate on the Conservative government's defense estimates. They had not miscalculated their strength: it was Attlee, not Bevan, who yielded the most ground in reaching a compromise when the matter of disciplinary action arose. By summer the Bevanites forced the leadership to retreat again, this time in connection with German rearmament. It was at the 1952 annual conference that the extent of the Bevanite force was most impressively bared. Not only did Bevan and five of his followers capture seven of the constituency party seats on the NEC, defeating Morrison, Dalton, and Shinwell in the process; what was more, a Bevanite resolution urging a reduction of the rearmament program and warning against dependence on the United States, which Gaitskell condemned as neutralist in tone and Attlee as doctrinaire in spirit, was barely turned back on a vote of 2,288,000 to 3,644,000.[54] In addition to the overwhelming support of the constituency parties, the resolution won over several of the big trade unions. Bevanism was clearly a power to be reckoned with, a movement that would shake the Labour Party to its foundations and nearly tear it apart in the process.

The emergence of Bevanism completed the disintegration of Labour's fragile consensus in foreign policy that had been eroding since autumn, 1950. Once again discord prevailed, just as it had in the 1945–48 period—only this time it was to prove even more far-reaching in its consequences. For six years Labour had governed the nation, during which it had fashioned a firm foreign policy and applied it with vigor; yet that policy had never really "bitten deep into the consciousness of the party." As a result, when Labour reverted to Opposition during the 1950's and early 1960's, it was no closer to agreement on fundamental questions of foreign policy than it had been in the past. Conflict, angry and protracted, was again its fate.

*Chapter nine*

## "In Search of Purpose"

In the fierce free-for-alls over foreign policy that convulsed Labour after 1951, the pivotal issues always reduced to the same gut matter: a massive crisis of purpose, an agonizing intellectual and moral dilemma concerning the party's aims and objectives in the political realm. Lacking any unifying consensus, Labour partisans suffered one *crise de conscience* after another, and the result was that they could not give clear-cut answers to recurring policy questions that invariably touched on underlying beliefs and basic moral values. Indeed, any attempt to be bold and decisive was fraught with hazard, liable—as Gaitskell discovered during the related controversy over Clause IV of the constitution—to result only in spreading disaffection and so pushing the party that much nearer to outright disintegration. Harold Wilson, in his own way, made a similar discovery, though the lesson that he drew has been rather different. Rather than grapple with matters of fundamental principle or try to clarify the party's purpose, he has preferred to take refuge in ambiguity and inaction and to avoid at all costs any effort to force decisions that would reopen festering divisions. Papering over cleavages with deft maneuvering and temporary compromises; edging along cautiously until controversy over policy alternatives loses its force because the situation in question has fully crystallized and demands some response, however improvisatory; pursuing blatant traditionalist policies abroad while invoking the old familiar socialist rhetoric; justifying, for instance, a costly and ill-conceived East-of-Suez engagement as Britain's socialist contribution to collective security, only to justify a hasty pullout as at long last opening the road to vigorous socialism at home—such has been the style of leadership, the mode of tactics, assiduously cultivated and faithfully implemented, of the two Wilson governments in foreign policy. Whether blurring of issues, temporizing, and forgoing initiative are too large a price to pay for these tactics remains to be seen. But what can be clearly seen even at this point is that as long as the Labour Party remains split on the central problems of the day, its leader has a hefty incentive to do nothing decisive lest he succeed only in intensifying conflict within the ranks.

This is, needless to say, a most unenviable spot for a political party to be in. What is particularly ironic is that such a fate has overtaken a party that was once so confidently cemented together by a powerful vision, a comprehensive socialist orthodoxy. How in the world did Labour partisans ever stumble into a moral and intellectual dilemma that now seems well-nigh inescapable?

The short answer is that, whereas the foreign policy of the two Attlee governments added up to a firm repudiation of socialist principles, a new vision—a new consensus—could not elicit agreement. To an observer unfamiliar with the previous patterns of conflict within the party, the intense disagreement that prevailed in this regard might seem puzzling. Hadn't the vision of the socialist pioneers proved to be utopian? Hadn't the Labour government in 1945 found that the problems confronting the nation were neither grasped nor still less illuminated by those who peered at the world through socialist eyes? And therefore was not the obviously sensible course to adapt the four socialist principles to the realities of power as experienced for six long years, retaining what was indisputably valuable in the old dogma but modifying it sufficiently to produce an operational doctrine—one that came to terms with the bipolar world and Britain's declining position in it?

The trouble is that only one faction in the Labour Party happened to read the history of the Attlee governments in this light. As far as it was concerned, there was not the slightest doubt that fearless rethinking, sweeping reconstruction—in short, not just adaptation but audacious and thoroughgoing revision—were in order. The old orthodoxies had failed, turned out to be unrealistic. The doubtful legacy of pro-Soviet sentiment, anti-American resentment, hankerings after third force greatness, and repugnance to armaments had not provided the nation with any helpful beacon when dealing with Soviet intransigence over German reparations, civil war in Greece, the Berlin Blockade, alliance relations, or aggression in Korea. Morally stirring or not, either the principles deriving from the socialist generation had therefore to be revised or they would continue to create the misunderstanding, confusion, and discord that had shaken intra-party politics between 1945 and 1948 and then again in 1951. Such in brief was the argument unpacked and defended by the revisionist, or the Gaitskellite, or more simply just the right wing of the party. In their eyes, facts were facts; and their opponents, by refusing to recognize them, by resisting modernization and the overhaul of dubious intellectual hand-me-downs, were, in Anthony Crosland's phrase, the true dogged conservatives of British politics—for they kept Labour from refurbishing its image and from rethinking its basic policies and attitudes, to the benefit only of the Conservative Party.[1]

To a second faction in the party, this whole line of argument was tendentious and muddled—and blasphemous as well. Far from the old orthodoxies having been proved inadequate between 1945 and 1951, they had never really been given a chance to control policy, for the simple reason that the Attlee governments had never tried to put socialist principles into practice—or, at rate, to put them into practice with much devotion or perseverance. And what accounted for this moral dereliction? On this score the Bevanites (the fundamentalists, the left) offered a battery of explanations. The leaders of the party had lacked faith in socialism; they had been corrupted by their tenure in the Churchill Coalition, they had allowed themselves to be outflanked by reactionaries in the Foreign Office, they had turned their backs on third force revolutionaries in Europe, they had sold out Britain's latitude of choice for a few hundred million American dollars. And worst of all, though as a logical consequence of these previous lapses, they had succumbed to hysteria in the autumn of 1950 and been prepared to jeopardize the whole foundation of the welfare state and future socialist prospects by hobbling the economy with a monstrous and unnecessary rearmament program. As far as the Bevanites were concerned, then, the underlying problem had nothing to do with socialist principles and everything to do with those who had seized the leadership of the party, diverted it from a bold socialist course, and pursued a bipartisan foreign policy well-nigh indistinguishable from Churchillianism.*

Nor was this all. For if the party leaders turned out to be so blatantly unreliable in the past, how could they be relied upon to plump for socialism in the future? To the fundamentalists, the question answered itself: they, the leaders, could not be counted upon, not as long as the Labour Party continued to function as it had for more than a decade since 1940. The only guarantee that genuine socialists could have would be one that they created for themselves; they would have to force the mass party, in the form of the conference, to assert itself and shackle the leadership in advance with detailed instructions. Predictably, to the revisionists' way of thinking, the Bevanite attempt to make the conference so rigid an ultimate authority was irresponsible in the extreme. It would not only deprive the PLP of flexibility, but aid the Tories electorally by substantiating the claim, raised by Churchill in 1945, that a Labour government was not a free agent. The plea for flexibility fell on deaf ears. "The purpose of this Conference," so a leading Bevanite insisted, is precisely "to clarify its position and tie this Executive down to socialist principles in foreign policy."[2]

There was nothing novel about the Labour Party's suffering angry conflict over foreign policy, prolonged or otherwise. But this time the conflict was fiercer, more drawn out, less conclusively resolved than in the past. For one thing, it coincided with a bitter and protracted struggle for the leadership, and the principal con-

---

* The charge of a Labour sellout to a Tory foreign policy was raised again and again by fundamentalists. For Michael Foot, for instance, "the aim of the right wing is to make British socialism mildly reformist in its domestic aspirations and bipartisan in foreign policy, accepting the Churchillian thesis of agreement with the United States at all costs" ("Mr. Bevan Remains"). One reason the charge was made so often was that it obviously put the revisionists on the defensive, so similar in most respects were their policy prescriptions to Conservative measures. Gaitskell once tried to deal with it by accepting its logic but denying the assumed causal connection: "I doubt if foreign policy will play a big part in the next Election—not because it is not important, but because Mr. Eden has, in fact, mostly carried on our policy as developed by Ernest Bevin, in some cases against the views of rank-and-file Tories" (*Tribune*, 8 October 1954).

tenders happened also to be the major spokesmen for their respective factions. Attlee himself trudged on until 1955, but the defects of his direction became increasingly glaring toward the end; his leadership was weak, confused, ineffective, conceding one thing to the Bevanites one day and then regretting it the next.* After 1955 Gaitskell took control, yet determined as he was to act decisively, his hold on the party was not fully consolidated until late 1962, at almost the moment that he died. The delay in consolidation had in large part, of course, to do with the ferocity of the controversies that he helped stir up, but in no small measure it was also because the most powerful trade union leader in the country, Frank Cousins, turned against him and became his most embittered adversary. For another thing, the fact that Labour lost three successive general elections, receiving a steadily declining percentage of the vote, added to the turmoil within the party. As an election drew near, a superficial unity would be hastily patched together, only to be torn apart with defeat and the consequent revival of the underlying controversies. On top of this, the more unpopular Labour's cause seemed to become in the nation, the less effectively Gaitskell was able to make use of the massive powers of patronage that any prospective Prime Minister can usually wield. For yet a third thing, the clash was all the more extensive because the two factions involved were approximately equal in strength. Thus, while each was powerful in its own right, neither was so powerful as to be able to impose its views on the other.

As a fourth and perhaps decisive cause, it is necessary to stress that the conflict over foreign policy was conjoined with a related fundamentalist-revisionist struggle over matters of domestic policy. Here was something entirely new in the long history of discord within Labour's ranks. Between 1914 and late 1917, for instance, the divisive issues were strictly questions of foreign policy. By the same token, Lansbury's ouster from the leadership in late 1935 did not so much as touch on domestic problems. Even when MacDonald was under fire in 1924, there was fairly general satisfaction with his foreign successes. But the conflict after 1951 was encompassing, cutting across the entire spectrum of party policy. Had

---

* It is almost impossible to find anyone, left or right in orientation, with a kind word for Attlee's faltering behavior after 1951. In this connection, see Hunter, *The Road to Brighton Pier*.

Labour not been historically a programmatic party, knitted together by a common socialist doctrine, the subsequent battles would never have been so bloody or so impassioned. But when questions of fundamental principle are felt to be at stake, passions are never easily restrained and compromise is not at all easily reached, let alone sustained once circumstances change. The revisionists did not, at first, even grasp the full extent of the challenge being directed at them. Gaitskell appeared genuinely puzzled by the vehemence of the debates waged at the 1952 Morecambe Conference, which was only the first of many such public confrontations. "The most worrying feature of Morecambe to me," he wrote shortly afterward, "was the fact that so many local party delegates seemed to favor a foreign policy which was not just slightly different from the official view, but totally opposed to it. The views they [the Bevanites] express are very much what the Communists would like them to express."[3] By the time of the momentous Scarborough Conference some two years later, there were no longer doubts on either side about what was at stake. "I'll fight the blighter," Bevan assured his followers, referring to Gaitskell, "year after year if necessary."[4]

"Raging fevers in the Party" was the term Dalton jotted down in his diary to describe the soreness and bitterness developing between the two factions.[5] It was no exaggeration. By the time of the unilateralist upheaval in 1960–61, the party was so split and tempers so frayed that the very fabric of Labour as a functioning political force seemed near the breaking point. To many on the left the party was no longer even in the hands of errant socialists, but had instead been captured by an anti-socialist, an outright traitor. Gaitskell, as they saw him by then, personified sterile reformism, arid parliamentarianism, the evils of an affluent society, and the horrors of nuclear weaponry. Rather than be led by someone of that ilk, they voiced the same angry protest that Bevan had on quitting the Attlee government back in 1951: they were not interested in winning elections and exercising power if the price to be paid was revisionism. What they wanted was a resolute socialist government and they were prepared to wait, if need be, a generation for the existing despicable capitalist order to crumble under pressure of its inner contradictions and growing competition from the Communist bloc.[6]

### BEVANISM AS FUNDAMENTALISM

I have emphasized that Labour's purpose was not at issue simply in relation to foreign policy and that there was equally a crisis in socialist thought concerning domestic policy. The stormy controversies in the two areas were, of course, complementary, with those who demanded a bold socialist breakthrough at home being the same ones, for the most part who demanded a plucky reaffirmation of socialist foreign policy.[7] There was nothing surprising about this overlap. From the beginning of Labour's history, socialist foreign power had been conceived of as a projection of the party's domestic principles onto the international scene. If it is thus somewhat artificial to isolate the disputes over foreign policy, discussing them apart from the larger struggle that went on, there is this justification at least: these disputes were not only as important as the tussles over nationalization and welfarism but perhaps of even greater magnitude and consequence.* Scarcely a year went by without some fresh controversy appearing: British rearmament, German rearmament, SEATO, Suez, membership in the EEC, development of a British deterrent, and unilateralism and neutralism. Even the party's election manifestos reflected the trend. Whereas the 1945 manifestos had relegated foreign and defense policy to the last section, in the 1955 manifesto, "Challenge to Britain," they had pride of place.

#### Fundamentalist Thrust

In domestic matters, the dominant issues were whether Labour would temper its historical moral commitment to the socialist commonwealth, accept egoism as an abiding component of human behavior, and reinterpret fellowship to mean equality of opportunity. In foreign policy, the overriding issues were whether Labour would temper its commitment to building an international commonwealth, accept self-regarding interests as inevitably at the fore in a nation's behavior abroad, and overcome its repugnance to force as an unavoidable determinant of international relations. At home the issues reduced to the question of nationalization: Could a socialist party tolerate a mixed economy that it itself helped build; abandon the goal of full public ownership in favor of some-

* As Jackson (p. 113) notes, PLP revolts after 1951 "were almost exclusively in the general field of foreign affairs."

public ownership, some centralized planning, and new regulatory agencies; and concentrate, accordingly, on making this mixture run more efficiently while at the same time introducing further social legislation in the name of social justice and equality? Or would it, instead, decide to press forward to the socialist utopia, indifferent to revisionist criticisms and convinced that anything short of that goal was an intolerable compromise. Concerning the international system, the issues reduced to related questions of bipolarity, ideological tension, and military competition: Yes or No, could a socialist party remain in an alliance dominated by capitalist America, with built-in hostility to the Soviet Union? Yes or No, could it agree to an alliance strategy that rested ultimately on the threatened use of nuclear weapons? Yes or No, could it—would it —carry the logic of the Attlee government's atomic bomb program to its conclusion, which meant sanctioning the construction of the H-bomb and an independent deterrent? Yes or No, could it abide by another Attlee governmental decision to rearm West Germany and recognize that former enemy and present capitalist nation as an honorable ally? And finally, Yes or No, could it, once the focus of the cold war shifted from Europe to Asia, support anti-communist interventions there by the United States?

These were complicated questions with far-reaching implications, not only for the Labour Party but also for Great Britain itself. As far as the fundamentalists were concerned, however, they could all be answered with a resounding negative.* Even to pretend that they could be answered otherwise was to freeze out options promising independent and more socialist policies. To demonstrate this by reformulating socialist principles in response to contemporary challenges was precisely the burden of the fundamentalist campaign. Yet even while undertaking this task, fundamentalist spokesmen continued to profess the eternal validity of old orthodoxies and tried beliefs: reformulation was necessary, but radical or extensive revision was not—any more, indeed, than was radical or extensive revision of Clause IV. It was thus true, as the revisionists averred, that their opponents were dogged (socialist)

---

* The early Bevanite publications were among the most straightforward statements ever produced, except in relation to membership in NATO itself, concerning which the Bevanites hedged their otherwise categorical pronouncements. See in particular "One Way Only" and "Going Our Way?"; Bevan, *In Place of Fear,* esp. pp. 127–56; and Bevan, "In Place of the Cold War."

traditionalists. But to go on from there and dismiss the campaign as an atavistic throwback was to miss the point of the exercise, which was to reinvigorate socialist traditions so as to prove their relevance to existing problems.

Where the United States was concerned, the tone was unsparingly critical. Dislike of American policy and politics was argued on several grounds: because the United States was capitalist, because it was materialist, because it dominated the British economy, because it was provocative or immature or "wildly anti-Communist"(as "Going Our Way?" put it). The list was endless but it contained few novelties. After all, since unease about American capitalism was already enshrined in socialist foreign policy, had flourished between 1945 and 1948, and then been vigorously reactivated during 1950–51, there was really little new that could be said on the subject. Still, no one could doubt the sincerity of fundamentalist misgivings or that their articulation had a powerful appeal reaching far beyond the ranks of just the Labour left.[8] How powerful was reflected, to cite only one instance, in an NEC resolution passed at the 1953 conference. In principle it reaffirmed Labour's commitment to the Anglo-American alliance, but it did so —as a former Minister of State for Foreign Affairs observed—in terms of several provisos, "scarcely any one of which corresponds with the policies of the United States."[9] No less telling was the obligatory condemnation of the "harm done to Anglo-American relations by political witch-hunting in the U.S.A." that Attlee pronounced in defending the resolution.

The anti-American appeal was all the more potent when coupled with exhortations for energetic independent British action, variations of which extended from the demand that Britain be more assertive with its ally to the ambitious plea that it become neutral and lead a third force of underdeveloped nations. The Bevanites were particularly eager to "stand up to the Americans," and in order to demonstrate how practical this was, they uncovered all sorts of powerful bargaining positions like American dependence on British bases.* In the beginning, however, most fundamental-

---

* "One Way Only," pp. 4, 10, 11. This Bevanite publication had bomber bases in mind. By the late 1950's American missile bases were the thorny issue, and in the early 1960's Polaris submarine bases were. A resolution opposing the construction of the latter was passed at the 1961 conference.

ists disagreed that Britain should quit NATO outright if it was drastically overhauled and reformed. Bevan himself took care to distinguish his position in this regard. In fact, one reason that he broke with his followers over unilateralism at the 1957 Brighton Conference had to do with his conviction that Britain needed allies but that, to influence them, it required weapons as powerful as any that they had. Still, the left's distaste for NATO grew as the years went by. Not only did a close relationship with the United States strike them as indistinguishable from dependency, which no effort at reform, however sweeping in aim, could ever really correct; in addition, the whole ideological defense of the West rang hollow in their ears. It seemed little more than the extension into foreign policy of the revisionist sellout to capitalism at home—a betrayal made doubly offensive by being linked to anti-communist hysteria in America and to West German rearmament and revanchism. Even Bevan continued long after Brighton to harp on the need for Britain to "rise and give the world the lead that the world is asking for."[10] When the unilateralist campaign edged round at Scarborough in 1960 to an outright neutralist policy, it was thus only using a crisper and more honest socialist logic.

Where the Soviet Union was concerned, the fundamentalist attitude was more ambivalent. Too much had happened between 1945 and the 1950's for any but fellow travelers to revert to the exhilarating enthusiasm of the earlier period. Not only was it taken for granted that there were real tensions between Britain and the Soviet Union, but criticism of the Soviet regime even in the post-Stalin period was voiced. Sometimes it was voiced loudly, as when Bevan joined right-wing Labour MP's in assailing Khrushchev and Bulganin during their London visit in April 1956. But the underlying attachment to the Soviet cause was never entirely extinguished, and it continued to influence left-wing behavior in the form of a chronic aversion to anti-Soviet policies. Occasionally this inability was rationalized by invoking the old orthodoxy that the Soviet Union, for all its undeniable excesses, was still a socialist state, no doubt errant for the time being but destined to realize its full humane potential at some not-too-distant future date. Its digressions from the democratic path and even its occasional aggressive outbursts were due, were they not, to the tasks of rapid economic development at home and to its fears of armed intervention from abroad? Bevan himself, for all his critical comment on the Soviet government, evinced a perennial optimism that democracy and pacifism were making mighty strides there.[11]

The fundamentalist attitude toward the Soviet Union was by no means so naïve as its opponents made out, and judged against the events of recent years, it may even be said to have been farsighted in certain respects. At any rate, it was no further off the mark than some of the vehement anti-Communist pronouncements made by headstrong revisionists in the trade unions. The point is, however, that the fundamentalists' analysis of the Soviet Union derived less from intensive and open-minded study of the facts of Soviet development than from an *a priori* conviction, rooted in socialist sentiment of the interwar period, that just happened to catch the drift of some changes in recent Soviet life. That this was so can be all the more easily grasped when the conviction is conjoined—as it invariably was in fundamentalist rhetoric—with deprecatory analysis of American developments. The attitudes involved on both issues formed a syndrome, a socialist ideology. A perceptive American remark about Bevan's makeup underscores the point in these terms: "There seemed deep in him the feeling that any society founded in private ownership, no matter how diversified and agreeable in its outward manifestations, was essentially wicked, and that any society founded on public ownership, no matter how cruel and arbitrary its outward manifestations, was potentially good."[12] It followed from this syndrome that cooperation with the Soviets was not only desirable but possible, and therefore that, if it had not yet materialized, this was due to rigid NATO policies, to American anti-Communism, to British dependence on the United States—in any case not to Soviet behavior or objectives. To the extent that the fundamentalists acknowledged any Soviet challenge at all, they continued in line with "Keep Left" and "Keeping Left" to see it primarily as social and economic, not military. Again, this view might in retrospect be judged to have been farsighted, but it could also be carried to ideological excess, as when Bevan analyzed the Soviet repression of the Hungarian Revolution *solely* in terms of economic and political development.[13] The reference to "Keep Left" and "Keeping Left" might remind us, moreover, that at the core of Bevanite opposition to rearmament was not just a careful appraisal of Soviet intentions but also a lively socialist fear that large military spending would dry up precious resources needed for new socialist advances on the economic front. By 1960 the unilateralists proved here as in other matters to be bold and sharp in their logic when they denied the need for a Western deterrent against a possible Soviet attack, because such an attack was illusory, the product of anti-Communist obsessions.

The remainder of the fundamentalist critique followed from these basic socialist tenets. (1) Since anti-Communism was unjustified on several grounds where the Soviet Union was concerned, it was even less justified in the case of China. On this point even many revisionists tended to agree. Thus when Attlee extended cautious and qualified approval to Eden's announced plans for setting up SEATO in April 1954, he found himself exposed to so steady a drumfire from the Bevanites that he decided it was only prudent, some months later, to urge Chinese membership in the proposed pact. The Chinese, he added, "apply their Communism with a good deal of elasticity."* (2) Concerning third force neutralism, the fundamentalists embraced it for reasons similar to those that had animated the third force advocates of the 1945–48 period. The locus of the force, however, changed in response to the evolution of the cold war from Western Europe to the underdeveloped areas and specifically to cover neutralist nations like Yugoslavia, Ghana, Egypt, India, and Indonesia. As we have seen, Bevan energetically championed the cause to no avail on his 1954 Indian trip. As we have also seen, the rebuke that Nehru administered to him did nothing to lessen his or his followers' enthusiasm, and they came to produce an elaborate socialist version of imperial nostalgia in proportion as British power in the world declined. Sometimes the emphasis was laid on the armed force that such a bloc might wield (a possibility that Bevan hinted at in his 1957 Brighton speech), but most often, in accord with good socialist reasoning, on just the moral suasion that it could exert by way of example.[14] Along with this moralistic attitude went a rooted refusal to acknowledge the reality of much of third world politics, its tendency toward author-

---

* *LPCR*, 1954, p. 72. At this point the revisionists rallied and managed to turn back a Bevanite resolution by a vote of 2,570,000 to 2,669,000 (*ibid.*, p. 78). Throughout the remainder of the decade the Labour Party remained fidgety all the same over Western policy in Asia, particularly in relation to China. In March 1957, for instance, almost half of the PLP signed an unofficial Motion urging the government to end the trade embargo on China.

itarianism, its internal divergencies, its suspicion of all Western industrialized countries. Such acknowledgement would have been unsettling, because it would have thrown doubt on the belief, boldly uttered by Bevan in his resignation speech and reiterated with fervor thereafter by others, that a Labour-governed Britain had unique moral and ideological goods for export. Yet even the right wing became infected by this nationalistic vision to various degrees, and it was not uncommon for a George Brown or a Denis Healey to talk of Britain's "distinctive worldwide role" even while deprecating the more fancied versions of their backbench brethren. (3) As for military matters, the position of the fundamentalists remained consistently anti-militarist whether the issue in question was British rearmament in the early 1950's, German rearmament in the mid-1950's, or the nuclear deterrent in the late 1950's and early 1960's. Since it was over these specific issues that the fiercest left-right controversies raged, a separate section will be devoted to them later.

Depicting the fundamentalist case in such summary fashion oversimplifies, no doubt, a complex body of utterance that was seldom clear-cut or coherent. A more elaborate account would have to distinguish between basic socialist attitudes, their intensity, and their degree of correlation with each other. But the point is that the attitudes held by the fundamentalists were comparatively few, and the Finer study makes it clear that the degree of correlation among them was sufficiently high to warrant the description of a syndrome.[15] In light of Labour's long-standing commitment to socialist principles, this finding is hardly surprising.

### Revisionist Counterthrust

The revisionist case, for its part, amounted to little more than a continuation of the policies pursued between 1945 and 1951, updated and modified according to the flux of events over the next decade. The revisionists were pro-NATO, pro-American, anti-Soviet, receptive to defense policies aimed at strengthening Western defenses, and suspicious of moral gestures.

At loggerheads with their opponents on all these scores, they grew impatient with the fundamentalists' moralizing and tended to write them off as hopeless ideologues. They regarded themselves, by way of contrast, as pragmatists, sharp-eyed empiricists in bracing touch with the reality of things. Yet this attitude was not only somewhat unfair to the fundamentalist cause* but misrepresented their own cause as well, for if the revisionists were pragmatic, it was pragmatism of an ideological sort—the kind defined by traditionalist principles. The revisionists might have been more sensitive to the pressures of the international environment, more aware of the declining latitude of choice open to Britain, more alert to the competition for power, prestige, and security going on in the postwar world than their fundamentalist opponents were; but their perceptions of all these matters were nonetheless highly colored by a doctrine, traditionalist foreign policy, that was itself a product of specific historical circumstances, an embodiment of a *Weltanschauung* ("a philosophy of necessity"), and a simplification of complex reality. And if the revisionists were more attuned to what in recent jargon are called "systemic" considerations, their understanding suffered certain defects that a too strictly systemic perspective can impose. The fundamentalists were not entirely wrong when they accused their rivals of being overly cautious, narrow in imagination, and averse to new departures in policy.

As in the 1945–51 period, the fundamentalists were particularly incensed by the similarity between revisionist and Conservative policies. On most issues the true division in British politics seemed to run more between the Labour frontbench and backbenches than between the Labour and Conservative parties. And yet there remained a difference between revisionist and Conservative foreign policy of an intriguing sort. Labour's compulsive ideologism meant that the revisionists were faced with a choice of either formulating their policy prescriptions with the use of socialist symbols and sentiments or watching their opponents monopolize these inherited emblems by default. The latter alternative seemed too risky; it would have handed the opposing faction an incalculable advantage. But in endeavoring to present nonsocialist policies in socialist terms, the revisionists ran another danger, no less risky. They tended to fall prey to their own socialist rhetoric—or so, at any rate, it seemed. For all their harping on bipolarity, the decline of British power, the need for close relations with the United States,

---

* No less an authority than Bevan himself conceded that the key issue was the perplexing question of how "to apply the principles of Socialism to a particular situation." *Tribune*, 1 April 1955.

and the perils of overboldness, they came by their very use of socialist symbols to adopt the language of a "philosophy of choice"
and thereby to conjure up visions of great initiatives in policy that
they probably knew in their more detached moments to be unrealistic. Here was a strange predicament: their fundamentalist critics
assailed the revisionists as unimaginative, and in fact the revisionists supported routine conservative or traditional policies; yet in
order to repulse their critics they had to defend those nonsocialist
policies as somehow being socialist and they stumbled, in doing so,
into more than one muddle owing to their resulting inability to
act decisively either by left-wing or by right-wing principles.*

This predicament was overlooked by most outside commentators
while the Labour Party remained in Opposition and the left-right
controversies raged unabated. As we shall see, it is still largely
overlooked. Yet what else would explain Labour's snub to the EEC
in 1962, with its blatantly unrealistic preconditions for membership, or the fanfare with which the East-of-Suez mission was proclaimed on taking office in 1964? In both instances the adopted
policies turned out to be widely at variance with existing international realities, and in both instances the Wilson government
has been compelled to reverse course—though not before squan-
dering precious resources and frittering away other, more promising alternatives.

### Dynamics of the Conflict

Bevanism and fundamentalism have so far been used as inter-
changeable terms. This is not careless language but good analysis,
for Bevan no more created Bevanism than it died out once he

---

* Thus, for example, the same collective security rhetoric that attended the
birth of NATO was used throughout the conflict to defend continued membership in the alliance, as though questions of international legality and morality
were straightforward and uncomplicated, and always resolvable to the West's
advantage. "We have always realized," said the 1959 election manifesto "Britain Belongs to You," "that power is required to make the rule of law effective.
That is why during the period of east-west deadlock we have stood resolutely
by our defensive alliances and contributed our share to western defence through
NATO." The fact is that NATO did not exist to enforce the rule of law but
to counterbalance Soviet power. What indeed are the laws that are supposed to
be implemented in disputes? The question is far from academic. The Berlin
crisis had just erupted and many Labour partisans, seeing a strong *legal* case
on the Soviet side, were more than willing to make concessions.

broke with his followers in 1957. It is true that because Bevan, Morrison, and Gaitskell were the preeminent spokesmen for their factions, their contest for the leadership had added significance. But the real struggle was over what each of the factions stood for —distinct conceptions of foreign policy that were and still are irreconcilable.

Far from being born with Bevan's challenge to the Attlee-Morrison leadership in 1951, this struggle was rooted in the battles between left and right that had been flaring in the party for decades. What distinguished the battles in the post-1951 period were the magnitude of the stakes and the ferocity of the confrontations. Before 1945, the conflicts over foreign policy had been intense and left bitter memories, but they had nonetheless taken place within clearly marked boundaries set by a unifying purpose, a shared socialist consensus. With what degree of speed could the socialist principles be applied to this or that situation? Could they in fact be made operational? And was a minority Labour government in a position to risk bold departures when it depended on nonsocialist support in Parliament? Such were the questions that agitated socialist minds and unleashed the recurrent bouts of soul-searching and recrimination in the pre–World War II days. But the situation altered for good with the acquisition of complete power in 1945 and the subsequent realization by the left that the problem was no longer whether the Attlee government would find ways to apply socialist principles, but rather whether it was interested in doing this at all. With the abandonment of socialist principles at stake, the party was now threatened by outright loss of consensus, and the turmoil over rearmament in 1950–51 made the threat an actuality. The struggle that was then waged over the next decade marked the stormy attempt by left and right alike to restore a consensus on their own incompatible terms. And because the currents of opinion that each represented were widely diffused throughout the party and had support at each level, the two warring factions faced each other more or less as equals.

Thus Bevanism is properly viewed as the refusal of a large body of the Labour Party to accept the drift toward revisionism that had been going on since 1945. Bevan did, of course, make a difference. He helped crystallize the massive discontent into a full-blown faction, ably led it for the next several years, and publicized its cause with his impressive speeches in the Commons and in party councils. Instead of dying upon his defection in 1957, however, fundamentalism not only survived but conducted an even more intensified campaign against the revisionist foe. It was in the 1958–61 period that the left-right clash reached its height of fury and came closest to driving Labour to the breaking point.*

In their endeavor to reverse revisionist trends, the fundamentalists had several advantages that compensated for their inferior numbers in the party's hierarchy. For one thing, their numbers were not so inferior in the various leadership councils that they could be overwhelmed. Bevan was in the Shadow Cabinet until his death (except for the year following his resignation in April 1954), and after 1955 he was joined by Harold Wilson, a wavering supporter of left-wing causes. On the NEC there were always six or

---

* Bevan's break with his followers at the Brighton Conference has, it appears to me, frequently been misunderstood, and not least by the Bevanites themselves. The issue precipitating the fallout was the Norwood unilateralist resolution; Bevan as Shadow Foreign Secretary denounced it in a powerful speech and swung the conference round against it. The glittering phrases that are remembered are his plea not to send a future Labour Foreign Secretary "naked into the negotiating room" and his sneer about a "moral spasm." What is overlooked is that he claimed to sympathize with the resolution's criticism of sterile arms races ("with none of these sentiments do I disagree, with none of them at all") and, even more important, that his rejection of unilateralism had distinct third force and other fundamentalist overtones. Like the third force advocates of the 1945–48 period, he recognized that independent British action would be meaningless unless backed by adequate military capabilities. Like them too, he believed that a British initiative could, in his words, "modify, moderate and mitigate" the polarization of the two superpowers. Quite clearly the question that separated Bevan from his followers was not whether to demand bold socialist policies but how to apply socialist principles to concrete problems. (See *LPCR*, 1957, pp. 181–82.)

None of this means that Bevan's major motive here was not to conciliate Gaitskell, now firmly in the saddle as leader, and to strengthen his hold on the Shadow Foreign Secretaryship—perhaps also to improve Labour's image in the eyes of the electorate by a show of unity. But to say this is not to contradict the above argument—on the contrary. For Bevan probably did not distinguish between his own personal ambitions and his conviction, which seems utterly sincere, that he alone could stamp a socialist mark on future Labour policies. There was no repudiation of fundamentalism but only a tempering of his devotion to the cause in the interest of Labour's fortunes as he envisaged them. And the fact is that by 1958 he helped secure leftward-leaning changes in the party's declared policy (about which more later). McKenzie is probably right, then, to hint at the likelihood that Bevan, before his death, was considering a new challenge to Gaitskell's leadership on the issue of nationalization. See *British Political Parties*, p. 609, n.1.

seven Bevanites, whose cause could during the unilateralist up-
heavals command the support of a few other sympathizers (thus
"Policy for Peace," a right-wing anti-neutralist statement on nuclear weapons, was passed by a vote of only 16–10 in February
1961). In the PLP the left was a persistent force varying between
one-quarter and one-third of the whole, though at times, as on the
vote to approve German rearmament in February 1954, it could
edge close to one-half of the total. By 1960 it was sufficiently powerful to produce an outright impasse within the Parliamentary
party, which virtually ceased, in consequence, to function as an effective Opposition for the next two Parliamentary sessions. Finally, the left was strongly rooted in the constituency parties and
could make an impressive showing at the conference because it also
enjoyed extensive support within the trade union movement.*
The Bevanites did not at first fully appreciate the latter factor. As
they saw it, the conference was being strangled by pugnacious
right-wing trade union bosses and their undemocratic block votes.†
This was not altogether correct even in the early 1950's, because
several unions, including members of the Big Six, often voted left,
and it was even less true as the decade went by. The anti-Bevanite
union leaders could not, for instance, prevent Bevan from winning
the party Treasuryship in 1956, though certainly not for lack of
trying. And by the 1960 Scarborough Conference there was a
startling reversal of fortunes, with the trade unions now arrayed
(as they had been over Clause IV the year before) against Gaitskell's policy while the constituency parties went heavily for it.[16]
In short, the fundamentalists may have been outmanned but not
by enough that they could be dragooned into submission.

A second advantage was an effective use of socialist symbols in
arguing fundamentalist views. The fundamentalists did not enjoy
a monopoly here because the revisionist leadership also appreciated the need to invoke the same symbols. But the revisionist at-

---

* For example, an April 1954 Gallup poll revealed that no less than 29 per
cent of Labour *supporters* (would-be voters) agreed with Bevanite views. Given
the difference in zeal between Labour voters and active members, it can be safely inferred that Bevanite support was much higher among the latter group. See
too, Jackson, pp. 264–65.

† "The Labour Movement," Mrs. Barbara Castle said in 1953, "is in danger
of dying a death of three million cuts—the block votes of four men." Quoted
in Harrison, p. 189.

tempts at this were always more strained and less successful, for the obvious reason that the gap between their policies and the socialist sentiments evoked by the symbols was not easily bridged. Again and again the revisionists were forced into verbal gymnastics, and again and again they were outperformed by their rivals. The *Economist*, friendly to the revisionist cause, expressed their dilemma perfectly when it observed that "the great majority of the party is out of sympathy with the stand its leaders are trying to maintain in foreign policy."[17] Being out of sympathy is not the same thing, of course, as being actively opposed, and the fact is that the majority could be brought around to compromise policies by various stratagems on most crucial occasions. But the toil involved in trying to mobilize effective coalitions against fundamentalist thrusts was enough to hamper more than one revisionist counterthrust.

A third advantage was the articulateness of leading fundamentalists and their access to the media. Compared with Crossman, Foot, Driberg, Mikardo, Castle, and Wilson, not to mention Bevan himself, a Deakin or a Morrison was severely handicapped in his ability to fire the imagination. Even Gaitskell, otherwise a decisive and otherwise determined politician, did not measure up to his rivals in this regard. The result was that the Bevanites, even when outnumbered, could make the running in the arguments. No one less than the secretary of the International Department of Labour's head office at the time has singled this out as an important factor in the Bevanites' ability to outmaneuver their rivals over German rearmament between 1951 and late 1953.[18]

A fourth advantage was that the party leaders, though for the most part revisionist in leaning, could not make effective use of their formal disciplinary powers. How, indeed, could they, when the party was so split and the sheer size of revolts in the PLP itself conferred a large degree of impunity upon its participants? When a fourth of the PLP bolted in the March 1952 defense debate, the leadership did move to reimpose standing orders,* just as it mobilized a majority several months later to ban all unofficial groups. But while these measures hampered Bevanite activity, they did not smother it, for the simple reason that it enjoyed too much sympathy with others, including a center group of uncommitted mem-

---

* They were again revoked in 1959, only to be quickly reinstated in 1961 following a backbench revolt on the armed forces estimates.

bers who often acted as mediators in ways that further frustrated severe punishment of dissidents.* As a consequence, revolts went on: 62 Labour members defying the official line in the March 1955 H-bomb debate, 43 defying it in the March 1960 defense debate, 72 flouting it in December 1960 on a unilateralist issue. Even when revolts did not actually crystallize, their potential was a factor that had to be reckoned with. In short, the power to discipline has to be distinguished from the formal authority to exercise it. Faced with obvious lack of enthusiasm for a policy against which rebels are demonstrating, that authority cannot be easily made effective; and in fact the resort to it is, arguably, a sign that the leadership may be acting from a position of weakness, not strength. Certainly this seems true when the divisions within the party involve the whole range of policy and when, therefore, disciplinary measures will probably only intensify rather than narrow the existing policy differences. In Bevan's own words "a firmer lid . . . is hardly the recipe for a boiling pot."[19]

A final advantage, perhaps the most important of all, proved to be the party's democratic structure. Labour's democratic traditions, its diffusion of policy-making powers over several bodies, and its encouragement to mass participation proliferated opportunities for carrying out the struggle because they hampered the ability of one faction or the other to score clear-cut or lasting decisions. A controversy would no sooner be settled in one forum than it risked being reopened in another.[20] The struggle over unilateralism was a particularly apt illustration of this process. One faction, after being repeatedly outflanked by the other, suddenly captured certain trade unions in 1960 and overturned existing PLP, NEC, and previous conference decisions at the Scarborough

* The most famous case was the backdown on the attempt in March 1955 to deprive Bevan of the whip and have him expelled from the party. The attempt was made following the debate on the government's decision to build the H-bomb, in which Bevan publicly rebuked the frontbench—Attlee in particular—and then joined 61 other Labour members in abstaining on the official Opposition amendment approving construction of the bomb. Though the Parliamentary Committee and the PLP approved Attlee's recommendation to have the whip withdrawn, it quickly became clear that a substantial section of the party, both in and outside Parliament, opposed the action. When the matter came before the NEC, the ultimate tribunal, Attlee therefore backtracked and Bevan was reinstated after giving promises of good future behavior —promises that cost him nothing. See Hunter, pp. 94–101.

Conference. The other faction then refused to abide by the decision, promised to fight it, fought in the PLP against implementing the new policy, organized a movement in the constituency parties to reverse the policy, exploited an ambiguous compromise declaration subsequently produced by the NEC, and finally triumphed at the next conference—whereupon the first faction then bolted and tried to counterattack. The result was that during the 1964 electoral campaign no one was quite certain what Labour would do with the nuclear deterrent. As this example shows, the party's democratic structure could aid the revisionist cause when it was in trouble. On the other hand, throughout the running left-right struggle, and particularly during the initial clashes, it was the fundamentalists who were most benefited, if only because the democratic procedures restricted the initiative available to the revisionist leaders lodged in the party hierarchy. Despite the numerous commanding posts that they controlled, the revisionists found themselves unable to stifle sustained challenges or to impose clinching decisions to their liking. Clearly, in a democratic party badly split over fundamentals, the leadership is not guaranteed anything except the ability to produce temporary and indecisive compromises.

From time to time Labour did make a show of impressive unity. But this was made possible only by the imminence of a general election. In 1951, in 1955, and again in 1959, the two factions would join together against the common electoral foe, patch together a common program, and march bravely in unison out on the stump—only for the subsequent defeat to shatter the tenuous accord and introduce a new and more vehement phase of discord. The aftermath of the 1964 election was, it goes without saying, rather different as a result of victory and the consummate political juggling of the new leader. Whether the resulting harmony proves enduring seems, however, more dubious as time passes, for reasons that remain to be discussed.

### STALEMATE

"The crisis in the party was, in the first place, the product of the confrontation of old Socialist commitments with new social and political realities."[21] This was no less true in foreign policy than in domestic affairs. The old commitments were to the four socialist principles, and the realities were those that the revisionists claimed to have encountered within the international system after Labour entered power in 1945.* The crisis arose and then endured because the attempt to rethink and reconstruct the existing principles in light of those realities did not succeed. Or rather it only half-succeeded. For to roughly half of the party, the attempt smacked of betrayal, and Bevanism developed as their reaction to it. In their eyes, the old vision—the old orthodoxies—were as appropriate as ever; it was simply a question of reformulating them to match the new problems of the postwar period. The no-holds-barred conflict that shook Labour from top to bottom after 1951, creating so much anguish and acrimony on both sides, must thus be understood as deriving from a situation in which an ideological party no longer possessed a consensus but continued to hunger for one. Both sides emphasized the need for a unifying purpose. Both claimed to have one in their respective ideologies. Neither could get the other to agree with it.

To say this is only to observe that the old vision of a socialist foreign policy showed a remarkable resilience in spite of repeated efforts to have it repudiated. Socialist principles continued to exercise a magnetic hold on approximately half of the party, in spite of superior revisionist strength within the PLP, of revisionist strongholds on the frontbench and in the NEC, and of a powerful revisionist following within the mass party. They further continued to hold in spite of six years of a vigorous revisionist foreign policy as carried out by the Attlee governments and of the subsequent claim, backed by most of the national press and by the Conservative Party in the name of bipartisanship, that the revisionists were the "responsibles," the "Governmentalists" within Labour ranks, and their opponents were the "irresponsibles," the "Permanent Oppositionalists." With a devotion to their cause that seemed to astound their rivals, the fundamentalists scorned the offerings of revisionist thinking and reaffirmed the relevance of original socialist thought. And continuing to reaffirm it right into the 1960's, they obliged even the Wilson leadership to remain shy of carefully conceived and fully detailed programs for the days when Labour

---

* In point of fact, though the revisionists were hardly prepared to concede this, the encounter had actually begun during the days of the Churchill Coalition.

would again take office. Thus, in October 1964, thirteen years to
the month since reverting to Opposition, a Labour government
committed to sweeping change entered power without any imaginative plans for future policy.

The consequences of the conflict have not often been seen in so
gloomy a light. To many outside observers, the left-right split had
been pretty adequately healed by the time Harold Wilson won the
leadership—healed, moreover, for the most part on revisionist
terms.[22] Was it not the case that whenever the clash between the
two currents of opinion was formulated in terms of a specific issue and submitted to a vote in the party's forums, the revisionists
tended to have the upper hand?

The answer is both yes and no. Yes, if we mean that the revisionists bested their rivals on significant questions like British rearmament in 1951, German rearmament, construction of the H-bomb,
continued membership in NATO, and unilateralism of an uncompromising sort. No, on the other hand, if we inquire into the
substance of those victories to uncover what they really represented. For the victories, if not necessarily *pro forma*, were so
hedged in by compromise and by qualification that no one could
say with assurance what Labour would actually do in power.
Would the PLP actually vote for German rearmament following
the narrow win for that policy at Scarborough in 1954? The PLP
in fact abstained when the Paris Agreement came before the House
in November of that year, thereby repudiating in effect the policy
that it had sanctioned months before at a stormy party meeting.[23]
What is more, that repudiation was underscored when three years
later the PLP, the NEC, and the conference all endorsed a disengagement policy that "took up a view not dissimilar from that of
the 1955 [fundamentalist] critics."[24] Would the party actually sanction manufacture of the H-bomb? The PLP vote in the March
1955 defense debate seemed unequivocal on this score, as did the
sound pasting that Bevan administered to the unilateralists at
Brighton in 1957. On the other hand, at the very next conference
the party's stand was a great deal more doubtful. Bevan, introducing the party's policy as Shadow Foreign Secretary, insisted that
Labour could not pledge itself one way or another in advance of
taking office. This appeared to imply that a Labour government
might not proceed with construction of the H-bomb, except that

Gaitskell, winding up the debate, ambiguously hinted that the previous policy still stood. Topping off the confusion, a prominent revisionist acclaimed Bevan for at long last producing a "distinctive socialist foreign policy . . . which unites our whole policy from left to right."[25] Again, assuming that the Conservative government built the bomb anyway, would the Labour Party actually maintain the British deterrent? On this question the decision-making forums developed a string of pronouncements that made the issue at Scarborough in 1960 and during the following year no longer unilateralism but neutralism, indicating as a result that Labour would abandon the deterrent. During the 1964 electoral campaign the leadership resorted to the smoke-screen prose of "renegotiating Nassau." In office it has, nonetheless, done nothing of the sort. Would Labour approve membership in the EEC or oppose it? In 1962, when Britain's bargaining hand was still fairly strong, Gaitskell united the warring factions on a policy of nationalism ("the end of a thousand years of history") and anti–European integration. Four years later the Wilson government decided that Britain's destiny did indeed lie with Europe, but the decision came at a time when a rebuff was almost certain.

The point of all this is not that internal division and consequential deadlock over policy have been unique to the Labour Party. The Conservatives have also suffered internal conflict over foreign policy and behaved in ambiguous and contradictory ways. All the same, Labour's divisiveness and stalemate have been of a magnitude that clearly sets it apart. This would be easiest to illustrate in domestic affairs, for it is here that the Conservative Party most strikingly revealed its powers of adaptability after 1945, rethinking the fundamentals of Conservative policy and so accepting the welfare state and the managed economy. Even in foreign policy, however, it succeeded in developing coherent and innovative measures that, if noticeably offensive to vocal sections of the party, nonetheless won their passive acquiescence in the end. One thinks here of the decisions to withdraw from the Empire and to apply for membership in the EEC. Both of these policies broke with established positions and strained party unity. Yet both were implemented with a firm hand and eventually rallied the dissidents. What accounted for the limited scope of discord? The short answer is that the leadership, by invoking the proper symbols of national greatness, militarism, prestige, and alliance commitments, managed to convince the party that its decisions were in the best of Conservative traditions. The fact that the Conservative Party is elitist and so confers a great latitude of initiative on its leaders also facilitated the maintenance of internal harmony. That Conservative governments made errors in judgment, even large-scale and costly errors, is something that I would be the last to deny—but it is largely beside the point. For we have been discussing not so much the wisdom or unwisdom of Labour's policies, as rather the party's ability to formulate clearly defined and purposeful policies without reopening old battles. In this regard the Conservatives have done a better job, whatever the appropriateness of the policies they produced.

### Unilateralism

Nothing spotlights Labour's persistent deadlock quite so brilliantly as the unilateralist upheaval of the late 1950's and early 1960's. The conflict that unilateralism generated was dangerously explosive, touching on all the inflammable controversies of the period and involving brawls of a vehemence without previous parallel. More than one member of the party spoke of a raging civil war.

Yet, if we can believe most contemporary press accounts and much subsequent party propaganda, this time there was a difference. This time one side (the revisionists) scored a smashing victory, consolidated its hold on the leadership, routed its rivals, and vindicated multilateralism.[26] In fact, the continuity in the pattern of previous clashes remained largely unbroken. Nothing, or at any rate very little of a lasting nature, was decisively solved. If the unilateralists were defeated at Blackpool in 1961, it was largely because the Gaitskellites had already stolen most of their clothes and produced a policy very close to the original program of the Campaign for Nuclear Disarmament.[27] In other words, a fuzzy compromise was once more the result—fuzzy, because one faction, the fundamentalists, were unhappy with it, while the victors, for all their campaign rhetoric in 1964, disowned it as unwise upon coming to power. Nor did Gaitskell really consolidate his leadership at the time. As much as Blackpool signaled a personal triumph for him, it was not until the following year and on an altogether different issue—the British application to the EEC—that he succeeded in (temporarily) uniting the implacably divided crusaders of both the left and the right behind him.

The string of concessions with which the revisionists hoped to accommodate unilateralist pressure, and at the same time salvage a responsible policy to their own liking, stretched back to March 1958. Until then, the established party policy was to support the British H-bomb program and the construction of an independent deterrent. But by 1958 disillusion with the cold war, fear of a future nuclear holocaust, anger with bipartisanship in foreign policy, and a general malaise with what soon became known as the affluent society began spreading rapidly throughout large sections of British life normally sympathetic to Labour's cause. In an effort to head off the agitating of the newly created Campaign for Nuclear Disarmament (CND) outside the party and the lobbying of the Victory for Socialism (VFS) within the PLP, the NEC and the TUC General Council promulgated a new policy statement that opposed H-bomb patrols from British bases, construction of American missile bases until fresh Big Three talks, and any further H-bomb testing.[28] The suspension of testing would be conditional, undertaken temporarily in expectation of reciprocation by others. But what if other nations did not reciprocate? The vagueness of this formula was underscored by a new joint statement issued in the following year. On the surface "Disarmament and Nuclear War: The Next Step" registered a retreat from multilateralism— a sort of conditional unilateralism whereby Britain would abandon its deterrent by forming a "nonnuclear club" of all powers except the Soviet Union and the United States. The retreat was real but purposely obscured. For in spite of the appropriate socialist slogans accompanying the scheme (Britain would by an act of selfless renunciation make a bold strike for world peace, Britain would give a new moral lead to others, etc.), the leadership took care not to specify how the club would be formed, let alone held together. These were hardly academic matters: the Chinese, for instance, immediately dismissed the scheme as "hypothetical, hypocritical and a humbug." Judged by the rights and wrongs of the complicated defense problems involved, Labour's new policy was "an incomprehensible compromise formula."[29]

Judged against a different standard, it was an effective makeshift—or so the leadership must have thought. For it did the trick of temporarily heading off a unilateralist groundswell within the trade unions and thus enabled the party to present a façade of unity during the 1959 electoral campaign. Still, like so many pronouncements of the period that were made to paper over the internal divisions, the nonnuclear club idea not only did not settle anything conclusively; it actually had the effect of driving the unilateralist conflict into a newer and more destructive phase.

By early 1960 the situation shaped up in this manner. The revisionist leadership, attached to multilateralism, had left itself vulnerable by espousing conditional British unilateralism. No doubt the concessions were not entirely voluntary, the unilateralist pressure on and within the party picking up increasing momentum since 1958. But to the extent that the leadership hoped to accommodate its opponents with indecisive formulas, it was mistaken. CND denounced the nonnuclear club because it reaffirmed a NATO deterrent policy, VFS because it did not cover the two superpowers. Another group, for whom R. H. S. Crossman and George Wigg emerged as preeminent spokesmen, was only too happy to scrap the British deterrent for whatever reason, provided that the resources saved would be diverted into larger conventional forces.[30] Although this prescription was well reasoned and attracted attention, it put off the unilateralists because it envisaged continued British membership in NATO and it put off the leadership because it envisaged reinstatement of National Service—an obvious electoral liability.

Beyond these matters, there was acute disagreement over the implications that retention or renunciation of the deterrent would have on Anglo-American relations. The early revisionist line had been to champion an independent deterrent as a means to greater influence over the United States. Attlee had argued to that effect in the 1955 March defense debate, George Brown repeatedly after 1957, and Gaitskell himself from time to time. Even Bevan had opposed unilateralism on similar grounds at Brighton. But to others, the very effort to maintain an independent deterrent was, owing to its costs and British reliance on American aid and know-how, leading to ever greater rather than ever smaller British dependence.* By 1960 there was total muddle on the issue, some still

---

* Crossman, as far as I can tell, was the first to argue this on the floor of the Commons (568 *H.C.Deb.* 1977 [17 April 1957]).

insisting that the deterrent spelled influence and independence, others that it meant bondage, yet a third group—by now prominent among unilateralists—in favor of both unilateralism and neutralism, on the ground that the former without the latter would be meaningless. The muddle was hardly reduced when, shortly afterward, the Gaitskellites reversed direction and began arguing that a scuttling of the British deterrent would be the way to greater British influence within NATO after all. By all accounts, the existing policy neither clarified the major issues nor pleased anyone, whether on the left or the right. As if to underscore the unsatisfactoriness of the situation, 43 Labour MP's revolted against the official Labour amendment in the March defense debate.* With one trade union after another repudiating the official policy as well, Labour seemed all but threatened with internal paralysis.

At this point the Conservative government, by its cancellation of the Blue Streak missile system, handed Labour an opportunity to resolve its confusion without intensifying the civil war. Or so for the moment it seemed. Did not the cancellation in favor of the American-developed Skybolt make nonsense of the government's pretensions to an independent deterrent? The Labour frontbench eagerly said so, and if by unilateralism is meant the abandonment of the British deterrent without reciprocal concessions from others, then Labour soon went unilateralist. In "Foreign Policy and Defense" the PLP, the NEC, and the TUC General Council repudiated the British deterrent on practical grounds: it was proving too costly, was no longer independent, duplicated the American contribution to NATO, and contributed to nuclear proliferation.† Here was a policy of unconditional unilateralism, similar in many respects to the original demands of CND and VFS. But the crusaders of the left had not been standing still since 1958: with each concession that the right had made in an effort to accommodate them, they had responded by upping their demands. The concessions enshrined in "Foreign Policy and Defense" now met with a similar reception. From the unilateralist viewpoint, the new policy was actually the worst of all worlds, for it compounded the sin of

---

* By 1960 there were roughly 45 outright unilaterialists within the PLP and an additional 70 who leaned in a unilaterialist direction (Finer *et al.*, pp. 25–26).

† *LPCR*, 1960, pp. 13–16. At a news conference after publication of the policy statement, Gaitskell and Brown said that a Labour government would let the existing V-bomber force expire into obsolescence.

reaffirming a NATO deterrent by envisaging total American control of all deterrent weapons. Thus, by the summer of 1960, the
issue confronting Labour was no longer unilateralism but neutralism. Far from unifying the party by heavy doses of unilateralism,
the new policy struck much of the left as an intolerable halfway
house, and no amount of socialist incantation could convince it
otherwise.

The failure of Gaitskell to win party approval for the Executive's policy at the Scarborough Conference is too well known to
necessitate rehearsal here. What deserves to be underlined is the
change in the leadership's tactics. Instead of obscuring the defeat
by means of new semi-magical formulas, the Gaitskellites dug in
their heels and vowed to fight for a clear-cut reversal of the conference's decision.* They recognized that the stakes had grown too
large: that the challenge confronting them cut much deeper than
cancellation of a weapons system. As Gaitskell crisply defined the
stakes in his speech of defiance, they involved the repudiation of
the entire edifice of Labour's foreign policy over the past fifteen
years—NATO, Anglo-American relations, armed balancing of the
Soviet Union, and multilateral East-West disarmament.[31] Rather
than continue to blur the underlying problems out of hope for
accommodation, the revisionist leadership thus acknowledged that
further compromises would only accentuate the already dangerous
policy muddle. As he had over Clause IV, Gaitskell was determined to speak explicitly and to fight for a clarification of purpose
even if, in doing so, he risked breaking the party apart.

How successful did he prove? The Scarborough decision was
reversed and the party, of course, held together. But as it turned
out, these goals were in part achieved because further concessions,
however halfhearted, were granted to the left wing. In "Policy for
Peace," a new NEC statement issued in February 1961, opposition
to the British deterrent was for the first time justified on *moral*
as well as on practical grounds: specifically, where "Foreign Policy and Defense" had insisted that Britain *could* not remain a

---

* The Executive statement was defeated by 3,339,000 to 3,043,000. A Transport and General Workers' Union resolution, vaguely neutralist in substance,
was carried by a smaller margin. A Woodworkers' resolution favorable to the
Executive was also defeated, and an Amalgamated Engineering Union uni-
lateralist-neutralist resolution was also carried, by a margin of about 400,000.
*LPCR*, 1960, p. 202.

nuclear power, the new policy also insisted that it *should* not.[32] Beyond that, the Gaitskellites were only too happy to trade on the confusion that arose concerning the blurred distinctions between the Executive's statement and a compromise draft submitted by R. H. S. Crossman and Walter Padley.* The Union of Shops, Distributive & Allied Workers, for instance, reversed its unilateralist stand by adopting the compromise draft, only to find when it arrived at the Labour conference that Padley had decided to bury the draft. This left the union no alternative to voting for the Executive statement. One should probably not make too much of these maneuvers; they were not significant concessions in comparison with past performances by the Gaitskellites. But they did show that even with a mass grass-roots campaign in the constituencies (the Campaign for Democratic Socialism), with patient wooing of the unions, with Gaitskell's vindication in the PLP when challenged by Harold Wilson for the leadership, and with all their pleas for a responsible policy, the Gaitskellites found Labour too internally divided to confront their opponents in as head-on a manner as they had initially threatened. In March 1961, the PLP decided to abstain in all divisions regarding the defense estimates, rather than risk making public the extent of conflict within its ranks.

That the revisionist victory was not so decisive as claimed at the time can be grasped from a different angle. For even leaving aside the question of how many unilateralist clothes the Gaitskellites donned in the process, Blackpool recorded discrepant decisions regarding NATO. If the Executive statement on foreign policy and defense carried by 4,526,000 to 1,756,000, two left-wing resolutions—one opposing the training of German troops in Britain as a NATO exercise, the other opposing Polaris bases on British soil—were passed by majorities of about 800,000 each.[33] The Labour Party was thus placed in the odd position of reaffirming NATO on principle, but of rejecting two specific (and in the case of

---

* Three drafts were submitted to the NEC by a committee of twelve, eight of whom were Gaitskellites, and each was voted on by the NEC. The Gaitskell-Healey draft was adopted by sixteen to ten and became the basis for "Policy for Peace." A Frank Cousins draft, a radical unilateralist statement, was defeated by eighteen to seven. The third draft was the Crossman-Padley proposal, which was close to the Gaitskell-Healey draft in substance but layered this over with heavy socialist details. It was defeated by fifteen to thirteen.

Polaris bases, vital) NATO policies. This jumble of contradictory aspirations was not tidied up until the new leader, Harold Wilson, capitalizing on his goodwill in left-wing circles, reaffirmed Gaitskell's refusal to feel bound by the conference decision on the bases.[34]

### Labour and the Deterrent Since 1961

Though the split between left and right persisted, the great defense controversy itself abated after Blackpool. The nuclear deterrent was but briefly debated at the 1962 conference and not at all at the 1963 conference. By the time of the 1964 general election, the party leadership contrived another formula that obscured the nuclear issue sufficiently to avoid offending any one large group.

The reasons for the slackening of the controversy can be briefly summarized. For one thing, by 1962 Labour became absorbed in another problem, the British application to the European Economic Community; and exploiting the opportunity, Gaitskell made peace with the left and prodded the party into a head-on quarrel with the Conservative government. Members obviously relished the chance to shift their forensic energies away from internal disputes toward the target of the common enemy, and the rebuff that de Gaulle administered to the Conservative policy only strengthened Labour's rediscovered Oppositional disposition. The more the party scented electoral victory in 1963 and 1964, the more incentive it had not to reopen old destructive battles. Of course, since nothing had been conclusively agreed on, the conflict over defense and foreign policy could flare up again without much catalytic provocation, but it was precisely here that Harold Wilson's skills at party management enabled him to perform so aptly as a political mediator. Quite apart from these considerations, there was also by 1963 a noticeable betterment in East-West relations, a growing detente that crystallized in the Test Ban Treaty. With the international atmosphere clearing, a major spur to the original unilateralist movement was removed, and Labour partisans of all leanings found it easier to relax. Along with this went a dawning perception that what Britain did or did not do no longer very much mattered. In 1958, even in 1960 perhaps, it was possible for Britons to believe that their nation still sufficiently counted to be able by its own actions to shape international developments of great moment. The revival of French influence, the resurgence of Western Europe, the emergence of a Chinese nuclear force, Vietnam, and above all a cozy Soviet-American dialogue *à deux* forced a realization by 1964 that scrapping the British deterrent was a matter of limited interest to others. With this realization the moral fervor of the earlier unilateralist challenge largely burned itself out.

For all that, the party's behavior once it entered power has proved most instructive from our viewpoint. If the underlying thesis of this work is right, then a policy hammered out in opposition by even casual reference to socialist principles might turn out to be undesirable in office. The pledge to end Britain's nuclear status, if not entirely socialist in substance, was nonetheless given in an attempt by the revisionist leadership to accommodate fundamentalist pressure. Made largely for reasons of internal unity, it might accord with British interests or it might not, but that depended entirely on the reading of the international situation that a Labour government would take at the proper time. The Wilson leadership seemed to be well alert to this distinction, and appreciating that too clear-cut a commitment to the 1961 policy might recklessly freeze out future options, it began gradually to tone down the commitment by a series of ambivalent pronouncements—not too ambivalent, to be sure, not enough at any rate to alarm the left, but enough to facilitate a future shift in policy should one be deemed desirable. To disguise the retreat from a unilateralist policy, Wilson was also helped by his reputation as a man of the left that included a challenge to Gaitskell's leadership in the turbulent aftermath of Scarborough.* The stealth with which the leadership operated made it difficult to say with any assurance, by early 1964, what Labour's defense policy really

* Wilson took care not to commit himself too much one way or the other during the 1960–61 debate. For instance, though he was reputed to sympathize with the unilateralists, he contested the leadership not on unilateralism but on the less controversial issue of Gaitskell's defiance of a conference decision. The most that we know of his true sentiments appeared in a *Sunday Telegraph* article of 5 February 1961, which reported that Wilson had submitted a draft of six points to the Committee of Twelve that produced the Gaitskell-Healey, Crossman-Padley, and Cousins statements. As one of his points, Wilson favored permanent cancellation of the British deterrent—not just for economic reasons but also as a matter of principle.

added up to. Although on the surface the party seemed to remain hostile to the British deterrent, both Brown and Wilson now allowed occasional contrary notes to creep into their Parliamentary speeches to the effect that a Labour government, while of course breaking with Tory defense policies, would not destroy the nuclear force but instead use it as a bargaining counter in setting up "a genuine Atlantic alliance nuclear organization."[35] In subsequent campaign rhetoric, this ambition was referred to as "renegotiating" or "denegotiating" the Nassau Agreement. Nothing more was said of "cancellation" or "abandonment" or "expiration"; in fact, the whole defense question was carefully played down.[36] When pressed by the Conservatives to clarify the party's intentions, the Wilson leadership employed the diversionary tactic of reopening the German rearmament dispute, hinting that the Conservative government's cautious support of the Multilateral Nuclear Force would mean "having a German finger on the nuclear trigger."[37] Wilson himself took the trouble to write the defense section of the party manifesto.

To say that Wilson and his colleagues were already having second thoughts about the compromise of the 1960–61 period would thus be more than a mild understatement. And predictably, once Labour did enter office, the international situation was read in ways that underscored these doubts. Outlining the new government's defense policy, Wilson called for creation of an Atlantic Nuclear Force that would include, among other things, most of the existing British V-bombers and those British Polaris submarines too near to completion to be canceled.[38] At the time the Prime Minister did not specify how many submarines that might be. It was necessary to investigate the matter so as to make economically sagacious decisions. When the results of the investigation were all in, it turned out that four submarines qualified, each armed with sixteen Polaris missiles with an explosive force of one million tons of TNT apiece. But if Nassau was not boldly renegotiated, did not the call for the Atlantic Nuclear Force testify to the Labour government's willingness to place its nuclear weapons at the disposal of the new organization, thus in effect fulfilling the party's pledge to end the independent deterrent? As much as party spokesmen contended this, the fact is that the government did not go appreciably beyond what the Conservatives had already conceded in giving up British independence. At Nassau Macmillan had assigned the British deterrent to NATO subject only to the right to withdraw it in the event of a grave national emergency. The ANF formula was different. It would assign the deterrent for the duration of the alliance, but since the alliance would break up as soon as a difference of opinion emerged over the defense of the vital interest of any member country, the difference was immaterial.

The argument must not be misunderstood. There was nothing sinister in the backdown from the 1961 Blackpool policy that the Wilson government staged. The options that should be held open or taken often look different when in power. At any rate, the surprise would be if they did not. And in truth, what good would come of implementing Labour's erstwhile policy? As long as France possessed a nuclear force, the act of nuclear renunciation would not only diminish British influence in Europe but throw away a useful bargaining lever that one day might pry open the way to membership in the European Economic Community. But this is a digression, for the merits or demerits of the government's current defense policy are not directly germane. The point here is rather that the Labour leadership entered office saddled with a partisan commitment that had been largely hammered out for reasons of internal unity and not because it was considered necessarily the best or most suitable policy. Having appreciated this, the leadership tried even before the electoral campaign to shake free. But it could not rid itself of the commitment forthrightly— or so Wilson obviously concluded; for the party appeared too internally divided, too doctrinally at variance, to risk an outright reformulation of policy.* Hence by stealth and by subterfuge the leadership drained the substance out of the policy while disguis-

---

* Richard Neustadt's "Memorandum on the British Labour Party and the MLF," a summary to the Johnson Administration of his candid, detailed discussions with the PLP frontbench, places this point beyond dispute. Dated 6 July 1964, the memorandum says that the Wilson leadership estimated the left wing to number at least one-third of the entire PLP strength, with a hard core of 15–20 MP's hewing close to a Communist line. According to the memorandum, the leadership knew, therefore, that left-wing opposition would become a problem as soon as a future Labour government sought to force issues to sharply defined decisions. Concerning the MLF issue in particular, Neustadt reported that Wilson would not want "to rush his calculations"; he needed time to determine how split the party might be in the event of a clear-cut decision, one way or another. The memorandum is cited in full in Andrew Kopkind, "A Document of the Sixties," *New York Review of Books* (5 December 1968), pp. 40–46.

ing this with socialist rhetoric, vague allusions, shadowy formulas, and partisan sniping. Even then, the leadership sensed that its hands were too much tied. Striving therefore to represent the ANF as a means of terminating the independent deterrent, Wilson and his colleagues ended up producing a cumbersome scheme that displeased Washington, struck de Gaulle as dishonest, offended the West Germans, and in general aroused widespread uncertainty in Western Europe concerning British intentions toward it.[39]

The nuclear issue remains unclarified to this day. Unwilling to apply a crisp socialist solution and to scuttle the deterrent and quit NATO, the Wilson government has been unable at the same time to promulgate clearly defined revisionist policies. As an example, it could abandon the deterrent in favor of larger conventional force contributions to NATO and for peacekeeping missions in the third world. Or, taking a different tack, it could boldly try to use the nuclear force as a bargaining ploy with the West Europeans. But in fact the government has shied away from either option. To choose the latter, it would provoke angry howls from a left wing already intensely suspicious of joining the EEC under any circumstances. And to choose the former, it would risk the outcry that Britain, by becoming more dependent than ever on the American deterrent, would become a satellite. Therefore, the government has done nothing since the days of the ANF proposal, preferring inaction to action that would be controversial and, in the present mood of the party, perhaps disastrous for Harold Wilson.

## *"In Search of Purpose"*

In spite of the brutal brawls of the 1960–61 debate, then, the outcome remains inconclusive. As basically a doctrinaire and ideological party, Labour still hungers for an underlying consensus; but divided on fundamentals since 1951, it cannot reach agreement on what the consensus should be about. Between Blackpool in 1961 and the general election in 1964, the contending factions contrived a temporary if uneasy truce in the growing expectation of electoral victory, under the skillful management of Harold Wilson. Between the 1964 and 1966 elections, they maintained the truce as a result of more leadership of this sort and for the additional reason that the party's Parliamentary majority was perilous.

Blurring issues, avoiding difficult choices, keeping all options open, overwhelming nascent opposition with forms of words that had now left-wing overtones and now right-wing overtones, Wilson put on a dazzling performance that seemed to justify all the journalistic accolades bestowed on him as the consummate political tactician of the day. But as time has passed and the excuse of a hairsbreadth majority disappeared, the performance has appeared increasingly deficient in one crucial respect: it has been unable to yield strong and imaginative policies. And the question that inevitably leaps to the fore is whether this defect derives from Harold Wilson's intellectual makeup and style of leadership or whether instead it is inherent in Labour's present and apparently inescapable situation. Is the Labour Party capable of sustaining a purposeful and innovative government?

Judged in terms of the very different style of leadership that Hugh Gaitskell practiced, the answer seems doubtful. Where Wilson has equivocated and evaded, Gaitskell spoke forthrightly, but in the end his bold effort to surmount the party's split by overwhelming one of the warring factions did not succeed either. Although the party did not disintegrate as some feared it might, the left-right division endured even at the moment of his personal triumph at Blackpool. As for the unilateralist commitment that emerged from the debate, there is no reason to believe that Gaitskell would have tried to dilute it any less than Wilson and his colleagues diluted it. For, to repeat a signal point, a compromise policy patched together as a means of modulating internal conflict may not be compatible with the needs of a nation's foreign policy. The problem that Wilson has stumbled over, which would no doubt perplex any Labour leader, is how to shake loose from that policy and act decisively without at the same time spreading massive disaffection inside the party. So far this problem has resisted all efforts at clean-cut solution. It is hard to see how it can be satisfactorily solved as long as on every major issue of the day—on the Common Market, on Vietnam, on East-of-Suez, on the nuclear deterrent, and previously on devaluation—Labour remains divided through and through. In such circumstances, how often will a Prime Minister risk trying to force a decision that will invariably be resented by large numbers of party members?

Nor does the formulation of the underlying problem stop here.

For if Labour's split gives the leadership an overwhelming incentive to caution, ambiguity, and dissembling, the practice results in policies stubbornly akin to those created by previous Conservative governments. Only where circumstances reach crisis point and so force a change rendered beyond dispute, as happened in the case of devaluation, have departures from the status quo been chanced. Not all the rhetoric of socialism can permanently obscure this basic fact, though for over two years, by a combination of ambivalent formulations and rehearsed rationalizations, the Wilson government did manage to keep everyone guessing or hoping long enough to prevent informed opposition from emerging. But such tightrope-walking has its limits. For if equivocation has helped to keep the party in line, it does nothing to heal the underlying split—and Labour partisans are unlikely to tolerate forever a government that offers only the satisfaction of playing down problems, postponing decisions, and temporizing by minor adjustments. No matter how much the Conservative Party may be at home with this style, the Labour Party, still eager for a distinctive consensus that continues to elude it, is not. Indeed, fidgetiness and ill temper have been plainly on the rise since early 1967. As the adverse votes on Vietnam and Greece at the annual conference and the subsequent strife within the PLP indicate, disaffection can spread in more than one way.

# Chapter ten

# Some Concluding Remarks

This book has been at pains to show that Labour's recurrent crises in foreign policy, whether during World War I or in the 1930's or between 1945 and 1949 or following 1951, can be properly understood only against the background of the party's commitment to a distinctive doctrine of international politics. That commitment stretches back to the beginning of Labour's history as an independent political force, and no one, with a handful of exceptions, publicly questioned its soundness until 1945. These exceptions divided into two groups. The first consisted of a tiny band of trade union leaders in the 1930's who, doubting the wisdom of socialist foreign policy in the light of existing international circumstances, pressed the party for a tough-minded stand on rearmament; yet even when their view prevailed, by late 1937, neither the rank and file nor the leadership acknowledged a need to go on and adjust all four fundamental socialist principles to the harsh realities that had been bared to their view. The second group was more important and exercised more far-reaching influence. It consisted of the party's leaders in the wartime Coalition government, who, owing to their new responsibilities, gained an entirely new perspective on foreign policy. Geographical position, international conditions, economic and military capabilities, and above all ingrained national habits and tested national traditions: such were the considerations that now dominated the Labour leadership's thinking, as, indeed, they had done for generations of British statesmen regardless of party; and the result was that by 1945

the Coalition Labour ministers had come to discard the four socialist principles as irrelevant to the conduct of Britain's affairs
in the world as it is. Yet no more than the trade unionist did the
leadership succeed at the time in reeducating the party's partisans;
the lessons of its own wartime experience were not imparted to
the rank and file. Labour members entered World War II with a
good conscience, unshaken in their conviction that all was sound
concerning socialist foreign policy, and when the war ended, they
were more convinced of this than ever.

After 1945, this innocent state of mind was abruptly shattered.
Until then, Labour enthusiasts had been free to argue that, whenever socialist foreign policy proved unequal to the situation, this
was due solely to the party's lack of sufficient power to implement
it fully. Even the not noticeably socialist foreign policies of the
first two Labour governments could be conveniently explained
away on this basis. Such ingenuousness was impossible to sustain
after 1945. Whatever the confusion to which the Labour leadership added during the general election, the new government did
not peer at the existing world situation through socialist eyes.
What principally stirred its concern and absorbed its energies was
the growing imbalance of power on the European continent; and
the thrust of its foreign policy aimed directly at correcting that
imbalance, exactly as the policies of previous British governments
had done throughout the ages. If a socialist foreign policy did not
materialize this time, the responsibility could manifestly be im-
puted only to a prudent and calculated decision that the policy
was simply inadequate to the tasks at hand. Hence the reforming
vision of the socialist pioneers was judged utopian. Nor was uto-
pianism, as things turned out, its sole deficiency. As a partisan doctrine failing to stir the enthusiasm of even the leaders of the Labour Party, socialist foreign policy proved to be not simply inop-
erative and useless but decidedly harmful. For in arousing fervent
expectations that were destined to remain unrealistic, it developed
into a source of severe strain among its Labour adherents.

The paramount problem after 1945, then, was whether the
party would adapt to the inescapable realities in foreign policy to
which the Labour government itself readily adapted. To an observer unfamiliar with the underlying pattern of recurrent party
conflict in this area, this problem might have seemed fairly tract-

able; the obviously sensible solution was not only to adapt but to do so with sufficient purpose as to retain what was indisputably valuable in the old doctrine, thus arriving at a satisfying synthesis. But the problem was not so easily manageable. Many Labour partisans saw the government's behavior as nothing short of betrayal, and in the face of biting criticism from its own ranks, the government had no choice but to proceed cautiously; it was not until mid-1947 that it felt confident enough to undertake a vigorous campaign aimed at discrediting its critics and winning the party round to full support of Ernest Bevin's policy. In this it was partially successful, although the march of events, particularly the upsurge in Soviet belligerence in 1947 and American Marshall Aid, was equally responsible for the leadership's consolidation of its authority. The result was that an adaptation of sorts in party outlook was effected, and for roughly eighteen months, a new, if fragile, consensus seemed to be evolving. Nonetheless there remained the pivotal question of the degree of adaptation involved. Was it complete and acknowledged as such? Or, stated differently, were the four fundamental socialist principles brought fully into accord with the hard realities of governing?

Judged against what ensued after 1950, when international events again took a sharply unfavorable turn, the answer must be decidedly in the negative. As in the past, Labour's fate in the area of foreign policy became riddled with conflict, only with the difference that this time the conflict proved more portentous than ever. Two massive factions, the fundamentalists and the revisionists, fought one exhausting but inconclusive battle after another. The clash between them was all the more accentuated in that the two sides were roughly equal in strength. Consequently, though each was powerful, neither was so powerful as to be able to impose its views on the other.

Had the Labour Party amounted to a mere coalition of interest groups, in which the socialists figured as only one wing, the problem of adaptation would have been comparatively tractable in that the common beliefs and values shared by the various components would have been hazy, amorphous, without comprehensive design or coherent pattern. There would be no distinctive doctrine to discuss, whether in foreign policy or in domestic affairs; there would only be a commitment to piecemeal social reform,

pragmatically conceived and empirically implemented. But even
though an interpretation of this sort has threatened to become a
conventional view, the fact is that the Labour Party evolved in a
much different fashion. It functioned as a mass democratic movement cemented together by a commitment to a particular orthodoxy, a comprehensive ideology, which profoundly colored the
attitudes of its members toward policy both at home and abroad.
Because the foreign policy of the Attlee governments added up
to a decisive repudiation of that doctrinaire commitment, the ensuing struggle within the party was fierce and prolonged for the
simple reason that it involved the explosive issue of fundamental
principles. At stake were questions of basic beliefs and basic moral
values.

Hence, the enormous conflict over foreign policy after 1951
amounted to a genuine crisis of purpose, a tormenting intellectual
and moral predicament. What did Labour stand for and what did
it seek in the political realm? This was the question that Labour
partisans posed to themselves, and to others, again and again; but
no longer agreeing on a common answer, they found themselves
torn apart whenever a controversial matter demanded a clear-cut
policy decision. To be sure, personal factors like the struggle for
the leadership influenced the conflict, as did new and dramatic developments on the international scene. But always the underlying
issue round which the controversies of the moment whirled was
the fate of the original socialist principles. To the fundamentalist
wing, these principles were as compelling as ever and at most
needed reformulation in contemporary terms. To the revisionist
wing, they were outdated aspirations that had turned out to be
utopian and therefore required extensive reconstruction. With the
party chronically split on every major problem of the day, stalemate—inability to formulate strong and innovative policies—resulted. To maintain a modicum of unity the leadership resorted
to compromises that obscured issues rather than confronting them.
Ambivalence and equivocation were no doubt more congenial to
Attlee and to Wilson than to Gaitskell, but when Gaitskell's frontal attacks on Clause IV and unilateralism not only failed to overcome the basic impasse but pushed the party to the brink of disintegration, he too retreated into compromise formulas as a way
of maintaining his leadership. What else can be expected from a

party that continues to hanker after consensus but is divided into two warring camps on its substance?

All too many observers have been reluctant to trace Labour's stalemate to the party's underlying doctrinaire outlook. They would like to believe that the party is not ideological by heritage but pragmatic, flexible, and adaptive—an ideal engine for continuous but experimental and nondogmatic reform. As they profess to see it, whatever ideological quirks Labour once evidenced have long since been repudiated, and the troubles that keep overwhelming a Labour government like the present one are therefore to be ascribed to the logic of the situation. It is Britain's restricted freedom of maneuver, its narrow margin of choice, its vulnerability to international movements beyond its control, that account for the government's recurring failure to get on top of events and to formulate radical and imaginative policies. No doubt the present situation of the nation is unenviable, but then the job of bold statesmanship is precisely to undertake creative measures for altering it. If the Wilson government has so far been delinquent in this regard, the causes are not solely to be located outside the present character of the party sustaining it.

# Notes

# Notes

**PREFACE**

1. Attlee, *The Labour Party in Perspective,* p. 227.
2. Wolfers, *Discord and Collaboration,* pp. 244–46.
3. See, for instance, Denis Healey, "Power Politics and the Labour Party," p. 164.
4. A. J. P. Taylor, *The Trouble Makers.*
5. *Ibid.,* p. 19.
6. *Ibid.,* p. 20.
7. Beer, *British Politics in the Collectivist Age,* pp. 126–52.

**CHAPTER ONE**

1. A classic statement of the policy is found in "Memorandum of Sir Eyre Crowe," pp. 204–6.
2. For this and other Gladstonian utterances, see *ibid.,* pp. 167–91.
3. For one such assessment, see Strang, pp. 153–56.
4. MacDonald, *National Defence,* pp. 115–16.
5. Attlee, *The Labour Party in Perspective,* pp. 226–27.
6. *LPCR,* 1934, p. 156.
7. *LPCR,* 1933, p. 189.
8. Dalton, *Towards the Peace of Nations,* p. 2.
9. Great Britain, House of Commons, *Parliamentary Debates,* Vol. 335, col. 535 (2 May 1938). Hereafter cited in the form 335 *H.C.Deb.* 535 (2 May 1938).
10. 330 *H.C.Deb.* 1797–98 (21 December 1937).
11. Beer, *British Politics in the Collectivist Age,* pp. 126–52, 234–36.
12. I have two intellectual debts that should be spelled out at this point. First, though several writers (including Labour members) have discussed Labour's foreign policy in terms of principles, the value of employing them as an analytical tool was most persuasively implanted in my mind by a reading of Richard Rose, "The Relation of Socialist Prin-

ciples to British Labour Foreign Policy, 1945–1951." In spite of considerable disagreement between Rose's views and my own, particularly in relation to Ernest Bevin's foreign policy after 1945, I have no doubts regarding the extent of my indebtedness to his thesis. The fourfold classification of socialist principles employed in these pages approximates Rose's brief summary (pp. 85–89 in his thesis) of the matter, though the exposition of these principles and the theoretical use to which I have put them are, needless to say, entirely my own. An earlier work that also analyzes Labour's policy in terms of principles, though only during the interwar period and less systematically than I have attempted to do, is W. R. Tucker, *The Attitude of the British Labour Party Towards European and Collective Security Problems, 1920–1939.* Subsequent research calls into question some of Tucker's arguments, but it is a work that has helped me considerably in formulating my initial ideas about Labour's foreign policy.

13. On ideology as a symbolic representation of social reality, see Geertz, pp. 48–76.

14. May, pp. 653–67.

15. MacDonald, *Socialism*, p. 120.

16. 22 *H.C.Deb.* 1924 (13 March 1911); 32 *H.C.Deb.* 74 (27 November 1911).

17. Hamilton, p. 92.

18. Dalton, *Towards the Peace of Nations*, pp. 124–25.

19. 167 *H.C.Deb.* 76 (23 July 1923).

20. Brailsford, *After the Peace*, pp. 47–52. Brailsford's writings in general carried considerable weight in Labour's ranks after 1917. His *Covenant of Peace* won the English Review prize for the best study of the League idea.

21. Henderson, *Labour's Way to Peace* (London, 1935), p. 31.

22. Winkler, *The League of Nations Movement in Great Britain, 1914–1919,* p. 259.

23. The quoted words are, again, Winkler's, *ibid.*, p. 260.

24. *LPCR,* 1922, p. 193.

25. Winkler, "The Emergence of a Labour Foreign Policy in Great Britain, 1918–1929," pp. 254–58. Henderson, in developing a League-centered policy, relied heavily on the International Advisory Committee, one of several such advisory committees that sprouted after 1918 and on which many of the ex-Liberal recruits were to be found. Cline, *Recruits to Labour*, chap. IV, is helpful on this point.

26. 281 *H.C.Deb.* 148 (7 November 1933).

27. 333 *H.C.Deb.* 1417 (24 March 1938).

28. Henderson, *Labour's Way to Peace*, p. 106.

29. Healey, "Power Politics and the Labour Party," p. 163.

30. British Labour Party, *Report of the Independent Labour Annual Party Conference, 1900*, p. 21.

31. See McBriar, pp. 119–30.

32. Quoted in Poirier, p. 107.

33. Bealey and Pelling, pp. 178–79.

34. "An Indictment of the Class War," *Labour Leader*, 9 September 1904, as quoted in Tsuzuki, pp. 153–54.

35. *LPCR*, 1912, p. 101; *LPCR*, 1913, p. 124.

36. Hamilton, pp. 166–70.

37. *Labour Leader*, 31 January 1918, as quoted in Dowse, p. 34.

38. Landauer, I, 804–5.

39. G. D. H. Cole, *A History of the Labour Party from 1914*.

40. *LPCR*, 1922, p. 200.

41. *LPCR*, 1926, p. 256.

42. Snowden, pp. 595–96, is illuminating here.

43. Beer, *British Politics in the Collectivist Age*, p. 159.

44. Dowse, pp. 34–37.

45. Cline, *Recruits to Labour*, pp. 67–99.

46. Cline, "E. D. Morel and the Crusade Against the Foreign Office," pp. 126–37, places Morel's challenge against the background of his earlier crusades.

47. Swanwick, pp. 374–75.

48. Quoted in Mayer, p. 49.

49. Tawney, "The Choice Before the Labour Party," p. 327.

50. *LPCR*, 1934, pp. 160ff.

51. *LPCR*, 1934, p. 176.

52. *LPCR*, 1935, p. 160.

53. Cripps, "The Political Reaction to Rearmament," p. 124.

54. *LPCR*, 1933, pp. 224–25, 277; similar resolutions were passed at the TUC conference.

55. *LPCR*, 1937, pp. 27, 268–70.

56. Dalton, *Memoirs, 1931–1945*, p. 89.

57. Graubard, pp. 242–43.

58. Hamilton, p. 197.

59. Quoted in Mowat, p. 5.

60. Bullock, I, 135–42.

61. Jenkins, *Pursuit of Progress*, p. 15.

62. *New Statesman*, 24 January 1948.

63. Dalton, *Memoirs, 1887–1931*, p. 230. Dalton jotted down this observation in 1929 while Parliamentary Under-Secretary at the Foreign Office.

64. Pelling, *The British Communist Party*, pp. 24ff.

65. *Ibid.*, p. 25.

66. A strongly worded but representative trade unionist's view of this struggle is found in Deakin, pp. 337–39.

67. Citrine, p. 344.

68. *LPCR*, 1934, p. 11.

69. *LPCR*, 1939, p. 215.

70. Beer, *British Politics in the Collectivist Age*, pp. 132ff.

71. Hobson, *Imperialism*, pp. 50, 59.

72. Quoted in Taylor, *The Trouble Makers*, p. 170.

73. *LPCR*, 1946, p. 106.
74. "Forward to Socialism," in Fenn *et al.*, p. 219.
75. *LPCR*, 1934, p. 175.
76. Woolf, *Economic Imperialism*, p. 9.
77. *LPCR*, 1934, p. 174.
78. Pelling, *America and the British Left*, pp. 7–66, traces the evolution of British opinion.
79. *Ibid.*, pp. 90–94.
80. Quoted in *ibid.*, p. 142. A penetrating analysis of the British left-wing state of mind in the 1930's is found in Hartley, pp. 2–43. The writings of George Orwell are, of course, indispensable in this respect.
81. Bevan, *In Place of Fear*, p. 3.
82. Laski, *The American Democracy*, p. 120. Helpful in running through Laski's utterances is Deane, especially pp. 302–19.
83. Epstein, *Britain, Uneasy Ally*, pp. 138–44.
84. Bullock, I, 358.
85. MacDonald, *Labour Leader*, 3 February 1911, p. 74.
86. *Socialist Review* (October–December 1914), p. 316.
87. *LPCR*, 1916, p. 32.
88. Jenkins, *Mr. Attlee: An Interim Biography*, p. 102.
89. Angell, "Pacifists and Cruisers."
90. Carr, pp. 41–62, is still one of the most penetrating accounts of this matter.
91. *LPCR*, 1944, p. 4.
92. *Labour Leader*, 19 December 1916.
93. Greenwood, pp. 46–47.
94. MacDonald, *The Foreign Policy of the Labour Party*, p. 20; Attlee, *Daily Herald*, 5 April 1935.
95. Taylor, *The Trouble Makers*, p. 199.

CHAPTER TWO

1. 305 *H.C.Deb.* 37 (22 October 1933).
2. For a succinct and searching examination of these matters, see Claude, pp. 238–43.
3. MacDonald, *League of Nations Official Journal*, p. 42.
4. Toynbee, pp. 17ff.
5. On the differences in French and British views of collective security, Labour's included, see Jordan, pp. 179–218, esp. the latter 20 pages.
6. 182 *H.C.Deb.* 298 (24 March 1925).
7. *LPCR*, 1924, p. 108.
8. MacDonald, *Protocol or Pact*, p. 5.
9. Winkler, "Arthur Henderson," pp. 315ff.
10. Parmoor, pp. 235, 240ff.
11. Hamilton, pp. 246–47.
12. Ramsay MacDonald, in 109 *H.C.Deb.* 719, as quoted in Taylor, *The Trouble Makers*, p. 144.
13. MacDonald, in 182 *H.C.Deb.* 342 (24 March 1925).

14. Cline, "E. D. Morel and the Crusade Against the Foreign Office," pp. 133–34.

15. Hamilton, pp. 238–40.

16. Cline, "E. D. Morel," pp. 134–35; Lyman, pp. 193–98.

17. Quoted in Cline, "E. D. Morel," p. 136.

18. W. R. Tucker, "British Labor and Revision of the Peace Settlement, 1920–1925," *Southwestern Social Science Quarterly* (September 1960), pp. 148–49.

19. Carr, p. 53.

20. Wolfers, *Britain and France Between Two World Wars*, pp. 328ff, 382ff.

21. Taylor, *The Origins of the Second World War*, pp. 57–58.

22. Concerning the Labour government's diplomatic achievements, see Dalton, "British Foreign Policy, 1929–1931," pp. 484–505.

23. *LPCR*, 1929, p. 210.

24. 229 *H.C.Deb.* 457–58 (29 June 1929).

25. *LPCR*, 1932, p. 228.

26. 259 *H.C.Deb.* 898 (9 March 1931).

27. *LPCR*, 1931, pp. 42, 184.

28. Winkler, "Arthur Henderson," p. 328.

29. Quoted in Taylor, *The Trouble Makers*, p. 185.

30. *LPCR*, 1933, pp. 186–93.

31. *LPCR*, 1932, p. 68.

32. 270 *H.C.Deb.* 526 (10 November 1932).

33. Bassett, pp. 553–57.

34. Winkler, "Arthur Henderson," p. 341.

35. Foot, *Aneurin Bevan*, p. 197.

36. Cooke, p. 191.

37. G. D. H. Cole, *A History of the Labour Party from 1914*, pp. 347–60. Foot (*Aneurin Bevan*, pp. 243–99) offers a lively left-wing viewpoint of these developments.

38. See George Lansbury, *My Quest for Peace* (London, 1938).

39. Postgate, p. 308.

40. Henderson, *Labour's Way to Peace*, p. 46. (Italics added.)

41. *LPCR*, 1934, pp. 152–53, for Henderson's comments, and pp. 245–46 for the report.

42. *LPCR*, 1935, pp. 153–93.

43. Postgate, pp. 300–305; Francis Williams, *Ernest Bevin*, pp. 188–98. Ponsonby, leader of the party in the Lords, had resigned before the conference in protest against the NEC statement.

44. Bullock, I, 560–61.

45. 315 *H.C.Deb.* 1171 (27 July 1936).

46. Attlee, in 305 *H.C.Deb.* 45 (22 October 1935).

47. *LPCR*, 1935, p. 5.

48. Attlee, in 320 *H.C.Deb.* 1211 (7 February 1937).

49. Dalton, *Memoirs, 1931–1945*, p. 88; 310 *H.C.Deb.* 1454 (26 March 1936).

50. Foot, *Aneurin Bevan*, pp. 414–15.

51. *LPCR*, 1936, p. 203.

52. Bullock, I, 511–12, 550–51; Pelling, *A Short History of the Labour Party*, pp. 77–79.

53. *TUCR*, 1935, p. 349.

54. Dalton, *Memoirs, 1931–1945*, p. 69.

55. *LPCR*, 1936, pp. 181–84, 203.

56. *TUCR*, 1936, p. 358.

57. Williams, *Ernest Bevin*, pp. 201ff.

58. Dalton, *Memoirs, 1931–1945*, pp. 133–40.

59. Foot, *Aneurin Bevan*, pp. 264–65.

60. Laski, "British Labor in Retreat," p. 344.

61. G. D. H. Cole, *A History of the Labour Party from 1914*, p. 332.

62. *TUCR*, 1937, pp. 472–74.

63. Dalton, *Memoirs, 1931–1945*, p. 140.

64. *LPCR*, 1936, p. 33.

65. Poirier, pp. 9–20.

66. Bendix, pp. 61ff.

67. Crossman, "Labour and Compulsory Military Service," p. 315.

CHAPTER THREE

Epigraph: Quoted in Miliband, p. 272.

1. Quoted in Kingsley Martin, *Harold Laski*, p. 169.

2. The quoted words are G. D. H. Cole's, *A History of the Labour Party from 1914*, p. 378. Attlee's speech was later printed as a Labour pamphlet and given the title of "Labour's Peace Aims."

3. Attlee, "Labour's Peace Aims"; "Why Kill Each Other?" (1939); Citrine, in *TUCR*, 1939, p. 355; "Labour, the War, and the Peace" (1940).

4. The argument here is a composite derived from three official party declarations: "The Old World and the New Society" (1942), "The International Post-War Settlement" (1944), and "From a People's War to a People's Peace" (1944). The latter was a manifesto issued at the conclusion of a conference of Commonwealth Labour parties held in London, September 1944 (see *LPCR*, 1944, pp. 212–14). Also relevant are two Fabian society publications offering an even more ardent socialist view: "Labour and Europe" and Leonard Woolf, "The International Post-War Settlement."

5. Dalton, *Memoirs, 1931–1945*, pp. 423–27.

6. *LPCR*, 1940, p. 8.

7. *LPCR*, 1940, pp. 13–14.

8. Quoted in Coates and Topham, p. 165.

9. Among the more witting enthusiasts, G. D. H. Cole speculated in *Europe, Russia and the Future* that the world would be better off for "Germany as well as Eastern Europe to be included in an enlarged U.S.S.R.," and Harold Laski dwelt in *Britain and Russia: The Future* on the advantages of a "Sovietised Asia." See too in this connection almost any issue of the *Tribune* and the *New Statesman* in the spring and summer of 1945.

10. McCallum and Readman, p. 97. See, too, C. R. Rose, "The Relation of Socialist Principles," p. 72.

11. *LPCR*, 1951, p. 127.

12. Bullock, II, 349.

13. 373 *H.C.Deb.* 1362 (29 July 1941).

14. 406 *H.C.Deb.* 908 (8 December 1944).

15. 413 *H.C.Deb.* 312 (20 August 1945).

16. 408 *H.C.Deb.* 1614 (1 March 1945).

17. See Dalton, *Memoirs, 1931–1945*, p. 457.

18. Fitzsimons, p. 198. Fitzsimons' view is cited without comment by D. C. Watt, in *Personalities and Politics*, p. 61.

19. *LPCR*, 1945, p. 104.

20. Dalton, *Memoirs, 1931–1945*, p. 423.

21. *Ibid.*, p. 457.

22. Jenkins, *Pursuit of Progress*, p. 32.

23. *Ibid.*, pp. 32, 33.

24. Waltz, p. 57.

25. For Bevan's views, see Foot, *Aneurin Bevan*, pp. 476–90.

26. *LPCR*, 1944, pp. 143–50.

27. *Ibid.*, pp. 131–32.

28. Jenkins, *Pursuit of Progress*, pp. 30, 31.

29. *LPCR*, 1945, pp. 107–8.

30. *Ibid.*, pp. 115–19.

31. Jenkins, *Pursuit of Progress*, p. 30.

32. *Ibid.*, pp. 31–32.

33. *LPCR*, 1945, p. 112.

34. For two such impressions, the one contemporary and the other retrospective, see Wyatt, p. 100, and Morrison, *An Autobiography*, p. 246.

35. *The Times* (London), 26 June 1945.

36. *New Statesman*, 12 May 1945.

37. McCallum and Readman, p. 98.

38. *The Times*, 3 July 1945.

39. *New Statesman*, 11 August 1945.

CHAPTER FOUR

Epigraph: Williams, *A Prime Minister Remembers*, p. 171. (Italics added.)

1. Williams, *A Prime Minister Remembers*, p. 71.

2. 413 *H.C.Deb.* 291 (20 August 1945).

3. Fitzsimons, *The Foreign Policy of the British Labour Government*, p. 31.

4. 417 *H.C.Deb.* 1342 (7 December 1945).

5. Dalton, *Memoirs, 1945–1960*, p. 57.

6. 413 *H.C.Deb.* 285–312 (20 August 1945).

7. Williams, *A Prime Minister Remembers*, p. 169.

8. Meehan, p. 73.

9. Byrnes, pp. 108ff.

10. In the opinion of one scholar of the period, Byrnes's whole policy

"was designed to arrange peace treaties promptly in order to permit American withdrawal from active participation in European affairs." William Hardy McNeill, p. 710. This evaluation may be a bit too categorical, since Byrnes seemed to vacillate in his attitude, being somewhat conciliatory at Potsdam, "getting tough" at London, and then becoming conciliatory again at Moscow (so much so, indeed, that he drew a rebuke from Truman). But by and large there is little doubt that both Byrnes and to a lesser extent Truman were more responsive to Soviet claims than Bevin and Attlee ever were.

11. *Ibid.*, p. 629.

12. 416 *H.C.Deb.* 762 (23 November 1945).

13. Quoted in C. R. Rose, "The Relation of Socialist Principles," p. 110.

14. Williams, *A Prime Minister Remembers*, p. 172.

15. Cmd. 7046 (1947), p. 16.

16. Churchill, p. 456.

17. The two words in quotation marks are taken from Feis, p. 596.

18. McNeill, p. 327.

19. At Yalta Roosevelt's hostility to British imperialism became so intense that he urged Churchill to convert the Empire into international trusteeships. When Churchill protested, he told his Secretary of State, in a subsequent aside, that Britain "would take land anywhere, even if were only rock or a sandbar." Edward Stettinius, *Roosevelt and the Russians* (London, 1950), p. 212.

20. This generally accepted interpretation of Truman's policy has recently been strongly contested by Gar Alperovitz, *Atomic Diplomacy*. Alperovitz argues that Truman soon broke with Roosevelt's aims when he learned of the atomic bomb, in the belief that this so strengthened the American hand that the U.S. could dictate to the Soviets the terms of postwar settlement in Europe. As a result, American diplomacy is alleged to have been the major disturbance of East-West cooperation. But whereas the thesis is interesting and Alperovitz vigorously expounds it, it remains unconvincing, and in no small measure because Alperovitz has to resort to rather strained surmise in order to sustain his argument. A major instance of this occurs on pp. 230–31, where in summary he seeks once again to argue away the known facts regarding what he himself calls "Truman's conciliatory actions during late May, June and early July." These actions, however, "did not represent [Truman's] *basic* policy . . . ; his actions during this period—symbolized by his attempt to *avoid the appearance* of 'ganging up' with Britain against the Soviet Union—were only a manifestation of his *tactical* retreat," etc. (italics added). Another defect of Alperovitz's interpretation is its use of memoirs, especially Byrnes's and Truman's. Alperovitz does not sufficiently recognize that both wrote their works in part to rebuff critics, American and British alike, who had charged them with being naïve in their relations with the Soviet Union. But whether Alperovitz is right or not does not matter here, for what is relevant for our purposes is the unquestion-

able suspicion prevailing in Washington at the time with respect to British schemes.

21. Feis, pp. 650–52.

22. Truman, p. 410, notes that at the time he had been unaware of the extent of the British economic plight.

23. Nicholas, pp. 39ff.

24. Williams, *Ernest Bevin*, p. 257.

25. For example, Halle, pp. 36–37, 99–108.

26. Quoted in Michael Foot, *Aneurin Bevan*, p. 434.

27. *Tribune*, 5 October 1945.

28. See the *New Statesman*, 13 November, and the *Tribune*, 12 November 1945.

29. Meehan, p. 70.

30. *Forward*, 26 January 1946.

31. *Manchester Guardian*, 12 March 1946. I am grateful to Rose, "Socialist Principles," p. 115, for having drawn my attention to this source.

32. 419 *H.C.Deb.* 132 (21 February 1946).

CHAPTER FIVE

Epigraph: Strang (Permanent Under-Secretary at the Foreign Office 1947–53), pp. 338–39.

1. See Dalton, *Memoirs, 1945–1960*, p. 105.

2. Viscount Montgomery of Alamein, p. 450.

3. Williams, *A Prime Minister Remembers*, p. 175.

4. McNeill, pp. 321–22.

5. Quoted in Williams, *A Prime Minister Remembers*, pp. 59–60.

6. Vandenberg, p. 244.

7. Millis, p. 144.

8. Quoted in Williams, *A Prime Minister Remembers*, p. 170.

9. See for instance, Montgomery, p. 408. Montgomery became Chief of the Imperial General Staff in June 1946.

10. Rosecrance, *Defense of the Realm*, pp. 8–11, 51–58.

11. Montgomery, p. 408.

12. "Keep Left" (*New Statesman* pamphlet, London, 1947), p. 40. Authors were R. H. S. Crossman, Michael Foot, and Ian Mikardo, but twelve other Labour MP's subscribed to its views in print.

13. A concise summary of the background of the incident is unraveled in McNeill, pp. 54, 56off.

14. Lie, p. 31.

15. For a recent study of British policy in Germany, see Watt, *Britain Looks to Germany*.

16. From October 1944 to May 1947, Britain supplied 132 million pounds sterling of aid to Greece and almost an equivalent amount to Turkey, much of it in scarce dollars. See Cmd. 8065 (1950).

17. See Dalton, *Memoirs, 1945–1960*, pp. 106–9, for the Treasury viewpoint.

18. Quoted in Fitzsimons, *The Foreign Policy of the British Labour Government*, p. 91.

19. On British policy toward Berlin, see Bevin's statements in *LPCR*, 1948, p. 195; 452 *H.C.Deb.* 2230–32 (30 June 1948); and 456 *H.C.Deb.* 910 (22 September 1948), the latter comparing concessions to the Soviets with appeasement at Munich. Bevan's proposal for an armed convoy is related in Watt, *Britain Looks to Germany*, p. 62.

20. Watt, "Germany," p. 98.

21. Beloff, *New Dimensions in Foreign Policy*, p. 17.

22. Millis, p. 185.

23. Mongomery, pp. 394–95.

24. 446 *H.C.Deb.* 395 (22 January 1948).

25. Truman, *Memoirs*, II, pp. 258–59.

26. Millis, p. 455.

27. *Ibid.*, p. 491.

28. See e.g., the speech of Philip Noel-Baker, Minister for Commonwealth Relations, 464 *H.C.Deb.* 2127 (12 May 1949).

29. Inis L. Claude, Jr., *Power and International Relations*, pp. 115–23; and Wolfers, *Discord and Collaboration*, pp. 181–205.

30. R. N. Rosecrance, "British Defense Strategy," p. 69.

31. Rosecrance, *Defense of the Realm*, p. 109.

32. Cmd. 6923 (1946) documents the government's reorganization of the defense establishment; a useful supplement is Johnson, pp. 304–15. See, too, Rosecrance, *Defense of the Realm*, pp. 34–152, for a general analysis of the Labour government's defense policies. The decision to build a British nuclear force is conveniently summarized and appraised in Goldberg, pp. 409–30, 600–619.

33. "Cards on the Table" (London, 1947), p. 18.

34. Hoffmann, p. 74.

35. *LPCR*, 1945, pp. 107–8.

36. 438 *H.C.Deb.* 2354 (19 June 1947).

37. *New Statesman*, 22 September 1945 (italics added).

38. 413 *H.C.Deb.* 665 (22 August 1945). Goodwin, pp. 51–57, provides a compact summary of the Labour government's policy.

39. The only resolutions critical of the government's foreign policy that secured a majority vote at Trades Union Congresses concerned Spain. See *TUCR*, 1946, pp. 469–73, and 1947, pp. 501–8.

40. Montgomery, p. 448.

41. Elaine Windrich, *British Labour's Foreign Policy*, (Stanford, Calif., 1952), pp. 179–82, p. 185.

42. 413 *H.C.Deb.* 196 (20 August 1945).

43. Williams, *A Prime Minister Remembers*, p. 175.

44. Williams, *Ernest Bevin*, p. 250.

45. *LPCR*, 1947, p. 176.

46. Fitzsimons, *The Foreign Policy of the British Labour Government*, pp. 179–80.

47. See, for example, the interesting account by Michael Foot, *Aneurin Bevan*, I, chap. 13: "The Fight with Bevin."

48. *LPCR*, 1946, p. 154.

49. *New Statesman*. The relevant issues are 31 August and 7, 21, 28 September 1946.

50. Meehan, pp. 95–103; Jackson, pp. 55–57.

51. 430 *H.C.Deb*. 577–90 (18 November 1946).

52. For a treatment of the manner in which Soviet belligerence began to backfire in late 1947, see Shulman, *Stalin's Foreign Policy Reappraised*.

53. See *LPCR*, 1948, p. 23.

54. Quoted in the *Manchester Guardian*, 3 May 1948.

55. *LPCR*, 1949, p. 18. In 1948 and 1949, the NEC expelled three other members of the PLP on somewhat similar grounds.

56. This was the number of MP's who signed an "Open Letter" to Bevin in July 1948 urging elaborate appeasement of the Soviet Union.

57. F. S. Northedge, *British Foreign Policy*, p. 141.

58. 473 *H.C.Deb*. 320 (28 March 1950).

59. "Comment by Kenneth Younger," *International Affairs*, January 1967, p. 25.

60. *New Statesman*, 17 January 1948.

61. 448 *H.C.Deb*. 2302–3 (18 March 1948).

62. C. R. Rose, "The Relation of Socialist Principles," p. 256.

63. *LPCR*, 1948, p. 172.

64. *LPCR*, 1948, pp. 177–79.

65. For a representative socialist view, see Mackay, *Heads in the Sand*.

66. Dalton's account, *Memoirs, 1945–1960*, pp. 312–36, is particularly revealing in these matters.

67. "European Unity" (London, Labour Party, 1950), pp. 3–8. The authors were the same pair, Hugh Dalton and Denis Healey, who had prepared "Cards on the Table," only this time they were careful to obtain the prior permission of the NEC before publishing the statement.

Healey, a firebrand socialist in 1945, became increasingly disenchanted with socialist principles, especially the one relating to international working-class solidarity. Aside from the already cited "Power Politics and the Labour Party," see his "International Socialist Conference, 1946–1950," *International Affairs* (July 1950) and "Beyond Power Politics."

68. André Philip, *The Times*, 27 August 1950.

69. Cited above, p. 120, n. 7.

70. C. R. Rose, "The Relation of Socialist Principles," p. 179.

71. *The Times*, 15 February 1950.

72. *Ibid.*, 16 February 1950.

CHAPTER SIX

1. Deutsch and Merritt, "Effects of Events on National and International Images," pp. 182–83.

2. *Ibid.*, p. 182.

3. For a cogent appraisal of these factors, see Janis and Smith, pp. 198–203.

4. Deutsch and Merritt, "Effects of Events on National and International Images," p. 183.

5. Laski, *Dilemma of Our Times*, pp. 60–61, 169ff. Laski's ideas regarding the cold war are examined by Deane, pp. 302–28.

6. *LPCR*, 1946, p. 106.

7. Thus Aneurin Bevan told the 1951 conference: "Let us also remember that the Soviet revolution would not have been distorted, would not have ended in a tyranny, would not have resulted in a dictatorship, would not now be threatening the peace of mankind, had it not been for the behavior of Churchill and the Tories ... the City of London, New York and all the rest of the capitalist world." *LPCR*, 1951, p. 121. See Leon Epstein's comments, *Britain, Uneasy Ally*, pp. 93–94.

8. Quoted in Deane, p. 322.

9. *New Statesman*, 13 April 1946.

10. *LPCR*, 1946, p. 157.

11. *Ibid.*, p. 167.

12. P. Calvocoressi, *Survey of International Affairs, 1947–1948*, pp. 100–101.

13. *Tribune*, 7 July 1946.

14. Wyatt, p. 140.

15. See Wyatt's observations, *ibid.*, pp. 140–43.

16. Osgood, pp. 32–51.

17. *New Statesman*, 9 April 1949.

18. See for instance Aneurin Bevan, 484 *H.C.Deb.* 733 (15 February 1951).

19. *LPCR*, 1950, pp. 141ff.

20. Bryan, Magee, *The New Radicalism* (London, 1962), p. 108.

21. Watt, "American Aid to Britain and the Problem of Socialism, 1945–51," pp. 53–82.

22. Epstein, *Britain, Uneasy Ally*, pp. 102–3.

23. Tom Driberg, *LPCR*, 1946, p. 173.

24. This point figured prominently in the "rebels" case of November 1946. See 430 *H.C.Deb.* 529 (18 November 1946).

25. *LPCR*, 1952, pp. 82–83.

26. 430 *H.C.Deb.* 533 (18 November 1946).

27. "Keep Left," p. 33.

28. *Tribune* publication (London, June 1951), p. 10.

29. Pointing out that "a great many people have fundamentally the same idea of what the American is like," Mass Observation, a London survey organization at the time, went on to say that the "key point in this picture is the conception of *the American who does not grow up.*" "Portrait of an American?," *International Journal of Opinion and Attitude Research*, I (June 1947), 96. The article also pointed out that opinion of the United States had been seriously deteriorating since the end of the war.

30. Thus, more than two decades later, a leading conservative historian could write: "While the [anti-imperialist] attitude of the Truman administration was partly no doubt just an attempt to win the votes of zealous American liberals and Zionists, it was also due to eagerness to eliminate

a major obstacle to the expansion of its own influence and business interests." Medlicott, p. 485.

31. See Hartley, pp. 53–74.

32. The shift is traced in detail by Epstein, *Britain, Uneasy Ally*, pp. 108–11.

33. "Keeping Left," p. 25.

34. 466 *H.C.Deb.* 566 (23 January 1948).

35. Epstein, *Britain, Uneasy Ally*, pp. 111–12. This and the previous two paragraphs have drawn liberally from Epstein's account.

36. Ernest Bevin, 476, *H.C.Deb.* 1096 (18 July 1949).

37. 495 *H.C.Deb.* 842 (5 February 1952).

38. *The Times*, 13 May 1948.

39. Hinchingbrooke, pp. 8–9. The state of mind reflected in such statements as these was and still is widespread, reaching much beyond fringe circles. Kenneth Waltz (pp. 148–57) has termed views of this sort "the immaterialist fallacy."

40. See Hudson, pp. 536–48. The question of Communism and China is discussed from a British view in Luard, pp. 42–82.

41. Luard, pp. 80–82.

42. Epstein, *Britain, Uneasy Ally*, pp. 204–12.

43. See almost any British newspaper in November and December 1950.

44. Truman, *Memoirs*, II, pp. 419–20.

45. See for instance 481 *H.C.Deb.* 1382–91 (30 November 1950).

46. The text of the letters is found in Williams, *A Prime Minister Remembers*, pp. 233–35.

47. 482 *H.C.Deb.* 1353 and 1357 (14 December 1950).

48. Rees, p. 323.

49. Truman, *Memoirs*, II, p. 435.

50. R. H. S. Crossman, *New Statesman*, 14 April 1956, p. 378.

51. The rebels' Amendment to the Reply to the Throne, 430 *H.C.Deb.* 525 (18 November 1946).

52. Aneurin Bevan on the reasons for his resignation, 487 *H.C.Deb.* 38 (23 April 1951).

53. Resolution carried by voice vote, *LPCR*, 1952, pp. 116, 142.

54. "Keep Left," p. 34.

55. *New Statesman*, 21 September 1946.

56. Epstein, *Britain, Uneasy Ally*, pp. 113–14; C. R. Rose, "The Relation of Socialist Principles," pp. 196ff.

57. "The International Post-War Settlement," p. 4.

58. *New Statesman* (29 September 1945 and all October issues) appears to have pioneered the discussion, urging the Labour government to create a "friendly bloc on the Western seaboard of the Continent."

59. *Tribune*, July 1946.

60. The latter figure is given by Watt, "American Aid to Britain, 1945–1951," p. 66.

61. The letter was subsequently published in the *Manchester Guardian*, 16 October 1946.

62. Bevin, who was out of the country at the time, later referred to his critics' gambit as a "stab in the back." *LPCR*, 1947, p. 179.

63. 430 *H.C.Deb.* 530 (18 November 1946).

64. *Tribune*, 22 November 1946.

65. Epstein, *Britain, Uneasy Ally*, pp. 122–23.

66. "Keep Left," p. 41.

67. *Socialist Commentary*, XII (February 1948), as quoted in Epstein, *Britain, Uneasy Ally*, p. 122.

68. *Tribune*, 16 April 1947. Rose, "Socialist Principles," pp. 302–7; Jackson, *Rebels and Whips*, pp. 58–60.

69. 6 February 1948. The change in third force opinion is traced in Epstein, *Britain, Uneasy Ally*, pp. 123–27. C. R. Rose, "The Relation of Socialist Principles," calls the socialist version of the Anglo-American alliance that was common in former third force circles, after 1948, the "two and one-half force."

70. 476 *H.C.Deb* 2040 (26 June 1950).

71. "Keeping Left," p. 19.

72. "One Way Only," pp. 10–13.

73. Quoted in Epstein, *Britain, Uneasy Ally*, p. 123.

74. *Tribune*, 25 November 1949.

75. Crossman, "Between Two Façades."

76. *LPCR*, 1952, p. 117.

77. Crossman, "Between Two Façades." For a penetrating critique, see Epstein, *Britain, Uneasy Ally*, pp. 125–26.

78. See, for instance, his remarks in *The Times*, 15 April 1954.

79. *The Times*, 17 January 1953.

80. *Ibid.*

81. *The Times*, 15 April 1954.

82. Attlee, *The Labour Party in Perspective*, p. 224.

83. "Keeping Left," p. 44.

84. Attlee, *The Labour Party in Perspective*, p. 224.

85. *Daily Herald*, 4 April 1935.

86. "Keep Left," p. 7.

87. *LPCR*, 1949, pp. 194–95.

88. C. R. Rose, "The Relation of Socialist Principles," pp. 349–50.

89. "Keeping Left," pp. 7, 22–23, 44.

90. See Dalton, *Memoirs, 1945–1960*, pp. 250–53; Morrison, *An Autobiography*, pp. 257ff, 287ff; and the important speech of Morrison in *LPCR*, 1949, pp. 153–57, 209–12.

91. See for instance the March 1950 issues of the *Tribune*.

CHAPTER SEVEN

1. Crick, p. 16.

2. On these points, see the informative discussion by Richard Rose, "Parties, Factions, and Tendencies in Britain," pp. 314–29, esp. 325–27.

3. See Richard Rose, "Complexities of Party Leadership," pp. 257–73.

4. Waltz, pp. 55–61. See, too, Jackson, especially the conclusions on pp. 308–9, for an elaboration of methods used by party leaders to maintain solidarity in the face of internal stresses and strains, arguments and counterarguments.

5. An informative discussion of these groups is found in Burns, pp. 861ff. On "Keep Left," in particular, see C. R. Rose, "The Relation of Socialist Principles," pp. 471–81.

6. For a general analysis of these matters, see Deutsch, p. 55.

7. 430 *H.C.Deb.* 576 (18 November 1946).

8. McKenzie, pp. 446–54.

9. *LPCR*, 1946, p. 57.

10. The incident is described at length in Burns, pp. 868–69.

11. D. J. Heasman, "The Prime Minister and the Cabinet," pp. 471–84, and "Parliamentary Paths to High Office," pp. 315–30; Mackintosh, *The British Cabinet*, chap. 13; Waltz, pp. 42–43.

12. Seymour Cocks, *Tribune*, 13 June 1947, as quoted in C. R. Rose, "The Relation of Socialist Principles," p. 452.

13. C. R. Rose, "The Relation of Socialist Principles," pp. 455–57. Rose's diagnosis of the perennial dissenters is suggestive, and I have drawn heavily on it in both this and the next paragraph.

14. Figures taken from Butler and Freeman, p. 44.

15. An examination of the power of British government in Parliament owing to sheer numbers is found in Crick, pp. 16–43.

16. McKenzie, pp. 446–54, especially 450.

17. McKenzie, p. 449; Burns, pp. 859–60.

18. See Morrison, *An Autobiography*, p. 254.

19. Dalton, *Memoirs, 1945–1960*, p. 23.

20. C. R. Rose, "The Relation of Socialist Principles," pp. 463–65, 478–81; Jackson, pp. 61–63.

21. "Duties and Powers" of the NEC, Clause VIII of the Labour Party Constitution (1953).

22. *British Political Parties*, p. 525.

23. Kingsley Martin, *Harold Laski*, p. 218.

24. Dalton, *Memoirs, 1945–1960*, pp. 325, 328, 331; C. R. Rose, "The Relation of Socialist Principles," pp. 410–20.

25. McKenzie, p. 525.

26. For that matter, the conference acted contrary to the NEC's recommendations on only nine occasions—all of them involving minor matters of domestic policy (McKenzie, pp. 511–12).

27. Roberts, pp. 95ff.

28. See Harrison, pp. 108–94.

29. *Ibid.*, pp. 224–61.

30. *Ibid.*, p. 340.

31. See for instance the statements of Deakin and Williamson in *TUCR*, 1950, pp. 419, 425.

32. *TUCR*, 1951, pp. 501–5.

33. Source: *LPCR*, 1946–51. I am grateful to C. R. Rose, "The Relation of Socialist Principles," p. 435, for the idea of such a table. It should be noted that in 1948 affiliated organizations, which till then could submit two resolutions and two amendments, were limited to one resolution and one amendment. See McKenzie, pp. 490–91.

34. *LPCR*, 1949, p. 193.

CHAPTER EIGHT

Epigraphs: Quoted in *The Times*, 7 May 1951; 487 *H.C.Deb.* 1137 (1 May 1951).

1. Statement made by Prime Minister Attlee in summarizing the appeal, 478 *H.C.Deb.* 595 (12 September 1950).
2. The Joint Chiefs of Staff, for instance, were insisting that "American proposals to NATO be made strictly conditional upon iron-clad commitments by the Europeans to their own contributions, and in particular, upon unequivolcal acceptance of any immediate start on German rearmament in a form technically acceptable to American strategists." Lawrence W. Martin, "The American Decision to Rearm Germany," pp. 28–29.
3. 478 *H.C.Deb.* 479 (26 July 1950).
4. Cmd. 7895 (1950).
5. 478 *H.C.Deb.* 479 (26 July 1950).
6. A retrospective analysis of the decision was given by Attlee, 478 *H.C.Deb.* 595 (12 September 1950). See too Mitchell, pp. 30ff.
7. 478 *H.C.Deb.* 595 (12 September 1950).
8. 478 *H.C.Deb.* 1146–50 (13 September 1950).
9. 483 *H.C.Deb.* 584ff (29 January 1951).
10. 483 *H.C.Deb.* 583 (29 January 1951).
11. 476 *H.C.Deb.* 2160 (27 June 1950).
12. Rosenau, p. 65.
13. Final communiqué, as quoted in Truman, *Memoirs*, II, p. 412.
14. See Attlee, 483 *H.C.Deb.* 584 (29 January 1951).
15. Mitchell, p. 40.
16. Rees, p. 324.
17. "Full Speed Ahead," esp. pp. 14, 21. See, too, Meehan, pp. 161–63.
18. *Tribune*, 26 January 1951.
19. *Tribune*, 9 February 1951.
20. *New Statesman*, 9 December 1950.
21. Epstein, *Britain, Uneasy Ally*, p.219.
22. British Institute of Public Opinion, press release, January 1951, as cited in Epstein, p. 219.
23. *New Statesman*, 4 December 1948.
24. *Manchester Guardian*, 17 February 1951.
25. C. R. Rose, "The Relation of Socialist Principles," pp. 343–44.
26. 484 *H.C.Deb.* 733 (15 February 1951).
27. 484 *H.C.Deb.* 736 (15 February 1951).
28. Quoted in Schilling, Hammond, and Snyder, p. 100.

29. *Ibid.*, p. 101.
30. *Ibid.*, p. 103.
31. *Ibid.*, p. 103.
32. See Dalton, *Memoirs, 1945–1960*, pp. 357ff; Morrison, *An Autobiography*, p. 245; Shinwell, p. 224; Williams, *A Prime Minister Remembers*, pp. 245–46.
33. Dalton, *Memoirs, 1945–1960*, p. 358.
34. The evaluation is Morrison's, *An Autobiography*, p. 265.
35. Dalton, *Memoirs, 1945–1960*, pp. 251–53.
36. Hunter, *The Road to Brighton Pier.*
37. Saul Rose, interview, October 1964. Mr. Rose, Fellow of New College, Oxford, was formerly Secretary of the International Department of the Labour Party.
38. *The Times*, 4 April 1951.
39. Mitchell, p. 178.
40. Beer, *Treasury Control*, pp. 29–30.
41. Dalton, *Memoirs, 1945–1960*, p. 364.
42. 487 *H.C.Deb.* 34–35 (23 April 1951).
43. 487 *H.C.Deb.* 36 (23 April 1951).
44. 487 *H.C.Deb.* 37 (23 April 1951).
45. 487 *H.C.Deb.* 36 (23 April 1951).
46. Mitchell, p. 59.
47. *Ibid.*, p. 274.
48. 491 *H.C.Deb.* 660 (26 July 1951).
49. 508 *H.C.Deb.* 1775–82 (4 December 1952).
50. The distinction is Richard Rose's (following Samuel Beer), "Parties, Factions, and Tendencies in Britain," p. 319.
51. *Tribune*, 4 May 1951.
52. Cited in Krug, p. 119.
53. *TUCR*, 1951, pp. 501–5.
54. *LPCR*, 1952, pp. 142–53.

CHAPTER NINE

1. Crosland, *The Future of Socialism* and *The Conservative Enemy.*
2. *LPCR*, 1954, p. 74.
3. "Further Thoughts on Morecambe," *Spectator*, 17 October 1952.
4. Quoted in Krug, p. 213.
5. Dalton, *Memoirs, 1945–1960*, p. 383.
6. See, for instance, Crossman, *Labour in the Affluent Society* and "The Specter of Revisionism," pp. 27, 28.
7. Beer, *British Politics in the Collectivist Age*, p. 226; McKenzie, pp. 596, 629.
8. In 1959 a well-known conservative-minded writer of American birth was moved to protest against what he called "the anti-American zoo." See FitzGibbon, pp. 9–13.
9. *LPCR*, 1953, p. 161.
10. 596 *H.C.Deb.* 1393 (4 December 1958).

11. For one of many such assessments, see Bevan's comments upon his return from Moscow in *The Times*, 5 October 1957, and in a *Foreign Affairs Quarterly* article published that month entitled "Britain and America at Loggerheads."

12. Schlesinger, p. 142.

13. 562 *H.C.Deb.* 1403ff (19 December 1956).

14. For a characteristic scheme, see Rex and Worsley, pp. 49–53.

15. Finer *et al.*, pp.15–75.

16. Hindell and Williams, p. 331. In the debate on German rearmament at the 1954 conference, Martin Harrison estimates that the NEC won only 24 per cent of the constituency vote (p. 225).

17. *Economist*, 19 July 1952.

18. Saul Rose, p. 140.

19. Quoted in Alderman, "Parliamentary Party Discipline in Opposition, p. 135.

20. Beer, *British Politics in the Collectivist Age*, pp. 228–39.

21. *Ibid.*, p. 235.

22. Robert McKenzie argues this with respect to both domestic affairs and foreign policy, p. 600.

23. Saul Rose, p. 144.

24. Finer *et al.*, p. 29, referring to "Disengagement in Europe."

25. *LPCR*, 1958, p. 201.

26. For a left-wing account that more or less accepts this interpretation, see Aitken, pp. 15–16, 19.

27. Marquand, p. 3.

28. "Disarmament and Nuclear War" (*LPCR*, 1958, pp. 5–6).

29. "Let Us Face the Future," *Political Quarterly*, July–September, 1960, pp. 237–38.

30. See, for instance, Crossman, 618 *H.C.Deb.* 1058–60 (1 March 1960).

31. *Ibid.*, pp. 198–99.

32. *LPCR*, 1961, pp. 6–7.

33. *LPCR*, 1961, p. 194.

34. *The Times*, 15 February 1963.

35. The quoted words are George Brown's, 648 *H.C.Deb.* 195–96 (13 November 1963). For Wilson's remarks, see 687 *H.C.Deb.* 444 (16 January 1964).

36. Epstein, "The Nuclear Deterrent and the British Election of 1964," pp. 155–56.

37. *Ibid.*, p. 156.

38. 704 *H.C.Deb.* 429–39 (16 December 1964).

39. Camps, pp. 147–56.

# Selected Bibliography

# Selected Bibliography

Aitken, Ian. "The Structure of the Labour Party," in *The Left: A Symposium*, ed. Gerald Kaufman. London, 1966.

Alderman, R. K. "Discipline in the Parliamentary Labour Party, 1945–1951," *Parliamentary Affairs*, XVIII (Summer, 1965).

—— "Parliamentary Party Discipline in Opposition: The Parliamentary Labour Party, 1951–1964," *Parliamentary Affairs*, Spring, 1968.

Alperovitz, Gar. Atomic Diplomacy: Hiroshima and Potsdam: The Use of the Atomic Bomb and the American Confrontation with Soviet Power. New York, 1965.

Angell, Norman. "Pacifists and Cruisers," *New Leader*, 29 February 1924.

Attlee, Clement. "The Socialist View of Peace," in *Problems of Peace*, Ninth Series, *Pacifism Is Not Enough*. London, 1935.

—— The Labour Party in Perspective. London, 1937.

—— Labour's Peace Aims. London, 1939.

Attlee, Clement, and Ernest Bevin. Britain's Foreign Policy. London, 1946.

Baird, John. *Left*, July 1946.

Bassett, Reg. Democracy and Foreign Policy: A Case History, The Sino-Japanese Dispute, 1931–1933. London, 1952.

Bealey, Frank, and Henry Pelling. Labour and Politics, 1900–1906: A History of the Labour Representation Committee. London, 1958.

Beer, Samuel H. Treasury Control: The Coordination of Financial and Economic Policy in Great Britain. London, 1956.

—— British Politics in the Collectivist Age. New York, 1965.

Beloff, Max. New Dimensions in Foreign Policy—A Study in Administrative Experience, 1947–1949. New York, 1961.

Bendix, Reinhard. Nation-building and Citizenship: Studies of Our Changing Social Order. New York, 1964.

Bevan, Aneurin. In Place of Fear. London, 1952.

———— "In Place of the Cold War." *Tribune* series, 17 and 24 July and 1 and 8 August 1953.

———— "Britain and America at Loggerheads," *Foreign Affairs Quarterly*, 5 October 1957.

Bevin, Ernest. The Labour Party's Policy on Foreign Affairs. London, 1946.

———— Foreign Affairs. London, 1947.

Brailsford, H. N. The War of Steel and Gold: A Study of the Armed Peace. London, 1914.

———— The Covenant of Peace: An Essay on the League of Nations. London, 1918.

———— After the Peace. London, 1920.

Britain Belongs to You. Election manifesto, 1959.

British Labour Party. Report of the Annual Labour Representation Committee, 1901–5.

———— Report of the Annual Conference of the Labour Party, 1906–67.

———— Report of the Independent Labour Annual Party Conference, 1900–1931.

———— Report of the Proceedings of the Annual Trades Union Congress, 1914–67.

———— *See also Labour Party pamphlets and election manifestos by title.*

Bullock, Alan. The Life and Times of Ernest Bevin. Vol. I, Trade Union Leader, 1881–1940. Vol. II, Minister of Labour, 1940–1945. London, 1960, 1967.

Bulmer-Thomas, Ivor. The Party System in Great Britain. London, 1953.

Burns, J. M. "The Parliamentary Labour Party in Great Britain," *American Political Science Review*, December 1950.

Butler, David E. The British General Election of 1951. London, 1952.

Butler, David E., and Jennie Freeman. British Political Facts. London, 1963.

Byrnes, James. Speaking Frankly. New York, 1967.

Camps, Miriam. European Unification in the Sixties: From the Veto to the Crisis. New York, 1966.

Cards on the Table. Official statement, 1947.

Carr, E. H. The Twenty Years' Crisis. 2d ed. London, 1946.

Challenge to Britain. Official statement, 1953.

Churchill, Sir Winston. Triumph and Tragedy. New York, 1954.

Citrine, Walter. Men and Work: An Autobiography of Walter Citrine. London, 1964.

Claude, Inis L. *Power and International Relations*. New York, 1963.

———— Swords into Plowshares: The Problems and Progress of International Organization. 3d ed., rev. New York, 1964.

Cline, Catherine Ann. Recruits to Labour: The British Labour Party, 1914–1931. Syracuse, N.Y., 1963.

———— "E. D. Morel and the Crusade Against the Foreign Office," *Journal of Modern History*, June 1967.

Cmd. *See under* Great Britain.

Coates, Ken, and Anthony Topham, eds. Industrial Democracy in Great Britain: A Book of Readings and Witnesses for Workers' Control. London, 1968.

Cole, G. D. H. Europe, Russia and the Future. London, 1941.

────── A History of the Labour Party from 1914. 2d ed. London, 1948.

Cole, Margaret, ed. Beatrice Webb's Diaries, 1912–1924. London, 1920.

────── Beatrice Webb's Diaries, 1924–1932. London, 1956.

Control of Foreign Policy, Labour's Programme. Official statement, 1919.

Cooke, Colin. The Life of Sir Richard Stafford Cripps. London, 1957.

Crick, Bernard. The Reform of Parliament: The Crisis of British Government in the 1960's. London, 1964.

Cripps, Sir Stafford. Why This Socialism? London, 1934.

────── "The Political Reaction to Rearmament," *Dare We Look Ahead?* London, 1936.

Crosland, C. A. R. The Future of Socialism. London, 1957.

────── The Conservative Enemy. London, 1962.

Crossman, R. H. S. "Labour and Compulsory Military Service," *Political Quarterly*, July–September 1939.

────── "Reflections on the Cold War," *Political Quarterly*, January–March 1951.

────── "Between Two Façades," *New Statesman*, 22 September 1951.

────── Labour in the Affluent Society. Fabian Society, London, 1960.

────── "The Specter of Revisionism," *Encounter*, April 1960.

D'Abernon, Viscount. The Diary of an Ambassador, III. New York, 1931.

Dalton, Hugh. Towards the Peace of Nations. London, 1928.

────── "British Foreign Policy, 1929–1931," *Political Quarterly*, October–December 1931.

────── Call Back Yesterday: Memoirs, 1887–1931. London, 1953.

────── The Fateful Years: Memoirs, 1931–1945. London, 1957.

────── High Tide and After: Memoirs, 1945–1960. London, 1962.

Deakin, Arthur. "British Trade Unions and the Communist Conspiracy," *National and English Review*, December 1952.

Deane, H. A. The Political Ideas of Harold Laski. New York, 1955.

Deutsch, Karl W. The Analysis of International Relations. Englewood Cliffs, N.J., 1968.

Deutsch, Karl W., and Richard L. Merritt. "Effects of Events on National and International Images," in *International Behavior: A Social-Psychological Analysis*, ed. Herbert C. Kelman. New York, 1965.

Diebold, William, Jr. The Schuman Plan: A Study in Economic Cooperation, 1950–1959. New York, 1959.

Disarmament and Nuclear War. Official statement, 1958.

Disarmament and Nuclear War—The Next Step. Official statement, 1959.

Dowse, Robert E. Left in the Centre: The Independent Labour Party, 1893–1940. Evanston, Ill., 1966.

Eden, Anthony. Memoirs: Full Circle. London, 1960.

Epstein, Leon. Britain, Uneasy Ally. Chicago, 1954.

——— "The Nuclear Deterrent and the British Election of 1964," *Journal of British Studies*, No. 2, 1966.

European Unity. Official statement, 1950.

Fabian Society. Labour and Europe. Research Series No. 71, London, 1943.

Feis, Herbert. Churchill–Roosevelt–Stalin: The War They Waged and the Peace They Sought. Princton, N.J., 1957.

Fenn, L. Anderson., G. D. H. Cole, *et al.* Problems of the Socialist Transition. London, 1934.

Finer, S. E., *et al.* Backbench Opinion in the House of Commons, 1955–1959, New York, 1961.

FitzGibbon, Constantine. "Anti-American Zoo," *Encounter*, July 1959.

Fitzsimons, M. A. "British Labour in Search of a Socialist Foreign Policy," *Review of Politics*, April 1950.

——— The Foreign Policy of the British Labour Government, 1945–51. South Bend, Ind., 1953.

Foot, Michael. "Mr. Bevan Remains," *Nation*, 16 April 1952.

——— Aneurin Bevan: A Biography. Vol. I, 1897–1945. New York, 1963.

For Socialism and Peace. Election manifesto, 1934.

Foreign Policy and Defence. Official statement, 1960.

Forward with Labour. Election manifesto, 1955.

From a People's War to a People's Peace. Official statement, 1944.

Full Speed Ahead, *Tribune* publication. London, 1950.

The Future Labour Offers You. Official statement, 1958.

Geertz, Clifford. "Ideology as a Cultural System," in *Ideology and Social Discontent*, ed. David Apter. New York, 1964.

Going Our Way. *Tribune* pamphlet. London, 1951.

Goldberg, Arthur. "The Atomic Origins of the British Nuclear Deterrent" and "The Military Origins of the British Nuclear Deterrent," *International Affairs*, 1965.

Goodwin, Geoffrey L. Britain and the United Nations. New York, 1957.

Graubard, Stephen R. British Labour and the Russian Revolution, 1917–1924. Cambridge, Mass., 1956.

Great Britain. Government Publications.

——— Cmd. 2200 (1924). *Miscellaneous No. 13.* Correspondence between H.M.G. and the League of Nations respecting the proposed Treaty of Mutual Assistance.

——— Cmd. 7046 (1947). *Economic Survey.*

——— Cmd. 7217 (1947). Treaty of Alliance and Mutual Assistance between His Majesty in respect of the United Kingdom of Great Britain and Northern Ireland and the President of the French Republic.

——— Cmd. 7534 (1948). *Germany No. 2.*

——— Cmd. 7677 (1949). Memorandum on the Measures Agreed by the UK, US, and French Foreign Ministers on the Programme for Germany.

——— Cmd. 7883 (1950). Collective Defence under the Brussels and North Atlantic Treaties.

——— Cmd. 7970 (1950). *Miscellaneous No. 9.* Anglo-French Discussions regarding French proposals for the Western European Council, Iron and Steel Industries.

——— Statements on Defence and Defence estimates, including Supplementary Statements, 1946–67.

——— House of Commons. Parliamentary Debates, Fifth Series. Cited in text in the following manner: Vol. No. *H.C.Deb.* col. no. (date).

Greenwood, Arthur. The Labour Outlook. London, 1929.

Guttsman, W. L. The British Political Elite. London, 1963.

Haas, Ernst B. The Uniting of Europe: Political, Social, and Economic Forces, 1950–1957. Stanford, Calif., 1958.

Halle, Louis J. The Cold War as History. London, 1967.

Hamilton, Mary Agnes. Arthur Henderson: A Biography. London, 1938.

Harrison, Martin. Trade Unions and the Labour Party Since 1945. London, 1960.

Hartley, Anthony. A State of England. London, 1963.

*H.C.Deb. See under Great Britain.*

Healey, Denis. Power Politics and the Labour Party, in *New Fabian Essays,* ed. R. H. S. Crossman. London, 1952.

——— "Beyond Power Politics," in *Fabian International Essays,* ed. T. E. M. McKitterick and Kenneth Younger. New York, 1960.

Heasman, D. J. "The Prime Minister and the Cabinet," *Parliamentary Affairs,* XV (1962).

——— "Parliamentary Paths to High Office," *Parliamentary Affairs,* XVI (1962).

Henderson, Arthur. Labour's Foreign Policy. London, 1933.

——— Labour's Peace Policy. London, 1935.

——— Labour's Way to Peace. London, 1935.

Hinchingbrooke, Viscount. "The Cause of Conservative Politics," *Quarterly Review,* January 1950.

Hindell, K., and P. Williams. "Scarborough and Blackpool," *Political Quarterly,* July–December 1962.

Hitlerism. (With T.V.C.) Official statement, 1933.

Hobson, J. A. Imperialism: A Study. London, 1902.

——— Confessions of an Economic Heretic. London, 1938.

Hoffmann, Stanley. "Paradoxes of the French Political Community," in *In Search of France: The Economy, Society, and Political System in the Twentieth Century,* ed. Stanley Hoffmann. New York, 1965.

Hudson, G. F. "Will Britain and America Split in Asia?" *Foreign Affairs,* XXXI (July 1953).

Hunter, Leslie. The Road to Brighton Pier. London, 1959.

International Policy and Defence. National Joint Council, 1937.

The International Post-War Settlement. Official statement, 1944.

Is This an Imperialist War? Official statement, 1939.

Jackson, Robert J. Rebels and Whips: Dissension, Discipline, and Cohesion in British Parties Since 1945. New York, 1968.

Janis, Irving L., and M. Brewster Smith. "Effects of Education and Persuasion on National and International Images," in *International Behavior: A Social-Psychologiacl Analysis*, ed. Herbert C. Kelman. New York, 1965.

Jenkins, Roy. Mr. Attlee: An Interim Biography. London, 1948.

—— Pursuit of Progress: A Critical Analysis of the Achievement and Prospect of the Labour Party. London, 1953.

Johnson, F. A. Defense by Establishment: The British Committee of Imperial Defence, 1885–1959. New York, 1960.

Jordan, W. M. Great Britain, France, and the German Problem, 1918–1939: A Study of Anglo-French Relations in the Making and Maintenance of the Versailles Settlement. London, 1943.

Keep Left. Official statement.

Keeping Left. Official statement.

Kelman, Herbert C. "Social-Psychological Approaches to the Study of International Relations: Definitions of Scope," in *International Behavior: A Social-Psychological Analysis*, ed. Herbert C. Kelman. New York, 1965.

Krug, Mark M. Aneurin Bevan: Cautious Rebel. New York, 1961.

Labour and the Crisis in Foreign Policy. Official statement, 1938.

Labour and Defence: A Statement of Policy. Official statement, 1939.

Labour and the Defence of Peace. National Council of Labour, 1935.

Labour and the International Situation. (With T.V.C.) Official Statement, 1938.

Labour and the Nation. Election manifesto, 1929.

Labour and the New Society. Election manifesto, 1951.

Labour Problems After the War. Official statement, 1917.

Labour in the Sixties. Official statement, 1960.

Labour, the War and the Peace: A Declaration of Policy. Official statement, 1940.

Labour's Appeal to the Nation. Election manifesto, 1923.

Labour's Foreign Policy. Official statement, 1958.

Labour's Immediate Programme. Official statement, 1936.

Labour's Russian Policy: Peace with Soviet Russia. Official statement, 1919.

Landauer, Carl. European Socialism: A History of Ideas and Movements: From the Industrial Revolution to Hitler's Seizure of Power. Berkeley, Calif., 1959.

Laski, Harold. "British Labor in Retreat," *The Nation*. New York, 2 October 1937.

—— Britain and Russia: The Future. London, 1942.

—— The American Democracy. London, 1949.

—— Dilemma of Our Times. London, 1952.

Let Us Face the Future. Election manifesto, 1945.

"Let Us Face the Future," *Political Quarterly*, July–September 1960.

Let Us Win Through Together. Election manifesto, 1950.

Lie, Trygve. The Cause of Peace. London, 1954.

*LPCR*. Report of the Annual Conference of the Labour Party, 1906–67.

Luard, Evan. Britain and China. London, 1962.

Lyman, Richard W. The First Labour Government, 1924. London, 1957.

McBriar, A. M. Fabian Socialism and English Politics, 1884–1918. Cambridge, Eng., 1962.

McCallum, R. B., and A. Readman. The British General Election of 1945. London, 1947.

MacDonald, J. Ramsay. Socialism. London, 1907.

—— National Defence: A Study in Militarism. London, 1918.

—— The Foreign Policy of the Labour Party. London, 1923.

—— *League of Nations Official Journal*. Special Supplement No. 23, Records of the Fifth Assembly Plenary Meetings, 1924.

—— Protocol or Pact: The Alternatives to War. London, 1925.

Mackay, R. W. G. Heads in the Sand: A Criticism of the Official Labour Party Attitude to Unity. London, 1950.

McKenzie, R. T. British Political Parties. New York, 1963.

Mackintosh, John P. The British Cabinet. London, 1962.

—— "The Reform of Parliament," in *A Radical Future*, ed. Ben Whitaker. London, 1967.

McNeill, W. H. America, Britain and Russia: Their Cooperation and Conflict, 1941–1946. London, 1953.

Marquand, David. "Passion and Politics," *Encounter*, December 1960.

Martin, Kingsley. "Marxism Reviewed," *Political Quarterly*, July–September 1947.

—— Harold Laski, 1893–1950. London, 1953.

Martin, Lawrence W. The American Decision to Rearm Germany. The Twentieth Century Fund on Civil-Military Relations. Mimeo., 1961.

May, Ernest. "The Nature of Foreign Policy: The Calculated Versus the Axiomatic," *Daedalus*, XCI, No. 4 (Fall, 1962).

Mayer, Arno J. Wilson vs. Lenin: Political Origins of the New Diplomacy, 1917–1918. Meridian Paperbacks, New York, 1963.

Medlicott, W. N. Contemporary England, 1914–1964. London, 1967.

Meehan, Eugene J. The British Left Wing and Foreign Policy: A Study of the Influence of Ideology. New Brunswick, N.J., 1960.

"Memorandum of Sir Eyre Crowe," 1 January 1907, in *Britain and Europe: Pitt to Churchill, 1793–1940*, ed. James Joll. London, 1961.

Memorandum on War Aims. Official statement, 1917.

Miliband, Ralph. Parliamentary Socialism: A Study in the Politics of Labour. London, 1961.

Millis, Walter, ed. The Forrestal Diaries. New York, 1951.

Mitchell, Joan. Crisis in Britain, 1951. London, 1963.

Montgomery, Viscount. Memoirs. New York, 1958.

Morrison, Lord Herbert. An Autobiography. London, 1950.

—— Government and Parliament. London, 1959.

Mowat, C. L. Britain Between the Wars. London, 1955.

Neustadt, Richard E. "Memorandum on the British Labour Party and the MLF, 6 July 1964," *New York Review of Books*, 5 December 1968.

The New Britain. Election manifesto, 1964.

The New Party Constitution. Official statement, 1918.

Nicholas, H. G. Britain and the United States. London, 1963.

Northedge, F. S. *British Foreign Policy: The Process of Readjustment, 1945–1961.* London, 1962.

——— The Troubled Giant: Britain Among the Great Powers, 1916–1939. New York, 1966.

The Old World and the New Society. Election manifesto, 1942.

One Way Only. *Tribune* pamphlet, 1951.

Orwell, George. "England Your England," in *A Collection of Essays.* Anchor, New York, 1954.

Osgood, Robert E. NATO: The Entangling Alliance. Chicago, 1962.

Our First Duty—Peace. Official statement, 1951.

Parmoor, Lord. A Retrospect. London, 1936.

Peace and Freedom. (With T.V.C.) Official statement, 1934.

Pelling, Henry. America and the British Left: From Bright to Bevan. London, 1956.

——— The British Communist Party: A Historical Profile. London, 1958.

——— A Short History of the Labour Party. London, 1961.

Poirier, Philip P. The Advent of the Labour Party. London, 1958.

Policy for Peace. Official statement, 1961.

Postgate, Raymond. The Life of George Lansbury. London, 1951.

Protocol or Pact? Official statement, 1925.

Rees, David. Korea: The Limited War. London, 1964.

Rex, John, and Peter Worsley. "Campaign for Foreign Policy," *New Left Review,* July–August 1959.

Roberts, B. C. Trade Union Government and Administration in Great Britain. London, 1956.

Rose, C. R. (Richard). The Relation of Socialist Principles to British Labor Foreign Policy, 1945–1951. Unpublished D. Phil. thesis, University of Oxford, 1961.

Rose, Richard. "Complexities of Party Leadership," *Parliamentary Politics,* XVI (1963).

——— "Parties, Factions, and Tendencies in Britain," in *Studies in British Politics,* ed. Richard Rose. New York, 1966.

Rose, Saul. "The Labour Party and German Rearmament: A View From Transport House," *Political Studies,* June 1966.

Rosecrance, R. N. "British Defense Strategy, 1945–1952," in *The Dispersion of Nuclear Weapons: Strategy and Politics,* ed. R. N. Rosecrance. New York, 1964.

——— Defense of the Realm: British Strategy in the Nuclear Age. New York, 1968.

Rosenau, James. "Pre-theories and Theories of Foreign Policy," in *Approaches to Comparative and International Politics,* ed. R. Barry Farrell. Evanston, Ill., 1966.

Sahm, Ulrich. "Britain and Europe, 1950," *International Affairs,* January 1967.

Schilling, Warner R., Paul Y. Hammond, and Glenn H. Snyder. Strategy, Politics and Defense Budgets: Three Case Studies. New York, 1962.

Schlesinger, Arthur, Jr. "Attitudes Towards America," in *Hugh Gaitskell, 1906–1963*, ed. W. T. Rodgers. London, 1964.

Shinwell, E. Conflict Without Malice.

Shulman, Marshal. Stalin's Foreign Policy Reappraised. Cambridge, Mass., 1963.

Snowden, Philip. An Autobiography, II. London, 1934.

Snyder, William P. The Politics of British Defense Policy, 1945–1962. London, 1964.

Strang, Lord William. Britain in World Affairs: The Fluctuation in Power and Influence from Henry VIII to Elizabeth II. New York, 1961.

Swanwick, H. M. I Have Been Young. London, 1935.

Tawney, R. H. The British Labour Movement. New Haven, 1925.

——— "The Choice Before the Labour Party," *Political Quarterly*, July–September 1932.

Taylor, A. J. P. The Trouble Makers: Dissent Over Foreign Policy, 1792–1939. London, 1957.

——— The Origins of the Second World War. London, 1961.

Time for Decision. Election manifesto, 1966.

Toynbee, Arnold. Survey of International Affairs, 1924. London, 1928.

Truman, Harry S. Memoirs. I, Year of Decision. London, 1956. II, Years of Trial and Hope. London, 1957.

Tsuzuki, Chushichi. H. M. Hyndman and British Socialism, ed. Henry Pelling. London, 1961.

Tucker, W. R. The Attitude of the British Labour Party Towards European and Collective Security Problems, 1920–1939. Geneva, 1950.

——— "British Labor and Revision of the Peace Settlement, 1920–1925," *Southwestern Social Science Quarterly*, September 1960.

*TUCR*. Report of the Proceedings of the Annual Trades Union Congress, 1914–67.

"U.D.C." The Diplomacy of Mr. Ramsay MacDonald. London, 1925.

Vandenberg, Arthur H., Jr., ed. The Private Papers of Senator Vandenberg. Boston, 1952.

Waltz, Kenneth. Foreign Policy and Democratic Politics: The American and British Experience. Boston, 1967.

Watkins, Ernest. The Cautious Revolution. New York, 1950.

Watkins, K. W. Britain Divided: The Effect of the Spanish Civil War on British Public Opinion. London, 1963.

Watt, D. C. "American Aid to Britain and the Problem of Socialism, 1945–1951," in *Personalities and Politics: Studies in the Formation of British Foreign Policy in the Twentieth Century*. South Bend, Ind., 1965.

——— Britain Looks to Germany: British Opinion and Policy Towards Germany Since 1945. London, 1965.

———— "Germany," in *The Cold War: A Reappraisal*, ed. Evan Luard. London, 1968.

Weber, Max. Gesammelte Aufsaetze zür Wissenschaftslehre. 1922.

Wheeler-Bennett, John. King George VI: His Life and Reign. London, 1958.

Why Kill Each Other? Official statement, 1939.

Willcock, H. D. "Public Opinion: Attitudes towards America and Russia," *Political Quarterly*, January–March 1948.

Williams, Francis. Socialist Britain. New York, 1949.

———— Ernest Bevin: Portrait of a Great Englishman. London, 1952.

———— A Prime Minister Remembers: The War and Post-War Memoirs of the Rt. Hon. Earl Attlee. London, 1961.

Willson, F. M. G. "The Routes of Entry of New Members of the British Cabinet, 1868–1958," *Political Studies*, VII (1959).

Winkler, Henry R. The League of Nations Movement in Great Britain, 1914–1919. New Brunswick, 1952.

———— "Arthur Henderson," in *The Diplomats, 1919–1939*, ed. Gordon A. Craig and Felix Gilbert. Princeton, N.J., 1953.

———— "The Emergence of a Labour Foreign Policy in Great Britain, 1918–1929," *Journal of Modern History*, September 1956.

Wolfers, Arnold. Britain and France Between the Two World Wars. New York, 1940.

———— Discord and Collaboration: Essays on International Politics. Baltimore, 1962.

Woodward, Sir Llewellyn. British Foreign Policy in the Second World War. London, 1962.

Woolf, Leonard. Economic Imperialism. London, 1920.

———— Foreign Policy: The Labour Party's Dilemma. London, 1947.

———— The International Post-War Settlement. Fabian Research Series No. 85, London, 1944.

Worswick, G. D. N., and P. H. Ady. The British Economy, 1945–1950. London, 1952.

Wyatt, Woodrow. Into the Dangerous World. London, 1952.

Younger, Kenneth. "Public Opinion and Foreign Policy," *British Journal of Sociology*, VI (June 1953).

———— Changing Perspectives in British Foreign Policy. London, 1964.

# Index

# Index